SAGE was founded in 1965 by Sara Miller McCune to support the dissemination of usable knowledge by publishing innovative and high-quality research and teaching content. Today, we publish over 900 journals, including those of more than 400 learned societies, more than 800 new books per year, and a growing range of library products including archives, data, case studies, reports, and video. SAGE remains majority-owned by our founder, and after Sara's lifetime will become owned by a charitable trust that secures our continued independence.

Los Angeles | London | New Delhi | Singapore | Washington DC | Melbourne

Advance Praise

As change management practitioners, we have witnessed organizations go through several phases of transformation over the last three decades, but nothing was more radical and sudden as has been the COVID-19 era. HR professionals who are looking for a one-stop source to answer their queries on digital transformation that delivers a WoW experience cannot miss this book. Will strongly suggest reading this book.

Shyam Vasudevan, OD & Change Management Practitioner

The timing of the book could not be more opportune than the contemporary COVID-19 period, wherein organizations and employees have discovered a new way of connecting and working with each other. As an HR leader, I could relate to the real-life examples shared in the book, and felt so connected with the thoughts shared in the book. Every HR professional would love to read this book.

Murthy D. N., Partner—HR & Talent Consulting, ACCTPRO Advisory Services, LLP, and Ex-Head-Regional HR, Deloitte Haskins

Dr Venkatesh, through this book on EX, has created an opportunity for all people professionals to ponder over the need for transforming organizations into digital workplaces where processes are designed to be employee-centric. Thoroughly enjoyed reading through the book. A must-read for all HR professionals.

Nirmala Garg, Ex-Senior VP (HR), Sutherlands Global Services

Prof. Venkatesh has structured the book in a lucid and comprehensive format, which makes it easy for the readers to relate to the concept and application of EX in modern workplaces. The industry examples make it easy for the reader to appreciate the topic. The book kept me engrossed throughout and has provided several actionables for my organization.

Ram S. V. V., *VP (HR), WNS Global Services*

An absolute delight to learn more about EX as Dr Venkatesh expertly delves into the practical and theoretical nuances of EX. This book provides an incisive insight into the digital tools, in addition to the behavioural and organizational literature, that one can leverage to create a holistic EX framework for today's multi-generational workforce. Highly recommended for both academicians and practitioners like HR professionals and senior leaders who are constantly adopting new ways to enhance employee engagement and employer branding. An excellent read for students and professionals interested in exploring the area of EX and its impact on organizations in this digital era.

Neha Gupta, *Knowledge Management Leader, Genpact*

WINNING *with* EMPLOYEES

WINNING *with* EMPLOYEES
Leveraging Employee Experience for a Competitive Edge

D. N. VENKATESH

Los Angeles | London | New Delhi
Singapore | Washington DC | Melbourne

Copyright © D. N. Venkatesh, 2021

All rights reserved. No part of this book may be reproduced or utilized in any form or by any means, electronic or mechanical, including photocopying, recording or by any information storage or retrieval system, without permission in writing from the publisher.

First published in 2021 by

SAGE Publications India Pvt Ltd
B1/I-1 Mohan Cooperative Industrial Area
Mathura Road, New Delhi 110 044, India
www.sagepub.in

SAGE Publications Inc
2455 Teller Road
Thousand Oaks, California 91320, USA

SAGE Publications Ltd
1 Oliver's Yard, 55 City Road
London EC1Y 1SP, United Kingdom

SAGE Publications Asia-Pacific Pte Ltd
18 Cross Street #10-10/11/12
China Square Central
Singapore 048423

Published by Vivek Mehra for SAGE Publications India Pvt Ltd. Typeset in 10.5/13.5 pt Sabon by Fidus Design Pvt Ltd, Chandigarh.

Library of Congress Control Number: 2021941239

ISBN: 978-93-91370-56-5 (PB)

SAGE Team: Neha Pal, Megha Dabral, Ankit Verma and Dally Verghese

I am grateful to Adi Guru for guiding me on the path of discovering and sharing knowledge.

I dedicate this book to my mother, who has been the guiding force in my life through trials and tribulations, for instilling in me discipline and keeping me on track, which helped me complete the book.

Thank you for choosing a SAGE product!
If you have any comment, observation or feedback,
I would like to personally hear from you.

Please write to me at **contactceo@sagepub.in**

Vivek Mehra, Managing Director and CEO, SAGE India.

Bulk Sales

SAGE India offers special discounts
for purchase of books in bulk.
We also make available special imprints
and excerpts from our books on demand.

For orders and enquiries, write to us at

Marketing Department
SAGE Publications India Pvt Ltd
B1/I-1, Mohan Cooperative Industrial Area
Mathura Road, Post Bag 7
New Delhi 110044, India

E-mail us at **marketing@sagepub.in**

Subscribe to our mailing list
Write to **marketing@sagepub.in**

This book is also available as an e-book.

Contents

Foreword by C. Krishna Kishore ix
Preface xiii
Acknowledgements xix

Chapter 1: Digital Organizations in a Connected World 1

Chapter 2: Managing Employees in the Digital Era 29

Chapter 3: Creating Experience-Levered Organizations 57

Chapter 4: Acquiring Talent with Positive Candidate Experience 91

Chapter 5: Nurturing Employee Experience through
Performance and Rewards Management 131

Chapter 6: Strategizing and Executing the Learning
Experience of Employees 183

Chapter 7: Leveraging Employee Experience for
Employer Branding 249

Chapter 8: Employee Experience of Gig Employees 301

Chapter 9: Employee Experience Analytics: Tracking and
Measuring Employee Experience Indicators 365

About the Author 417

Foreword

Modern times can be divided into the pre-COVID-19 and post-COVID-19 eras. The business world inevitably has been transforming into digital workspaces, briskly for sure. Organizations are planning and executing their digital transformation journey based on multiple parameters, such as business scenario, culture, leadership and people processes. Those with young talent are consciously more innovative and more open to design and deliver systems and processes, thus taking a balanced view of their employees and other key stakeholders.

The pandemic scenario has triggered change across the world and the focus for businesses is survival, and growth taking the backseat. The paradigm shift has brought to centrestage the need for employee-centric focus on employee experience (EX) in the life cycle of an employee.

Professor Venkatesh Naga's book has captured the transformation both from strategic and operational perspectives, which helps readers have a sight of 'both the woods and the trees' without losing sight of either for a moment. The approach to focusing on EX has been structured in a rather strategic way. First, the readers get introduced to the digital transformation and the emergence of digital workplaces. The book then brings the attention of the reader to perspectives and insights in managing employees in the digital world. Readers then are introduced to 'experience' as a strategy driver/lever for businesses, scoping all related aspects for organizations, with a special focus on people.

The next chapter explains in detail how organizations can win the 'war for talent' using 'CX' (candidate experience) as a competitive tool, and how this can in turn result in multiple payoffs, like employer branding (EB) and attraction and retention of talent. The narrative then shifts to EX and its impact and EX as an outcome of the 'performance and rewards' system in an organization. The competitiveness of an organization is only as good as that of its talent, which makes the former dependent on the involvement of its employees in learning and self-development. The chapter on 'LX' (learning experience) convers this entire canvas in a captivating way.

The adage 'Seeing is believing, and believing is seeing' is applicable to the modern world unlike in the past when the applicable adage was 'Your work should speak for itself'. The changed paradigm calls for not just doing a great job but also showcasing it right in the right forums, right away confirming the value added to the stakeholders. This is more so in the case of organizations' relationships with prospective employees and reinforcement of emotional connection with the existing employees. The chapter on leveraging EX for EB takes a 360° view of various facets of the HR function and the need for its seamless integration in both design and execution and in its showcasing to the external world using a well-crafted EB strategy.

The biggest challenges faced by leaders and organizations in the VUCA (volatility, uncertainty, complexity and ambiguity) world are pace and type of change, which call for agility and flexibility in all spheres of operations. The gig economy is an answer for all these challenges. We have examples of online aggregators, like Swiggy and Ola, where the business model is majorly based on gig workers, and mainstream organizations are adapting/integrating the gig strategy into their operating model, to bring in agility with flexibility. The chapter on the EX of gig workers drives home the importance of caring to deliver EX for gig workers, to derive value from them and retain them.

'Anything that does not get measured does not get done' applies universally and eternally. For organizations to transform into great workplaces that offer a 'wow EX' to their employees and stakeholders, they need to plan a transition road map with definite timelines and metrics that define responsibilities with accountability. The chapter on EX analytics offers comprehensive insights on how organizations can identify and define metrics in their evolutionary journey.

This book, which starts as a journey towards discovery for the readers, for sure helps to refine their understanding of all the three spheres of concept, strategy and execution for desired deliverables. This is a must-read for all HR professionals, managers and upcoming leaders who aspire to leave a lasting brand value in the market with strategies for transformation of talent.

C. Krishna Kishore
Group Head & Sr Vice President-HR, Greenko Group

Preface

The advent of the digital world and impact of social media has made it necessary for organizations to provide positive experience to their customers across the customer life cycle. The customers today are spoilt by choice, as marketers vie with each other to garner the attention of prospective customers even as they try to retain existing customers to ensure that they strengthen their organization's market share to win the competitive battle. Technology has made it possible for organizations to design and offer customized service relationships to their customers.

In a connected world, there is no room for watertight operations and silos, and what starts as a trend in one part of a society or organization catches up with other areas as well. Social media is playing a facilitating and integrating role in this respect. In a way, it has made the world more open and transparent, with connection and communication becoming instantaneous. People are open to sharing their experiences and the emotions attached with those experiences now more than ever before.

The focus on EX in contemporary organizations is driven by multiple factors, such as digital trends (social media), consumerism and the arrival of millennials and Gen Z at workplaces. The combination of all these factors has resulted in EX becoming a central theme among both leaders and HR professionals across organizations, sectors and geographies. Researchers have started focusing their attention on this emerging aspect, and authors are presenting their views. I have observed that in relation to the international arena, the focus on EX in India is on the lower side. It is in this context that I thought it pertinent to write a book on EX with flavours of international and Indian perspectives. The book has nine chapters in all and is structured to facilitate the readers in navigating the topic.

The first chapter, 'Digital Organizations in a Connected World', introduces readers to the aspects such as redefining boundary-less world. Factors like social media and the adoption of co-creation as a strategy by organizations to design/deliver products/services to their stakeholders (both internal and external employees). It discusses in detail the impact of 'appification' and its implications for organizations in engaging and dealing with both customers and employees. The chapter also touches upon other related topics, like virtual teams and social commerce. It discusses in detail the transition into Industry 4.0 and the consequent impacts on people, processes and customers.

The second chapter, titled 'Managing Employees in the Digital Era', starts with description of connected workplaces, due to factors like the technology and hybrid business models. Tech service organizations have used a mix of on-shoring, off-shoring and near-shoring, to service their clients better. It discusses in detail the steps involved in cultural-change management, which organizations have to undergo to service both their internal and external stakeholders. The chapter explains the impact of social capital on Employee Life Cycle Management. The aspects like inclusive people management practices, including crowdsourcing, are covered. The chapter explains how 'experience' can become an antidote to 'talent fluidity'. The readers will gain insights on how to design and deliver a positive and inspirational 'talent experience' through identifying and offering talent services and serving/satisfying the needs of talent. The chapter explains in detail the need for the leaders and HR in organizations to adopt the 3C framework to engage talent. The impact of Gig Talent on the business strategy of an organization is explained in detail. The chapter ends with a discussion on how organizations could assess the value of talent and the impact of such assessment on their business.

The third chapter is titled 'Creating Experience-Levered Organizations'. It starts with an exposition on how EX can be a driver of customer experience. There is a need to identify the stakeholders and their needs to embark on a journey to design and deliver experience-focused business and people processes. The need for organizations to have a robust feedback system that captures the 'stakeholder voice' as an integral part of the experience strategy is discussed in detail. Readers can learn to assess the maturity of feedback system in an organization by using the Feedback Maturity Management Model. The experience strategies adopted by players across sectors (IT [information technology], ITeS [information technology–enabled services], retail, e-commerce, healthcare, hospitality) are documented and discussed to help readers gain cross-sectoral insights. The linkage between culture and experience orientation of an organization along with steps have bene explained to make it easy for readers to understand and appreciate steps needed for their organizations especially by mapping and navigating the supportive and anti-forces through the transformation.

The fourth chapter, titled 'Acquiring Talent with Positive Candidate Experience' covers both the strategic and operational aspects of creating and delivering a positive experience for candidates in an integrated way through the stages of the recruitment life cycle (RLC). Apart from its impact on hiring indicators, CX has an impact on other dimensions, like EB and employee retention. The impact of the expectations of millennials on hiring is discussed. Readers get to learn about the 3I framework for CX and the steps to integrate recruitment technologies into the hiring process across the RLC stages. The topics like leveraging CX and the steps involved in integrating EB with CX are discussed.

The fifth chapter, titled 'Nurturing Employee Experience Through Performance and Rewards Management', starts with a focus on inclusive leadership strategy, with the Line of Sight (LoS) model discussed in detail. The employee expectations around performance management across the performance life cycle are touched upon and then discussed in detail. There is need for organizations to discover their performance rhythm in its transformation from traditional to tech-driven employee-centric approach. The need for organizations to partner with employees for skill building and to deliver positive experience is highlighted with performance systems. The need for integrating employee performance and rewards through the touch points of employees is covered, to help readers, appreciate and implement takeaways as practitioners in their organizations. The opportunities for organizations to leverage digital technologies in helping their employees perform better and the various tech-tool options available for this purpose are discussed in detail.

The sixth chapter, titled 'Strategizing and Executing the Learning Experience of Employees', covers the paradigm shift in learning and the evolution of technology-based learning and its integration with business needs due to increased adoption of competency-based learning. The paradigm shift in learning and the learning ownership transfer from employers to employees are discussed in detail, along with various models of learning design and learning-effectiveness assessment. Readers get introduced to the career discovery model and COVID-19's impact on learning strategies and processes. The section on the learning maturity model would help readers do a quick check on the level of learning maturity in their organizations. The chapter also covers appification of learning and micro-learning.

The seventh chapter, titled 'Leveraging Employee Experience for Employer Branding', starts with decoding EB, along with explaining its impact and importance. It discusses the EX expectations of employees across the employee life cycle (ELC) stages and through the employee journey. Readers get insights on how to integrate EX with EB along with the steps involved.

The eighth chapter is titled 'Employee Experience of Gig Employees' and focuses on the same. It starts by detailing the environmental and economic factors that have led to the discovery and adoption of talent by organizations. The balancing act that needs to be carried out by organizations in offering EVP and EX, to ensure differentiation and equity at the same time, is covered. The aspects like inclusion and transparency, which have a bearing on the EX of gig workers, are explained with details from across sectors. The role of employers in offering social security is discussed both from regulatory and organizational accountability perspectives. The strategic drivers of gig-talent strategy and alternatives available for organizations in customizing it to the context of their business and culture are explained in detail. The issues involved in dealing with gigs and their EX expectations, which set the actionable agenda for HR functionaries have been explained.

The ninth chapter titled 'Employee Experience Analytics: Tracking and Measuring Employee Experience Indicators' starts with the need for and importance of tracking and analysing EX. The factors at the organizational and employee levels which need to be factored in while identifying EX metrics are discussed. The EX analytics frameworks that organizations could refer to while embarking on or reviewing their EX analytics strategy are described. The concepts like employee services intelligence and hyper-localization and their impact on EX analytics are explained. The EX indicators that need to be tracked across the ELC stages and employee touch points are lucidly explained. The steps involved in firming up an EX strategy are covered. Readers get to know about the nuances of EX data and analytics and EX maturity models.

Acknowledgements

My passion for learning and sharing was engendered during my early education days, thanks to my teachers (gurus) who have inspired me with their unique strength. The MBA programme has sharpened my focus on helping employees and aligning them with organizational strategies.

The HR functional experience of over two decades and academic/research experience have given me opportunity to witness evolution of HR function from re-christened HR to actual HR function, with focus on people development. The advent of HR service delivery brought in employee feedback. However, the focus remained on process metrics. The advent of the digital world and social media, coinciding with the arrival of millennials and Gen Z, has brought to centrestage the aspect of EX. The need for HR as a function to focus on EX has become imperative.

As an HR professional who has seen the HR or people function from both the practitioner's and the academic or researcher's perspective, I thought of writing this book, which is a hybrid of theory and practice. The inputs/feedback from next-generation leaders, which I noted while facilitating the learning of PGDM students at GIM (Goa Institute of Management), gave me insights on their expectations from their prospective employers. Additionally, my role as placement chair at GIM gave me a unique opportunity to witness the approach of corporates in attracting and engaging talent.

Writing this book has indeed been a journey of mixed emotions, of discovery and joy at some points and low moments when pressed for time, with competing responsibilities. The constant engagement and conversations with Ms Neha Pal from SAGE

Publications helped me stay on track with the timelines for this writing project.

More than to anything else, I strongly attribute the ideas, efforts and completion of this book to the blessings of Adi Guru, the divine lord of knowledge.

1
Digital Organizations in a Connected World

The emergence of the digital era and connectedness of the world has created a new context and operational environment for organizations. Further, it poses a set of challenges for organizations and has set their change agenda as well. The change agenda covers 'strategy reset', 'process reset' and, most importantly, 'people reset'. Organizations are navigating through these areas in their tryst with 'digital strategy'.

The advent of digital technologies has changed the world from 'static' to 'interactive', 'connected' and 'collaborative' across geographies and time zones. Organizations today are working in a paradigm that has not previously been seen in human history. Technology, which started as a supportive tool for improving process efficiency, has now become a tool that influences processes to be redesigned. The processes of strategy design and execution, which were periodical, have now become dynamic and real-time processes. The strategy design process required painful collection of data, which was largely post-facto and post-mortem analysis. In a sense, organizations were interpreting and working on data for their future preparedness, which obviously was not the best way to plan for the future. In the connected world, it is possible to capture data across spectrum viz., consumer pulse on social media, supply chain status through digital tracking mechanism. Organizations can predict and prepare for the people aspect as well, based on business trends, employee skill, performance, development and engagement indicators.

Beyond Boundaries

Are organizations of today agnostic to boundaries, and have they become boundary-less in the true sense? Yes, they have, for multiple reasons, including that e-commerce has made it easy even for small businesses to reach out to global markets effortlessly, without major investments. Another major reason is digital media, which helps people not just relate to and connect with each other but also adopt consumer habits. Another aspect of this boundary less business model is remote working, which allows organizations to source talent and expertise from vast geographies, from where they exist, and service customers across the world. Organizations today have broken the myth that all aspects of creating/manufacturing a product have to be located at one place for operational flexibility. Today organizations operate based competence advantage.

For this reason, organizations do not resort to creating products/services on their own but partner with other organizations, which have expertise in specific areas, while they focus on their 'core' business. In a sense, organizations today are 'networked organizations'—an aggregation of various organizations interconnected with each other. The other reasons for boundary transcendence include: (a) expanding the business; (b) strengthening the market presence; (c) gaining a foothold in attractive markets; (d) availing incentives by governments; and (e) minimizing risk. In a competitive marketplace, organizations look at global markets for expanding their market presence. In an era where global conglomerates decide on sovereign policies, it is imperative for organizations to have the scale to withstand the competition. Given the constraints, such as existing market potential limitations and tough competition, organizations adopt the blue ocean strategy by assessing which markets have greater potential and are relatively easy for the organizations to capture them. The competitive economics at the national level is another motivator for organizations. Leaders at the international level are vying to welcome organizations into their countries to give a positive spin to their economies and in the process provide the benefits of economic development to their citizens. Organizations do not always take a unidimensional approach but take a combined view of various factors when making their decisions. They consider a combination of factors, such as resource availability, market attractiveness of a market based on its inherent potential, its local advantage and its connectivity to other countries in the region, to become a regional hub as in the 'hub-and-spoke' model.

Mobility is the key driver of the boundary-less world that we are witnessing today. This mobility is due to the social mobility of talents who are able to realize their dreams of global careers. It is not that only talent travels in search of careers, but the same applies to organizations as well. If the cost economics work in their favour, organizations would not blink twice before setting up their operations across geographies based on such business strategies as 'near shoring' or 'offshoring'. The strategic reasons can include cost arbitrage, cultural compatibility and proximity to the markets/customers to be serviced by the organization.

Winning Hearts with Social Media

Social media, which came into existence as an 'entertainment and hobby' space, has now become a core strategic component of organizations. The pre-eminence and dominance of social media can be linked to human psychology. Humans by nature love to interact and spend time with each other, bonding and sharing/exchanging information. Unlike the past, thanks to social media, it has become easy for people to connect and hang out on virtual platforms, for reasons such as paucity of time, convenience, challenges in physical mobility on account of city pollution and traffic, etc. It is observed that an average person spends between four and six hours on social media. In the previous era, for cold-call marketing, marketers used to identify the time and locations to reach out to existing and prospective customers, either to upsell/cross-sell to existing customers or to reach out to prospective customers. Though the marketers were making efforts, the efforts involved were daunting and demanding due to the time and efforts involved. Another reason for social media's prominence is that unlike the past, people in the modern world are unwilling to connect with or entertain a stranger in person due to the security risk involved.

From a marketing perspective, organizations have realized the advantages of connecting and reaching out to customers through social media. The first step in this direction was making their presence felt through branding on social media. The initial static presence quickly evolved into the video format as consumers started connecting with visual communication more than with static communication. Both organizations and customers realized the advantage of quick and instant two-way communication. This aspect created opportunities for organizations to involve customers in the testing of pilot launches and take quick feedback from them. This has led to the concept of 'customer intimacy', of getting closer to the customer on a real-time basis. The customer has evolved from being an external party who would consume products and services to becoming a partner of organizations.

The major challenge faced by organizations in relating to customers was faith and buy-in from them to the communication efforts. Thanks to the availability of abundance information, customers have adapted to the habit of cross-validating claims by organizations through feedback from fellow customers on several informal channels and websites, including social media. This 'trust deficit' has presented a challenge and an opportunity for organizations to rethink its connection and relationship with the customer. Another key aspect in the digital era is the trust of customer in 'peers' and 'informal feedback' as more dependable sources of information in relation to formal channels.

Organizations have studied these trends and have decided to strategically source the responsibility of brand advocacy on the customer. Customer advocacy initially happened through the formal channels of organizations. Organizations used their sales channels to receive customer feedback and make it available on their channels at the point of sale. The first point of cross-validation of feedback by the customer is the 'point of sale'. This has a profound impact on the purchase behaviour of the customer. However, in cases of high-value purchases, customers prefer to check the feedback from multiple sources. The sources include majorly the social networks and focused websites that provide comparisons of competing products.

It has thus become essential for organizations to monitor and manage their presence not just on their formal channels but on other channels as well. For this, organizations have started reaching out to their customers for advocacy of their products/services. This has led to the advent of 'customer advocacy', which has become the new format for the branding of organizations. It has become important for digital marketing teams to have designated team members to handle this job.

Figure 1.1. Customer Engagement Paradigm Shift

Co-creating Products

From an organization's perspective, the earlier method of designing a product/service and keeping it under wraps till its launch does not guarantee the success or acceptance of the product/service. The competitive dynamics have made it imperative for organizations to take the pulse of or get feedback from customers at every stage of product/service design. The first step is to collect feedback on existing products and analyse it for areas of improvement or get ideas for improving the next version of the products. For new product design, organizations have created 'ideathon' as a format to collect ideas from customers. This gives an idea to the product and service design team about customer expectations. The involvement of customers at the ideation stage gives an opportunity for firms to design products and services that have better acceptance, due to their being in tune with the needs of the customers. The next step in co-creation is customer involvement in the pilot launch. Co-creation has its applications in product/service/context/value design. The co-creation of value is a result of the delivery/offer of products/services which exactly meets the needs of customers. The higher the satisfaction of a customer's needs/preferences, the higher would be the derived value for the customer. A customer who derives higher value becomes a 'brand ambassador' for an organization and, in the process, discharges the role of 'customer advocacy', thus providing brand equity, which results in competitive advantage for the organization. For co-creation to be used as a successful strategy, organizations would have to redesign their structure and process to connect with customers seamlessly on a real-time basis.

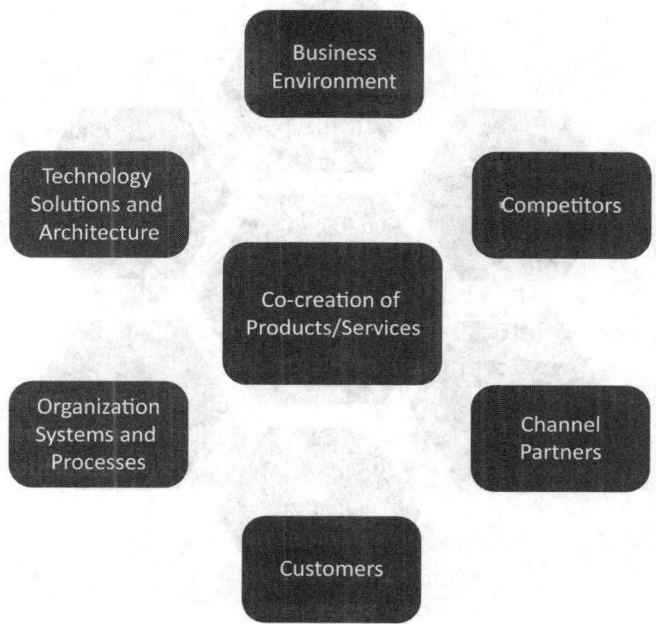

Figure 1.2. Co-creation Ecosystem

For co-creation to be effective and functional, it is important that an organization integrates and connects with all the factors impacting the same. The strategy team in an organization has the responsibility of tracking the business environment to analyse the organization's direct and indirect competitors. The channel partners are key to connecting with customers. The channel partners include both those operating in physical channel and more importantly the digital channels. The seamless connect for the organization with customers has to be channel agnostic and real-time. This calls for organizations scaling up their non-digital channels and making them at par with digital channels. Any disconnect between the two can lead to customer dissatisfaction, which can be costly for an organization. Organizations are designing processes to connect with customers and receiving their feedback across channels/platforms. Handheld devices and 'appifications' are at the forefront of this integration.

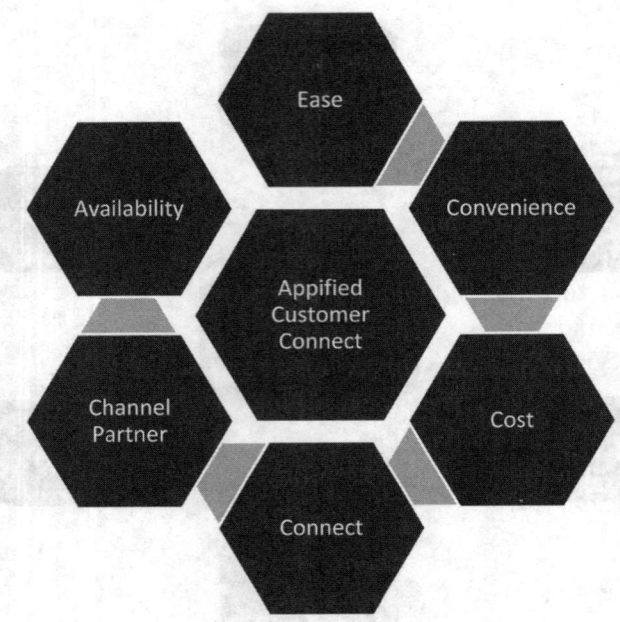

Figure 1.3. Appification and Factors

The 'appified' version of customer connect is making it less capital-intensive. There are multiple advantages of designing and implementing an 'appified' customer interface/connect system to connect with customers, the first and foremost being the ease of the customers in connecting and sharing their feedback on a real-time basis. In the era of digital connections, customers prefer instant connection and hate to be dependent on anyone else. They love to give their feedback at the 'point of experience'. This is where the app steps into the picture and provides convenience to the consumer to connect with organizations and share their feedback. The advantage of the 'appified' customer connect strategy is that it can be designed, rolled out and tracked on a real-time basis at an affordable cost. The centralized technology architecture model SaaS (software as a service) allows organizations to quickly update their app without discomfort to any segment—technology administrators, business leaders and managers and, more importantly, the customers.

Virtual Teams

When we describe the evolution of mankind, we always refer to BC (before Christ) and AD (*anno domini*). But now when we refer to the modern world, we will have to use the phrase 'before and after COVID-19'—more so in the case of virtual teams. Virtual teams in the pre-COVID-19 (coronavirus disease 2019) era were a rarity and were restricted to people working across geographies and timelines. COVID-19 has brought a sea change in the entire context. People working in the same office and location are now adjusting to working in virtual teams. Virtual teams have their pros and cons.

The question that may arise in one's mind is 'how to leverage virtual teams and make them tick and work'. Leaders and managers used to leading teams in the conventional format would find it difficult to operate with virtual teams. The top leadership and HR (human resources) leadership have a major role in anchoring the transition of their organization and

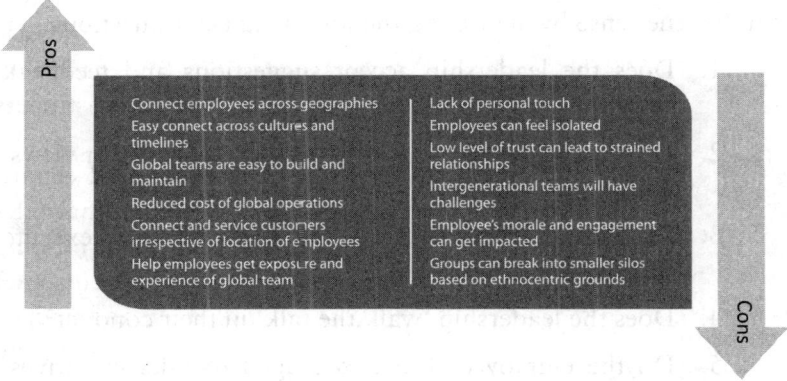

Figure 1.4. Pros and Cons of Virtual Teams

managers to the virtual world. The top leadership's responsibilities include:

- Constantly communicating with the managers and employees;
- Sharing their personal experiences, including both hits and misses;
- Setting an agenda with clear timelines and indicators;
- Designing and rolling out a dashboard that makes transparent the traction of the organization;
- Motivating and incentivizing managers who will lead this virtual transformation; and
- Encouraging top performers to share their success stories in virtual town halls.

The HR team has the responsibility of playing an anchor role in the virtual transformation of an organization. Organizational culture plays a major role in the success of virtual teams. Though there are several models for organizational culture, the most integrated approach that can support the effective functioning of virtual teams in organizations is the OCTAPACE model.

The first and most fundamental cultural aspect in an organization is 'openness'. One can validate whether an organization is 'open' in the true sense by answering the following eight questions:

1. Does the leadership accept suggestions and feedback from the employees?
2. Do the employees openly share their 'contrarian views' without hesitation?
3. Do the managers trust the employees' abilities to execute their responsibilities?
4. Does the leadership 'walk the talk' in their conduct?
5. Do the employees feel encouraged to take initiatives/ contribute new ideas?

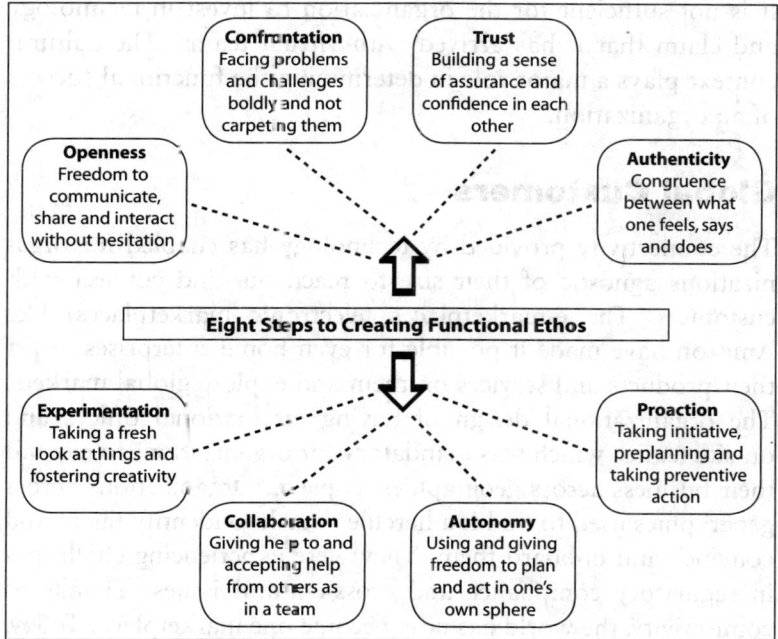

Figure 1.5. OCTAPACE Model
Source: https://images.app.goo.gl/8SH3fKwvfB6UskRt6

6. Do the employees feel empowered in their role with 'Operating Space' and 'Needed Power and Authority'?
7. Do the employees collaborate with each other while working in teams?
8. Does the organization have a structured process to review the status quo and facilitate processes of innovation and experimentation?

An organization can be successful in operating with virtual teams, only when at least five of the eight dimensions can derive productivity from virtual teams. In the COVID-19-affected situation, while all organizations may transition to and operate in 'virtual teams', very few can actually derive mileage from them.

It is not sufficient for the organization to invest in technology and claim that it has arrived with virtual teams. The cultural context plays a major role in determining the functional success of an organization.

Global Customers

The connectivity provided by technology has enabled for organizations agnostic of their size to reach out and connect with customers. The e-marketplaces (electronic marketplaces) like Amazon have made it possible for even home enterprises to list their products and services on them and explore global markets. The organizational design of having international offices and on-site teams, which was mandatory for organizations to expand their business across geographies, is passé. Organizations across geographies used to find it a herculean task to identify talent and convince and onboard them. They were experiencing challenges in regulatory compliance and cross-cultural issues. Thanks to connectivity, the world has now become one marketplace. Today, start-ups based in the developing markets like India are rolling out their products first in the United States, tasting success and then focusing on the domestic market. These start-ups have dispelled the age-old saying that 'victory on the home front' is a key requisite before one sets out to conquer other frontiers. Does this mean doing business is a cakewalk for organizations today and there are no challenges? Not really, since connectivity involves toil to understand customer preferences/choices and customizing products and services before offering them to customers. Social media is another platform that has made it easy to identify and reach out to global customers. Social media platforms, such as Facebook, Twitter and Instagram, have made it easy for organizations to design and roll out targeted campaigns for global customers.

Social Commerce

In modern times, the virtual world, which is surreal, has become more real and powerful than the real world for social, cultural and psychological reasons. Technology has broken down several old barriers but has created new barriers as well. People are now addicted to living and connecting and engaging with each other in the virtual world. The events like the COVID-19 pandemic have accentuated this trend. In a sense, social platforms, due to the kind of transactions that take place over them, have become marketplaces apart from connecting people. This trend has created a new opportunity/channel in the form of social commerce. Since its initial usage in only branding and advertising, social commerce has evolved into a complete marketplace, allowing customers to review products and shop as well. The potential for social commerce can be gauged from the following facts:

- Among shoppers, 23 per cent are influenced by social media recommendations (so why not sell straight from that recommendation?)
- Among millennials (who will soon be the major buying market), 51 per cent are likely to make a purchase over social media.
- Among shoppers, 84 per cent review at least one social media site before purchasing (so it makes sense to sell where they are going to research).
- There are 1.47 billion daily active users on Facebook alone.
- Among Instagram users, 60 per cent say they find new products on the platform (so it makes complete sense to also sell them on the same platform).
- Among online shoppers, 30 per cent say they are likely to make a purchase from a social media network like Facebook, Pinterest, Instagram, Twitter or Snapchat.
- Social media messenger sales are massively outperforming the current ROI (return on investment) champion of email.

(Source: https://www.bigcommerce.com/blog/social-commerce/)

Having looked at the commercial insights, it is time to focus on the impact of social commerce on organizations' design and processes. Organizations are trying to proactively create teams, to begin with, to start the business, and as the volume picks up, they are creating full-fledged departments. From a functional-effectiveness perspective, organizations are tweaking their structures and processes to create central supply chain teams that can handle omnichannel business. One key aspect of focus would be to change facilitation for legacy teams to connect, bond and work with teams working in the social commerce area.

Data Capital

The definition of 'capital' has been evolving with industrialization. The first generation of business in the early 19th century considered 'finance' as the key driver of business. The competition, at both the national and organizational levels, was to raise the capital to fund business needs and expansion. This led to the establishment of financial markets, including stock markets across major cities, such as London, New York, Paris, Bonn and Hong Kong.

The advent of the second wave of industrialization saw the dominance of production techniques. Organizations invested heavily in the research and development of machinery which

- Finance Capital
- Technology Capital
- Knowledge Capital
- People Capital
- Data Capital

Figure 1.6. Types of Capital

helps improve productivity. The excessive focus on productivity led to a lot of backlash from employees, leading to the rise of unionism and employee unrest globally. Leaderships and managers had an obsession with productivity parameters. Employees felt deprived of their human identity, and this was a cause of heartburn and unrest.

The advent of the third wave of industrialization saw the focus shift to 'knowledge capital'. Organizations felt that 'knowledge' was the source of competitive advantage for corporations. The realization of the importance of knowledge was concurrent with the evolution of information technology (IT) in the world, with businesses focusing on automation. The focus on 'process re-engineering' and 'people skilling' drove the automation agenda.

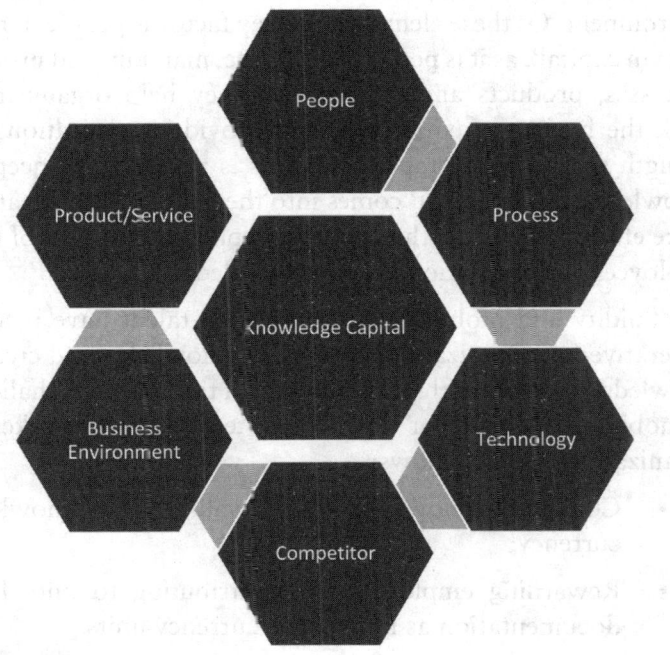

Figure 1.7. Knowledge Capital and Factors

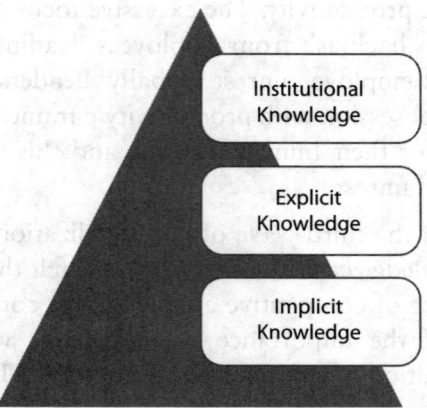

Figure 1.8. Types of Knowledge

Knowledge capital has six key dimensions: people, processes, products/services, competition, technology and the business environment. Of these elements, the key factor is people, termed 'human capital', as it is people who create, maintain and produce processes, products and technology. They help organizations track the business environment and provide organizations the strength to face the competition. This is where the concept of 'knowledge management' comes into the picture. Organizations make efforts to capture the tacit and explicit knowledge of their employees and institutionalize the knowledge.

The fluidity and mobility associated with talent have made it imperative for organizations to capture knowledge and create a knowledge repository that can help them tide over the challenge of mobility of talent. For this, the strategic initiatives taken by organizations are as follows:

- Converting knowledge to and valuing it as knowledge currency;
- Rewarding employees for contributing to knowledge documentation as knowledge currency units;
- Using both formal and informal communication for creating knowledge;

- Converting informal conversations, like chats, into knowledge resources;
- Implementing crowdsourcing strategies for the creation of a knowledge repository; and
- The learning teams are playing the role of curating and sharing knowledge.

Industry 4.0 and Its Technological Pillars

As technology makes deep inroads into industry, the focus is on integrating technology in operations across the production life cycle to optimize resources and improve operational efficiency. The initial focus was on the mechanization of processes, and later, the focus was on improvement in mass production capacity. In the third stage, the focus was on automation and introduction of computer technologies. The advent of mobile technologies and networks led to connected systems and the Internet of Things (IoT), ushering in Industry 4.0.

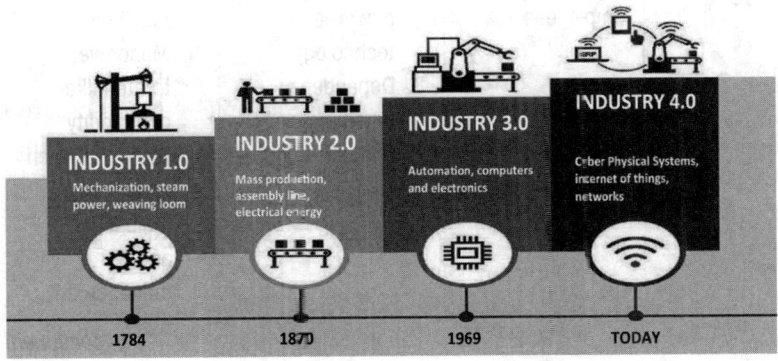

Figure 1.9. Industry Evolution. The Industrial Revolution: From Industry 1.0 to Industry 4.0
Source: https://images.app.goo.gl/wxYY97Q1TYQ2vQAG8

Each of the above transformations had an impact on organizational design, organizational processes and people.

Industry Evolution and Impact on Organizational Design, Process and People

Industry Stage	Organizational Design and Dimensions	Work Process	People Processes/Skills
Industry 1.0	Small enterprises; person-centric; restricted to one geography	1. Basic 2. High level of person dependency	1. Largely manual skills 2. Ability to understand instructions and execute tasks
Industry 2.0	Large enterprises; introduction of bureaucracy and hierarchy to manage employees	1. Introduction of assembly lines and exploration of mechanization 2. Machines powered by technology 3. Dependency on employees reduced	1. Ability to deploy automation 2. Ability to work with power-enabled machines 3. Manpower treated like commodity 4. Tussle between employees (unions) and management

(continued)

(continued)

Industry Evolution and Impact on Organizational Design, Process and People			
Industry Stage	Organizational Design and Dimensions	Work Process	People Processes/Skills
Industry 3.0	Global enterprises connected across geographies; cross-culture and cross-geography; complex structure	1. Automation of processes 2. Supply chains spread across geographies and integrated	1. Employees valued as critical talent 2. Knowledge and skills valuation 3. Processes designed for people connect and centricity
Industry 4.0	Networked organizations; blurred boundaries; backward and forward supply chain integration; employee ownership	1. Co-creation with supply chain partners 2. Customers becoming co-creators 3. Connected networks and technologies becoming process anchors	1. Gig workers becoming business partners 2. Employees and supply chain partners being involved in business process, design and execution

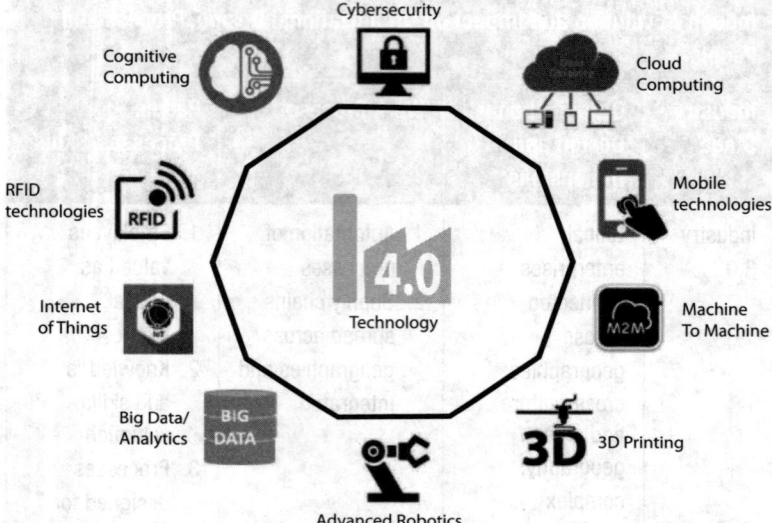

Figure 1.10. Technologies for industry 4.0. | Download Scientific Diagram

Source: https://images.app.goo.gl/kznmJGSbScK7UNJr5

The key feature of Industry 4.0 is the integration of several types of technologies based on the business context and need.

The technology and purpose of deployment is based on the business context and need. The various purposes for which businesses deploy technology tools/applications are as follows:

1. **Cognitive computing:** Cognitive computing (CC) is based on the scientific disciplines of artificial intelligence and signal processing. It works on a whole gamut of platforms, such as machine learning, reasoning, natural language processing, speech recognition and vision. These applications involve many human and machine interactions. The applications try to understand and respond to business needs akin to human response. The typical applications of CC are in the processing of

emails and documents, analysis and interpretation of data, etc. To cite a few examples, in the field of education, it is being used to supplement learning with personalized assistance for learners (students), which would be humanly impossible for teachers. Similarly, in the field of healthcare, it can be deployed to interpret various medical indicators and reports of a patient to help the medical practitioners decipher the information and decide on a course of treatment.

Organizations are trying to supplement employee efforts through CC to support their core business operations. CC is being deployed both on the front end and through advanced applications. On the front end, it is being deployed to respond to Level 1 and Level 2 IT support. The deployment on the front end has solved multiple challenges for organizations. Organizations were struggling to recruit, train and retain employees and deliver consistent and predictable services to their partners/customers. At one go, CC has eliminated these challenges on the people front and, on the other hand, also ensured consistent service delivery at predictable costs. The advanced applications of CC include supply chain and service delivery analytics and customer insights and analytics. The dependence on people had presented multiple challenges to organizations, ranging from availability and skills of talent to the performance efficacy of the talent. The effectiveness of analytics was dependent on people, which posed a risk for organization in the competitive climate. However, with CC coming into the picture, organizations can automate analytics and the leadership can become 'analytics-empowered' and thus can take effective decisions based on real-time analytics and insights.

2. **Cyber security:** Cyber security involves the design and implementation of security systems to protect computer

networks containing data relating to organizations and customers from external hacking efforts. The criticality of IT networks is due to the integration and reliance of entire businesses on IT networks and applications. To address security needs, organizations have been creating separate teams within IT functions/teams. In addition, they have been deploying external experts, ethical hackers, to test the robustness of their systems. Any unfortunate incident can adversely impact the brand and business of an organization. The cyber security team works in tandem with the HR and learning teams to educate employees on compliance.

3. **Mobile technologies:** The initial phase of technology was based on laptops and desktops. The advent of mobile networks has led to phenomenal developments in the technology landscape. Mobile handsets, which came into existence for the purpose of communication, have assumed an 'all-powerful' and 'all-pervasive' status due to multiple reasons. The wide gamut of reasons include availability, accessibility and cost-effectiveness, for organizations, supply chain partners and customers. Another key factor is the availability of customers for prolonged periods in captive mode. It is relatively easy for organizations to deliver 24x7 service delivery by onboarding their employees to process, as it is convenient for them as well. The adoption of mobile technologies is interlinked with the preparedness of organizations in terms of cyber security. Mobile technologies are akin to a double-edged sword. Apart from their positives, there are risks associated with data and network security. Mobile technologies break the organizational barriers and makes sensitive organizational networks and data anytime and anywhere. In the absence of strong cyber security controls, organizations are bound to lose control over their data, which are a source of competitive advantage.

4. **Machine to machine (M2M):** The original technology adaptation visualized integration of human and machine efforts in product/service design and delivery. As organizations explored opportunities for improving their efficiency, they discovered that communication between machines without human intervention can lead to greater effectiveness. The advent and growth of M2M has been in conjunction with that of communication technologies, as the technology is dependent on M2M communication using either wired or wireless technologies. The other interlinked technologies are AI/IoT/CC. The evolution of these parallel technologies have helped the advancement of M2M. The applications of this technology are manifold; examples include intelligent cars that operate on a self-drive basis, smart homes, where home attributes can be remotely operated, warehouse and inventory management to trigger dispatch and re-order requests, smart city surveillance, etc.

5. **3D printing:** The technological advances in manufacturing the need for organizations to reduce the deadlines for new product design and production. The conventional approach for creating physical prototypes consumed a lot of time, apart from having resource and cost implications. Product design calls for multiple iterations before a final product is designed. The advent of three-dimensional (3D) design helped in addressing these challenges. The technology involves CAD/CAM (computer-aided design/computer-aided manufacturing).

6. **Advanced robotics:** The need for process automation led to the advent of robotics, which has now evolved into a full-fledged technology application and is termed RPA (robotic process automation). RPA covers a wide gamut of business needs, like the need for bots for basic interaction at Level 1 IT support. The advanced applications include AI-powered interaction, indoor

navigation and remote human interaction. Robotics is now used in critical and precision medical intervention and geographic surveillance/monitoring. Organizations like Amazon have deployed robotics in warehouse management.

7. **Big data analytics:** The increased automation has led to the creation of a large amount of data, and it has become necessary for organizations to process and analyse the data. Initially, analytics was handled using spreadsheets and Microsoft Excel. However, as time progressed, organizations faced challenges around the cost of maintaining large teams to process their analytics. The second major challenge was time lag due to the time consumed by these teams to process and provide decision insights for the leaders to craft their strategy. In a sense, leaders ended up getting dated data and found it frustrating. The competitive world makes it imperative for leaders to have real-time data insights along with futuristic and predictive analytics. The introduction of mobile and connected technologies has led to the generation of gigantic volumes of data. Trying to process such volumes of data is humanly impossible, and this is where big data analytics (BDA) comes into the picture. BDA has the advantages of: (a) cost reduction; (b) faster and better decision-making; and (c) new products and services. BDA, due to its pay-offs and benefits, has been deployed across sectors, ranging from government, healthcare and education to utilities and media and entertainment. Organizations have adopted two types of strategies to integrate BDA into their business. The first is to create a specialized team (centralization strategy) for analytics as a centre of excellence which supports the analytics needs of an organization. The second is a hybrid strategy of 'diffusion and integration'. The analytics team is diffused and assigned to various

businesses/departments. The BDA adoption strategy is dependent on the factors such as business needs, financial investments and organizational culture and design.

8. **Internet of things:** The connected world, along with AI, led to the evolution of IoT. The interconnectedness of devices has created opportunities to design applications within and outside organizations, to provide seamless connections and design service architecture that is independent of human intervention and capable of operating independently aided by the technology. A few applications of IoT include smart homes, driverless cars, smart surveillance and remote health monitoring for senior citizens. The adoption of IoT by organizations has necessitated the redesigning of systems to capture, process, analyse and act to support both business and customer needs.

9. **Radio-frequency identification technologies:** Radio-frequency identification (RFID) is another technology application that helps organizations track goods at various stages on a real-time basis. Its applications include security access, inventory tracking, goods movement tracking and people movement tracking. The tracking mechanism helps leaders get real-time status, information and analysis and make informed decisions.

Industry 4.0 calls for preparedness of organizations at multiple levels. The three-tiered SPP (strategy reset, process reset, people reset) model helps organizations in their preparedness.

- **Level 1 (strategy reset):** The first level of preparedness is fundamental for organizations, which calls for strategy re-engineering. Organizations aiming to adapt to Industry 4.0 have to transform from being 'closed' to being 'open'. They have to change their perspective from 'do it alone' to 'do with all'. Under the former perspective, organizations try to operate and do all

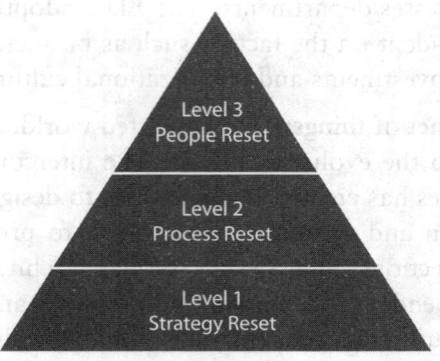

Figure 1.11. Industry 4.0 and Levels of Organization Preparedness

aspects on their own and try to limit external interactions. The fundamental premise of Industry 4.0 is the interrelations and interactivity with the external environment. This calls for organizations to include external partners in their business processes, be it in product design, the supply chain or the service chain. The operating model of organizations has to undergo a radical transformation for them to integrate external stakeholders/partners.

- **Level 2 (process reset):** After reviewing their strategy and operating model, the next area of focus for organizations is to review the business processes. The conventional process that creates a 'restrictive and closed environment' needs to be modified to include external partners, process the data coming from these partners and provide feedback on the effectiveness Vs challenges with existing business processes. The wider is the cast of the process and data capturing, the more reflective will be the analytics, product design and service to meet the needs of the customers.

- **Level 3 (people reset):** After the strategy and processes are reset, the critical action item for organizations is people reset, which is the key to achieving the goals of Industry 4.0. 'People reset' involves a series of steps to be taken jointly by the leadership and HR teams in an organization. The first step is to communicate the need for and urgency of the organization to undertake the transformation in order to survive and thrive in the competitive marketplace. The next step is to clearly communicate the road map and timelines, along with ensuring preparedness, at both the individual and organizational levels. This is the crux of the 'change management' process. The reason for this is that people tend to have apprehensions, real or presumptuous, due to which they develop antipathy towards change. This can adversely impact both the individual and the organization at large. The next step is holding the hand of and guiding employees through this change. This job is not just that of the top leadership and HR but also that of all the people managers. The top leadership and HR have the responsibility of training and empowering the people managers with the knowledge, skills and, more importantly, the confidence to carry their teams along on this journey. Along with these initiatives, the leadership and HR have the responsibility of designing and implementing performance and reward systems to reward the cooperation extended by employees to the change of process.

'In essence, nothing can be more exciting times than the digital times and digital area, both for organizations and employees. The key survival strategies are future gazing and adaptation in these turbulent times.'

Points to Ponder

1. Can traditional organizations coexist with digital organizations?

2. Does a multi-generational workforce complicate the 'change paradigm' for organizations?

3. Have the roles of leaders, HR and line managers become more integrated in the digital era?
4. What can be the key competencies for people managers in the digital era?

2
Managing Employees in the Digital Era

The digital era has redefined the context of the workplace. Today, workplaces are globally integrated, bringing in diversity in all dimensions. Social media has transitioned from a communication platform to a connection platform. Employees today aspire to be connected and serviced across multiple platforms and expect support 24x7. These dimensions have opened up both challenges and opportunities for organizations, more so for the leadership and human resources teams.

Connected Workplaces

The digital era has brought in a sea change in modern workplaces. Organizations have now become connected workplaces with the help of multiple technologies in place. The age-old definition of organizations stands dismantled, and today organizations can be spread across geographies and time zones. The same team can now be scattered over geographies, work across different time zones and yet work on the same common goal. One may think: where is the need or driver for this connectedness in organizations? Is it just hype or does it make business sense—if yes, then how and why? Organizations today are now servicing customers across geographies. Customers today need services/products delivered under aggressive timelines. This has necessitated creating integrated teams. The concepts of near shoring, offshoring and on-shoring have come into workplaces. The revised organization offers integrated workplaces. The geographical distribution of scattered teams based on skills, task distribution/allocation. Teams' connectivity helps them leave a trail of updates on their tasks and help other members pick up the thread and continue with the work stream. Seamless integration of teams calls for more than just 'technology connect'.

The real connection of teams calls for 'people-to-people connect'. This is where leaders and HR come into play. They have the responsibility of creating a culture conducive for virtual teams. A stumbling block for digital transformation is the legacy mindset of both leaders and managers due to reasons of ethnocentricity and personal idiosyncrasies. The leadership tends to write off technology and depend on the old ways of working, due to the latter's comfort factor. By doing so, they harm not only their interests but also those of the organization and the employees. To facilitate the cultural transformation, a structured 'cultural change management' is to be initiated by organizations. The cultural-transformation journey needs to be carried out in a phased manner.

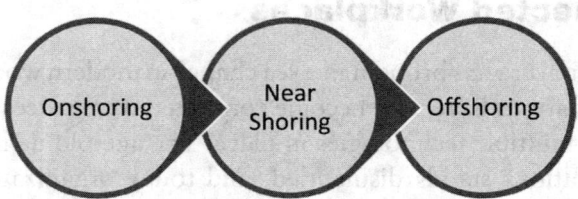

Figure 2.1. Integrated Workplace

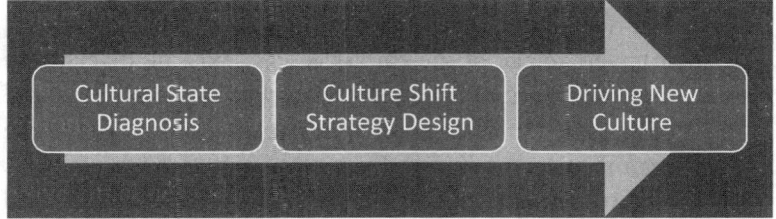

Figure 2.2. Cultural Change Management

1. **Diagnosing the culture state:** The diagnosis can be carried out by either the HR team internally or an external organization development (OD) expert. For reasons of objectivity and a clinical approach, an external OD expert is preferable. A study to identify the stumbling blocks to both the cultural transition and the 'shift of gears' is needed to help an organization transform culturally. The four major stumbling blocks often seen in organizations are (a) dated systems/procedures; (b) culture of compliance; (c) inability to adapt to new technology; and (d) the leadership's unwillingness to provide space for innovation and change.

2. **Designing the culture shift strategy:** The OD expert needs to work along with the top leadership on the 'cultural-shift strategy' through identifying the desired behaviour and carrying out a programme to engage employees in behavioural change. The focus areas for a cultural shift are (a) HR process redesign, especially in the areas of performance and rewards management. Performance management makes it easy for an organization to document and communicate the expected behaviour and the rewards associated with it.

3. **Driving a new culture:** The leadership has the responsibility of leading the change from the front through 'being role models' and 'walking the talk'. The factors influencing acceptance or resistance to change in an organization

are: (a) age of the organization and the leadership; (b) average age of the employees; (c) existing diversity in the organization; (d) agility/flexibility in the systems and processes; and most importantly (e) markets in which the organization operates. Executing a 'paradigm shift' is akin to managing an orchestra with diverse musicians and musical instruments. The leadership will have to work along with the OD expert to address these dimensions. In some cases, harsh decisions, like letting go of 'tenured leadership', would have to be taken to drive the change. The key to deliver success can be adoption of Lewin's force field analysis model.

Identifying the resistance forces and proactively handling them is the key to remove the resistance to cultural change and bringing in digital transformation. The existence of tenured leadership can be a boon or bane based on its technology orientation. We have senior leaders, like Mr Ratan Tata, who are pro-technology and have driven technology adoption in their businesses, even at advanced ages. Rigidity in leaders will thwart followers from ideation and innovation. Talented employees who are capable of driving the digital journey may end up leaving the organization in frustration. In essence, lack of flexibility in approach by

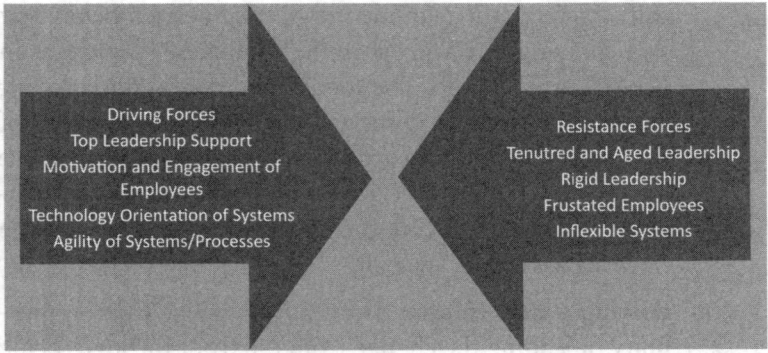

Figure 2.3. Force Field Analysis

the leadership and lack of flexibility in systems are two major 'show-stoppers' that can hold back the digital transformation of organizations.

Social Media: Before and After

The impact of social media is so profound that people are forced to differentiate between 'World before and after social media'. Social media has contributed to connectivity, communication, collaboration and the capacity to influence. Human beings by nature like to communicate and draw their energy from connecting and communicating with each other. People can connect with others, irrespective of geographies and time zones, and share what they feel about their life, experiences, thoughts and anything that has influenced them and about which they feel strongly or otherwise. The phenomenon of sharing with each other had a different cultural connotation before social media. However, in the social media driven world, extroverts, who are open to sharing with others, share effortlessly through social media, and introverts, who find it difficult to share things in person, have discovered a sense of comfort in sharing in the virtual world. There has been a marked change in human behaviour through sharing on social media, which has given people the power to influence others or build a strong virtual identity for themselves. The 'power of sharing' is the driving force for people, but the objectives for doing so vary among individuals, based on their personal preferences. This aspect of sharing has helped people collaborate for a cause and endowed them with the 'virtual capacity' to impact, achieve or bring into focus or maybe even change anything.

This power of social media has impacted employees in organizations in multiple ways. Employees today, unlike in the past, love to express due to their strong propensity to express themselves. The absence of such options can lead to employees

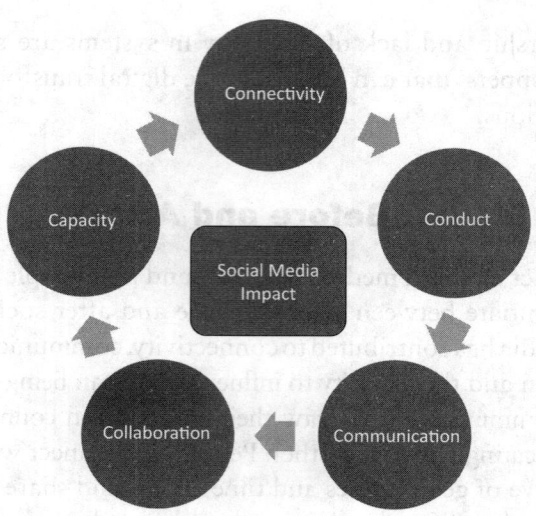

Figure 2.4. Social Media Impact

either slipping into 'withdrawal mode' or ending up expressing themselves on open social forums, which can seriously harm the image and interests of an organization. Organizations today are integrating and leveraging this aspect in multiple ways, based on their cultural and business contexts, for productive purposes. In the initial stages, organizations created intranets to allow employees to communicate with each other. The advent of mobile technologies has helped employees connect for both personal and professional reasons, through apps like WhatsApp, etc.

Organizations are leveraging connection to facilitate collaboration between employees, for the purposes such as ideation, innovation and teamwork. They are tapping into employee potential for ideation, innovation and productivity. The initiatives like 'crowd sourcing' are being taken for such aspects as policy design, product/service innovation and cracking of business challenges. The first step for organizations is to draft a strategy to 'leverage employee and social media potential'. The strategy can be anchored on four dimensions: (a) ideation; (b) innovation; (c) problem solving; and (d) branding.

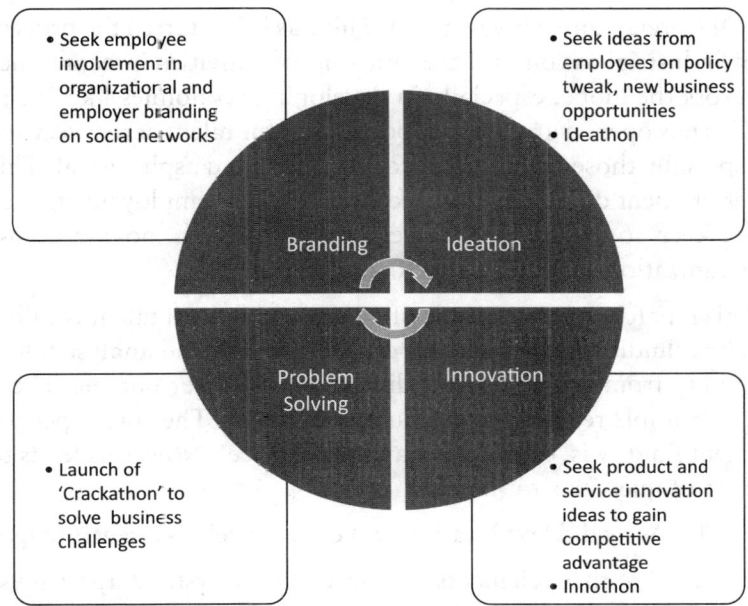

Figure 2.5. Leveraging Crowdsourcing for Connecting Employees

Organizations use a mix of these four 'employee engagement' pillars to connect and tap into employees' potential. It would be inappropriate to say one size fits all, as it is for the leadership of an organization to assess their context and use their inputs to craft their social media strategy mix. Inclusive organizations are involving employees in the design and execution of their social media strategy, as a measure of employee empowerment and engagement. Employees in the digital world do not like to be 'mere executors' of leadership decisions but love to be part of the decision-making process.

Fluid Talent

The advent of the digital world has led to countries maturing in the governance or moderating their liberation and 'opening up their economies' as a strategy to make themselves attractive for

FDI (foreign direct investment). This has kick-started the process of industrialization and the spurring of activities in economies across the globe, especially in developing economies like India. This has opened up career opportunities for talent across sectors, especially those who are skilled, confident and aspirational. This set of talent do not feel obliged towards their employers, as they are keen to realize their career dreams through moving across organizations and across sectors.

This flux (change in attitude of talent) and flow of talent is called talent fluidity. It would be superficial to study and analyse talent fluidity from only the select dimension of career pursuit. There are multiple reasons for the fluidity of talent. The core aspect of talent fluidity is 'exploration and experience'. Now, this leads to a set of questions for leaders:

1. Why did 'exploration and experience' take centre stage?
2. Are there elements one needs to understand apart these two elements?
3. Should these elements influence crafting of people strategy in organizations?
4. Can organizations create ecosystems to nurture and retain talent?
5. Are there best practices in the marketplace to be adopted by organizations?

The talent in the world are exposed to global trends and opportunities. Unlike previous generations, the current set of talent love to explore careers in a non-linear and unconventional way. They love roles across departments/functions not just in one organization but across organizations/sectors and geographies. They look for varied experiences as a method of adding value to their profile, as the market places a higher value on talent with diverse and rich experience. Talent has two key aspirations from careers. The first is the aspiration to explore different kinds of roles in careers, and second to gain personal and professional experience. This make talent command value in the job market.

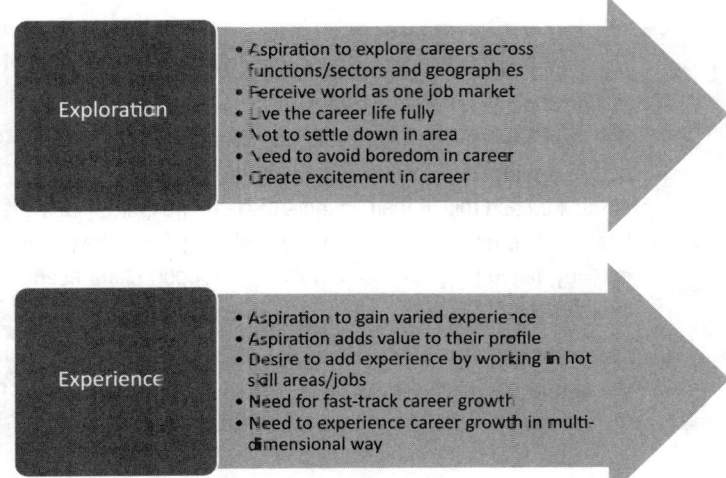

Figure 2.6. Employee Exploration and Experience

Leaders and the HR fraternity have realized the evolving trends and have started to redesign their HR strategy to bundle exploration and experience into employee careers, as part of the talent management framework.

> Best Practice at Infosys: The organization has realized these trends and the need to drive 'talent fluidity' within the organization. The talent strategy is interlinked to the business strategy of 'zero distance' between employees and clients.
>
> The 200,000-plus workforce tends to work closely in teams across geographies to serve its clients. The dimensions of talent fluidity at Infosys are:
>
> 1. Talent flow across skills: As the impact of the digital era on tech businesses started increasing, emphasis was placed on new-age digital skills, such as AI, ML, BDA, etc. The HR carried out a talent analysis to assess the preparedness of the organization for legacy versus new skills and created a road map for the transition of talent in new skill areas.

2. Preparation for emerging roles: Strategizing for the emerging business needs of the organization is implemented, and the preparedness of talent for emerging roles, in terms of skill sets, is mapped. The learning team then creates 'learning paths' for each role. It then anchors the learning journey of the talent in its process of reskilling and upskilling. Once the talent is ready, talent mobility into new roles to support client needs is facilitated.

3. Leadership support: The role of the leadership is critical in the design and execution of 'talent fluidity'. The leaders have to play a multi-pronged role, the first being gazing into the future of business trends and talent needs. The second role is collaborating with the HR in communicating with the talent and motivating them to be future-ready through upskilling/reskilling. The third role is helping the learning teams create learning paths for the talent. The last role is working along with HR in the mobility of talent for future roles.

https://www.i4cp.com/productivity-blog/talent-fluidity-in-action-at-infosys

Talent Services: Solutioning and Customization

The digital era has created an opportunity for talent to create an identity independent of their organizational roles. The other social and cultural factors such as nuclear families, exposure to global trends and customized products and service offerings are making the talent aspirational. The one-size-fits-all HR Policies does not serve organizations any more.

- **Sociocultural factors:** The family structure and social structures have undergone a sea change over the last few decades. The former has become nuclear, and both parents are working professionals, which limits their availability to their children. As a result, children have learnt to be independent from a young age. They learn a lot more from their peers and social media. The ability of young adults to connect, network and communicate is far higher in comparison to that of previous generations of young adults.

In their interactions with organizations, consumers have become more demanding and have gotten used to customized and focused attention. As a result, people are carrying similar behaviours to the workplace as employees. They expect a similar kind of focus and attention to their needs and aspirations and tend to review the employer–employee relationship periodically, based on their individual experience. Thanks to transparency and connectivity, employees have access to the experience of other employees, both within and across organizations. Thus, organizations have the responsibility of factoring in not just their services to their employees but those of the competition as well.

- **Economic factors:** External economic factors have a major role in the workplace dynamics between the employer and employees. Baby boomers are edging towards the end of their career. Gen X has assumed leadership roles across organizations. Based on their experiences with the previous generation, Gen X makes plans for financial savings to meet both their personal needs and those of their children. Millennials, unlike the previous generation, are well taken care of in terms of the basic needs of life (food, clothing, shelter and education). The freedom and choice experienced by them is much higher than that by previous generations. Gen X, because of their exposure to millennials at home, are supportive and understanding of the latter's needs.

Millennials, due to these factors, are choosy about their career choices and employment experiences. They have the habit of constantly validating their life experiences in terms of those of their peers. The economic stability and experience-based view of life are parameters that organizations need to take into cognizance while designing and implementing people policies and practices.

- **Technology factors:** Digital technologies have had a major impact on organizations, not just from the customer perspective but from the employee perspective as well. Employees in the digital era are constantly in touch with external trends of people practices and career opportunities. The empowered are aware of their power of voice and opinion and constantly look for opportunities within their organization. The advent of app-based work processes and interactions has redefined interpersonal interactions. Users of apps can connect and share their opinions/feelings on any topic/issue and check where they stand in terms of the rest.

  HR teams in organizations are innovating and re-engineering the HR process across the HR life cycle, in terms of recruitment, performance system, learning, etc. The key reasons for the design and deployment of apps for HR applications are 'ease of access', 'user convenience' and 'user empowerment'.

- **Competitive dynamics:** Organizations in the industrialization era used to focus on gaining or controlling access to resources for competitive advantage. With the advent of technology, organizations now focus more on process efficiency and excellence. In the digital era, organizational strategy is focused on 'experience centricity', and emphasis is placed on creating a positive experience for all the stakeholders, from customers and supply chain partners to employees. The experience gained by organizations in designing 'experience centricity' with customers and supply chain partners is being adapted to the 'positive experiences' of their employees. The experiences of customers and supply chain partners are interlinked with

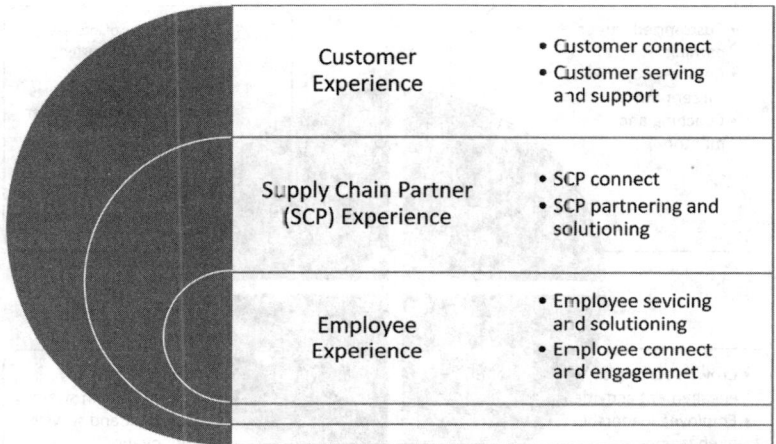

Figure 2.7. Competitive Dynamics and Employee Experience

and dependent on the kind of experiences that employees have with their bosses (organization). Probably, we could say that the 'core strategy lever' for experience-based organizations is driven by the employee experiences organizations design and deliver to their employees.

As a result, organizations are now seeing their employees as internal customers. This paradigm shift is forcing organizations to revisit the way they connect with and service their employees. The service delivery architecture has been seamlessly adapted to connect and serve employees. Service delivery metrics, like TAT (turnaround time) and CSAT/ESAT (customer/employee satisfaction), have become part of corporate metrics and HR dashboards. People metrics are being assessed in business performance review discussions.

Delivering Talent Experience

The integrated talent services model is multidimensional and scopes the four key needs of employees: (a) career needs;

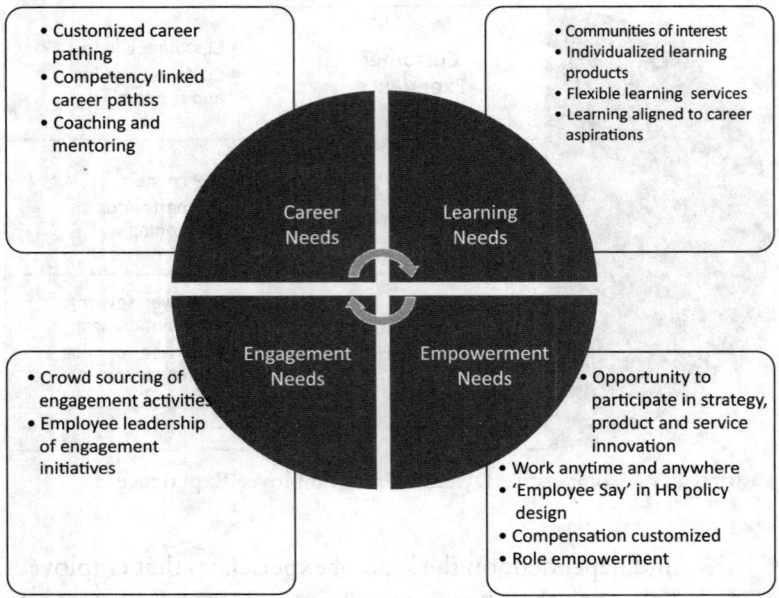

Figure 2.8. Talent Experience and Dimensions

(b) learning needs; (c) empowerment needs; and (d) engagement needs.

1. **Career needs:** Diversity at the workplace, which used to be a 'good thing to have' has now become imperative both for meeting business and talent needs. Geopolitical factors are forcing organizations to be inclusive in terms of diversity in all dimensions—gender, sexual orientation, culture, geography, skills, age and experience. Organizations are required to comply with regulatory mandates for diversity to operate in any geography/location. Customers today demand being served by employees who are familiar with their cultural context, in order to have a positive experience.

   The market reality is leading to business heads seeking talent for their business. The talent in the digital era are very focused on their career aspirations and goals. Their association with an organization is conditional to fulfilment of their career goals. The reasons for the talent-focused approach to career include competitive dynamics in the job market, peer pressure and personal orientation and aspirations.

It would not be inappropriate to say that the primary loyalty of talent is to their career goals and their secondary loyalty to their organization. Business and HR leaders have realized that having a linear or predefined career path and adopting a prescriptive approach would not gel well with the talent. As a result, initiatives are in place whereby new hires, after settling down for 6 months in an organization, are advised to explore the career opportunities/options available to them in the organization and draw up their career journey. In order to anchor/support the talent in career decisions, organizations have identified and designated domain experts and senior leaders, who are available as 'career coaches'. This approach allows organizations to offer 'individualized careers' to their employees. The onus of deciding and designing their career now rests with employees. An organization can provide options and avenues, but it is for the employee to make an informed choice with the organization's support. This approach to career planning leads to higher levels of employee satisfaction.

2. **Learning needs:** The conventional format of learning was structured around the classroom and focused on organizational priorities, and learning programmes were mapped to the roles of employees. The learning linkage was to the roles/positions and not to the role incumbent. In one sense, the entire approach was impersonal. Learning effectiveness was measured largely through the learning objectives set by a trainer for such a programme versus the learning of a learner. The 'transfer of learning'

to the business context was not measured. The net result was a 'wedge' between businesses (managers/learners) and the learning system.

In the digital era, both business managers and learners are looking for 'need-based learning'. The learning ecosystem has undergone a paradigm shift. The responsibility of learning has moved from creation to collection, curation, creation of accessible learning products and communication with employees to assess and track the learning of and its utilization by employees. The employees today look for on the job learning and learning opportunities linked to their current roles and future career aspirations. The learner expects to have the convenience of flexibility in learning and customization.

3. **Empowerment needs:** Talent in the digital era do not want to be mere executors of instructions. They love to be involved with their organization at multiple levels:

The first level of empowerment involves the ability of employees to design their jobs. It may not be practical for an employee to get 100 per cent freedom to design their job from scratch. However, it is possible to provide the freedom and space for them to design their job to

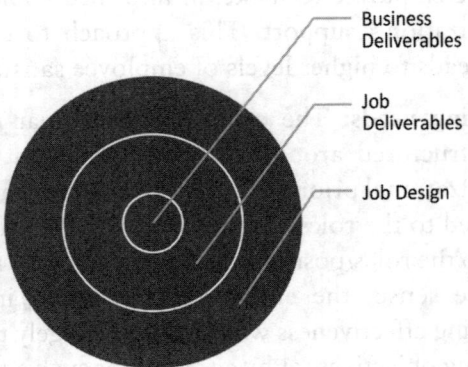

Figure 2.9. Empowerment and Employee Expectations

the extent of 15–20 per cent through initiatives like job enrichment or job enlargement. Talent in the digital era tends to outgrow their responsibilities quickly, and this is the reason for the disengagement and attrition in a significant percentage of employees. After completing a year in a job, an employee is aware of the job responsibilities and context due to the first-hand experience. The employee is the best resource to gain inputs on the scalability of jobs both horizontally and vertically.

The second level of empowerment involves job deliverables. Jobs for which the deliverables are pre-decided either by the system or the reporting manager tend to a create a constrained feeling within the talent. An employee would feel empowered when the reporting manager works along with them in co-creating the deliverables. There are cases of failure when a boss ends up leaving it completely to the employee to decide on the deliverables, leaving the employee directionless and disillusioned. Thus, there is a need for a balanced and calibrated approach, to balance the organization and employees' interests.

The third level of empowerment is where employees get invited to contribute to business strategies and deliverables. The era of leadership led strategy-related decision both in terms of design and execution are passé. Today, thanks to technological connections through apps, it is possible for the leadership to connect with a larger pool of employees and seek their inputs on issues like product/service design and roll-out. Ideas from the grassroots (front-line employees) would help organizations get insights on the market reality and improve the accuracy of their strategies/plans.

4. **Engagement needs:** There is huge published literature on employee engagement. The approach has been primarily based on organizational and employee psychology. There are organizations, like Great Place to Work,

that have developed their own framework to study engagement. A simplified approach to assess employee engagement needs is the 3C framework—connect, care and contribute. To validate the 'connect' of an organization with its employees, the following questions would be handy:

- Does the organization leverage digital technologies to connect with its employees?
- Is the communication real-time?
- Does the organization leave employee connection completely to the reporting manager?
- Does the organization have a structured approach towards employee connection?
- Does it have a mechanism to review and track its connection with its employees?
- Is the communication between the organization and its employees a two-way communication?
- Does the senior leadership connect with the employees? If yes, is the connection structured and regular?

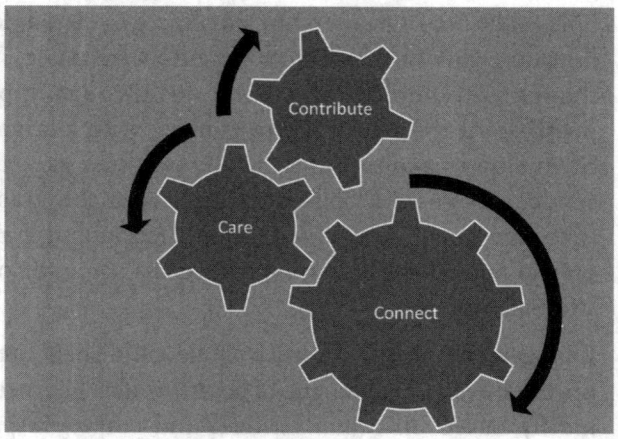

Figure 2.10. Employee Engagement and Expectations

The term 'care' is the key dimension to keep the bond or relationship between an organization and its employees intact. The definition of 'care' has undergone a sea change from employee perspectives. Employees today look for caring support from their organization in both the personal and professional spheres. Employee well-being, which was hitherto a good initiative in organizations, has become part of the core 'employee value proposition' (EVP). The 'care' dimension in an organization can be assessed using the following questions:

- What are the constituents of the EVP that the organization offers to its employees?
- Can the employees share their feedback with their bosses, uninhibited?
- Does the organization capture the 'voice of the employee' and act on it?
- Do the employees find it easy to share their grievances and get them addressed?
- Does the organization periodically measure its employee-engagement levels?
- If it does, does it depend only on engagement surveys or does it have alternate approaches as well?
- Does the organization have 'employee well-being index' in place; otherwise, how does it track its employees' well-being?
- Are the organization and its employees are on the same page about the 'care' dimension?
- Does the organization care to support the competence development of its employees?

Apart from the employer–employee angle, the 'care' dimension has other angles too. It has to be part of the 'DNA' of an organization. Employees today make an assessment of their organization based on how it treats its other stakeholders, such as customers, supply chain partners and society at large.

Figure 2.11. Caring Organization and Stakeholders

Corporate citizenship behaviour includes CSR (corporate social responsibility), which is part of the 'care' dimension of an organization.

The 'contribute' dimension refer to the 'value-add' that an organization and its employees offer to each other in a reciprocal relationship. It is but natural for an organization to assess its 'ROI' on its people assets. The 'contribute' dimension in an organization can be assessed using the following questions:

- Is the communication top-down or two-way in the organization?
- Do the bosses/managers invite suggestions from employees?
- Do the bosses/managers identify and value the skills of their team members?
- Do the bosses/managers assign responsibilities to team members based on their skills?

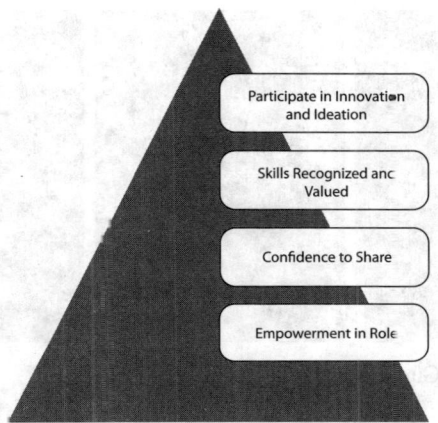

Figure 2.12. Employee Contributions and Dimensions

- Is there a climate of empowerment for employees to think, add value and deliver in their jobs?
- Does the organizational culture support the spirit of innovation/creativity?
- Does the organization take initiatives to invite suggestions from employees?
- Does the organization involve employees at large in the product/service design stage?

On-Demand Talent: Gig Workers

One aspect of the digital economy which has helped organizations deal with the competitiveness, complexity and dynamism in the marketplace is the flexibility in people staffing and talent availability. According to estimates, the digital gig economy has generated a gross volume of approximately $204 billion from worldwide customers during the year. The gig economy is expected to grow at a compound annual growth rate (CAGR) of 17 per cent and is forecasted to clock a gross volume of USD

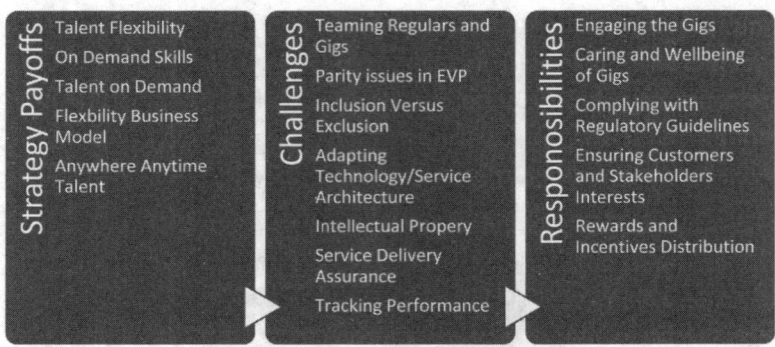

Figure 2.13. Gig Strategy—Perspectives

455 billion by the year 2023. McKinsey Institute, in its estimates, forecasted that the US GDP could grow by 2.3 per cent and could reach 2.7 per cent of full-time employment by 2025.

(The Pros and Cons of the 'Gig Economy'—Northern Trust—Commentaries—Advisor Perspectives; https://images.app.goo.gl/yZguUAkfDHNWGHw59)

From a strategy perspective, gig workers bring in pay-offs for organizations. Besides, they bring in responsibility as well.

- **Strategy pay-offs:** There are several strategic reasons for an organization to opt for the gig model of talent. The first aspect is the flexibility of talent for the organization. In the competitive sphere, businesses have been exposed to turbulence, calling for frequent resizing and right-sizing of talent/employees. However, it is not easy, due to various factors, like employee motivation and related issues. This has created the need for alternate staffing models, and the gig model has come in very handy for organizations. Gig workers can be quickly scaled up or down in response to business needs, impacting the talent at large. Another dimension of the dynamic business environment is the constant changes in skills/competencies. It is time-consuming and cost-intensive task to hire, train and retain talent to meet the skill needs. Gig workers provide an opportunity for organizations to shop for talent off the shelf and deploy them in the 'plug-and-play' mode. This dimension offers the opportunity for organizations to have a flexible business model, to source, onboard and deploy talent across geographies based on business/client needs.

- **Challenges:** Having seen the pay-offs, it is time to review the challenges associated with gig talent to understand the reality. The first challenge to be addressed is integrating and teaming up gig workers with regular employees. The regular employees may refuse to accept and include the gig talent into projects and work streams. The gig employees could experience a sense of exclusion, resulting in their frustration, and they may end up leaving the organization. This could negatively impact the organization by defeating the purpose of onboarding gig talent. In addition, it could lead to service lapses and product failure, inviting the wrath of customers. The other challenge faced by the leadership and HR is the constant comparison in employee offerings (EVP) between the full-time and gig employees. It's akin to balancing on Damocles sword. It is necessary to have equity, so that neither party feels cheated/exploited. The other challenge of employing gig workers involves technology and service architecture. Before onboarding the gig talent, organizations would have to carry out process re-engineering to seamlessly integrate them and facilitate teamwork between gig and full-time employees. Neglect of this dimension could termed right around the system, extending to human dimensions. Re-engineering the systems has three objectives. Intellectual property, assuring service delivery by tracking performance on a real-time basis. The induction of gig talent can lead to breach of the confidentiality clause contracted with clients and business partners. To avoid such breach, organizations need to sign 'back-to-back' contractual agreements, linking contractual clauses pertaining to clients with clauses of gig employment contracts. One key risk associated with deploying gig talent relates to service assurance. The fluidity of talent induces risks of talent mobility, on the one hand, and client dissatisfaction, on the other. The last-but-not-least challenge is tracking the real-time performance of gig talent. Unless organizations design systems around the selection and hiring of gig workers, have clarity in their reporting relationship, clearly articulate gig workers' performance goals and track their performance on a regular basis, they may end up with the gig talent hanging loose, leading to a host of issues, ranging from an unproductive workforce and demotivation of other employees to failure to satisfy customers.

The question is: how does one manage this challenge? The challenge has to be managed.

- **Responsibilities:** An organization, in order to benefit from gig talent, has to strategize and discharge responsibilities at three levels. The leadership and HR have to create a culture of openness and diversity in the organization, through 'walking the talk', and in their communications and interactions with the employees. The next key aspect of culture that the leadership needs to be cognizant of is 'transparency'. The leadership has the responsibility of communicating the urgency of and need for engaging gig talent.

  Once the cultural dimension is built, the next task is to align the organizational policies, in both the business and HR domains, with the hiring and engagement of gig talent. Unless specific goals are defined in the policies, they may end up becoming aspirational statements without any traction. Once the policies are formulated, it is equally essential to design and implement monitoring

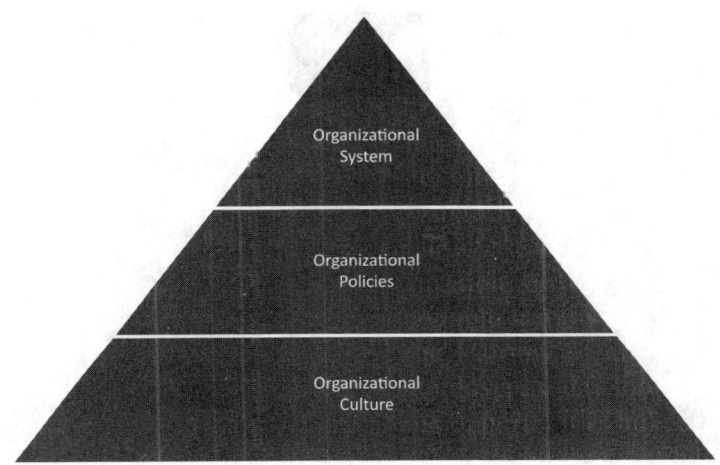

Figure 2.14. Gig Talent Management Pyramid

systems, to track the progress and impact of the stated gig policies of the organization.

Talent Valuation: A Key Business Indicator

The primary driver of the value of an enterprise is the quality and value of its talent. This has provided the scope for 'valuing the talent' in an organization. Talent valuation as a concept can be studied through three broad approaches.

- **Cultural approach:** In the cultural approach, the organization focuses on creating and nurturing a culture of respecting every employee. The leaders lead the culture-building initiative by 'walking the talk' through respecting every employee whom they get in touch with, especially the teams that work with them directly.

- **Systems approach:** In the systems approach, the focus is on establishing systems that aim to identify talent, create a talent repository, value the talent for their uniqueness and deploy them in a role according to a role–person fitment formula. The strategic intent is to

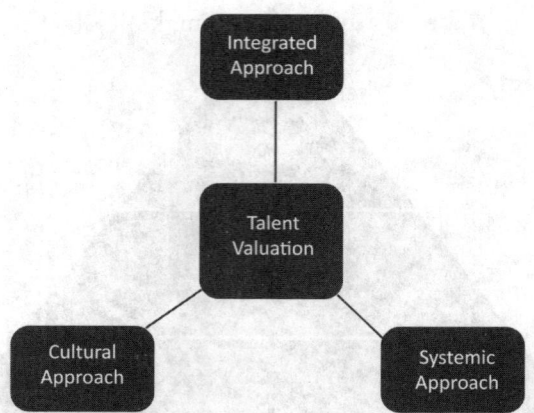

Figure 2.15. Talent Valuation Approaches

help the organization get 'added value' from the talented employees, through role fitment. The organization tries to derive its competitive advantage from the talent.

- **Integrated approach:** The integrated approach is a hybrid of the cultural and systems approaches. In this approach, the organization tries to create a culture of identifying and respect talent. Subsequently, it tries to create a system to align the talent with it, to get 'value-added' contributions from the employees. Thus, the focus is on building value for the organization through getting ROI from the talent valuation and investments. Another key differentiator in this approach is the tracking of the financial value of the talent in conjunction with the 'value added' to the balance sheet of the enterprise.

The state of preparedness for the talent valuation journey can be assessed using the following questions:

- Does the organization have a culture of respecting every employee with unique talent?
- Does the organization have a system to regularly assess the competencies/skills of its employees and create a 'talent repository'?

- Does the reporting manager make it a point to discuss the competencies of their team members and provide feedback on their competencies and a development plan?
- Does the manager discuss their employees' career aspirations vis-à-vis their competencies?
- Does the organization track the 'Value-Adding Roles and Employees' to the performance of the organization?
- Does the manager consider the competency level of their team members while deciding/recommending regarding their compensation?
- Does the organization have a system of calculating the talent capital and tracking its appreciation/depreciation on an annual basis?
- Does the organization have an accounting practice of calculating the value of its talent capital and representing it in its balance sheet?
- Does the organization analyse the business performance vis-à-vis talent valuation?
- Does the organization track its market capital vis-à-vis talent capital valuation?
- Does the organization have policies and systems to invest in developing its talent valuation?
- Does the organization have a key to metrics that impact talent valuation?
- Does the top leadership include 'talent value' as a regular agenda item in their business review meetings?

In essence, management of talent in the digital era presents opportunities and challenges. The multidimensional sociocultural factors, competitive dynamics in the market and technology changes have completely changed the way organizations connect and deal with employees. Organizations need to leverage technology to track and deliver a positive employee experience, value talent and track their business performance and deal with a talent mix, with gig talent becoming part of the workforce.

Points to Ponder

- How can organizations deal with challenges in digital workplaces?
- Can co-creation as a people strategy help organizations in the digital context?
- How can organizations leverage and integrate gig talent for competitive advantage?
- How can organizations leverage talent experience for their branding?
- How can organizations institutionalize talent valuation as a cultural phenomenon and not merely as a financial-analysis tool?

3
Creating Experience-Levered Organizations

The digital era has brought in the need for openness in all aspects of human life, more so for organizations. Unlike the past, every interface/act/initiative of organizations, without their involvement due to social media, professional networks. The openness has ushered in transparency in both internal and external processes. Unlike in the past, organizations today are redesigning themselves around 'experience', which acts as a competition differentiator.

Demystifying 'Experience'

> A customer walked into a retail outlet and tried to shop from the racks. She observed that a lot of items were lying disorganized in the racks, and the trolleys were lying all around, which made it difficult for her to

> navigate the aisles and identify the goods that she was looking for in the racks. She noticed that a few store attendants were gossiping about how aggressive the store manager had been with them that morning when they had tried to explain the reason for arriving at work 10 minutes late due to delay in public transport. Another colleague lamented that the previous month, during the appraisal meeting, the store manager had appeared to be on a 'fault-finding' mission more than providing any inputs for self-development or career development.

Having seen a snapshot of the two dimensions, one from a customer perspective and the other from an employee perspective, it is important to understand 'experience' with the help of the following questions:

1. What does 'experience' stand for in the context of an organization?
2. What is the difference between a 'narrow approach' and a '360° approach' to 'experience' by an organization?
3. How does 'employee experience' impact 'customer experience'?
4. Is 'experience' a strategy driver or part of 'core strategy' in the digital world?
5. How does 'experience' impact brand equity and valuation?
6. Who are the stakeholders involved in creating an 'experience-levered organization'?

Experience, in the context of an organization, refers to the summation of the feelings, be they positive or negative, that any

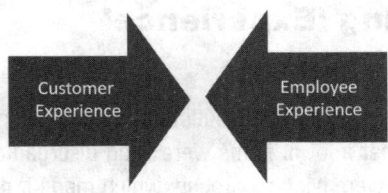

Figure 3.1. Competitive Levers

stakeholder has on getting in touch with an organization, be it as an investor, customer, employer or supplier connected with the organization. It is influenced by a wide gamut of factors. A narrow approach to employee experience would look at it in the context of HR process, which impacts the organization the most. Leaders/managers could use the 20–80 principle to identify the key processes/areas and invest energies and resources in them to ensure that they are analysed and redesigned to deliver superior experience in relation to the past. One may think: is it not akin to missing the wood for the trees? Well, it definitely is, as organizations may end up creating islands of excellence. This may help an organization in the short run with small wins, but in all likelihood, the organization may end up getting frustrated and revert to 'old way' due to people inertia.

For any change that an organization may want to initiate, there are always contrarian forces that wait for a debacle, seize the moment and kill the new initiative. This could be Ok from an internal corporate power tussle, where the parties can celebrate the 'Wins' or 'Losses' based on which side they stand by? In essence, the organization in entirety would end up losing the battle in the competitive marketplace.

Then, the question is what approach an organization should adopt to move in the direction of becoming an 'experience-levered' organization. The solution lies in adopting a '360° approach' that scopes all the stakeholders connected and interfacing with the organization. The organization would have to review the feedback from all the stakeholders connected with it, identify the opportunities for improvement and work on

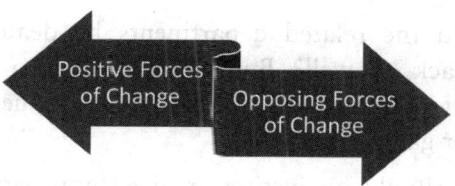

Figure 3.2. Employee Experience and Competing Forces

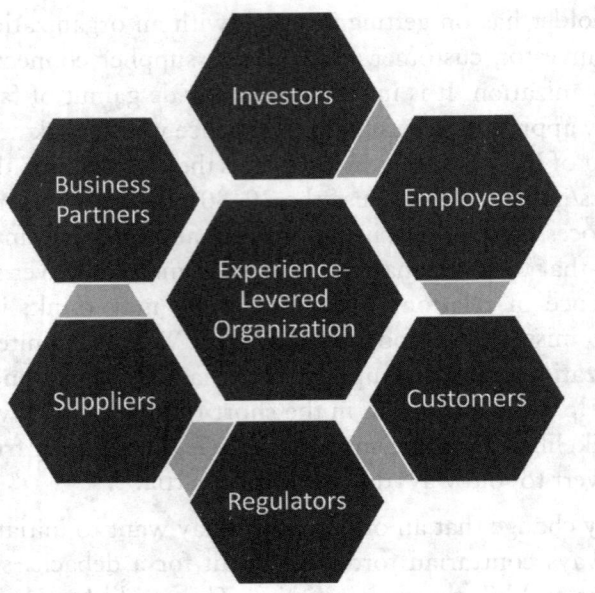

Figure 3.3. Experience-Levered Organization and Stakeholder Impact

them to deliver a superior experience to all of them when they interface with it.

This brings into focus the importance of feedback, regarding which a few pertinent questions need to be asked:

- Why is feedback so important especially in the digital era?
- Who is supposed to collect feedback in an organization?
- Who should process the feedback and identify opportunities for improvement?
- Should the related departments be dealing with the feedback as well? But would doing so not lead to 'conflict of interest', leading to dilution due to corporate power games?
- How should an institutionalized approach towards a 'feedback management system' look like?

Human Feedback Systems

In the connected world that we live in, stakeholders are keen that organizations listen to their 'voice' in the first place, 'act' on it promptly and close the loop with them. In the absence of fulfilment of their expectations in any of the steps/stages, they would not blink twice before going on social media and sharing their experiences, which sometimes go viral and have a devastating impact on the image of organizations, seriously jeopardizing their operations or even ending their valuation in the marketplace.

Several organizations have designed and implemented systems that capture feedback but have failed at 'acting promptly' or 'closing the loop' with the person sharing the feedback, which is more frustrating from the feedback-giver's perspective and can actually harm the organization adversely. It is better for organizations to not make 'half-baked' or 'half-hearted' attempts at feedback generation, as these do more harm than good. It is important to look at the impact of AI or ML on feedback systems. Several organizations have automated 'feedback systems' using chatbots for achieving the multiple objectives of manpower optimization, cost-effectiveness and provision of standardized and qualitative experience to 'feedback-givers'. However, the processes so designed are sometimes inhuman and frustrating from the customer's perspective. This is where ingenuity comes into the picture—while designing automated systems.

DEALING WITH A CHATBOT: AN INSIGHTFUL EXPERIENCE!

A medical director of a large hospital tried to connect with a leading insurance company to resolve an issue of one of his patients. He was directed to a chatbot which went in a structured way, asking for customer details. After checking the details, the chatbot shared that the claim had been rejected. The doctor tried to have a conversation, but when he tried to have an advanced conversation he got stonewalled, and the chatbot tried to take feedback on the service delivered.

Experience as a Strategy Lever

The first step towards 'automation of processes' is to visualize the possibilities for which a customer may connect. The next step is to understand the possible queries that come from customers. The last but most important step is to provide scope for an 'escalation' step, rather than 'stonewalling' a customer. Unfortunately, most automated feedback systems are designed to deal with basic and transactional queries and close-loop the interface. Unless the escalation mechanism is integrated into automation, the so-called automation can only help get a low number of wins in terms of a few transactional metrics, such as number of complaints received versus number of complaints resolved, CSAT, queries resolved in TAT, etc. The so-called dashboards track only these dimensions. The moot question is: should leaders be happy with a green colour coding for these transactional metrics and celebrate 'transactional excellence', interpreting it as 'operational excellence'? Should they do so, they would be living in a 'fool's paradise'.

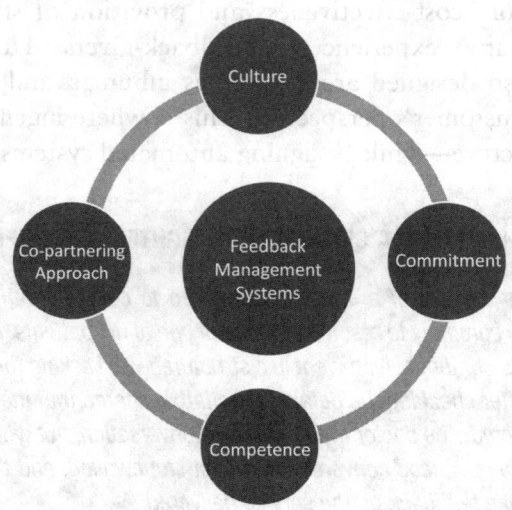

Figure 3.4. Four C's of a Feedback Management System

Dealing with Feedback Dilemma

The key question that leaders battle with while dealing with feedback is who should be dealing with the aspects of collecting, processing and acting on feedback. There is no clear answer, as it is dependent on a couple of factors that impact leadership decisions. Leaders could rely on the '4C approach' to arrive at a workable decision best suited to their context.

Culture is a key factor influencing the decisions involving the design and roll-out of feedback management systems. The culture of an organization can be interpreted using the OCTAPACE model. The impact of each of the cultural dimensions on the feedback management system can be analysed using the following table.

Cultural Dimension	Organizational Insight	Impact on Feedback Systems Design
Openness	Leaders and teams are comfortable being open to sharing feedback and information transparently.	A conducive environment can empower teams managing the process or servicing to collect and process feedback.
Collaboration	Leaders and teams are comfortable working with each other both for routine and critical deliverables.	Feedback systems can be created using cross-audits of the same team/function or between functions
Trust	Leaders and employees have a reasonable amount of trust and belief in each other about what they say to and share with each other.	Leaders can make a choice between empowering the team owning/delivering a process/service to own feedback and designing cross-functional teams.

(continued)

(continued)

Cultural Dimension	Organizational Insight	Impact on Feedback Systems Design
Autonomy	Leaders/managers make it a point to provide a fair amount of autonomy to their teams/employees.	Positivity in this dimension empowers employees/teams to collect and process feedback.
Proactiveness	Employees are encouraged to be proactive and to design and implement workplace improvement initiatives.	Positivity in this cultural dimension empowers employees with the end-to-end responsibility of collecting, processing and acting on feedback. This creates a positive impact on the customers/stakeholders. This helps in guarding against demotivation of employees/teams due to mistrust or powerlessness.
Authenticity	Leaders and employees 'walk the talk', which reinforces trust in mutual and reciprocal workplace relationships.	Leaders can choose to either empower the same team or form cross-functional teams.
Confrontation	Leaders and employees have a dialogue with each other on areas that they do not agree upon.	A high score in this dimension makes the situation conducive for cross-auditing.

(continued)

(continued)

Cultural Dimension	Organizational Insight	Impact on Feedback Systems Design
Experimentation	Leaders support employees' ideation of and experimentation with initiatives aimed at improving the effectiveness of systems/processes.	A high score in this dimension along with trust and autonomy are required to entrust employees with the responsibility of dealing with feedback systems.

A high level of commitment among its employees actually helps an organization get positive feedback from its stakeholders. Even if there were to be adverse feedback, the employee at the point of feedback would be able to take quick corrective action, thus eliminating the scope for escalation of the customer/stakeholder grievance.

QUICK CUSTOMER SERVICE DELIVERY AT A BANK

A customer, while returning home from office, realized he needed cash for shopping next day. He stopped the car near a bank ATM (automated teller machine) on the way and withdrew cash, and he drove away forgetting his debit card in the ATM.

After driving for 10 minutes, he realized his folly and drove back to the ATM and searched for his debit card. Not able to find it, he asked the security guard if he had seen it, but the guard responded in the negative. He immediately called up the branch manager and informed about the loss of his debit card. To his dismay, the customer received text messages of debits for a liquor purchase and other purchases in bulk amounts. He escalated the matter to the branch manager, who quickly assured him that the corrective steps of blocking the debit card and crediting back the wrongly debited amount would be taken. The customer thanked the branch manager for the quick help.

The level of competence of the employees who are deployed in the customer/market-interfacing role influences feedback systems' design. An organization that tries to optimize costs through lowering its hiring standards would end up hurting itself. In the first place, its employees would not be able to service its customers to their satisfaction. Second, the employees would not be able to handle grievances/issues of its customers. The organization may create a separate team to handle such issues, but this would not serve the purpose, as customer experience is dependent on the service at the 'point of interaction' or the 'moment of truth'. In these times of instant gratification, customer experience is primarily driven by the first-level contact who can handle end-to-end communication.

For an organization, carrying out all its activities by itself does not work in its favour in the competitive digital era. Organizations today look at focusing on their core business, and for non-core operations they identify partners to work with, based on their business needs. The feedback aspect calls for organizations to partner with specialized external organizations on feedback systems. There are multiple advantages to adopting such an approach, which has become all the more important due to

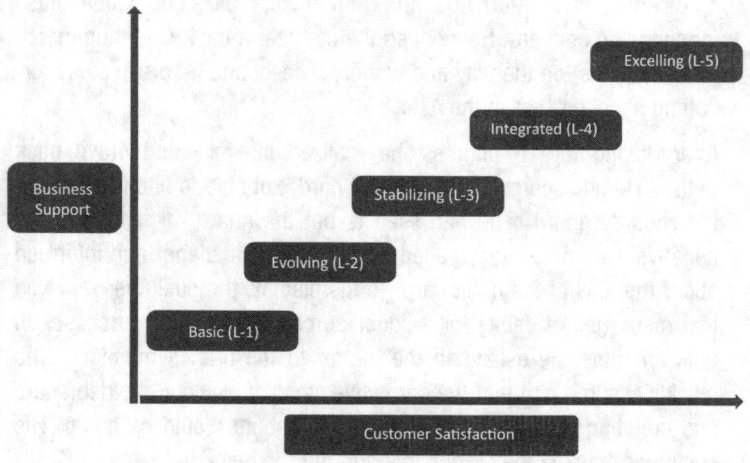

Figure 3.5. Feedback Management Maturity Model

digital interactions with customers either through the Internet or through an app.

The other aspect of a feedback system in the digital era is very complex, as it calls for high-level tech tools that leverage AI and ML to track feedback on social media platforms, like Facebook and Instagram, reach out to the customers concerned and try to resolve their grievance. One key aspect of feedback through social media is that the feedback, whether positive or negative, stays as a permanent footprint. The evolution of an organization's feedback management capability can be assessed using the Feedback Management Maturity Model (FMM Model)©.

Having looked at the FMM Model, it would be interesting to take a look at the types of feedback systems, along with their status and impact on organizations and customer experience, as captured briefly in the following section.

Feedback Management Mechanism Level	Status of the Organization	Impact on the Organization	Customer Experience
Basic	1. There is no defined process in place. 2. There is no system in place. 3. Handling of feedback is left to the capability of respective employees. 4. There is no tracking of the quantity and quality of feedback.	The organization would receive a lot of negative feedback. It would lose customers and market share due to ineffective handling of feedback.	Most often, customer would have a negative customer experience (CX). Dissatisfied customers would end up sharing adverse feedback through both word-of-mouth and social media.

(continued)

(continued)

Feedback Management Mechanism Level	Status of the Organization	Impact on the Organization	Customer Experience
	5. Employees are not coached or trained to develop feedback management skills.		
Evolving	6. Organization starts designing simple processes. 7. Feedback is tracked manually. 8. SLAs (service-level agreements)/ TATs (turn-around times) are loosely defined.	The organization would receive mixed feedback, as the effectiveness of the feedback system is dependent on the person/s involved.	CX would be mixed and positive, as the organization is making an effort to listen to feedback and work on it.
Stabilizing	9. Organization automates the feedback management system. 10. Dashboards are created to track feedback management.	The organization would start receiving positive feedback for its products and services.	CX would be positive. Customers would be giving positive feedback as long as their needs are met.

(continued)

(continued)

Feedback Management Mechanism Level	Status of the Organization	Impact on the Organization	Customer Experience
	11. Business and leadership reviews focus on feedback and action items.	However, there would be a few escalations, due to both people- and process-related lapses.	
Integrated	12. Organization integrates the feedback coming through online and offline systems/channels. 13. CX management is led by a senior resource to design, deliver and track CX across the channels/products/services and may involve external organizations that specialize in the area. 14. There is a very clear focus on CX.	The organization would have mostly positive feedback. It would be modelled by its competitors for benchmarking of their processes/products/services.	Customers would have a seamless experience in dealing with the organization, irrespective of the platforms/channels through which they try to connect and get their issues sorted out.

(continued)

Creating Experience-Levered Organizations | 69

(continued)

Feedback Management Mechanism Level	Status of the Organization	Impact on the Organization	Customer Experience
	15. SLAs and TATs are clearly defined. 16. Real-time tracking is carried out using dynamic dashboards.		
Excelling	17. The organization/leaders start discussing and communicating strategic advantages of CX. 18. The organization creates a 'centre of excellence' to drive the initiative at a strategic level. 19. Business metrics and CX are correlated and analysed. 20. Employees have CX as part of their KRAs.	Employees/associates of the organization would have a sense of pride for being associated with the organization. The organization would become a market leader in its space through constant innovation and upgradation.	Due to consistently positive CX, every customer would become a brand ambassador for the organization.

(continued)

70 | WINNING WITH EMPLOYEES

(continued)

Feedback Management Mechanism Level	Status of the Organization	Impact on the Organization	Customer Experience
	21. The organization in a way institutionalizes CX as a way of life. 22. The organization leads its competitors in strategizing and offering superior CX.		

Experience: Strategy Insights

The evolution of experience from its humble beginnings to becoming a strategy-influencing factor and then to a strategy lever is interesting, which has been influenced by socio-economic and technology factors. The FMM Model above indicates the journey that organizations could undertake in this direction.

Information Technology/Information Technology Enabled Services Industry

The impact of experience is not the same on all sectors. The organizations in tech and tech-enabled sectors were the first to adopt 'Experience Strategy' due to their business context. The designations of Project Manager and Client Relationship Manager have existed in the IT/ITeS (information technology enabled services) industry space for the last 20 years. In these sectors, due to the nature of the business environment, these roles were created to connect with, engage and service clients through the project life cycle. The engagement rigor between project manager and the client in terms of sharing the periodic information and review with the client on a periodic basis. The focus on providing an agreed-upon level of service according to the contracted TAT helps ensuring that clients have a positive experience in the business relationship. Since the advent of digital technology, organizations have moved towards providing clients with real-time project updates in place of periodic updates.

Retail Sector

The retail sector started with a focus on in-store experience as a strategy. The leadership interpreted in-store experience as the competitive differentiator. The dimensions influencing the shopping experience such as store layout, ease of identifying and accessing products, product diversity, pricing and discounts were evaluated and designed. One of the key aspects influencing the customer experience is the billing time and process. In the next level, energies were invested to improve the billing experience through the addition of more billing counters, billing during the weekend and automation of the billing process with product scanners. The twin challenges of managing the rush during weekends and festive shopping seasons and optimizing manpower staffing between weekdays and the weekend continued to remain a challenge. Amazon has introduced 'Just Walk Out' shopping in the United States.

> Amazon's 'Just Walk Out' Shopping: A customer can register on the Amazon app, walk into an Amazon store, pick up the items that they need and walk out without stopping at the billing counter. Amazon's technology automatically scans the goods as the customer picks them up from the shelves, bills the customer and debits the corresponding amount from the Amazon account of the customer.

Source: https://www.amazon.com/b?ie=UTF8&node=16008589011

E-commerce

E-commerce as an industry has evolved over the last decade in India. Initially the major players focused on the value propositions of 'convenience' and 'value for money', using deep discounts to lure customers. The entry of several new players led to neutralizing the novelty around these two value propositions. Added to this, the rate of cash burn became unsustainable and, in addition, regulatory restrictions forced e-commerce players to look at more options. The bid for upping the 'experience' forced them look at 'service and product innovation'. Technology has played a major role in this journey. Today, a customer can track the status of their order in real time and make changes to it or communicate regarding it with the seller. Players, like Amazon, that have several products/services are bundling products/services through subscription models (Amazon Prime), providing exclusive content (books/movies/shows/music), priority delivery, free delivery and exclusive discounts. This has now been extended to pharmacy and insurance too.

AMAZON LAUNCHES INSURANCE SERVICES IN INDIA

Amazon customers can take auto insurance for their two-wheelers and four-wheelers in India in collaboration with Acko General Insurance. Amazon Prime customers can pay the premium through Amazon Pay and complete the whole end-to-end transaction in two minutes without any paperwork.

The other features include hassle-free claims, one-hour pickup, three-day assured claim servicing and one-year repair warranty, apart from the option of instant cash settlements for low-value claims.

The strategy of Amazon seems to be clear — re-engineer the product/process, create a 'wow experience' that other players have not been able to and bundle it with the products.

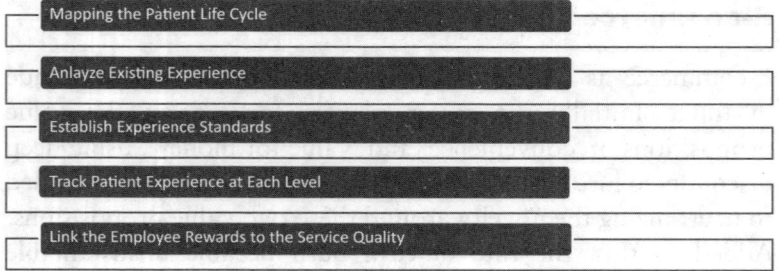

Figure 3.6. Experience Management in Healthcare: Steps

Healthcare

Healthcare as a sector has come of age, shedding its dated, brick-and-mortar high-handed approach towards patients. Today, an average patient is more informed about disease causes and treatment options and implications, thanks to the knowledge available on the Internet. Patients' experience while buying/availing other products and services is setting high expectations on the service quality of healthcare service providers. The steps involved in patient experience management are as follows.

> **APPIFICATION OF PATIENT EXPERIENCE:**
> **LEE HEALTH MEMORIAL, SOUTH FLORIDA**
>
> Lee Health Memorial is one of the leading health service providers in South Florida, with a network of six hospitals, more than 100 outpatient clinics and a free-standing emergency department.
>
> To brace against and differentiate itself from the competition, it developed a mobile app to make the patient experience positive. Coming to a hospital is a negative experience for both patients and their family members. The mobile app guides them through the treatment process. The app is designed to store patient health records as well, saving patients

the hassle of storing and carrying their health record. Further, doctors can access past data from the app to decide on a treatment course. The app is used to collect feedback at every stage of the treatment.

Source: https://www.inpixon.com/case-studies/lee-health-hospital-wayfinding-mobile-app

Education and Training

Education being a traditional sector, the inertia levels in the sector are high, due to the various factors like rigid hierarchy and strict bureaucracy. Thanks to AI, the entire education process has become user-friendly for both educators and leaners. The advantages of leveraging AI for the 'learning experience' are:

- **Personalized attention:** Limitations of time and space do not allow educators to give personalized attention to individual students. In this regard, ML and AI have been leveraged to create 'hyper-personalization'. This allows identifying learning needs, abilities and preferences to deliver the desired learning experience to learners. The learning content is broken into micro-modules that learners can access using chatbots.

- **Voice assistants:** Voice assistants such as Amazon Alexa, Apple Siri and Microsoft Cortana supplement educators. Leaners can access learning materials on their own, either while reviewing the learning after a session or for additional learning on the topics taught in a class.

- **Aid to educators in administrative tasks:** The often-heard complaint from educators pertains to their being involved in administrative tasks, such as admissions, student administration and evaluation of learning. In this respect, the design of tech tools has provided comfort to both educators and learners. Educators can automate the routine tasks like scheduling and evaluation of tests and set reminders for the tasks. These processes have been automated, easing the pressure on educators. On the learner's front, they can now carry out such tasks as registering for courses, checking their scores and querying on performance feedback at any time of their convenience.

- **Breaking of barriers:** The basic challenge with traditional learning is that it restricts and limits learning to the location/campus of the learning resources. This barrier has been shattered in the tech-driven learning environment. Today, a learner can access lessons and learn from anywhere and at any time of their convenience.

DIGITAL LEARNING REVOLUTION WITH COURSERA

The advent of globalization, on the one hand, and that of technology, on the other, have opened a new window called digital learning. Unlike previous generations, the current generation aspires for global learning opportunities to realize their global career ambitions.

Coursera was one of the early innovators in online education. It has tied up with the world's top universities, like Stanford University, to deliver courses to learners across the globe. Learners can sign up for the courses offered across a wide spectrum and complete them within the scheduled time frame, with the flexibility to learn at a time of their convenience and 24x7 access. The learners do not have to pay any fee for accessing the knowledge, but they have to pay for getting a certificate to authenticate their learning while seeking jobs or for career advancement. Coursera termed this initiative 'Freemium'. It has been continuously working on product innovation. One step it took for this was to cut short the duration of courses to make them user-friendly. For improving its revenue flow, it has tied up with corporates to understand learning needs and customized product offerings. One such example is its tie-up with pharma major Novartis, thanks to which employees of Novartis can have unlimited access to the product catalogue of Coursera. It is a win-win strategy for both Coursera and corporates. For the former, such tie-ups help improve its revenue flow, and for the latter, they help

> serve their learning needs and upskill their talent through a world-class learning service provided at affordable prices and on a flexi-investment format. The tie-up with Coursera helps Novartis track the effectiveness of its initiatives through various metrics, such as the number of employees signing up for various courses across disciplines, course completion rate, learning scores, etc.

Source: https://www.ifc.org/wps/wcm/connect/304 1eb88-e5dd-43d0-aab9-11cff1742db6/IFC-CourseraCaseStudy-May2020.pdf?MOD=AJPERES&CVID=n83-Doo

Hospitality

The seasonality associated with the hospitality industry has made it an interesting sector to study the impact of environment. Socio-technical changes have impacted the industry's strategies, structure and systems for the design and delivery of services to customers. The advent of room aggregators has come as a boon for all mid-sized and small-sized operators, who have gained visibility from customers across the globe. Their needs to invest in the marketing of their rooms, services and a large front office to take care of billing and servicing of customers have been resolved at one go. Room aggregators like OYO have simplified the entire process and brought in enhanced 'customer experience' through apps, which have helped customers make transactions on the go or even after entering a hotel.

Large properties and hospitality chains like Taj and Marriot have deployed AI and ML for redefining 'experience' to the customers. Today, their front offices have chatbots that take care of servicing customers.

The chatbots permit customers to choose their language of communication, unlike in the past when they had to depend on international languages. AI helps hotels discover the habits and needs of customers based on past patterns and offer them services proactively, and in the process create a 'wow'

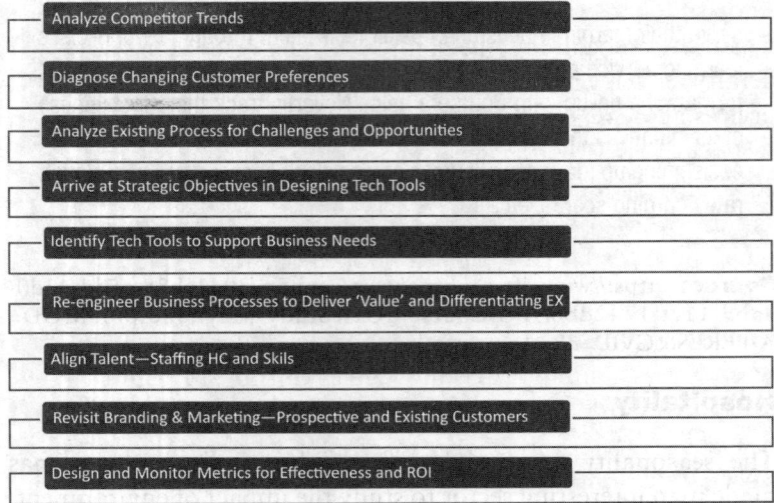

Figure 3.7. Tech-Aligned Business Strategy

experience for their customers. The services with scope for personalization include those related to music, books, food and beverage, access to clubs, etc. It is easy for decision-makers to get lost in the maze of tech tools, and for deriving the right benefits from the latter, they need to adopt a 'tech-aligned business strategy'.

The key to winning over customers is dependent on whether the strategy of an organization is designed to be 'at par' with the competition or offer 'next-level experience' to their customers. The ability of organizations to scan the environment and design and offer an 'innovative experience' holds the key to their gaining a competitive edge in the marketplace.

In the digital world, given the fact that product and service innovation is dynamic and ever-changing, it is imperative for organizations to design agile systems that can adapt to new tech-enabled tools and services without resulting in huge investments. To achieve this objective, organizations should identify tech vendors/service providers in the 'SaaS' or 'PaaS' (Platform as a

Service) domains offering auto product service upgrades. This approach has multiple pay-offs, like reducing the efforts to identify and upgrade systems and getting upgraded products or services at lower price.

Travel

The travel industry, which is closely linked to the hospitality industry, has adapted to digital technologies along with the hospitality industry. The travel industry was largely dominated by tour operators and by public sector transport (road/rail/air transport). The wave of liberation and privatization led to a host of private players stepping into these spaces. The positive aspect of this has been that today travellers have a host of options available to them. This complicated life for travellers and required them to chase multiple players to identify, compare and book their tickets. This struggle has led to the online aggregators like redBus in India.

BIRTH OF AN ONLINE TRAVEL AGGREGATOR: REDBUS

Mr Phanindra Sama started his tech career in the Indian Silicon Valley city, Bengaluru (BLR), as a software engineer. For a festival, he decided to travel back to his hometown, the South Indian city of Hyderabad. He had to travel in person to meet all the bus operators in BLR to check on the availability of tickets, which was troublesome. At the end of his efforts, he discovered that travel operators quoted differentiated prices, some of which were unreasonably high. Mr Sama analysed his 'experience' and discovered the pain points involved in bus travel, which included: (a) painful physical efforts to book tickets; (b) non-availability of a seat of their choice to customers; (c) no transparency in pricing; (d) pricing power resting with the bus operator; (e) no bargaining power for customers; and (f) the struggle faced by customers to get information on the quality of services rendered by a bus operator.

> In the light of all these issues, Mr Sama decided not to travel to his hometown, but these challenges triggered in him the thought of starting an 'online bus ticketing' platform through an app. The app would provide customers with the following facilities: (a) knowing all the bus operators operating buses from Point A to Point B; (b) comparing ticket prices; (c) checking the availability of seats; (d) checking the prices for seats in different rows, booking travel tickets and getting a soft-copy confirmation of the transaction through an SMS (short message service) message, email communication and a message in the login account created by a customer on the app; (e) checking the boarding and alighting points and making a choice on the same; (f) providing passenger feedback on a few parameters, such as timeliness, bus cleanliness, behaviour of the crew and facilities' availability; and (g) making changes in travel plans, such as rescheduling, cancelling tickets or changing the boarding plans through calling the operator.
>
> Mr Sama initially had to personally travel to each bus operator in BLR to convince them to join the online platform. After the initial success in BLR, he extended the platform to major South Indian cities connected to BLR, and from there to all the major towns and cities. Initially, the public sector undertakings were unwilling to join the platform, but as the platform gained popularity among travellers, even the public sector road transport services joined the portal to increase their seat occupancy and revenue with the help of differentiated seat pricing. The business model offered a path-breaking experience to bus operators and travellers.

In the context of product/service design in the digital space, it is important for organizations to identify the 'unmet needs' or 'challenges faced by stakeholders/customers' and design their business model around them. Such a strategy is bound to help organizations gain a competitive advantage in the marketplace based on their 'customer experience' level. One key aspect that leaders need to be mindful of in the digital space is that the so-called disruption has a limited shelf life, as competition is bound to catch up fast and it is bound to lose its 'novelty'. Hence, it is sufficient for organizations to design and offer a 'disruptive experience' just one time, through improving/scaling up their 'experience innovation' in the same or related areas, to stay ahead in the game and lead the competition.

Organizational Culture and Experience

Now that we have understood the importance of the process of 'designing and delivering a disruptive experience to customers/stakeholders, it is pertinent to understand the role of organizational culture in building and managing an organization around 'experience'. It is culture that lies at the 'core' of the 'experience strategy'. Though there are several models to decipher the linkage between the two, let us look at the OCTAPACE model for understanding the interlinkage between organizational culture and experience.

Cultural Dimension	Impact on 'Experience Orientation' of the Organization
Openness	1. Is the organization 'open' to ideating initiatives that are aimed at enhancing the 'experience' of its customers/employees and other stakeholders? 2. Is the leadership 'open' to ideas/suggestions given by the employees aimed at enhancing 'experience'? 3. Are the employees 'open and receptive' to new processes and systems designed and implemented towards enhancing 'experience'?
Collaboration	1. Does the leadership nurture 'teamwork' and 'co-working' among the employees? 2. Do the employees/functions work with each other in business processes?

(continued)

(continued)

Cultural Dimension	Impact on 'Experience Orientation' of the Organization
	3. Does the organization have in place people policies and reward practices that appreciate and reward employees for teamwork? 4. Do the employees support each other in efforts aimed at providing superior experience to stakeholders?
Trust	1. Do the stakeholders believe the organization on what it says or promises? 2. Do the stakeholders find their faith and trust in the organization reposed/reinforced after availing of products/services offered by it? 3. Do the employees trust each other while working together? 4. Do the employees find their co-workers standing by them in their hour or need, especially while dealing with external stakeholders?
Authenticity	1. Do the employees see their leaders 'walk the talk'? 2. Are the employees 'real' with each other in sharing their feelings? 3. Do the employees find support in adhering to the systems/processes? 4. Do the employees get encouraged or get punished for being 'authentic or real'? 5. Do the employees 'promise' what is possible to their stakeholders?
Proactiveness	1. Do the leaders/managers encourage employees to take initiatives? 2. Does the leadership focus on and emphasize preventive or corrective action while delivering a positive experience to the organization's stakeholders? 3. Are the people policies designed to nurture and reward the 'ability to take initiatives'? 4. Do the employees refer to their bosses or take steps on their own, within the policy framework, to render a positive experience to their stakeholders/customers?

(continued)

(continued)

Cultural Dimension	Impact on 'Experience Orientation' of the Organization
Autonomy	1. Does the leadership nurture a culture of 'empowerment' among the employees? 2. Do the organizational policies/systems provide a broad framework and give space for employees to take decisions and act based on customer needs?
	3. Does the organization impose on the employees rigid rules and a strict code of getting sign-offs from their managers for most actions while dealing with customers in the service delivery process?
Confrontation	1. Do the employees get encouraged by the leadership to identify issues and bring them to notice for solving them? 2. Do the employees fret in their communications with each other or discuss amicably diverse views on problem solving? 3. Do the employees feel comfortable to challenge each other in brainstorming or problem-solving situations to provide better solutions? 4. Do the employees have the freedom to correct each other in case they identify an issue while delivering services to the organization's customers?
Experimentation	1. Does the leadership encourage employees to try out new ideas aimed at product/service improvement? 2. Do the policies nurture or reward innovation and experimentation? 3. Does the organization have a practice of showcasing and celebrating the innovation and experimentation by its employees?

INNOVATION AT APPLE AND CUSTOMER EXPERIENCE

Apple is known for its product innovation and provision of a superior 'experience' to its customers through its products. Its culture of innovation was planted by Steve Jobs and continues to thrive under Tim Cook. The key cultural dimensions of Apple are supported by its mission statement:

> Apple designs Macs, the best personal computers in the world, along with OS X, iLife, iWork and professional software. Apple leads the digital music revolution with its iPods and iTunes online store. Apple has reinvented the mobile phone with its revolutionary iPhone and App store, and is defining the future of mobile media and computing devices with iPad.

The execution of the mission of Apple is anchored by its vision statement:

> We believe that we are on the face of the earth to make great products and that's not changing. We are constantly focusing on innovating. We believe in the simple not the complex. We believe that we need to own and control the primary technologies behind the products that we make, and participate only in markets where we can make a significant contribution. We believe in saying no to thousands of projects, so that we can really focus on the few that are truly important and meaningful to us. We believe in deep collaboration and cross-pollination of our groups, which allow us to innovate in a way that others cannot. And frankly, we don't settle for anything less than excellence in every group in the company, and we have the self-honesty to admit when we're wrong and the courage to change. And I think regardless of who is in what job those values are so embedded in this company that Apple will do extremely well.

The cultural characteristics of Apple are: (a) top-notch excellence; (b) creativity; (c) innovation; (d) secrecy; and (e) moderate competitiveness. To nurture excellence in Apple's culture, Steve Jobs started the practice of hiring only the best talent in the market. Apple employees are encouraged to compete with each other to design superior products. In the area of innovation, Apple encourages employees to innovate at a rapid rate the emphasis being on fast innovation to help Apple launch newer versions of its products and provide superior value to its customers.

In terms of secrecy, the organization has strict guidelines that prevent employees from disclosing product details due to the competitiveness in the market. The dimension of moderate combativeness helps the organization challenge its employees and inspire them towards superior innovation.

Preparing Organizations for 'Experience'

The journey of an organization to become 'experienced-levered' is based on four key factors:

1. **Cultural transformation:** The first step towards transforming an organization is to analyse the business context from both the current and emerging scenarios. The next step is to carry out a deep dive into the culture, covering the dimensions such as ethos, collective values and assumptions. Once the current-state diagnosis is

Figure 3.8. Experience-Levered Organization: Four Factors

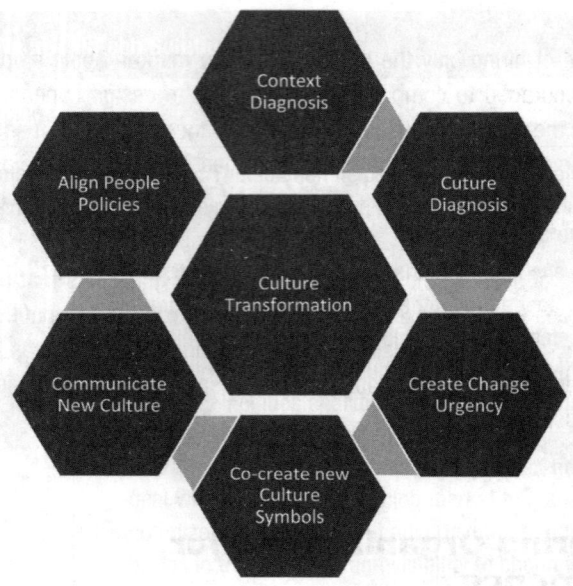

Figure 3.9. Experience-Levered Organization and Cultural Transformation: Factors

carried out, the next step is to create a sense of urgency in the organization and align and combine the energies of employees across levels to help them realize the need for change. The most important aspect is to involve as many employees as possible, across levels, in the journey of recharging and redefining the culture of the organization.

Bringing about a cultural transformation in an organization is easier said than done. For every supportive force, most likely, there would be double the number of opposing forces trying to protect the status quo and becoming champions of inertia in the name of continuity, for sheer personal and political reasons. The cultural-change process can be facilitated through understanding the organizational context using 'force field analysis'.

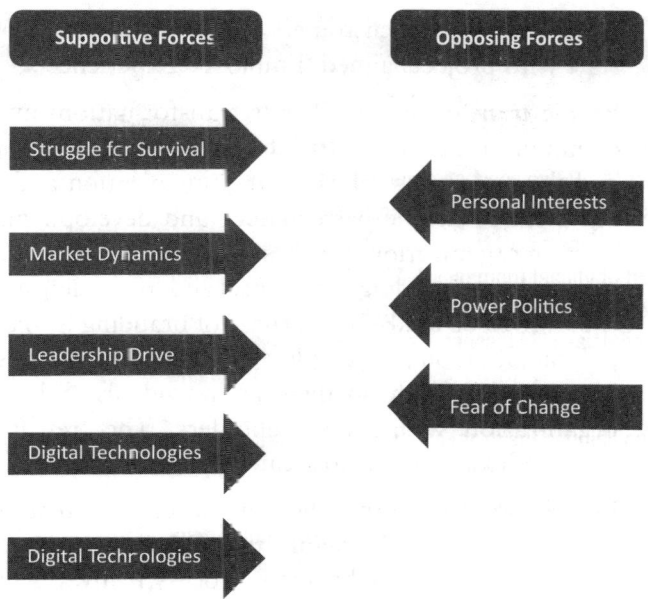

Figure 3.10. Force Field Analysis by Kurt Lewin

The key to transform an organization into an 'experience-levered' organization is to build synergies of supportive forces and neutralize the opposing forces. A few ways for the leadership to manage the change would be: (a) constantly communicating the need for change; (b) communicating the consequences of maintaining the cultural status quo; (c) identifying employees who are supportive of the change and mobilizing them towards the change; (d) creating success stories, communicating and celebrating; and (e) rewarding champions of change for their positive and compliant behaviour.

The key factor to cultural transformation is constant leadership in both spirit and deed—the presence of leaders and their championing of the cause both in communication and through their efforts towards projects directed at creating 'positive experiences' for their stakeholders/customers. This is the best way to start with projects aimed 'Employee Experience'.

2. **People transformation:** People transformation involves communicating the cultural components, like values and the underlying ethos, of the organization and linking them to people performance and development. To reset an organization towards 'positive experiences', the two tools of 'branding experience' and 'rewarding experience' are to be used. The purpose of branding is to create pull factor among the employees, by making the positive impact it has both on them as individuals and on the organization with its stakeholders. The 'rewarding' aspect of experience is to create positive reinforcement.

3. **Process re-engineering:** The core lever for creating an 'experience-levered' organization lies in process excellence. The focus for business process is always linked to the top line and bottom line and rarely to customer experience. Two of the key hindrances to experience design and delivery are the dated structures and processes in an organization and the lack of role clarity and empowerment among employees. The process should be re-engineered through carrying out 'experience mapping' to capture the customer experience across the product/

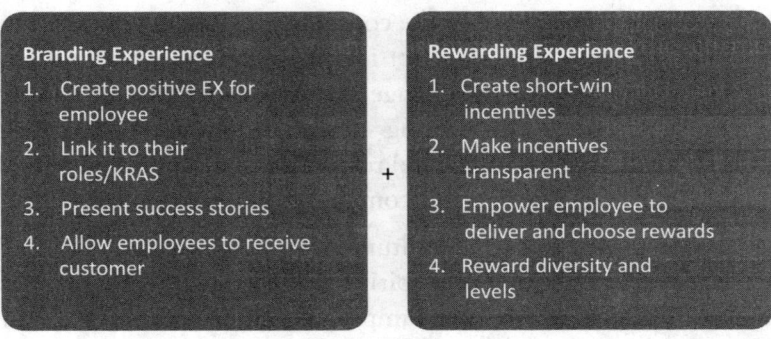

Figure 3.11. Branding Versus Rewarding Experience

service value chain. The approach should be a mix of inside-out and outside-in strategies to predetermine the experience levels to be delivered by the employees interfacing with customers. The experience delivery must be tracked on a real-time basis with the help of an 'experience index'. To translate the planned experience delivery into practice, it needs to be linked to the KRAs (key result areas) of employees.

4. **Technology alignment:** The regular approach of organizations is to automate processes as they are, in their eagerness to complete the process of automation. The net result is that neither the organizations nor their stakeholders, including the customers, get the desired results. The process of technology alignment needs an integrated approach in conjunction with other linked dimensions impacting it.

The success of tech alignment can be judged based on ability to deliver desired results and provide agility for quick adaptation to the emerging market and organizational needs.

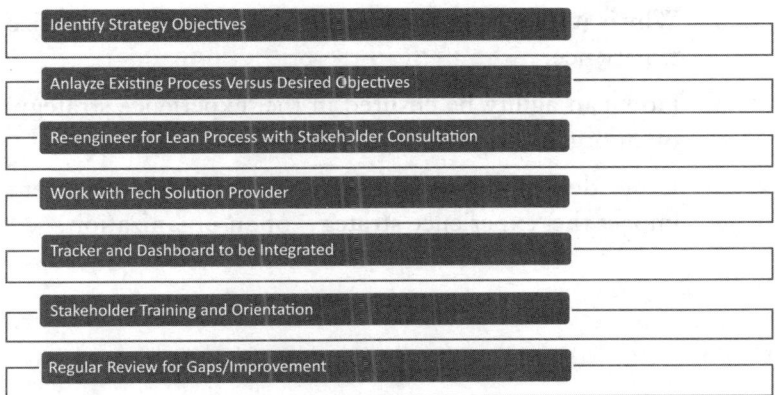

Figure 3.12. Tech Alignment: Steps

In essence, becoming experience-levered is no longer a 'good-to-have' aspect but an imperative for organizations to stay ahead of their competition. The approach adopted by an organization towards 'experience design and delivery' is dependent on two key factors, the first being the business strategy of the organization and the second being the culture of the organization. Organization can choose to adopt either a 'be-at-par' approach or a 'lead-the-market' approach. The former is relatively easy, as the organization can study its competitors or other organizations. However, the latter is tough, as the organization has to be strategic and innovative simultaneously. The strategy aspect helps it visualize the emergent future, while the innovation aspect helps it design and deliver a 'disruptive experience' and, in the process, emerge as a market leader.

Points to Ponder

1. Is 'experience' an over-hyped management fad?
2. How can leadership style and culture play a facilitating role?
3. Why is it important for an organization to contextualize experience?
4. How can agility be ensured in the 'experience strategy' of an organization?
5. How do employee engagement and empowerment impact the 'experience strategy' of an organization?

4
Acquiring Talent with Positive Candidate Experience

What to Expect...

This chapter starts with a discussion on the conventional hiring approach, its flip side and the issues in it. It touches upon the digital hiring canvas and its impact on candidate experience. It discusses in detail about crafting digital strategies for hiring, executing them and assessing their effectiveness. It explains why organizations need to focus on positive candidate experience and its importance for and impact on employees and the branding of an organization. It covers the impacts of positive candidate experience in talent attraction and retention.

Acquiring Talent in the Digital Era

Talent acquisition has come of age, from being an operational and transaction-driven function to becoming a strategic function.

The function operated largely from a reactive and execution mode earlier. Teams would wait for the hiring mandate from the hiring manager to start the process.

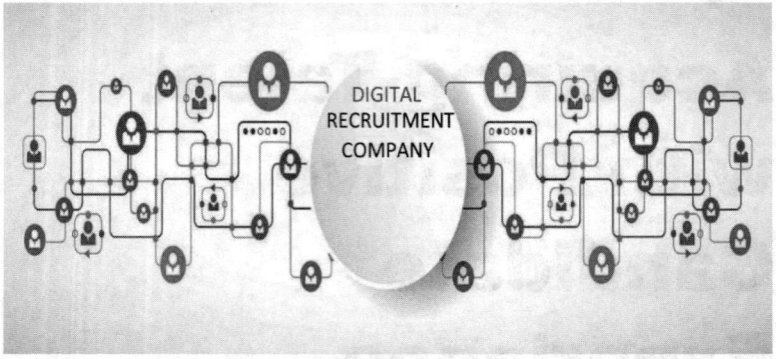

Figure 4.1. Design of Digital Organization
Source: https://images.app.goo.gl/gFg8USvDHoL4DqH5A

The comparative paradigm shifts in hiring in the digital era are captured below.

Dated Hiring Practices	Digital Hiring Practices
1. Wait for mandate from hiring manager	1. Business partnering though hiring
2. Try to source from referral, portals or consultants	2. Hiring has become talent solutioning
3. Process applications received	3. Use analytics (descriptive, diagnostic, predictive and prescriptive) for planning and effectiveness tracking
4. Wait for hiring manager's feedback	4. Forecast, plan and be ready to hire in shorter TATs
5. Deal with candidates based on their schedules	5. Use multi-platform integrated hiring model for hiring
6. Branding was limited to periodical adverts or press releases	6. Have HR, employer branding and hiring strategies synchronized
7. No efforts to measure employer brand equity	7. CX is the key focus Area
8. Hiring strategy is largely pushing	8. Metrics for hiring get defined and mapped for transactional and strategic dimensions
9. Time consuming processes	9. Social media is a key hiring driver
10. Effectiveness measured on rudimentary	10. Crowd-sourced employer branding
11. Huge dependency on external events	

Figure 4.2. Digital Hiring: Paradigm Shift

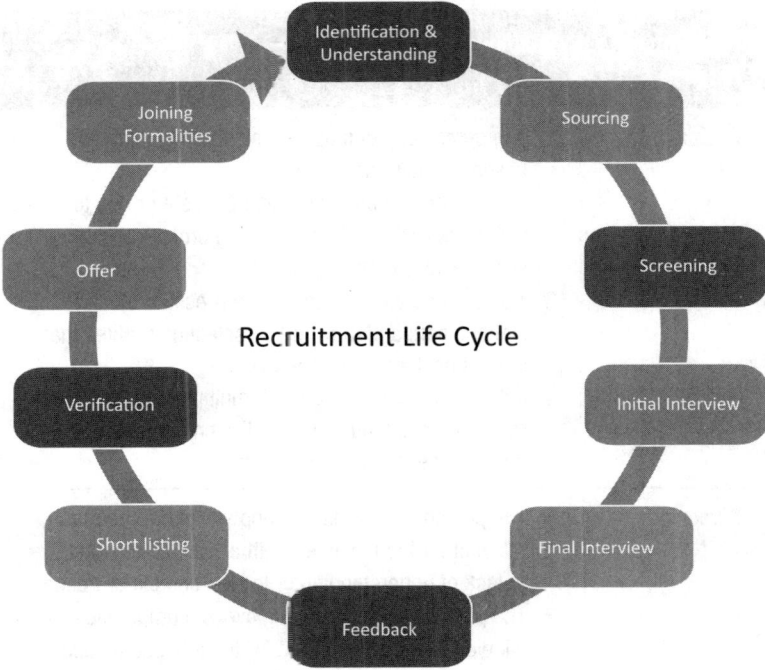

Figure 4.3. Recruitment Life Cycle Stages

The dated hiring practices were draining for the organization, the hiring team and all the stakeholders, as it was HR-intensive through all the stages of recruitment. This led to a situation of high people dependency across all the recruitment life cycle (RLC) stages and issues cropping up as a result.

From a candidate experience (CX) perspective, timely connection and communication at each stage of the RLC elevates the overall hiring experience.

Recruitment Stage	People Issues
Sourcing	1. The person can end up choosing wrong channels based on their gut feeling. 2. The person can pick up wrong CVs, either due to lack of skill of identifying suitable profiles or due to personal bias creeping in. 3. The person can succumb to the pressure of stakeholders and may end up selecting profiles that are not best suited for the role. 4. If the person is burdened with multiple profiles, they may end up putting some profiles on the back burner, marking them low on the priority list.
Screening	1. The person can validate wrong skills that are not relevant for the job, due to either lack of knowledge or lack of understanding of the job context or needs. 2. The person can validate the level of competencies at a lower level than required for the job, due to lack of due diligence. 3. The person can make the initial screening process but end up with an unpleasant experience, due to skill deficit or attitudinal issues.
Interview process	1. The person may lack negotiation skills to coordinate with the hiring manager and may end up protracting the waiting time for the candidate. 2. The person may not be able to guide the hiring manager on the profile, due to lack of communication or convincing skills.
Selection and shortlisting process	1. The hiring PoC may end up losing a shortlisted candidate due to dithering and delay. 2. The person may end up making the shortlisting communication shoddy for the candidate. 3. The person may not be able to clarify the status or process timelines for the next steps.

(continued)

(continued)

Recruitment Stage	People Issues
Offer negotiation process	1. The person may end up undervaluing the skills and experience of the candidate, leaving the candidate dissatisfied with their treatment, which can result in the latter rejecting the offer and the organization, in the process, losing the candidate. 2. The person may end up giving a wrong break-up of CTC, either due to lack of understanding of organizational policies or lack of appreciation of candidate's exiting salary break-up or expectations regarding the salary. 3. The candidate may accept the offer but consider the organization as a secondary option and search for other options, ditching the organization at the last minute and leaving the latter high and dry.
Onboarding process/ joining formalities	1. The person may fail to communicate the details of joining formalities and leave the candidate guessing about the next steps. 2. The person may not be able to guide the candidate appropriately on the steps in joining, leaving the process incomplete. This can lead to the candidate facing issues around background verification. 3. The HR may not be able to structure a holistic onboarding process and may leave the candidate 'groping in the dark', leaving room for formation of 'cognitive dissonance'. This can lead to the candidate forming a wrong perception and opinion about the people and culture in the organization and the overall organization. The end result can be frustration, which at its extreme can lead to early attrition, in turn resulting in a huge loss for the organization (productivity loss/hiring expenses going down the drain).

In essence, excessive dependence on people leads the hiring function to become unpredictable and unreliable, which does not augur well for both the organization and the stakeholders, including employees. In a competitive and dynamic situation where organizations are striving to improve predictability on all fronts of management and decision-making using technology and analytics, hiring/recruitment/talent acquisition cannot be left far behind.

Candidate Expectations and Experience

Changing Landscape

Candidate expectations have been undergoing changes due to socio-technical and demographic factors. To drive home this understanding, I quote verbatim candidate feedback on their selection process, sourced from Glassdoor, but withhold the names of the organizations for obvious reasons:

I applied online via job posting on a job boar. I was contacted by a recruiter via email the following morning and a time was scheduled that same evening to have the HR screening. Next steps were to be interviews with Hiring Manager, Use Case round and a behavioural round.

When the recruiter called me in the evening, he said my resume was already reviewed by the Hiring Manager and my skills matched exactly with what they were looking for. The job was in NY and I was based out of LA, so I was asked if I was open to relocation. I agreed immediately. No relocation assistance was even discussed. I was asked to provide a few time slots so that the next interview with the Hiring Manager could be scheduled. I emailed right after the call with my availability but the next morning the recruiter replied that the business team had identified a local candidate and they would directly make the offer to that person!

Question to Management—How do you make a direct offer to a local candidate (possibly a referral) when the ideal situation consisted of four rounds of interviews? Also, how professional is it to reject a candidate (willing to relocate without assistance) on the grounds of finding local talent?

Very smooth process. Done all over zoom due to pandemic, but was interviewed by direct supervisors in said role and felt that the leadership would be competent in the position if hired

First round was a series of code questions from leetcode. It involved four easy questions and one moderate question. You had two hours. The next interview was done through video, because of the COVID-19 pandemic. I liked the interview, because it was strictly technical. No questions like, 'Describe a time you demonstrated leadership'. These questions are stupid, because they measure a candidate's ability to interview, not to do a job.

I had to record my answers for the three questions provided. There were three attempts for each question it was a little awkward talking to myself and I felt weird; it can get you nervous as well.

Constant updates and contact with the organization on my status. All contact was via email. HR was receptive to answering any questions I had about the ongoing process. Overall it took about a month to get through the entire process. I was put in touch with many people within the organization.

It was the best interview process I've ever seen. The interviewers were very professional, and answered all of my questions perfectly. Very satisfying experience. I loved how knowledgeable they were about the company, and all the information they gave me.

Good and friendly people who made the interview and application process easy. The recruiters were honest and able to provide me with answers to all the questions that I had for them.

Had three rounds of interviews and received a verbal offer. Was really excited, planned a whole cross-country move. Then got a call late one night about three weeks later, saying actually never mind we're restructuring so we're pulling the offer. Would have been helpful if they had figured out their hiring needs BEFORE extending an offer, but what can you do. Please know that a verbal offer from them doesn't mean anything, and you should 1,000 per cent keep looking until you have something in writing. Really disappointing experience.

Figure 4.4. Candidate Expectations

A word cloud has been generated based on the real feedback (from Glassdoor) on organizations to summarize the candidate expectations that determine CX.

It is now necessary to look at candidate expectations at each stage of the RLC, as presented in the following table.

Recruitment Stage	Candidate Expectations
Pre-application	1. Organization to be visible as both a good business organization and a 'great place to work' 2. Organization to have positive feedback from its stakeholders (especially employees and customers) 3. Organization to be at a growing stage 4. Organization to be part of a growing or maturing industry 5. Organization to be known for its positive work culture (strongly rooted in values and ethics) 6. Organization to have leaders who are looked at as role models both within and outside the organization 7. Peers in the organization to be known to be helpful and friendly 8. Organization to be known for valuing diversity and inclusion in all aspects 9. Organization to be known for its corporate social responsibility activities 10. Employees to share a positive experience at being associated with the organization 11. Organization to be seen as a happening place in terms of recruitment 12. Organization to be known as a place that attracts and retains talent 13. Organization to be known to deliver a positive EX 14. Organization to be offering a differentiated and unique EVP

(continued)

(continued)

Recruitment Stage	Candidate Expectations
Application	1. Job advertisement to be unique and attractive 2. Job advertisement to be clear on job specifications and deliverables 3. Job advertisement to communicate the work context 4. Job to be easy to apply to 5. Application to not involve too many steps 6. Too much information not to be asked 7. Information to be provided on the professional networks like LinkedIn 8. Ability to reach out to the organization in case of query 9. Ability to receive acknowledgement for the application 10. Ability to witness the selection process and the steps involved
Shortlisting	1. Ability to track the application status on a real-time basis 2. Ability to get information on the next steps in the selection process on a real-time basis 3. Candidate to be consulted for scheduling the next steps
Interview	1. Interview panel to adopt a relationship management approach towards the candidate through the selection process 2. Interview panel to be considerate and empathetic 3. Interview panel to be professional in their approach 4. Panel to make sure that the waiting time is not long and stick to the announced schedule 5. If there are multiple rounds in the interview process, panel to make sure that the gaps between the rounds are not long 6. Panel to be accommodating in scheduling/rescheduling the interview on request for changes in case of genuine reasons

(continued)

(continued)

Recruitment Stage	Candidate Expectations
	7. The selection process to be customized to the position 8. Panel members to be aligned with each other to avoid redundant or deviant questions 9. Panel to provide the opportunity to the candidate to seek clarifications 10. Ability to leverage technology for some rounds, where it is feasible 11. Possibility of having at least one round of interview/interaction with leadership members
Offer of employment	1. Candidate's expectations to be sought and valued as far as possible 2. Organization to make an attempt to understand the need for customization of compensation structure 3. Organization to seek all the required documents at one go, rather than randomly seeking them 4. Organization to conduct discussions in a conducive and relationship-oriented environment and not in a high-handed way 5. Organization to share a draft offer and check the candidate's pulse before rolling out the final offer 6. Organization to be flexible on the aspects like the date of joining (being realistic and making it conducive for the candidate) 7. Organization to follow up with the candidate on a regular basis regarding the latter's acceptance of the offer
Onboarding	1. Organization to be in touch with the candidate till the candidate joins 2. Organization to check on the aspects like relocation needs and support 3. Organization to help the candidate connect with the prospective reporting manager and team members

(continued)

(continued)

Recruitment Stage	Candidate Expectations
	4. Organization to structure the orientation to give the new hire a 360° view of the organization 5. Organization to have a 100-day programme in place to check on and ensure the settling down of new hires

Having looked at the issues in the traditional recruitment format, it is now imperative to examine the reasons for the paradigm shift in CX and its implications for organizations. Technology has become all-pervasive, and digital technologies have become the primary focus in both our personal and professional lives. Today, an average individual spends more than six hours on the mobile handset, which is greater than the time one spends with one's family. Mobile phones have become a gateway for connection of human beings with the society at large, be it with friends, family or peers and bosses at one's organization. The way people used to interact in the traditional context is no longer valid in the mobile-driven world. This has necessitated organizations to look at appification of connection with the external world, be it in marketing products and services or connecting and communicating with their current and prospective employees.

Hiring Millennials and Gen Z

In addition to the advent of technology, the other social trend in recent times has been the rising prominence of millennials and Gen Z in the world. These two generations view life and navigate their personal and professional lives in a different way compared to the earlier generations. They expect to deal with their prospective employers using a mobile application. HR teams (hiring/onboarding) and hiring managers too like the aspect of

Figure 4.5. Mobile Hiring

access and oversight using a mobile application, as it helps them stay connected and respond to candidates on a quicker TAT. Mobile applications designed to support hiring process are in demand both with candidates and all other stakeholders.

The design of the mobile-friendly recruiting system is different from that of conventional hiring tools. The key drivers of effectiveness of the system are: (a) UX (user experience), which includes ease of access and use; (b) quick TAT; and (c) less information seeking.

It is important to understand the specifics associated with both millennials and Gen Z while designing a hiring process for them.

Millennials	Gen Z
Engaging millennials needs a different approach and calls for communicating the larger goals of the organization.	Strategic communication on the core values, strategies and insights of the organization must be undertaken.

(continued)

Acquiring Talent with Positive Candidate Experience | 103

(continued)

Millennials	Gen Z
They are willing to switch jobs without worrying about its impact on their career and salary, as long as the new job offer appeals to them.	They are a digital-native generation. They prefer connection with their employers/prospective employers through social media.
Their connection with the elements of 'flexibility' and 'innovation' is higher. The focus of the hiring-process designer must be on providing flexibility in the hiring process. A 'run-of-the-mill' process may not appeal to them. Hence, the emphasis must be on innovation in the digitized process.	They tend to look for options through their network. As a result, employee referrals become a major source of hiring for the organization. This calls for a revamp of the employee referral programme, in terms of both the process and the technology.
They value 'trust' from both their existing and prospective employers. Trust is created in them when they see openness and transparency in the overall process. The organization must ensure that the people involved in the process are 'walking the talk' while dealing with the candidates in the hiring process. For instance, the job advertisement must aptly and accurately capture and communicate the true job profile, without any 'padding' for appealing to the prospective candidates. Discovery by a candidate of such falsification can lead to their aborting the process or exiting the system after being hired.	They prefer being hired from their campus rather than having to hunt for a job by themselves. They look at their employers as career advisors and not so much as 'job-givers'. This calls for more interactivity, connection and accessibility as compared to that offered to previous generations.

(continued)

(continued)

Millennials	Gen Z
They value 'collaboration and teamwork' in organizations. The hiring team, while scheduling the hiring process, must ensure that all the stakeholders are on the 'same page' while dealing with the candidates. The candidates can feel a disconnect if they discover 'discord' between people involved in the hiring process.	The key drivers for them are 'speed of hiring', 'multi-channel approach' and 'face-to-face connection'. The digital hiring process needs to satisfy these three expectations of the candidates for a better CX.

Digital Tools and Talent Acquisition

Talent acquisition has evolved from a simple Excel-driven function to being driven by digital tools supported by AI. The reasons for implementation of digital tools by an organization are manifold.

1. **Process efficiency:** The traditional hiring operations had issues in process efficiency, as the process depended on resources to feed information at every step in the RLC. For instance, a recruiter had to struggle to surf through thousands of CVs (curriculum vitae) manually to identify the best fits for an open position. On the contrary, in the digital era, the recruiter sets the selection criteria in an automated tool, for the latter to surf through the volume of CVs to identify the best fits. The recruiter, based on his past experience can set target number of CVs to be sourced Vs open position for closing the position, to have enough buffer that would help the resource fill the position easily. The recruiter then adds their remarks on the shortlisted CVs and sends them to the next person

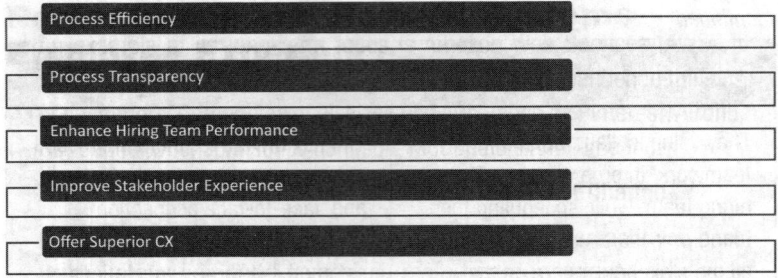

Figure 4.6. Digital Hiring Tools: Factors

in the recruitment process flow. In the earlier format, the recruiter had to manually capture candidate details along with the recruiter comments and mail them to the next designated person in the process flow, and they had to follow up with manual emails or personal follow-ups to check the status of the CVs sent. In the digital world, a system sends automated reminders to the resources for their feedback as per the TAT set in the system.

2. **Process transparency:** The digital hiring process brings in transparency and enhances accountability at every step. In the earlier process, the hiring manager had to query on aspects like the shortlisting criteria and their impact on the CVs shortlisted. Now, the hiring manager can see these details in the process flow, based on the self-help query tools in the system. Earlier, hiring managers could get away with rejecting candidates by saying that their CVs are not acceptable, and the recruiter had to struggle to understand the expectations of the hiring manager. In the automated process, the hiring manager is expected to share the details like job deliverables and job specs along with the hiring mandate. These hiring specs form the basis for the shortlisting by the recruiter.

In case the hiring manager rejects candidates, they would be held accountable for the rejection of CVs that were shortlisted on the basis of the very job specs provided by them.

Earlier, a regular dispute between the hiring team and other stakeholders involved the calculation of the TAT. There were questions around whether the TAT was to be calculated from the date of discussing the mandate or from the date of formally sharing the required details with the hiring team. The system eliminates the scope for such debates, as it automatically calculates the TAT based on pre-defined criteria that become binding on all the parties concerned.

Further, earlier, there was scope for manipulation of CV shortlisting either at the initial stages or in subsequent stages by the people involved in recruitment. This is not possible any more, as the list and priority of candidates get recorded at every stage and it would be difficult for people involved in the hiring to tweak or alter the order of priority. The system and tech audits reveal the tweaks, if any, thus bringing responsibility and accountability into the system.

3. **Enhanced hiring team performance:** The manual hiring process results in tenured team members getting lower workload due CV load for certain positions. As a result they ended up contributing lower productivity (i.e, lower number of the positions closed) Vs other team members. This led to heartburn and team conflicts due to differentiated workloads. The digital system takes away the pain or hiding factor of CV load. The recruiter can complete CV sourcing and shortlisting and screening based on pre-defined specs using AI tools in a jiffy. The hiring team, which earlier struggled with the manual tasks like CV sourcing and

shortlisting, is now relieved of such time-consuming activities.

Another challenging aspect for the hiring team was communicating to the candidates process updates or process outcomes at every stage of the hiring process, along with managing the process, which was stressful for the team. The hiring team tends to focus more on managing the process than on communicating with the candidates. This led to a gap or delay in candidate communication, which led to a situation like candidates moving on to other options. It can lead to candidates giving negative feedback on social media for an organization, which adversely impacts the 'brand' of the organization and both the quantity and quality of applications, results from lower functional efficiency by the hiring team. Digital tools enable the hiring team to finalize and release feedback concurrent with the hiring process 'on the go', on a real-time basis, relieving the team of the backlog of communication load at the end of the process. From a candidate's perspective, the spontaneous feedback helps them make alternate choices, leaving a positive trail of CX.

4. **Improved stakeholder experience:** The hiring team, by virtue of their job, are expected to deal with multiple stakeholders, ranging from channel partners, branding agencies, hiring managers and hiring logistics resources to candidates. The manual process required the hiring team to coordinating manually with each of the stakeholders, resulting in hits and misses on a randomized basis. The situation was akin to 'juggling multiple balls', which obviously led to a few balls being dropped in the process. These ended up becoming costly misses for the hiring team, based on the context, priority and power of the stakeholders. The team ended up engulfed in power struggles and pacification of the miffed stakeholders. This

does not happen anymore, as the digitally enabled hiring process takes care of multi-stakeholder management, leaving little room for misses. For instance, the hiring team, while coordinating the schedules of multiple interview panel members, may end up missing out on communicating with all the members on the schedules and location logistics. Alternately, it can miss out on sharing updated details with all the panel members, resulting in hiring mishaps or firefighting situations.

5. **Superior candidate experience:** Digital technologies enable to assess the three I's—'instantaneous', 'intensity' and 'individualization'—in the communication with candidates at every stage of the hiring process.

It would be interesting and insightful to understand the '3I model of CX delivery'. The model has three key dimensions, the first being 'instantaneous' communication. Candidates expect instant communication in the digital era. Satisfying this expectation is humanly impossible for the hiring team, as the applications' bandwidth do not permit them to do so. In this regard, AI-enabled digital tools help the hiring team communicate

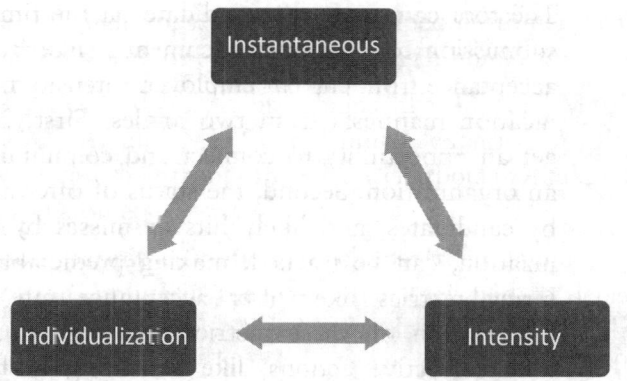

Figure 4.7. 3I Model of Candidate Experience Delivery

with or revert to the candidate at every stage, as soon as a process step is completed. For instance, when a candidate applies online, an automatic acknowledgement would be sent to them. After screening the profiles, the automated system can trigger the delivery of selection or rejection message to the candidates. In the steps like online assessment, a candidate gets an instantaneous result—selection/rejection—based on their score in the test.

The 'intensity' of connection refers to the number of times the hiring team connects/communicates with a candidate through the entire selection process. Earlier, the larger the volume of applications, the tougher it would be for the hiring team to satisfy candidates' needs. Digital tools, on the contrary, make it easy to fulfil the needs of candidates across all the stages of the RLC. The later stages, like offer negotiation, may need some aspect of human involvement, but the larger portion can be automated. For instance, the onboarding process can be digitally automated. The offer letter can be sent through a tool, advising a candidate to accept the offer using the tool. The subsequent steps like document submission can be guided, acknowledging the receipt. The tool can guide the candidate on the timelines for submission of various documents, like resignation acceptance from current employer. Intensity in communication manifests from two angles. First, candidates get an opportunity to connect and communicate with an organization. Second, the status of offer acceptance by candidates, and likely hits or misses by the organization, can be tracked, making predictable the key hiring metrics like 'offer acceptance rate'. Getting information on these metrics helps the organization take corrective actions, like activating a shortlisted-candidates pipeline.

Aligning Talent Acquisition to Technology

Utilization of tech tools in the hiring/recruitment space has evolved from the use of simple Excel sheets to workflow automation to enterprise resource planning to tools being seemingly integrated across all stages of the RLC. Most organizations tend to automate or implement tech solutions/tools in an 'off-the-shelf' format, without aligning the system to the process. Successful tech-tools implementation has three critical components: tech alignment, process alignment and people skilling.

- **Tech alignment:** Tech-solution developers design products or solutions either from a generic perspective or based on a situation. The 'reality' in an organization can be different. For instance, tech tools may call for centralized storing and accessing of information by all stakeholders. This could mean breaking down the 'silos' and 'power centres' in the organization. Hiring teams conventionally drew their power from 'opacity' and 'inaccessibility'. Bringing in a tool into the system without preparing a fertile ground would be a recipe for disaster. At this point one may wonder:

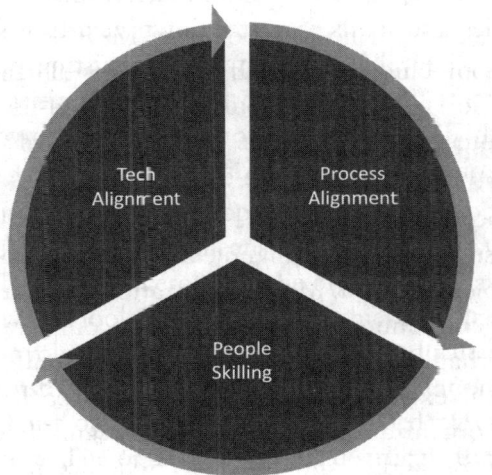

Figure 4.8. Digital Hiring: Tech Alignment

- To what extent should the system or tool be customized?
- Does not customization lead to diluting the 'benefit value' or 'utility value' of the organization, thereby lowering the ROI?
- Should the organization not adopt the 'off-the-shelf' strategy for the twin advantages of 'lower acquisition cost' and 'lower implementation cost', helping it align to market practices?
- How could one avoid the 'potential conflict' between tools and technology?

The answers to these questions are not 'black and white' and have 'shades of grey'. The factors impacting the decision-making process are the leadership's resolve and support to technology, automation, past track record in implementing technology processes and change orientation. Other factors include receptivity in the system, organization's competitive spirit to lead the market in new-technology adoption.

If the organization gets bogged down by internal issues and tends to water down new-tech solutions, to completely be in tune with the existing processes and systems, it is bound to lose opportunities in terms of both deriving value from technology investment and aligning to market trends.

- **Process alignment:** The next major challenge is the existing process alignment to the proposed tech implementation. Most organizations play at extremes of the continuum, either going for a complete and radical overhaul to employ tech solutions or tuning completely to the existing system. The first approach is feasible if the organization has a culture of regularly carrying out process audits and process re-engineering to enhance process effectiveness. Opting for a 'big bang' without such a track record would lead to either of two probable scenarios. In the first one, employees could get vocal about the issues and non-suitability of the solution. They could pool in all their energies to mobilize the opposing forces and thwart the implementation efforts. The other scenario involves their silent non-cooperation. In this scenario, employees would shun use of the system deployed and continue to use the old system, thus defeating the efforts.

- **People skilling:** The most critical factor impacting tech-solution implementation is the skills of people in the system and their attitude towards the technology. Organizations that operate in the tech sector and related sectors have an advantage, as they have tech adoption in their DNA. The age of the talent and their tech skills and the kind of talent being recruited also impact the tech adoption and skills of employees. Employees working in tech sector are tech-savvy and quickly adapt to the new tech trends. Employees take initiatives to up-skill themselves periodically, to keep up with the technology trends.

  Organizations need to adopt a multi-pronged approach towards training their employees, through the initiatives such as: (a) providing on-the-job training; (b) regularly nominating employees to HR tech events; (c) sponsoring skill development programmes for employees; and (d) rewarding employee performance.

Digital Recruitment Strategy: Insights

Digital recruitment is an often-heard buzzword in HR circles, but most often organizations end up taking the microscopic approach of focusing on just one or two stages of the RLC and rarely take the integrated approach. The decisions are always taken based on immediate pain points/bottlenecks and not from

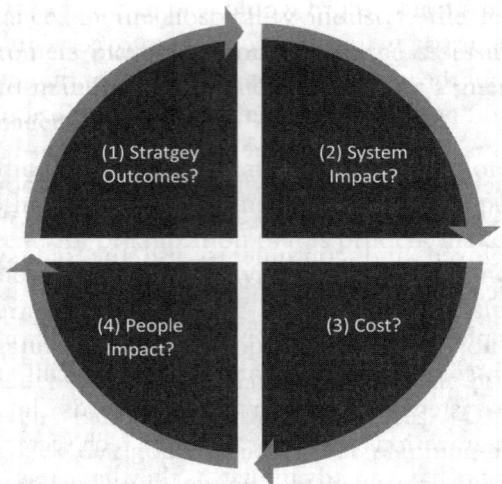

Figure 4.9. Digital Hiring Strategy: Factors

a long-term perspective. Though there a couple of other aspects that could be factored in formulating a comprehensive digital-recruitment strategy, the four primary decision dimensions are:

The organization needs to be clear in the first place about what it seeks to achieve through adopting digital technologies as a strategy? Is it aiming to achieve recruitment cost optimization, process effectiveness or enhancement of CX? Inward-looking organizations tend to focus on cost- and process-related objectives, whereas outward looking ones prioritize CX enhancement and employer branding (EB) as their strategy objectives.

The second decision dimension involves how and to what extent the existing system gets impacted by the digital strategy for recruitment. It depends on whether an organization opts for an integrated and comprehensive or a modular approach, based on its pain points or priorities. Comprehensive adoption could lead to complete revamping of the system. As a consequence, it would impact the existing hiring team in terms of head count, displacement of some team members due to lack of a tech-savvy attitude, etc. If the adoption takes place through a modular approach, it would be specific to the team members who are responsible for recruiting deliverables.

The third decision dimension is cost. Organizations would have to assess their ability to spend on technologies. A comprehensive solution would obviously be a costly proposition. Organizations that are constrained due to the cost factor can opt for a comprehensive solution but in a modular way, taking one step at a time and spreading the digitization over time.

The most important decision dimension is the people factor. Organizations would have to assess the capability of their existing teams to transition to the digital-strategy context. A small skill deficit can be handled through upskilling and reskilling. In the case of a large skill deficit, an organization would have to redeploy the challenged team members, either within the HR team or in other functions, providing them alternative roles. In case redeployment is not possible, the organization would have to make the tough decision of 'letting go' of talent.

After evaluating the factors impacting the strategy, the next step for the organization would be to take a comprehensive look at all the aspects it needs to take into cognizance before crafting a digital-recruitment strategy. These include assessing whether the strategy is customized to the context of the organization. A strategy that is out of sync would not be able to deliver results. Trying to ape competitors just to catch up with them would only result in draining energies and resources.

Organizations need to take a comprehensive and far-sighted view of the digitization efforts. In case they take the modular approach, they have to ensure that the strategy can be scaled up based on needs. The decision-makers must remember that CX is the key strategic objective. Lack of focus on CX could result in compromise in design and execution of tech systems which will not help organization to achieve the hiring objectives of talent attraction and enhancement of employer brand.

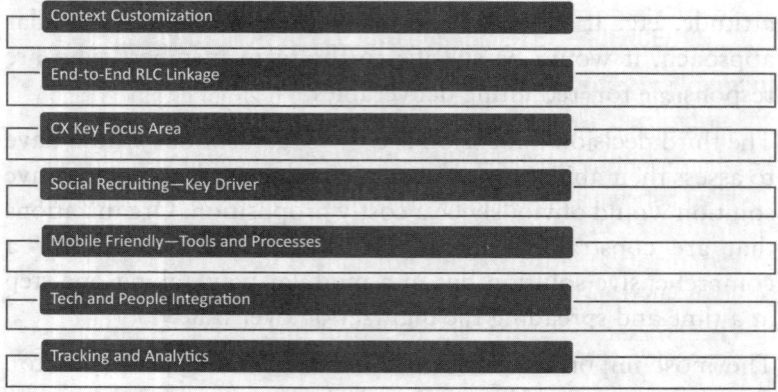

Figure 4.10. Candidate Experience: Factors

Talent across generations are active on social media, resulting in lion's share of hiring happening through social media, which makes it necessary for organizations to accord importance to social recruiting as one of the key drivers of recruitment. The other decision is mobile friendly orientation of the tech solution. Talent searches for jobs on mobile phones and applications are completed 'on the go', and hence the mobile phone becomes the primary tool for the entire hiring process. This calls for 'front-ending' of process, for all the key stakeholders/process participants.

A successful digital hiring strategy integrates people and tech capabilities, to deliver better desired outcomes for an organization. It should provide for empowerment for people to customize tools based on their needs. Technology tools need to offer opportunity for customization in functionalities like reporting and analytics.

Proper execution of a digital strategy calls for functionality of tracking and analytics. Most tech-solution providers do offer these functionalities, but they are always designed from a generic view and may not always service/support the objectives of an organization. There is a strong interlinkage between reporting/

analytics and strategy objectives. The alignment of reporting and analytics with the strategic objectives helps an organization track the effectiveness of the strategy along with realization of the strategic objectives. The other aspect is that the reporting and analytics needs of organizations tend to change over a period of time. Any tool that results in dependency on tech solution providers, takes away user comfort and consequently the utility value of the product.

Digital and Artificial Intelligence Technologies and Candidate Experience

The quest for digital technologies in hiring for organizations results from candidate expectations and the need to improve quality of hiring and EB. A few factors that drive the importance of digitizing the hiring process are as follows:

1. The continuation of hiring purely through assessment of CVs and interviews would result in only 50 per cent success.

2. Conventional hiring practices lead to exceeding the hiring TAT by at least three weeks, resulting in increased hiring costs and productivity loss for organizations.

3. Innovation in the 'hiring process' has become essential for organizations to face their competition.

4. At least 40 per cent of organizations are leveraging technology for predictive hiring.

5. More than 50 per cent of organizations are using AI-enabled recruitment software.

Having looked at the causal factors of AI-enabled hiring, it is now important to look at the different tech solutions available to organizations for the same.

Hiring Need	Tech Solutions
1. Sourcing	
Recruitment advertising	1. **Clickio:** The solution helps advertisers derive value from their advertisement, providing strong support for analytics. 2. **VONQ:** It is a recruitment marketing solutions company that offers products for a variety of functions: job marketing, volume recruitment marketing, EB, etc. The support extended by the company includes analytics on recruitment, multi-posting and labour market insights. 3. **JOVEO:** The recruitment marketing product helps deal with complexity in the job market to manage and optimize one's recruitment advertisement budget, brings in transparency and visibility to channel efficiency and helps derive positive ROI on recruitment investments. 4. **Recruitics:** A highly analytics-leveraged recruitment technology solution provider, it offers recruitment advertising, programmatic job advertising and EB solutions. 5. **Appcast:** The recruitment solutions provided by Appcast include Appcast Xcelerate (programmatic job advertisement distribution), Clickcast (Programmatic job Ad optimization), Global Hiring via The Network. It additionally offers solutions to job sites and job agencies. 6. **JobMate:** It helps with posting multiple jobs, bundled with reporting and applicant tracking features that help optimize the recruitment investment and efforts.
Social recruitment	1. **Recruitment edge:** The tech solution searches for and aggregates the best-fit candidates from across platforms, including professional networks, social networks and its own resume database.

(continued)

(continued)

Hiring Need	Tech Solutions
	2. **CareerArc:** The tech platform, apart from providing social recruitment solutions, focuses on EB amplification across social networks. It identifies and delivers job postings to the target talent across social networks. It also offers outplacement facility to help organizations with rightsizing, through the features such as social network assistance, skill assistance and career guidance facilities. 3. **HiringSolved:** It is an integrated hiring solutions provider that offers solutions for talent acquisition management, HR leadership, recruiters and resources and recruitment process outsourcing and Integrations. Integration solutions are offered for HR tech stacks across resources and platforms. 4. **AmazingHiring:** It is an exclusive tech-talent hiring platform that helps in hiring tech talent two times faster than conventional platforms. It offers pre-screened talent for a given position (assures 150 candidates, with two definite hires). In addition, it offers candidate management services across the RLC stages. 5. **Inhire:** It is an exclusive tech-hiring solution provider in Poland. 6. **TalentBin:** It is a tech-hiring solution provider by Monster to identify and hire talent in quick TATs.
Chatbots	7. **Paradox:** It is an AI-enabled recruiting assistant that allows screening, scheduling and engaging with candidates. 8. **jobpal:** It helps organizations connect with candidates seamlessly through multiple methods, such as chat, email or phone calls. It promotes openness and accessibility of the organization to the potential candidates.

(continued)

(continued)

Hiring Need	Tech Solutions
	9. **Mya:** It has three major product stacks. The first one is Recruitment Process Automation, which reduces the time spent in the application, screening and interview processes through connecting recruiters with qualified candidates. The second product offered is a career-site assistant. Candidates typically love to connect and interact with organizations at the time of surfing for jobs and while applying. This product caters to this unfulfilled need of candidates and in the process enhances CX. The third product, 'Outreach Automation', helps recruiters source CVs from across channels and thus frees them from CV sourcing and enables them to spend time on interacting with the candidates.
10. Selection process	
1. CV scraping	
HireAbility	The AI-enabled resume-parsing product screens CVs by extracting 200-plus fields from CVs after screening 80 million CVs across 40-plus dialects around the globe. The multi-field-based programming helps the recruiter screen CVs using multiple filters effortlessly and thus makes the selection process comprehensive.
Textkernel	This ML-based CV-parsing product offers internal services to both corporates and staffing agencies. For corporates, it optimizes HR processes, helps internal-talent mobility, enhances CX and employer sourcing through an ATS (applicant tracking system) and helps manage the exit of employees. For staffing agencies, it offers a wide gamut of services, including: (a) connection of people with jobs; (b) business development; (c) job matching; (d) candidate matching; and (e) outplacement and outreach.

(continued)

(continued)

Hiring Need	Tech Solutions
DaXtra	DaXtra's product stacks include the following. DaXtra capture: It captures specific candidate information from CVs. DaXtra search: It is an intelligent CV-searching product using semantic search features. DaXtra parser: It helps in searching for CVs faster. DaXtra magnet: It helps an organization build its recruitment database by linking to multiple platforms, like LinkedIn, job portals, job boards, etc. Apply and MATCH: This product is tailored for job seekers to tweak their application based on job specifications. DaXtra components: It integrates the entire workflow around CV parsing, searching, matching and aggregation.
2. Pre-employment assessment and predictive hiring	
Harver	It is a hiring software product custom-made for volume hiring needs to eliminate hiring biases and assess candidates using a wide gamut of criteria that include tests for evaluating cognitive ability, linguistic ability, multitasking ability, culture fit and personality, open questions, video portfolio, etc.
Hundred5	An assessment product, Hundred5 helps test the skills of candidates effortlessly and fast.
Pymetrics	A multi-feature AI-enabled product, Pymetrics provides the following facilities. Guidance: The product helps candidates navigate through assessment tests and, based on their results, guides the candidates to matching jobs. Selection: It helps recruiters identify candidates based on multiple selection criteria.

(continued)

(continued)

Hiring Need	Tech Solutions
	Redirection: When a candidate is found to be not suited for a job, it redirects them to alternative jobs. Insights: It offers data insights to recruiters on CV features, fitment, candidate scores in assessments, etc. It helps the recruiters make data-driven decisions.
Talview	An AI-enabled video interviewing tool, Talview helps recruiters shortlist candidates through video interviews and assessments.
Toggl Hire	It is a testing product that helps recruiters assess candidates through a wide variety of tests.
3. Video interview tools	
Spark Hire HireVue VidCruiter OutMatch	These tools use AI technology to conduct video interviews of candidates and shortlist candidates based on pre-determined criteria. They eliminate the recruiter bias that can creep in during the interview process.
4. Onboarding tools	
Enboarder	This integrated product suite has products catering to onboarding, remote onboarding, remote working, reboarding, transition and offboarding.
monday.com	It is a s product that has built-in HR functionalities that visually integrate recruitment, onboarding and employee management.
Talmundo	The onboarding feature of this product connects recruiters with new hires and anchors the onboarding process.
BambooHR	The product suite, apart from other features, has an onboarding feature that helps new hires complete paperwork, including electronic signature, seamlessly.

The tools discussed in the above table primarily contribute to the enhancement of CX through leveraging and integrating digital technologies across the RLC stages. These tools offer multiple advantages to organizations:

These tools have transformed the recruitment function both internal and externally. They contribute to enhancing the EB of organizations in the talent market.

Candidate Experience: Talent Pools and Talent Marketplaces

The current business environment is complex due to workforce diversity on several aspects, ranging from generation, race, culture and age group to skill set. Talent markets and talent pools provide a way of classifying talent, taking into consideration these differences.

Talent Pools and Candidate Experience

A talent pool refers to a set of candidates that a recruiter or recruiting organization tends to pool at one place. The pooling can be on the basis of job profiles or candidate profiles/skill

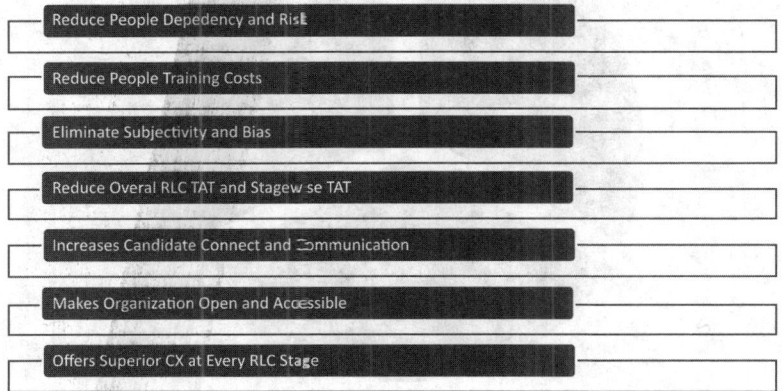

- Reduce People Depedency and Risk
- Reduce People Training Costs
- Eliminate Subjectivity and Bias
- Reduce Overal RLC TAT and Stagewise TAT
- Increases Candidate Connect and Communication
- Makes Organization Open and Accessible
- Offers Superior CX at Every RLC Stage

Figure 4.11. Tech Hiring Tools for Candidate Experience: Pay-offs

sets. Organizations are designing integrated tech tools to source and aggregate talent through different sources. The sources range from blind applications, previous applicants, (employee referrals), inbound recruiting (candidates willing to receive communication from an organization). The candidate expectations vary across each of these cases. For instance, candidates referred by employees may want to be notified about new positions and job specs. Also, employees would like to know the status of the candidates referred for a given position or may like to add them to the potential-talent pool for a given job profile or skill set.

Talent Marketplace

Today, employees (talent), unlike in the past, would like to explore different career options within their organization before looking outside. This trend has driven organizations to transform themselves into talent marketplaces and not just job service providers. The talent marketplace model has three dimensions

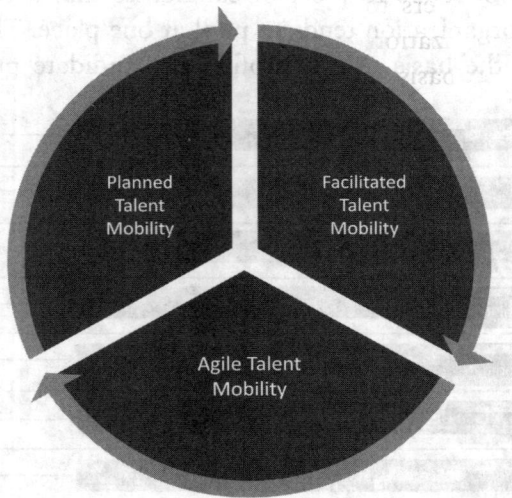

Figure 4.12. Talent Mobility: Three Dimensions

from the organizational perspective: (a) planned talent mobility; (b) facilitated talent mobility and (c) agile talent mobility.

Planned talent mobility involves mapping employees to career paths and notifying them of the opportunities to the positions mapped for them. Facilitated talent mobility refers to organizations opening up career opportunities due to business needs/restructuring. Agile talent mobility refers to employees working on multiple projects and shuffling their roles through multitasking.

Most organizations, while designing the digital hiring process, factor in only the external hires and not so much the internal talent. This leads to dissatisfaction and frustration among the existing employees. The digital hiring process should be able to facilitate 'internal talent mobility' to truly transform an organization into a 'talent marketplace'.

Employer Branding and Candidate Experience

EB refers to the perceived image/impression of an organization in the minds of both existing and prospective employees. It calls for the organization to capture its UVP (unique value proposition) and EVP (employee value proposition) and make an attempt to make customized communication based on the talent pools, segments and markets.

UVP refers to the unique features/aspects of an organization. It could refer to the uniqueness of its business model, products/services, position in the marketplace, etc. EVP refers to the 'returns' that an employee gets for being associated with the organization. The EB strategy is an integration of UVP and EVP and involves a fine balancing act between the two. For instance, an organization trying to overemphasize UVP ignoring EVP may end up getting poor responses to its recruitment efforts. Candidates may be impressed with an organization but do not get a convincing answer to the question: 'What's in it for me?'

Figure 4.13. Integrating Candidate Experience with Employer Branding

Alternatively, an organization overemphasizing EVP may elicit responses from candidates who look for benefits for themselves but are not willing to contribute to the organization. This could lead to the issues like 'cultural misfit', whereby an employee could be talented but would not be able to gel with the team, and may end up resulting in 'infant/early attrition'.

The steps involved in integrating EB with CX are:

CX enhancement has multiple benefits for EB, but the key benefits are: (a) ability to attract the right quantity and quality of talent; (b) positive word-of-mouth communication; and (c) employee retention.

CX and EB have strong interlinkages in the connected word. Candidates who have a positive experience are bound to share their experience both in person and through social networks. A positive CX helps an organization build, nurture and expand its 'positive footprint' on digital platforms. This helps especially with the hiring of millennials and Gen Z, who depend more on informal communication than on formal communication. A positive CX helps an organization 'crowdsource' its EB efforts.

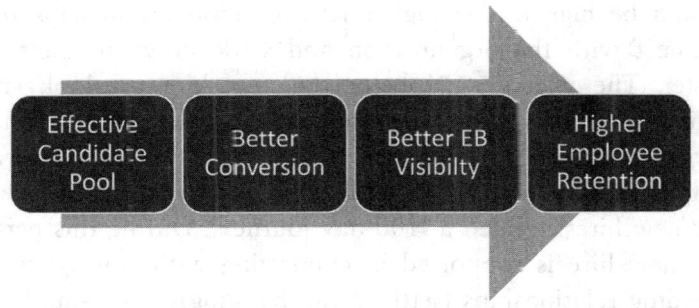

Figure 4.14. Impact of Candidate Experience on Employer Branding

EB is a double-edged sword for the hiring team. The hiring team and the employees involved in the hiring process are expected to 'live up to' candidate expectations. Candidates are bound to validate their experiences in relation to the EB. Positive conformity enhances their 'brand affiliation', and the opposite triggers frustration that manifests in 'emotional outbursts' on social media, which could leave a permanent 'negative trail' for an organization, thus damaging its EB.

Organizations are required to adopt a two-pronged strategy to ensure 'on-track performance' with respect to CX. The first step is to capture CX, measure it on a regular basis and link a positive CX with rewards for the employees involved. Simultaneously, 'corrective actions' should be taken against employees who have not been able to contribute to a positive CX. The second step is to capture the 'voice of the candidate' and share it on social media. This ensures authenticity and engenders trust among candidates.

Candidate Experience and Employee Experience Interlinkages

Candidates who have a positive CX would be keen to join the organization, and their level of motivation and engagement would be higher. The higher level of motivation helps them connect with the organization and settle down in their role faster. The positive CX helps the new hire overlook small 'blips' that they may encounter during the settling phase. Organizations that appreciate the linkage between CX and employee experience (EX) tend to have a structured approach for new hires, termed a '100-day journey'. During this period, the new hire is supported in connecting with colleagues and building relationships (settling and bonding), understand their role (role rooting) and, most importantly, aligning to the culture and context of the organization (culture sync).

The new hire, in a way, tends to get either 'positive' or 'negative' reinforcement based on the hiring experience. A positive experience tends to have a positive impact. In contrast, a candidate with a not-so-positive experience would get into the mindset of 'evaluation/judgement'.

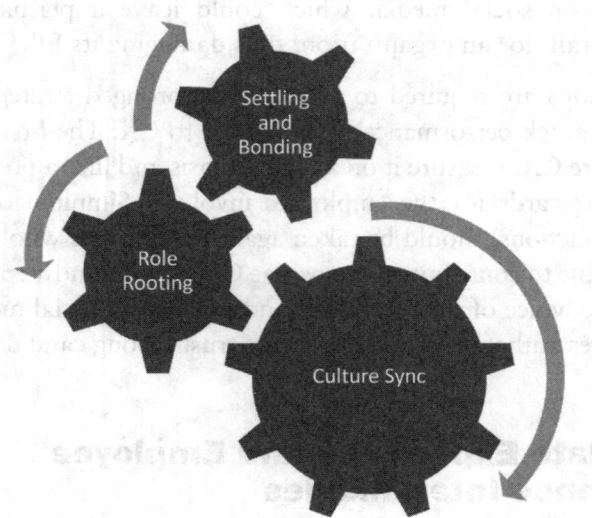

Figure 4.15. Candidate Experience and Employee Experience Interlinkage

Closing Thoughts

Talent acquisition has been transformed from being a purely supportive function into a strategic role that integrates with the business and communication strategy. In short, from being a 'back-room' boy, it has now assumed the status of 'face of the organization', especially for the existing and potential employees. Becoming tech-intensive with a focus on CX has become a competitive necessity. Digital technologies are no longer a 'good-to-have' option but are a 'must-have' option for hiring teams. Technology, apart from facilitating CX, is helping improve the efficiency of hiring teams. It is helping hiring become transparent and 'showcase' its contribution to both internal and external stakeholders.

Points to Ponder

1. Does an organization need to be 'culture-ready' to adopt digital hiring technologies?
2. Should the digital transition be led by a chief Executive Officer (CEO) or Chief Procurement Officer (CPO) of the organization?
3. Do digital technologies impact organization through a 'forced change'?
4. How could ROI on digital technologies be demonstrated to stakeholders by the hiring team?

5
Nurturing Employee Experience through Performance and Rewards Management

This chapter covers some issues that organizations face in the design and implementation of performance and reward policies/systems. It touches upon the various touch points and employee expectations that influence the employee experience.

Performance Paradigm Change

Performance system is at the core of the functioning of an organization. The effectiveness and performance of an organization is directly correlated with the effectiveness of its performance system. Performance in a way is an integrating and facilitating tool in an organization. There are several factors that impact the design and function of a performance system.

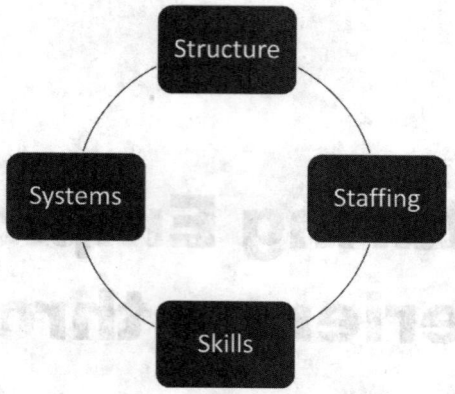

Figure 5.1. Performance Management: 5S Model

1. **Strategy:** The strategy of an organization has a significant impact on the performance system in the organization. An organization that has an aggressive business strategy would opt to have a performance with an in-built 'stretch factor' for its employees. Organizations that take a calibrated approach, which set performance goals, need moderate efforts by their employees to meet the goals. The performance focus of an organization can have an impact on the types of goals than it sets for its employees.

   The focus area for strategy is dependent primarily on the leadership and culture of an organization. A people-centric leader would emphasize the people dimension. For instance, Vineet Nayar, who headed HCL Technologies between 2007 and 2013, adopted the strategy of 'employee first', with an underlying philosophy: 'You take care of your employees, and they will take care of your business'.

Figure 5.2. Strategy Focus Areas

STRATEGY INSIGHTS AT GENERAL ELECTRIC

General Electric is known for its obsession with performance excellence. The foundation for this performance-centricity was laid by Jack Welch. The organization, which was symbolic for its performance, had its own share of 'ups and downs'. Once known for excellence and performance, it became an 'overgrown' giant in subsequent years.

Three underlying strategy insights here are:

1. Any growth from a single technology or market is bound to end. Companies that are cognizant of this reality and are prepared shall endure in the marketplace.

2. Successful strategies eventually get copied by many. Organizations that update continuously would be able to sustain their growth.

3. Smart corporate strategies are always nimble and flexible rather than constraining.

Nurturing Employee Experience through Performance | 133

The strategy dimensions at General Electric kept the giant on its toes. The organization went through a journey of evolving and improving its performance system. Organizations that are mature tend to adopt a balancing act between the four strategy focus areas. A few organizations have attempted maintaining a 'balanced scorecard' (BSC), as both a strategy and performance management tool. The advantage of BSC is that it helps align strategies and performance management systems with each other. The key pay-offs for organizations in adopting a BSC approach towards performance management systems are:

The three key levers for an organization's performance are strategy design, performance alignment and rewards distribution. BSC is an integrated approach that links these elements. It would be pertinent to discuss here the BSC pay-offs discussed above.

a. **Balanced organizational priorities:** The leadership in an organization tend to accord higher priority to one of the four strategy factors (profit, people, process and customers) in the design and/or in the execution of strategy. For instance, Amazon is known for its

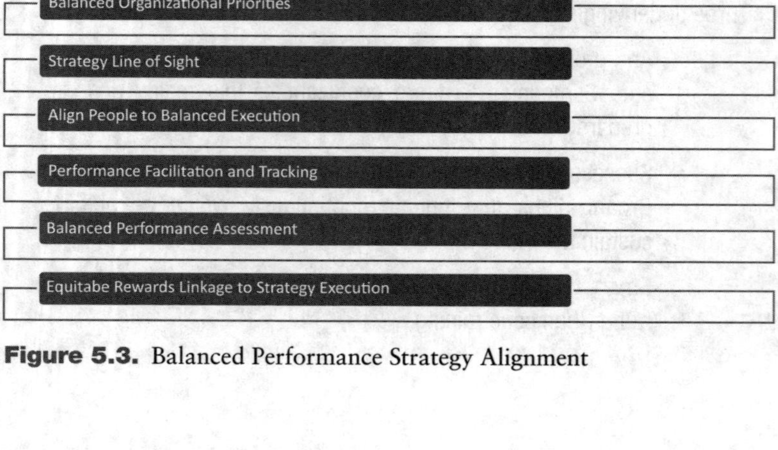

- Balanced Organizational Priorities
- Strategy Line of Sight
- Align People to Balanced Execution
- Performance Facilitation and Tracking
- Balanced Performance Assessment
- Equitabe Rewards Linkage to Strategy Execution

Figure 5.3. Balanced Performance Strategy Alignment

'customer obsession', and its customers are very happy with the quality of services Amazon offers. But this is just one side of the story. The other side is that Amazon suffers from high attrition across teams, more so in service delivery teams. The following employee feedback reviews posted indicate the imbalance that exists in Amazon.

> **WORK IMBALANCE AT AMAZON: EMPLOYEE REVIEWS ON GLASSDOOR**
>
> - 'Sometimes need to work for **long hours**'
> - 'Overtime transparency **no work life** balance'
> - 'Timings not good, no growth'
> - 'Too many people and hard to get recognition.'
> - 'The company wants to fire you more than retain you. This culture has been institutionalized especially in this office. Look at the average tenure of experienced people joining amazon. It is barely one year. **This is not by chance, but by design, and it has been designed by same immature managers in order to save their own jobs'**

The above feedback sourced from Glassdoor indicates the impact of lack of balance in the four-strategy dimensions in Amazon. Though the organization may succeed in the short run, there are two major factors to consider on the flip side: (a) cost of the success; (b) sustainability of the success. The cost of the success would be high, as the organization would end up spending heavily on hiring and training new employees and in the process inflating the people expenses, which eats into the bottom line of the organization. Sustainability becomes a question mark as well, and at some point, the organization would not be able to maintain its lead, as it would struggle to maintain its market share or retain its growth rate.

b. **Strategy line of sight:** The major reason for discontent among employees across organizations is that they are clueless about the impact of their KRAs on the organizational goals, leading to employee disconnect with the strategies and goals of organizations. The employees end up working on their KRAs based on their personal value system. This results in unpredictability in strategy execution by the organization, leaving the stakeholders dissatisfied with the performance of the organization. Cornell University, in a white paper, focused on 'line of sight' (LOS) and identified the causes and outcomes of LOS in an organization. Based on the research, an integrated model that encapsulates the linkage between strategy design and execution and the performance of employees in an organization, the LOS model of performance management.

The LOS Model integrates the Strategy design, Communication Methods and the impact on employee at emotional and professional levels, Impact on organizational at individual employee level and organizational levels.

The strategy, apart from being balanced across the four key factors, has to be crisp and concise. Organizations create great strategies but fail to communicate. The effectiveness of a strategy depends on whether it can be 'easily understood' by the employees at the front line and, more importantly, whether it can 'inspire stellar performance' by the employees. For example, sharp and clear communication is seen in Amazon's strategy statements.

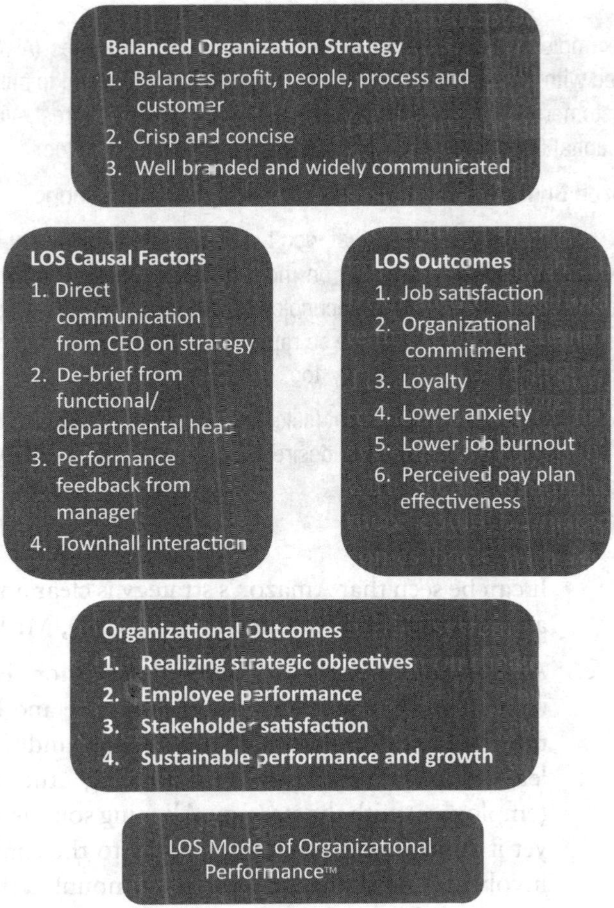

Balanced Organization Strategy
1. Balances profit, people, process and customer
2. Crisp and concise
3. Well branded and widely communicated

LOS Causal Factors
1. Direct communication from CEO on strategy
2. De-brief from functional/departmental head
3. Performance feedback from manager
4. Townhall interaction

LOS Outcomes
1. Job satisfaction
2. Organizational commitment
3. Loyalty
4. Lower anxiety
5. Lower job burnout
6. Perceived pay plan effectiveness

Organizational Outcomes
1. Realizing strategic objectives
2. Employee performance
3. Stakeholder satisfaction
4. Sustainable performance and growth

LOS Model of Organizational Performance™

Figure 5.4. Line of Sight Strategic Performance Model

AMAZON STRATEGY INSIGHTS

Amazon Focuses on the Long Term, Not the Short Term

'We are comfortable planting seeds and waiting for them to grow into trees', says Bezos. *'We don't focus on the optics of the next quarter; we focus on what is going to be good for customers. I think this aspect of our culture is rare'.*

> An example of its long-term focus is Amazon Web Services (AWS). It started with start-ups and developers and now has expanded to millions of customers. Companies of all sizes use AWS, such as Pinterest, Airbnb, GE, Capital One, Johnson & Johnson, McDonald's and Time Inc.
>
> **Amazon Builds Its Strategies on Things that Do Not Change**
>
> Base your strategy on things that won't change.... Whereas if you base your strategy first and foremost on more transitory things—who your competitors are, what kind of technologies are available, and so on—those things are going to change so rapidly that you're going to have to change your strategy very rapidly, too.
>
> Bezos notes that customers want 'selection, low prices, and fast delivery'. He shares how these three desires of the consumer are likely not going to change.

It can be seen that Amazon's strategy is clear and crisp and is communicated directly by its CEO, Mr Bezos.

c. **Alignment of people for balanced execution:** Leaders normally say that 'crafting an Innovative and Executable strategy' is a tough job. Smart and focused leaders place emphasis on 'aligning' the people (employees) with the strategy. Aligning sounds simple, yet it is profound and complex due to the challenges involved. The challenges can be surmounted through understanding 'what it entails'. There are four key factors involved in aligning employees to a strategy.

Leaders have to keep these factors in mind while communicating with or cascading their experience to employees. The effectiveness of the communication in aligning people would be dependent on a leader's ability to customize the message based on the target audience. There can be one generic communication that gets uniformly broadcasted to the entire organization. It needs to be followed up with

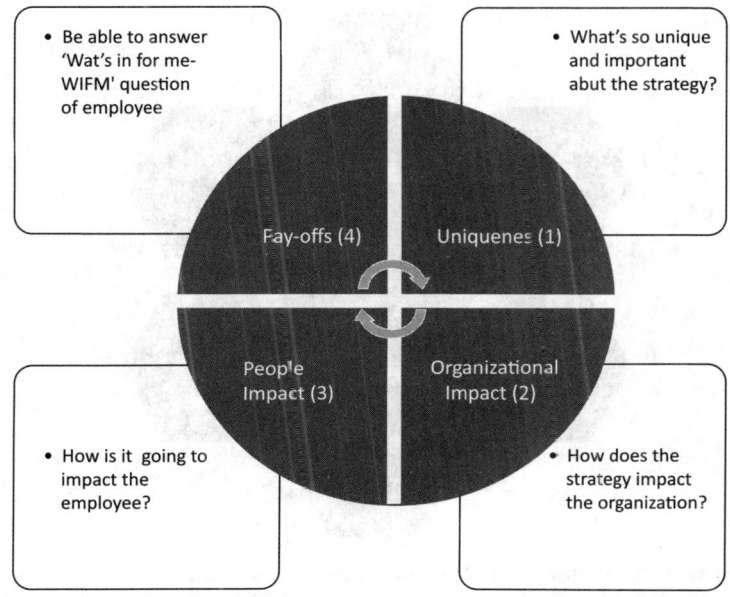

Figure 5.5. Employee Alignment and Strategic Performance Model

'tailored communication' based on the audience. For instance, a leader, while communicating with the leadership team, can emphasize the first two factors of alignment, that is, its uniqueness and impact on organizational elements. However, while communicating with frontline employees, the focus has to be on the other two factors—the people impact and pay-offs. The top leader's message needs to be reinforced by the other leaders in the hierarchy, especially the immediate managers. An average employee always views and perceives their organization based on the experiences they share with their reporting manager.

d. **Performance tracking and facilitation:** The lever controlling the execution of strategy is impacted by the tracking and measurement of employee performance. Thanks to digital technologies, it has become

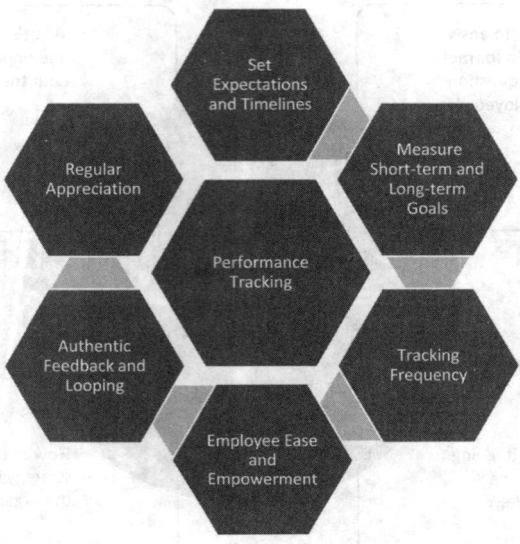

Figure 5.6. Performance Tracking Factors

possible for organizations to track and facilitate employee performance. The design of the perforance tracking system holds the key to its effectiveness. The features determining the effectiveness of the system are as follow.

Setting the expectations is the first step in tracking and managing the performance of employees. An approach of consensus would create a climate of positivity and motivate employees to work towards the set goals. If the goals are not equitably distributed or are out of sync with the reality, the organization would not see any traction in achieving the set goals. Aspects such as periodicity of performance reporting by the employee versus the goals, format of reporting and content of the reporting in terms of metrics should be covered.

Carrying out a balancing act between short-term and long-term goals is important, to provide performance focus and guidance to the employees. For instance, in case of area sales managers (ASMs), sales revenue can be measured frequently, as compared to team engagement scores. Trying to load both short-term and long-term goals leads to the issues like reporting overload and confusion on performance focus areas. It would be like 'gunning at multiple birds with one shot' and might end up being a futile attempt. Employees would end up being confused and would do a shoddy job, defeating the very purpose of performance reporting and tracking.

The frequency of tracking employees' performance helps eliminate both surprise and stress for the employees. Clarity on timing would help an employee with the collection of data needed for the reporting and processing. Effective reporting calls for not just collecting data but processing the data as well. The data insights would help make performance review discussions meaningful. An employee upon whom sudden performance reporting is thrusted would end

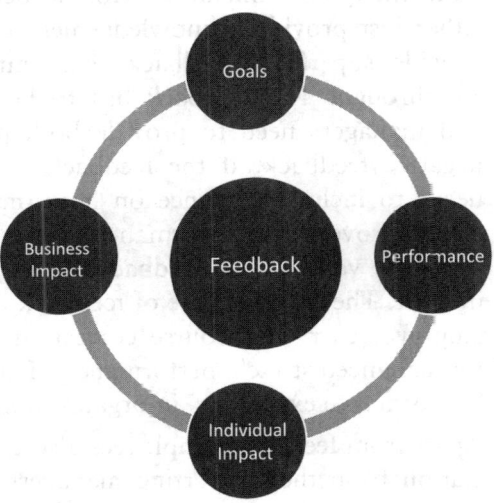

Figure 5.7. Performance Feedback and Factors

up either collecting piecemeal data or presenting raw data. Such a scenario can result in the reporting manager either misjudging the employee's performance or making their analysis on faulty assumptions. Nothing can be more disastrous than this for the interests of both the organization and the employees.

The extent of 'space' managers give to their employees to ideate and come up with performance metrics creates a sense of 'self-destiny' among the latter. The culture and leadership style of the organization plays a major role in deciding these factors. Another important aspect is the 'ease' of reporting for employees. If the reporting system consumes an equal amount of time as the job itself, it cuts into the productivity and lowers the motivation of the employees.

One key area of concern among employees is not receiving feedback on the performance reports and analyses submitted by them. The absence of feedback takes away the commitment and excitement of employees. Feedback per se has two dimensions: authenticity and timeliness. Most leaders/managers either just provide acknowledgement of receipt or provide superficial feedback that employees can see through. The feedback has to be qualitative, and managers need to provide both positive and negative feedback. If the feedback is negative, it needs to include guidance on how the employees can improve their performance. Time delays take away the value of the feedback, as employees lose interest. The core purpose of feedback is to help an employee carry out course correction or scale up for enhanced/stretch performance. This is key to 'performance excellence' in organizations.

Apart from feedback, employees also expect appreciation from their reporting managers. Autocratic leaders tend to perceive getting performance reports without closing the loop with the employees as a matter of right. Lack of appreciation takes away the zeal and commitment of employees.

e. **Balanced performance assessment:** One of the issues that employees often raise in the context of performance assessment is 'lack of balance'. It is not as simple as it sounds. The balancing act has multiple dimensions, ranging from balancing between goals and priorities allocated between the goals, balancing the assessment of employees, etc. For instance, a regional sales manager (RSM), while assessing the performance of an ASM, could factor in the following dimensions:

  i. Sales target versus achievement;
  ii. Product category–wise targets versus sales;
  iii. Overall profit margin versus product-wise profit margin;
  iv. Team engagement score—target versus actual;
  v. Team retention—target versus actual; and
  vi. Customer/stakeholder satisfaction score—target versus actual.

If the RSM were to focus on the first three performance indicators, the ASM would focus on both self-performance and management of the team. This would lead to a situation where employees end up become revenue spinners. Alternately, employees may end up developing a perspective of 'only ends matter, not the means'. Such an understanding can become dangerous for the organization, as employees would look for shortcuts to achieve results. This could involve compromising on ethics and values with their customers, leading to loss of reputation and trust. Trust once lost cannot be regained by an organization. The organization would struggle to maintain its performance and would end up on a declining curve in both financial terms and market share/growth.

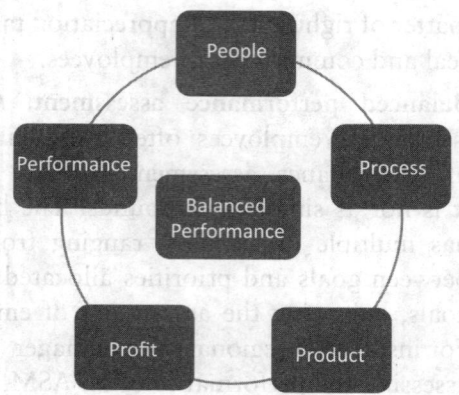

Figure 5.8. Balanced Performance: Five Ps

f. **Linkage of equitable rewards with strategy execution:** It is human psychology to expect rewards in turn for the contribution made. There are several theories that have established this fact. For reference, let us look at theory of expectancy.

The theory is apt for one to understand the linkage between effort, performance and rewards from an employee's perspective. According to this theory, an employee needs to have the conviction that their efforts would produce the desired results. 'Instrumentality' here refers to the expectation of the employee that the delivery of a certain level of performance would help in their getting rewarded. The most critical factor is 'valence', which basically refers to the value that an employee attaches to the reward. The value of the reward here has a couple of dimensions: (a) is the reward commensurate with the performance; and (b) is the reward 'equitable' vis-à-vis the efforts and contributions of other employees.

If an employee perceives the reward to be less than what is offered to other employees for similar

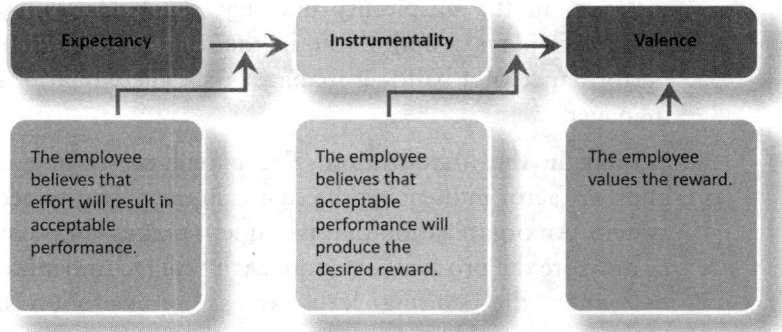

Figure 5.9. Vroom's Expectancy Theory
Source: https://images.app.goo.gl/eg72A9p9moxt64ij6

efforts/contributions, the employee would not value the reward, though it may be commensurate with their efforts.

2. **Structure of the organization:** The structure of an organization has an impact on the type of performance system in the organization. A hierarchical and large organization would have the typical structure of appraisees, appraisers and reviewers. In addition, it could also have a moderation committee and appeal committee in place. The moderation committee would typically review all the high-rated and low-rated employee performance cases, to ensure that the system has been implemented properly. It acts like an inbuilt systemic check to protect employees from being overrated or underrated due to subjective bias or considerations.

In an organization that has a matrix reporting system, the performance feedback is collected from all the stakeholders and is evaluated based on the weights assigned to each of the performance feedback-givers. In organizations that are designed around customer segments, the feedback of the customers plays a major role. For instance, in the hospitality industry, the feedback by customers plays a major role in the assessment of the performance of a banquet manager or a guest relations manager.

3. **Staffing in the organization:** The extent of staffing is another factor influencing the rigour in the performance system. An organization that is prudent makes it a point to measure the productivity from each role incumbent to determine the staffing level across positions/levels. Organizations that adopt the 'optimization' approach would have a performance system that brings in the 'stretch factor' for the employees. Organizations that lack of rigour in manpower planning and staffing would end up having excess staff, which results in employees signing up for suboptimal performance goals.

4. **Skills and organizations:** In this competitive era, organizations are trying to attain and maintain their competitive edge based on the talent they possess and their skills. In the rapidly evolving situation, it is imperative for organizations to assess and track the skills of their employees on a periodic basis. For instance, in an organization that has adopted a competency-based talent management strategy, the entire employee life cycle is linked to competencies. Employees are hired only if they possess the competencies needed for the role. It is not enough to hire talent and presume that the talent would automatically contribute to the performance of the organization. The steps involved in competency-based performance management are:

The first step involves identifying the competencies needed for a job/role. If the job is pre-existing, then the relevant competencies can be identified using 'job analysis' methods. In case it is a new role, competencies

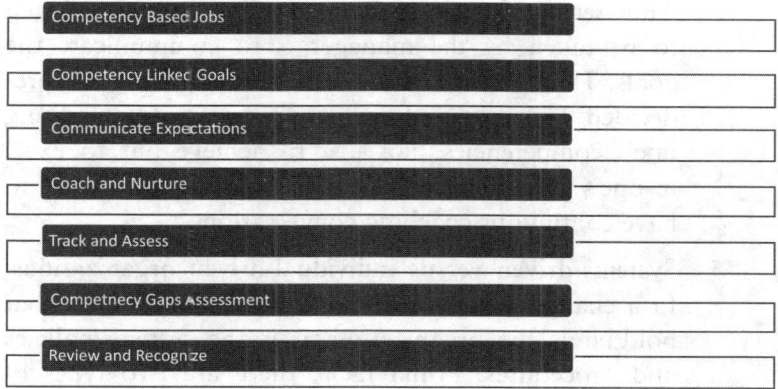

Figure 5.10. Competency-Based Performance Management: Steps

can be identified based on competencies mapped in other organizations where the role exists. The next two steps are closely interlinked. The reporting manager, while setting the goals, needs to keep in mind the competency level of the employee concerned. For instance, a business unit head, while allocating projects to project managers, would, among other things, take into cognizance the competency/skill level of the project manager. An organization would prefer an employee with similar experience while assigning talent to a new, prestigious and large client, bagged recently by the organization.

Similarly, while setting stretch goals for the years, among a given set of employees, the reporting manager will have to consider the competency level of the employees. The regional manager in an insurance organization would take into view the capability of area managers while assigning targets on the aspects such as the number of new policies to be signed, the insurance premium to be collected, per month, per quarter, etc.

After setting the goals, the connecting and critical step to be taken by the manager is to communicate the goals. The focus is not just on informing the goals pre-decided but the need for leveraging and integrating one's competencies, not just to achieve but to excel in one's performance. The reporting manager needs to have continuous coaching conversations.

5. **Systems-driven versus individual-driven organizations:** In a changing organization, if there is one aspect that hold/binds the organization, it is the systems/policies and procedures. Prima facie, there are two types of organization. Those of the first type are driven by individuals, and those of the second are driven by systems. In an 'individual-driven' organization, everything in the organization is managed and operated according to the 'whims and fancies' of the person who is at the helm. On the other hand, in a 'systems-driven' organization, all the spheres of operations are designed and executed according to well-defined policies and procedures. There is a clear set of differences in the way these two types of organizations are run, as shown in the table below.

Individual-Driven Organization	Systems-Driven Organization
The organization revolves around the leader.	The organization functions according to the defined systems.
Employees experience a sense or fear.	Employees are assured.
Employees remain clueless and always wait for instructions/directions from the leader.	Employees are clear on: (a) what to do; (b) why to do; (c) how to do; (d) how what they do would be assessed; and (e) what the consequences/rewards would be.

(continued)

(continued)

Individual-Driven Organization	Systems-Driven Organization
The loyalty of employees lies with the Individual. There is the danger of development of a 'cult style' in the organization, which could end up in sycophancy, resulting in negative and disruptive politics. Energies of the employees are directed towards getting access to the leader, doing what they are told to do, being liked by the leader and being in the good books of the leader, to get favours, like career progression and rewards.	The loyalty of the employees lies with the organization and the system. The collective understanding in the organization is that the organization is more important than its individuals and that everyone who works in the organization is a custodian and has accountability for planning and executing responsibilities in conformity with the laid-down systems that aim to protect the interests of the organization and the employees at large.
Culture and performance/ rewards: The overall culture could become and remain 'dicey and disruptive', with politics of 'one-upmanship' and being favoured by the boss prevailing. The organization would be split into two parts: 'loyalists' and 'anti-loyalists' to the leadership. People would get branded and included/ostracized based on their conformity or deviance.	**Culture and performance/ rewards:** The overall culture would be one of 'integration', where the collective efforts are directed towards managing and operating the systems for their designed purpose and providing collective benefits/rewards to the employees, based on their performance efforts, in accordance with the systems.

This discussion could lead to a set of questions: (a) can leaders not arise and exist in systems-driven organizations? (b) are strong leaders the antithesis to a systems-driven organization? This is not an 'either–or' scenario, as the systems-driven format and the individual-driven format can coexist. Good leaders, while they may start with the 'individual-driven' format of running their organization, understand and appreciate the need for systems and the need to make the systems 'sustainable' and lasting beyond them, for which they would design and implement systems with the collective participation of employees. They do this for two reasons. The first being to drive the importance of the systems and the second being self-driven (employee-driven) conformity to the systems, as systems that are designed by employees bring in employee commitment due to the ownership involved. A systems-driven organization, on the other hand, can operate in the 'individual-driven' way if the leadership is groomed in the organization and allowed to rise to the helm. The only caveat in this regard is that leaders who emerge from the systems should not end up manipulating the systems in their favour, which would jeopardize the entire cultural fabric of the organization. In fact, strong systems-driven organizations ensure that the systems have 'inbuilt checks' to counter these tendencies.

It is now time to dig deep into the systems-driven format of running an organization, its impact on performance systems and the consequent impact on EX.

The first step to making an organization systems-driven is to define systems/policies and procedures covering all aspects of the organization. The systems to articulate Why to do, What to do, When to do, How to do, Outcome Impact of the Tasks on the person team following the system. A slip in any of these counts can lead to 'perceptual distortion' in the minds of the employees, which can result in suboptimal performance outcomes at both the organizational and individual levels.

Redesigning systems would not lead anywhere unless there is communication with the employees about the

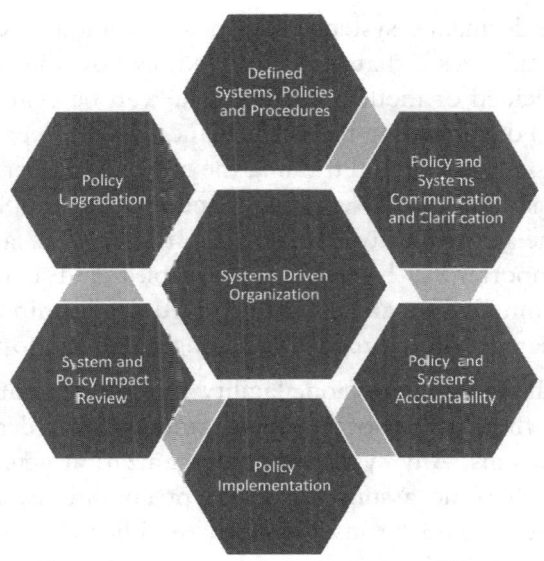

Figure 5.11. Systems-Driven Organization

systems, who are responsible for implementing the systems and policies. The leader has the responsibility of reinforcing the need for implementing the policies in both spirit and deed. Apart from communicating about the systems/policies, it is important to share the employees' accountability towards the implementation and review process. This would include the aspects like system and individual performance indicators that need to be complied with. During the policy implementation phase, three key elements are to be taken care of: transparency, equity and agility and adaptability. Transparency would ensure that all the people who deal with implementing the system and the people who are impacted by the system know why, what and how the system would operate, to avoid misconceptions and negative grapevine. The second aspect is equity, which has two dimensions—perceived equity/justice and delivered equity/justice—especially relevant to people systems. In terms of performance systems, the most common grievance of employees is that they do not know how the ratings are decided or moderated. The issue can be dealt with by: (a) documenting the performance evaluation standards; (b) educating and training the manager on performance systems; and (c) educating and training employees on the entire performance cycle stages, steps and, most importantly, both the deliverables and expectations from all the stakeholders involved (leadership team, HR team, reviewer, reporting manager and employees).

The third dimension, 'agility and adaptability', refers to the approach of the organization, towards dealing with systems. Any system in an organization gets designed with some assumptions and preconditions. However, there could be instances where either the stakeholder comes back with feedback on issues in the system or the situation undergoes a change, requiring changes in the system. This calls for 'bringing changes in the system on the go'. In the absence of this, an organization

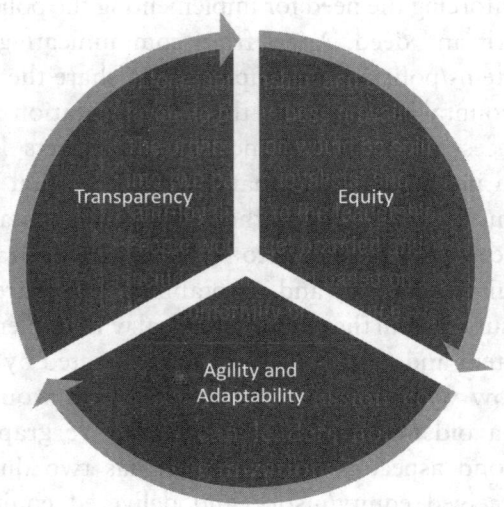

Figure 5.12. Performance Management: Effectiveness Dimensions

may end up with adverse feedback of being rigid and non-accommodating.

Performance System—Evolution and Continuum

- Closed performance system: The performance systems in organizations have been evolving with the passage of time. Earlier, for annual confidential reporting, reporting managers used to assess the performance of employees secretly and single-handedly take decisions on employee ratings. Employees were completely clueless as to the criteria and basis of their performance rating. Their relationship with reporting managers was one of fear. Reporting managers exploited the system to subjugate employees to them. The net result was a sense of mistrust among the employees towards the manager, the performance system and the organization. The performance system thus became captive in the hands of reporting managers, and such words as equity, fairness and justice were unknown in the realm of organizations.

- Open performance system: The second phase of performance systems included open discussions on performance between the managers and employees at the end of a year. The system was a form of tokenism, as the employees were never told about the goals/KRAs at the beginning of the year but had to work based on those of the previous year. The so-called discussion was merely communicating the decision of the manager(s) to the employees. Employee did not have to guess about their rating.

- Structured performance: The third stage of evolution was performance goal setting at the beginning of the year and performance review at the end of the year. The open discussion between the managers and employees covered what went well and what more could be done.

The employees had to struggle to recall the performance delivery feedback throughout the year. The managers had their own limitations, as they could not recall the employee performance levels throughout the year. As a leeway manager went by their overall impression of the employee or halo effect or influenced by recency factor in recalling the recent events. The employees felt frustrated because of four reasons: (a) their struggle to get feedback on their performance throughout the year; (b) managers' review being biased or based on recent data; (c) lack of scoping of entire year's performance; and (d) lack of mid-course correction opportunity.

- **Periodic performance review:** The fourth stage of evolution of performance systems led to evolution periodic performance reviews. Depending on the business context, organizational culture and type of performance

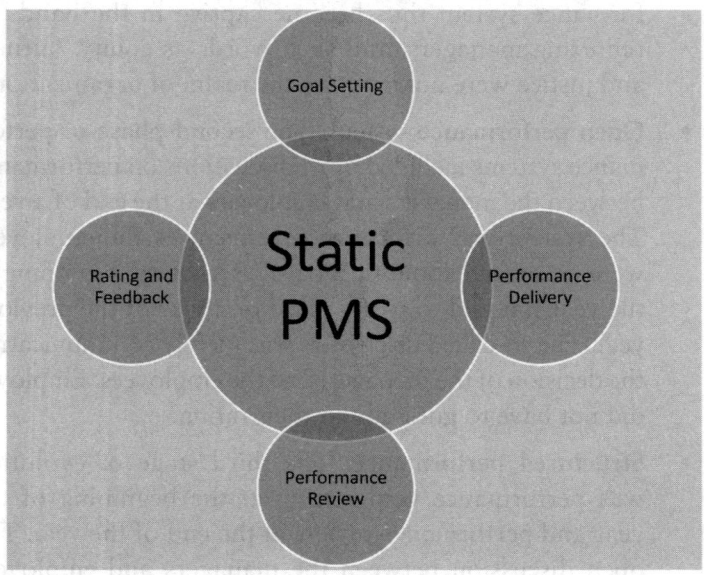

Figure 5.13. Static Performance Management: Factors

system, organizations treated the periodic reviews as either informal or formal. The informal-review format was used for periodic performance feedback and coaching, at the end of each month/quarter/half-year/year. This format of structured and periodic performance reviews helped all the stakeholders involved—managers, employees, leaders and the organization. The managers could keep a track of the traction in the goals due to the employees' efforts. The employees got an opportunity to get feedback on their performance at regular intervals. The feedback and review helped them attempt mid-course correction, without losing out on an appraisal. From the organization's perspective, they helped it in performance tracking and consistency. The performance dashboard got updated based on the aggregated data. The leadership got an opportunity to make changes in strategy design/execution, based on the organizational performance data, which were compared with macro-economic performance indicators.

- **Hybrid performance system:** Performance systems have a combination of both formal and informal performance

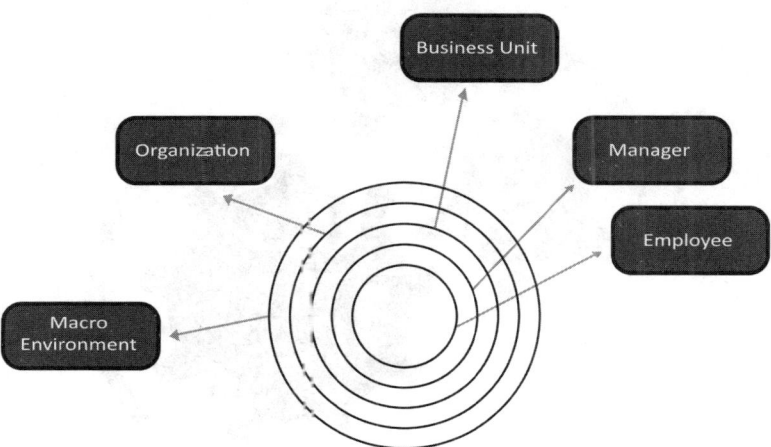

Figure 5.14. Performance Geosphere

reviews. The organization sets performance goals while the formal systems used the rating for aggregating for the year-end performance review of the employees. In a way, organizations orchestrate the performance rhythm based on their culture, business context and business needs, along with job and employee profiles. For instance, the sales manager of a pharmaceutical company would insist on getting weekly sales reports from medical representatives, as tracking and reporting weekly performance hold the key at his level and for the organization. The manager may pick up the phone and have a quick individual or team review, based on their personal operating style. They would have formal monthly/quarterly reviews based on the performance systems designed in the organization. The hybrid approach of performance system design provides 'operating space' for both the employees and the reporting manager. In a sense, the *Performance Rhythm* does a balanced orchestration between formal structures and yet provide

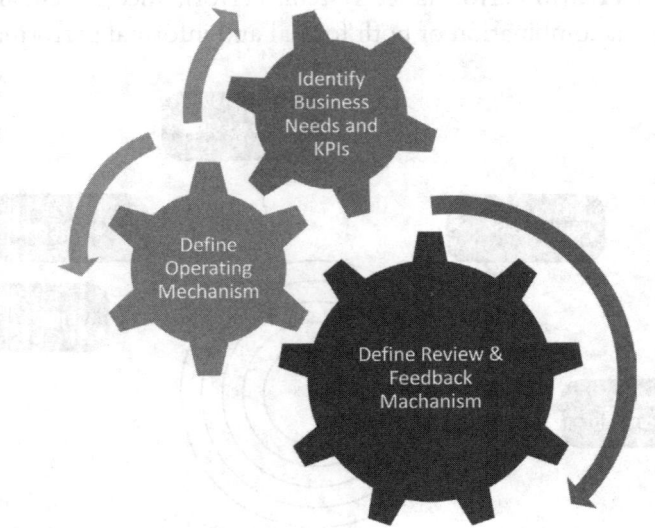

Figure 5.15. Performance Rhythm

space for managers and employees. This kind of approach provides the opportunity for strengthening the relationships between the reporting manager and the employees.

- **Development performance systems:** Organizations, while designing and implementing periodic– and hybrid–performance review systems, realized the need for incorporating the 'development dimension' into the performance reviews, as they felt that merely giving feedback of performance would not help an employee unless it was accompanied by development inputs for the employee on 'how to improve, what to improve and when to improve'. For development coaching to be impactful, it needs to have three major angles (performance angles) scoped into the conversation: skills, attitude and performance. While the manager provides development inputs, the discussion can focus on what skills are needed by the employees to be effective in their job, along with the level of skills needed for the job. For instance the Consulting Partner of a consulting firm, is expected to provide feedback to the junior consultants the skill feedback on strategy design and execution,

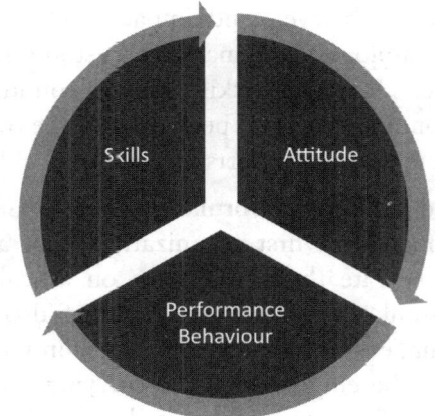

Figure 5.16. Coaching Triangle

client consultation and engagement, data analysis and report writing skills. While providing feedback on skills, for a junior consultant to get the context and insights, the partner could pick up a current project the latter is working on. This kind of contextual feedback would drive a quick message into the junior consultant.

The skill feedback discussion needs to be accompanied by the attitude and performance behaviour angles. Mere focus on skills would result in an employee focusing on just the skills and not so much on his/her orientation towards the job. For instance, in a retail major, the store manager, while providing performance feedback to the floor sales staff, can provide insights on attitude and its impact along with the feedback on their skills and performance. In this case, the manager can rely upon recorded videos of employee behaviour with the customers walking into the store. The usage of 'live videos' by the manager would help the sales staff get the message of interlinkage of skills, attitude and performance behaviour.

'Performance behaviour' here refers to the 'performance on the act'. The skills of the employee are invisible, their attitude can be seen and perceived, while their performance is observed and impacts all the stakeholders: other employees, the manager, customers and the organization. In a sense, skills are the foundation, attitude the bonding lever and performance the overall outcome of the employees' efforts in their job.

- **Forced ranking performance system:** General Electric was one of the first organizations that asked its managers to rate their employees on a scale of 1–5 and stack-rank them. The stack ranking, also termed forced ranking, ensured that the managers in GE would differentiate the employees while carrying out performance reviews. The managers typically played it safe by giving all their employees a rating of 3, to balance between the management and employees and strike a middle ground. This led to a situation where both top and low performers enced up with medium-performance ratings. The situation was complicated as managers' ratings were dependent on employee feedback for them and the engagement scores of their teams. The political dynamics in the process resulted in suboptimal performance of the system.

Forced ranking was subsequently adopted by other organizations across the globe. The system per se created more negative energy and outcomes for organizations than positive outcomes. It led to a lot of bloodshed and had an impact on the morale of both managers and employers. The managers had to forcibly rank some percentage of their teams as bottom performers, to meet their targets on performance ratings. This led to a situation where even a marginal difference in performance between employees led to them being rated as low performers. The negative effects of this system are:

- **Multidimensional performance systems:** As the operating environment became complex, organizations realized that providing performance feedback to

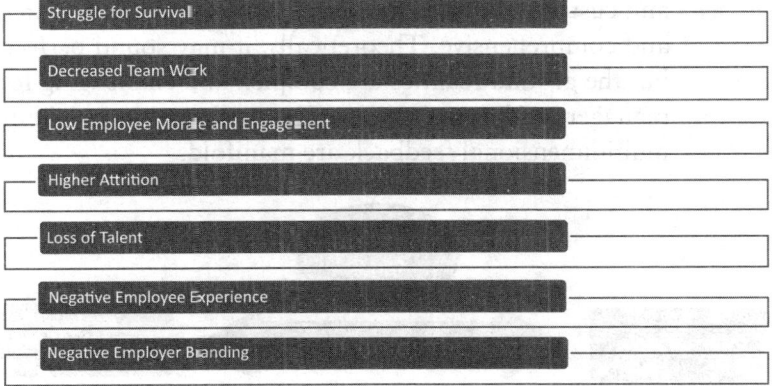

Figure 5.17. Forced Ranking: Negative Effects

Nurturing Employee Experience through Performance | 159

employees based on the reporting manager's review was purely 'unidimensional'. Though the manager may source feedback from other stakeholders, this becomes secondary, and employees may only accept their feedback with a pinch of salt. The employees may attribute the feedback to the personal bias/judgement of the manager, thus taking away the impact of the feedback. After realizing this dimension, organizations have scoped feedback from all the sources with whom employees interface. Such multidimensional feedback evolved over a period of time. It first covered feedback from peers, then from team members and subsequently from other stakeholders in the organization, like other teams/functions/departments with whom an employee needs to interact as part of the job profile.

In an environment where the performance of an organization is dependent on how the organization connects with, relates to and services external stakeholders, having a performance system that is internal/inward-looking would make an organization opaque and non-responsive. The inclusion of feedback from the external stakeholders such as suppliers, supply chain partners and customers makes the performance system integrated and comprehensive. Theoretically, it may sound perfect, but the ground realities are complex and challenging for managers and organizations. The challenges in providing multidimensional feedback are manifold.

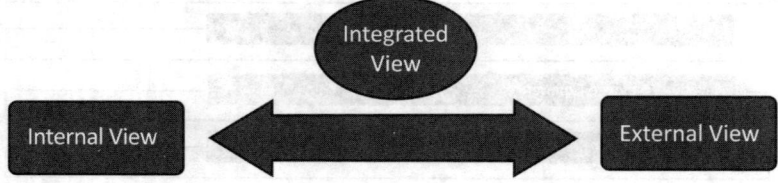

Figure 5.18. Performance Management: Integrated View

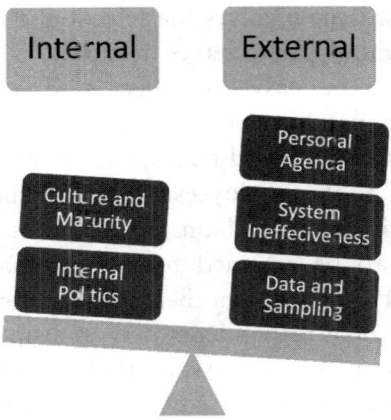

Figure 5.19. Multidimensional Performance Feedback

- **Internal challenges:** The primary precondition for multidimensional feedback is the maturity of employees to understand and appreciate the system. The employees are expected to provide objective feedback to each other. This comes from the culture and legacy of the organization. Organizations that have openness and transparency as a bedrock would be able to roll out and implement a multidimensional performance system (MDPS). If the culture in an organization does not have elements of cooperation and collaboration, then implementing an MDPS would lead to the issues like employees trying to sabotage each other through giving low performance ratings, resulting in bloodshed among them. The impact of peer assessment would be felt by the organization throughout the year, with employees trying to settle scores with each other. The organization, instead of gaining positive benefits from the system, would end up unleashing a wave of negative energy that becomes a source of 'performance destruction'.

- **External challenges:** The collection of performance data from external stakeholders has its own set of challenges.

The first issue involves the selection of the stakeholders from whom performance feedback is to be collected. It would be easy to collect feedback on employee performance for customer facing teams. In the case of support or back-end teams, the internal process can be mapped to the employees working in the manufacturing or service supply chain. The next issue involves the weight to be assigned to the external feedback and internal feedback. Another issue with external feedback is that some respondents may end up giving feedback without any seriousness. It would be a disservice for the employees to be assessed based on such feedback.

Performance System and Employee Experience

Learning and Skills Partnership

The conventional performance system was oriented towards the employer's needs of ensuring performance delivery. Managers had an orientation towards 'judging' employees for their performance contributions. This brought in a wedge between the managers and team members. An employee's relationship with their manager becomes one of 'boss versus me', and their relationship with the organization becomes one of 'organization versus me'. The transition of the employee into such a mindset takes away the collective spirit in the organization. The current generation of employees look for 'nurturing' approach from their reporting manager. They look forward to having their performance reviewed and being provided inputs to 'scale up' their performance, through either optimizing their 'skills utilization' or 'upskilling'. From an employee's perspective, this process would lead to self-development, which is a core EVP, as it holds the key to future career development. The performance conversation would involve the manager discussing the job specs, including an analysis of the skills needed for the job versus

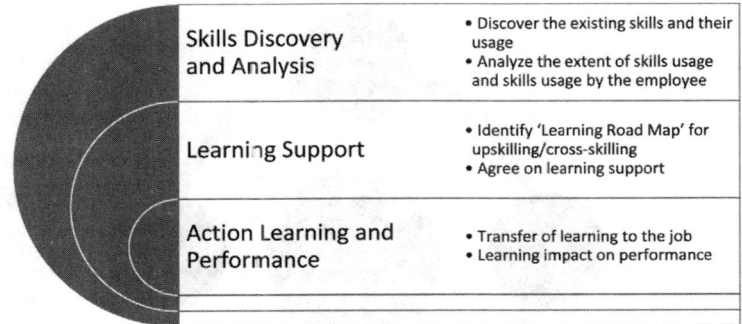

Figure 5.20. Skills and Learning Partnership

the existing skills, based on the employee's past performance. This would lead to 'joint discovery' of a 'learning road map' (LRP) for the employee. The LRP would include what to learn, when to learn, how to learn and whom to 'transfer the learning' to. The transfer here refers to an employee bringing either 'on-the-job' or 'off-the-job' learning to their job. In a way, it becomes 'action learning' linked to the 'job performance' of the employee.

Performance Partnership and Alignment

In the regular performance system, the performance rhythm is periodic in nature, and its advantages, to both the employees and the organization, are limited, the reason being its 'post-factor' or 'post-mortem' orientation. This shortcoming was overcome by organizations through their integrating a 'continuous feedback mechanism' (CFM) as a step towards continuous performance improvement. The steps in CFM are: (a) performance discovery; (b) performance engagement; (c) performance feedback; and (d) performance alignment.

In 'performance discovery', the reporting manager and the employee work jointly to identify the performance goals for the employee for a performance period. They discuss and arrive

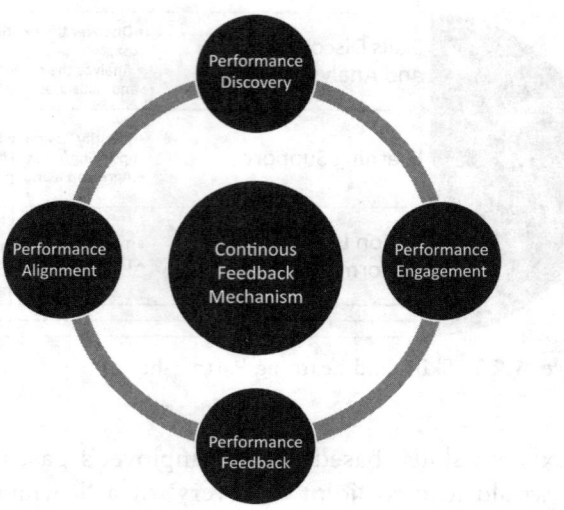

Figure 5.21. Continuous Feedback Cycle

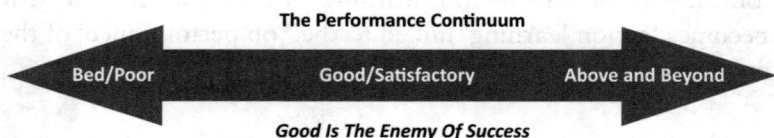

Figure 5.22. Performance Paradigm

at consensus on the level of performance delivery needed by the employee to deliver on the targets. In 'performance engagement', the manager anchors the performance journey of the employee through regularly having 'performance check-ins'. Check-ins are the new format of anchoring employee performance. They help both the manager and the employee to see the real-time plotting of the employee's performance on the performance continuum.

Figure 5.23. Performance Check-In

The check-in conversations are akin to doing a quick pulse study of the organization and have multiple benefits.

The reporting manager and the employee, through the periodic conversations, take away the apprehensions around the typical structured performance review but transform the content into a 'friendly' discussion where information on performance traction is exchanged. The check-ins help the employee get a feeling of 'empowerment', as they find the manager non-threatening and supportive. Employee decides on 'what to do, when to do and how to do' and shares with the manager. The conversations help the manager and employee undertake 'course correction' based on the context and challenges faced. The level of engagement between the manager and the employee would be high, as both would be able to experience a higher level of rapport and mutual comfort in their working relationship. From the employee's perspective, there would be a feeling that the organization is investing in nurturing their performance and skills. The tenor of the conversations would be of coaching the employee to excel in the job. The check-ins on a real-time basis, that is, as and when the employee completes tasks, help align the employee's performance to the job context and the needs of the organization.

Real-Time Performance Systems

The competitive and complex nature of the business world has invalidated the traditional format of periodic performance reviews. The new normal is 'real-time' performance monitoring. In this approach, an employee completes a task/project and submits a self-assessment of their contribution. The manager reviews it and shares feedback with the employee. The performance recording, documentation and feedback get completed for every task the employee completes. This instantaneous feedback takes away the need for periodic discussions and the pressure associated with them. At the end of a performance period, the employee has to aggregate the weights to the tasks/KRAs worked upon and submit a self-assessment. Their reporting manager would share overall feedback based on the traction/performance of the employee. The process becomes very transparent, and in a way, the performance review becomes part of the regular job and not a periodic job. Performance 'check-in' is a frequently used method, and in tech organizations, it is used in every project. The benefits of real-time performance systems are the provision of real-time performance feedback to employees, deeper engagement of managers when working with employees and a new culture of 'performance excellence' for the organization.

Celebrating Performance and Rewards

As the adage goes, 'All work and no play makes Jack a dull boy'. Research shows that an average employee expects some form of appreciation at least once in 7 days. The question is how many managers invest and commit themselves to this cause. There has been a lot of innovation in celebrating performance and rewarding employees for their contribution. Celebrating performance is a way of rewarding employees. Employees/teams get a treat immediately on completing a job. The types of rewards and the purposes for which they can be given are presented in the table below.

Type of Reward	Format	Purpose
Informal	Verbal praise	Appreciation of employees on the spot
	Peer feedback	Colleagues' appreciation of employee contributions
	Team get-togethers/parties	Hosting of a party by the manager either for a specific cause or for periodic bonding
	Birthday/anniversary	Celebration of unique events, like birthdays and marriage anniversaries
	Festive celebration	Celebration of festivals with the events like food fests, etc.
	Appreciation day	Employees are encouraged to share their feedback either online or appreciation corner
Formal	Certificate of appreciation	Appreciation of employees for their special or periodic contributions
	Project completion	Appreciation of employees on successful completion of projects assigned
	Best-performer badge	Awarding of one-time or periodic performance badges to employees
	Monthly/quarter/half-yearly/annual performance awards	Rewarding of employees during the concerned period
	Recognition as domain expert	Identification of employees as a domain expert based on their tenure in their role or performance or special skills

(continued)

(continued)

Type of Reward	Format	Purpose
	Town hall appreciation	Half-yearly/annual meeting of the leadership with the employees
	Declaration of culture/value champion	Recognition of employees for conformity or for championing the values and culture of the organization
	Exemplary-performance awards	Rewarding of employees based on their contributions
	Spot rewards	Appreciation given to employees for specific achievements, like receiving great customer feedback, closing a sales deal, etc.
Financial	Monthly/quarterly/half-yearly/annual incentives	Financial rewards given to employees for performance during the period
	Annual performance bonus	The annual bonus given to employees for their performance
	Deferred bonus	Provision of a deferred bonus that is payable to employees in the future
	Deferred incentive	Provision of incentives that are payable to employees
	ESOPs	Rewarding of employees with stock options for their merit and contribution and to provide value appreciation in the future, also aimed at retaining employees
	Pay hikes	Annual pay hikes given to employees based on the factors like their potential or performance

(continued)

(continued)

Type of Reward	Format	Purpose
	Learning voucher	Organization, with a view to nurturing learning and upskilling among employees, providing them with an incentive-equivalent learning voucher, using which employees can register and complete courses
	Gift vouchers	Employees being provided with rewards as gift vouchers instead of as cash, which they can use to buy products/services, like vacations, dinners, etc.
	Reward points	Reward points help to plan for rewards. Employees can shop on the intranet on the basis of their points and choices.
	Learning programme nomination	Organization, focused on employee development, offering to employees rewards-equivalent learning programmes that the latter can identify based on their learning needs and entitlement
Career	Next-level promotion	Promotion of employees to the next level based on their performance and potential
	Job enlargement/ enrichment	Provision of upscaling opportunities to employees through increasing the scope of their job either at the same level or at a higher level, which helps in grooming them to rise to the next level and nurturing the organization's talent pipeline

Performance and Reward Systems—Employee Experience

After understanding the performance and rewards paradigms (past, current and emergent future) it is important to understand the methods/processes for designing and delivering a superior EX for employees. EX is not episodic or snapshot but is continuous through the entire performance & rewards. The touchpoints between employees and their organization impact not just the experience at that point but also the overall EX at the end of the process. The EX model for touchpoints linking performance and rewards is presented in the figure below.

It is important to understand employee expectations while designing and implementing performance and reward systems. This can be carried out over various levels.

- **Level 1—Goal setting (employee experience touch points and enhancers):** Goal setting is rooted when an employee moves into a role either through a job transfer

Figure 5.24. Performance and Rewards: Employee Experience Touch Points

or as a new hire. It is the responsibility of the manager to help the employee settle down in the job and help them understand the role expectations/deliverables and stakeholder expectations. Most employees tend to err in their performance due to lack of understanding of their role and expectations.

After the employee settles down in the job, the next expectation of the employee is to have their goals set. The role of the manager is to inspire the employee through the mission/vision and co-create the goals and achievement road map. The employee expects a sense of 'freedom and empowerment' in setting the goals and the methods to accomplish the goals. They detest the managerial approach of micro-management, which stifles the employee and leads to frustration. The other type of managers are those preoccupied with themselves and do not provide any time or attention to their team members. The team members tend to 'grope in the dark' and end up discovering their performance goals through trial and error.

The EX enhancers of employees (a) support in settling down in the job; and (b) help in setting of goals that are inspiring and challenging. Both these factors contribute to a positive EX.

- Level 2—Performance check-ins (employee experience touchpoints and enhancers): The employee expects their

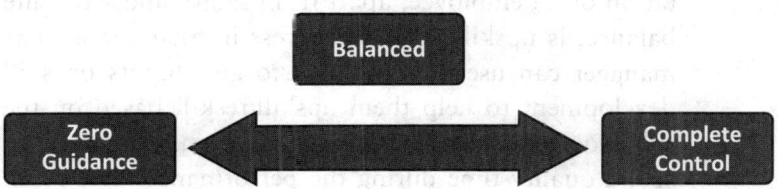

Figure 5.25. Performance Support by Managers

manager to connect with them while they deliver their performance and to provide coaching support through casual and informal conversations. The conversations can revolve around open-ended questions:

- o How is the job going?
- o Are you facing any challenges?
- o How are you addressing the challenges?
- o Do you need support?
- o How are the stakeholder responses?

Based on the employee response, the manager can provide inputs. A few managers tend to overreact by providing detailed guidelines/steps to handle the challenges, taking away the 'joy of learning and discovery' of the employee, and the employee would actually feel that they are being micro-managed. A mature manager, on the other hand, would give directions and help the employee discover the solution and execute it. During the check-ins, if the manager identifies a significant performance/contribution, the manager could use the opportunity to spot-appreciate the performance. Nothing energizes an employee as much as being recognized for their performance immediately. Spot appreciation motivates/inspires an employee to excel and scale up their performance.

- **Level 3—Skill and career development (employee experience touchpoints and enhancers):** The key expectation of an employee, apart from salary and work-life balance, is upskilling and progress in their career. The manager can use the check-ins to give inputs on skill development to help them upskill/reskill based on the role requirements. The manager must make it a point to spend quality time during the performance reviews on having a detailed discussion on career aspirations and skill mapping. The manager needs to help the employee discover their skill gap and draw a skill development plan based on the latter's aspirations. An approach of 'spoon-feeding' would result in the employee perceiving it to be too directive.

- **Level 4—Performance evaluation (employee experience touchpoints and enhancers):** Performance evaluation is undergoing a change in its positioning and structure. The check-ins/periodical performance evaluations, help employees avoid repetitive and redundant discussions. The focus should be on discussing the overall performance, the way forward, in terms of both planning for the next year and career moves, and skill development based on either the current role or career aspirations. An employee's expectations from the performance evaluation process are that:

    o Their performance be evaluated based on pre-set goals and standards. Any attempts to deviate would lead to the employee feeling cheated.

    o The evaluation be a combination of both 'absolute' and 'comparative' dimensions. The employee's first expectation is that their contribution be recognized, valued and assessed in the context of their skills, role requirements and pre-defined expectations. At the same time, the employee expects their manager to use the evaluation standards used for other employees in similar roles, so that their performance is not undervalued or underrated.

    o They be provided opportunities to showcase their contributions not just in their team but also in large events/forums that give visibility to them across the organization.

    o They be appreciated for their contributions and tips be shared with them for them to scale up to the next level.

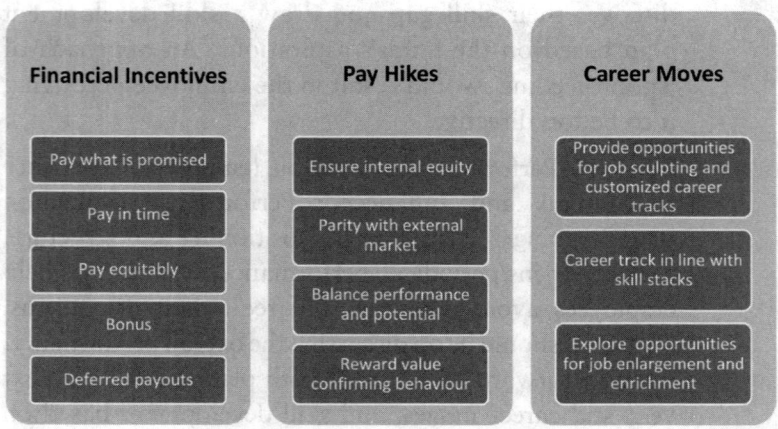

Figure 5.26. Rewards Touchpoints and Employee Experience Enhancers

- **Level 5—Rewards (employee experience touchpoints and enhancers):** The end objective of any performance process is the rewards, which include incentives, annual pay hikes and career moves. The expectations around these three reward components defining the EX are:

    o **Incentives:** The structuring of compensation has a major role in EX around both performance and rewards. Well-designed short-term incentives help an employee to stay on track, as they become milestones in their performance journey. Long-term incentives first help the employee in getting a sense of self-assurance about their contribution and satisfaction at being recognized for their contribution and, more importantly, inspire the employee to sustain and scale up their performance. Long-term incentives can take the shape of annual performance bonuses and deferred bonuses to motivate employee(s) to sustain their performance and stay with the organization. Another format of incentivizing employees is through an ESOP (employee stock ownership plan) that helps them realize the link between their earning and value creation for the organization. ESOP helps in building and nurturing the employer–employee relationship and productivity over the long run.

o **Pay hikes:** Employees look at the pay hike with a lot of expectations after delivering performance for a complete year. The three dimensions of their pay-hike expectations are equity, fairness and justice. The interpretation of employee expectations regarding these three dimensions can be gauged by answering the following questions:

- Is the employee paid in sync with their performance and potential?
- Is the employee paid equivalently versus other employees?
- Is the employee's performance valued appropriately?
- Is the potential of the employee factored in appropriately?
- Are logical reasons on decisions related to pay hikes communicated with the employee with empathy and human touch?
- Is employee feedback sought after delivery of pay hikes?
- Is the employee feedback on pay hike acknowledged, valued and acted upon?
- Are the organizational factors impacting pay hikes communicated to the employees and are they sensitized to them?

It is important for an organization to balance the process and the people. Most organizations tend to focus on the process and forget about the people. The pay-hike process is designed to satisfy the leadership or organizational needs, ignoring the people dimensions. On the other hand, excessive focus on the people would lead to an organization ignoring the process robustness. The employees would perceive this as ad hoc and lacking a scientific approach, which would result in a negative EX.

- o Career moves: At the end of the appraisal process, or as a fallout, employees expect their manager/organization to provide them with direction for their future. It is expected that the manager discusses with the employee how the latter would like their role to evolve to leverage their skills (upskilling/reskilling). The result can be extending the scope of the job with additional responsibilities, either at the same level or at a higher level. Employees who have a tenure of 3–4 years are bound to have aspirations of moving up to the next level. It is important that such expectations are addressed to ensure a positive EX.

Integrated Employee Experience Model for Performance and Rewards

Organizations, while designing and delivering employee initiatives/services, have to keep in mind three dimensions: (a) self; (b) skills; and (c) career. The 'self' aspect is addressed

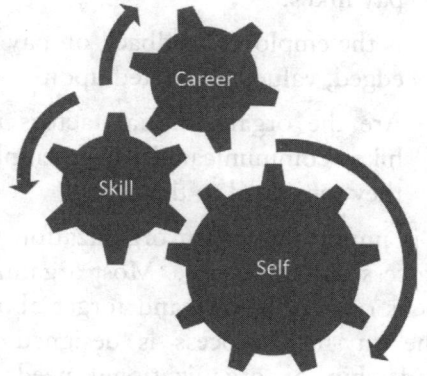

Figure 5.27. Performance and Rewards Integration

through empathy shown by the manager/HR who connects with an employee during the performance and rewards process. The skills are a facilitating link between the employee and the organization. For a win-win relationship, the organization/manager has to focus on both optimizing the usage of the existing skills as the employee settles down in their job and upskilling the employee for a future role at the next level. The end objective of the performance-and-rewards activity is to co-create a positive future full of hope and possibilities for the employee.

Digital Technologies in Performance and Rewards—Employee Experience

Digital technologies have redefined organizational processes of product/service design and delivery for both external and internal stakeholders. An organization can interact with its employees on a real-time basis for regular and periodic communication. If properly designed and integrated with performance and rewards, these technologies can deliver a significant and positive EX for employees. For instance, while planning for a performance review, if an employee wants to check back on their hits and misses of the previous year, they can access both aggregate information and information on critical incidents that either pushed up or pulled down their performance. Employees can carry out scenario planning, before deciding their performance goals, by playing with various combinations of KRAs and difficulty levels of goals, to check on the stretch factor needed. The system can help an employee check whether the proposed goals for the forthcoming year are at par or above par with respect to the team average in the previous year. In a sense, the employee gets a feeling of gamification and scenario modelling while carrying out such planning. From the manager's perspective, if they intend to check in on the employee and co-create goals, before sharing the goals with the employee they can seek the latter's feedback on goal setting. The system allows for the gamification angle as employees can see the inputs from others, collective insights, impact of the collective insights on team/ organizational performance, etc. In short, the process allows employees to have an LoS into the future, both theirs and that of their business unit/organization.

An employee can log in their performance on the go, whether in office or elsewhere, and seek their manager's feedback. The performance conversation gets recorded and can be accessed by the employee and the manager through a mobile app. An integrated performance feedback system can help manager give feedback to the employee. The manager and employee jointly set and track action items on learning and performance goals. Instead of conventional and formal submission, real-time conversation is facilitated by digital tools. The effectiveness of the system can be checked by the leadership/HR by carrying out text and conversational analyses to analyse the quality of conversations between the managers and the employees.

Learning tools can be easily integrated with the performance app to support 'on the job learning'—through subject matter expert (SME) chats, peer chats and performance support search tools. An employee can post their queries on issues/challenges faced and possible solutions. These facilities nurture a culture of 'shared learning' in the organization. Digital performance tools help employees 'learn on the go' and 'learn and deliver'. The stakeholders involved—employees/managers/HR/leadership—can see real-time aggregation and analytics through performance dashboards. This gives an opportunity for 'scenario planning' and 'mid-course correction' in the strategies and goals.

An employee, at the end of a year, for the annual performance self-assessment, does not have to revisit or share the details of their performance during the year, as they get recorded. The employee can run a query for aggregation, to check on their personal performance scorecard in relation to the goals. They can check on the manager's feedback as well, to finalize their self-assessment. The manager can review the employee performance and learning,

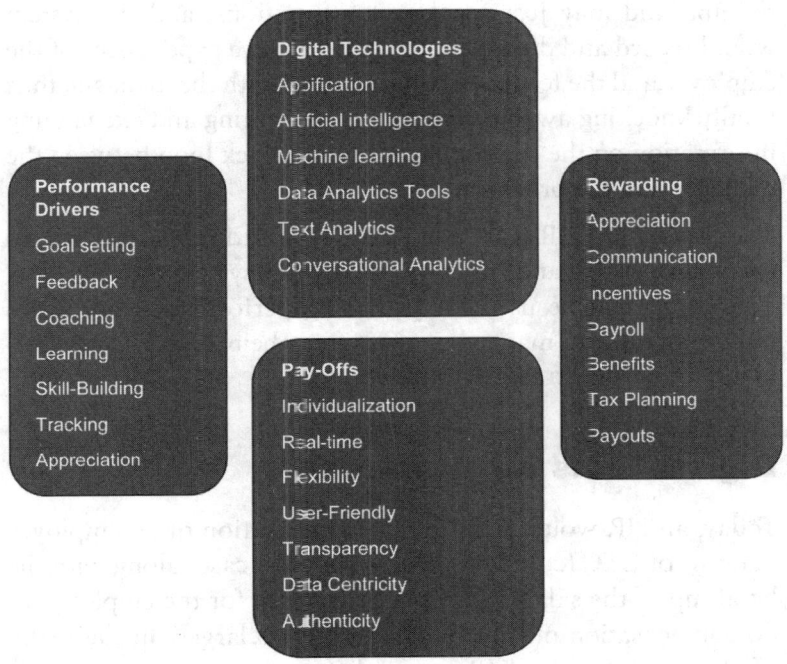

Figure 5.28. Digital Performance and Rewards Ecosystem

along with providing their feedback to finalize the former's rating and record comments on the aggregated feedback.

These features of digital performance tools facilitate the connection between managers and employees through real-time interaction and information and feedback sharing. These elements drive a 'cultural change' in the organization, from being leader/manager-centric to becoming people-centric.

Future Gazing on Digital Performance Tools

We have just seen the tip of the iceberg and there is an exciting future to unfold itself in the area. Digital tools can scope in stakeholder feedback. They can have features like voice-enabled performance documentation and review using AI and ML. An employee or a manager does not even have to enter details on the app and may just speak out instructions, and the system would record and document the performance experiences of the employee and the feedback conversations with the manager, thus totally knocking away the pain of documenting and exchanging information on the performance and feedback loop between the manager and the organization.

The leadership/HR can use text/conversational analytics to check on performance traction along with system effectiveness. The inputs can be used for providing performance advisories to employees and managers, apart from being used in scenario planning during strategy formulation.

Digital Tools for Rewards

Today, an HR would finalize the compensation of an employee in terms of CTC (cost to company), in most cases along with the break-up of the salary, allowing little room for the employee to do compensation planning, which remains largely in the realm of the compensation/HR team. A few organizations provide the flexi-basket option for their employees to decide on CTC allocation for the components in the basket.

In future, the compensation/HR team would decide the CTC and policies guiding the compensation and advise employees to do their compensation planning. The employees would get access to salary fitment tools, with the CTC being fixed beforehand as per the leadership decision. An employee can toggle and craft their customized compensation structure for the year. The system can be AI/ML-enabled, allowing an employee to interact to discuss their expectations and get help from the system.

Compensation components like 'sharesave' plans, where an employee subscribes to save on a regular basis to invest in equity of their organization, they can perform regular checks on the aspects like money saved, number of shares purchased, etc. In the case of incentives that are based on reward points, the employee can check on the points accumulated and reward options available and place an order to get rewards of their choice.

There has been a slight shift in the rewards paradigm and the shift is likely to intensify further to break the ivory tower around compensation and make it transparent for employees. In short, employees can plan and get what they are entitled to without 'knocking on the doors that be'. This induces a sense of empowerment and thus reinforces positive EX among the employees.

Concluding Thoughts

Performance and rewards are critical for an organization from the EX perspective. The employees can stay connected and motivated only when there is guidance on performance and delivery. Digital tools are bringing in a cultural and systemic transformation around performance. Rewards, which are still a 'suspense thriller' in most organizations, leave employees guessing and helpless. There has been a wave of changes in both the performance and reward systems, due to the factors like changes in employee profile/demographics and competitive dynamics and, more importantly, due to technology in general and digital technologies in particular. The changes are breaking away the barriers (psychological/power/distance) between employees and their organizations. Employer–Employee relationship is evolving from 'Us versus Them' to 'We Together', and in the process delivering EX for all the stakeholders.

Points to Ponder

1. How do performance and rewards impact EX?
2. What are employee expectations around performance and rewards?
3. What issues should an organization consider to co-create performance and rewards systems?

4. How do the business and people strategies of an organization impact EX of performance and rewards?
5. What are enhancers of EX of performance and rewards?
6. How does the integrated model impact EX of performance and rewards?

6
Strategizing and Executing the Learning Experience of Employees

This chapter focuses on how learning as a function has undergone a transformation in the digital world. It deals with the context of, challenges faced by and adaptations made by learning teams. The learning function per se has transformed into a facilitating function due to the strategies such as 'crowdsourcing', 'co-creation' and 'curation'. The function now has a distributed architecture instead of a centralized architecture. The so-called centralized service delivery architecture has to be modified to fit into the new normal. COVID-19 in a way has accentuated the digital transformation of learning, not just in workplaces but even in academic institutions. The next generation would be stepping into workplaces with digital-learning exposure. Organizations would have to transition and digitally transform their learning system to serve both the existing and next-generation employees.

Learning Systems: Evolution and Tracks/Phases

First Phase (Before the 20th Century)

Workplaces have been undergoing changes ever since the 20th century. The first phase of learning systems occurred in the organizational context of manufacturing, where there was large reliance on blue-collar workers. Organizations could scale up only when they had enough hands to run the machines. This resulted in an apprentice-training team taking root in the system. The team had the responsibility of identifying, onboarding and training apprentices and facilitating their job readiness. The format of training was a mix of classroom training for theoretical inputs and then the apprentices' transfer to the production floor to work under production supervisors and be trained for the job. After completion of the training, the apprentices are evaluated on both their classroom and on-the-job learning. If their learning and performance were found satisfactory, they were absorbed into the job.

Second Phase (Early 20th Century)

As organizations matured, they realized the need to train their employees not just before hiring and immediately after hiring but also through their period of employment in the organization. The training need came into the picture due to three reasons:

- **Low performance:** If a production supervisor notices that an employee is under-performing either, they would nominate the employee for training on the specific skills in which the employee was found to be lacking.

- **Reskilling for new processes/products:** Organizations, as they grew and as part of their expansion, rolled out new products/processes. However, for a successful roll-out, the employees had to be trained to be able to learn, adapt to and deliver on the new job.

- **Upskilling for the next level:** Organization to balance between aspirations of tenured employees and expectations managers. To meet the twin objectives, the employees were trained on specific skills identified for the next level to help them smoothly transition to a role in the next level.

Third Phase (Mid-20th Century)

This was the period when the HR way of managing employees came into focus. The need for training managers and employees on soft skills to facilitate positive and cordial relations between them came into focus. The HR personnel started designing and delivering training programmes on team building, communication, conflict management, etc. This was in addition to the off-the-job classes that employees were nominated to take care of their technical skills.

Fourth Phase (the Late 1960s)

The 1960s were the period when computers were in their initial avatar and organizations started introducing computers to support business processes. This brought in the need for employees' training to help them learn to use computers for the business processes. This was also the time when organizations started exploring geographical expansion and also evaluating internal talent for their managerial/leadership needs. In addition, organizations felt the need to undertake career planning for employees and train employees based on their career needs.

Fifth Phase (the 1990s)

This period saw the dawn of corporate networks and the introduction of the PCMM (People Capability Maturity Model) framework in the industry. The PCMM framework emphasized identifying competencies specific to an organization and assessing, developing and managing employees based on the competency mapping aligned to positions/roles in the organization. Thanks to technology availability, organizations identified the opportunity to use web-based training, especially for on-the-job training. The focus on productivity and performance led to reduced manpower, which impacted managers' ability to send employees for off-the-job training. Web-based training moved the pendulum in favour of on-the-job training. It offered payoffs for organizations in multiple aspects.

- **Design cost:** For the learning design expert, the design cost was lower, as web-based learning helps the learning content developer use tools more effectively in comparison to classroom training. The content can be designed with the elements such as animation and

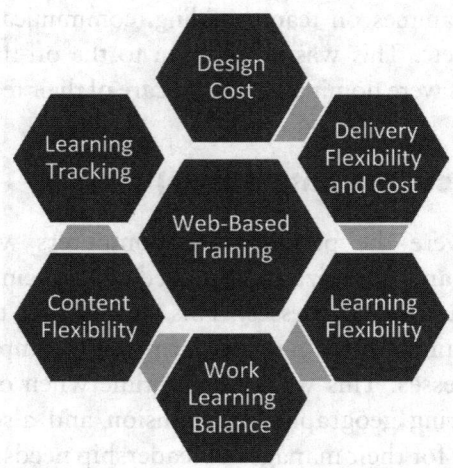

Figure 6.1. Web-Based Training: Factors

interaction, to help the learner connect and learn more effectively.

- **Delivery cost and flexibility:** Classroom training has multiple cost components, ranging from infrastructure cost and travel cost to stay cost (for residential programmes). The invisible cost that inflates the overall cost is that due to loss of productivity when an employee has to attend a classroom training programme.

- **Learning flexibility:** The learner has the flexibility to learn at their convenience, as web-based training has two formats: asynchronous and synchronous. In the asynchronous format, the learning is recorded and stored in an accessible format. The learner can access modules at their convenience. In synchronous training, participants are required to attend the training online.

- **Work–learning balance:** The biggest advantage of web-based training is that it allows an employee to balance synchronous and asynchronous learning. The employee does not have to log out from work or spend long hours in travel. These elements stay on at the top of the mind of the employee, cause stress and thus impact their learning. Post return from the learning, the employee ends up with excess hours to handle the excess workload. These factors have inherently built up a feeling of detestation in the minds of employees towards training. In web-based training, these points are taken care of, increasing the pull factors towards training for the employees.

- **Content flexibility (standardization and updates):** The centralized design and delivery model of web-based training makes it easy to revise the learning product frequently, based on the factors like learner feedback and stakeholder feedback. The centralized learning design and delivery helps standardize the content, unlike decentralized training, which consumes a lot of time in terms of reaching a consensus and adapting the trainers to the changes. Every trainer has their own independent views and approaches, due to which they make tweaks in both content design and delivery. This could lead to variance in learner takeaways, which lead to employees ending up with variant understandings of concepts and with different levels of skills.

- **Learning tracking:** Web-based learning makes it easy to track various dimensions, such as the number of participants registered, the number of learners attending an overall programme, the number of those taking individual modules, etc. Feedback dimensions can be sliced into multiple aspects, such as feedback response rate, module-wise and overall, etc. The tracking indicators feed in data for course correction, helping the trainers improve their effectiveness.

Sixth Phase (Digital Era—21st Century)

The 21st century has seen the advent of the Internet, appification and digital technologies. The pace of technology changes is much faster today, forcing organizations to stay ahead in terms of employee skills and competencies. Competencies and business strategies have become further integrated. The top five factors impacting the learning space are:

Learning Experience: Competency-Based Learning

The competitive advantage of an organization is dependent on the competencies of its talent. The top leadership in organizations are reviewing competency preparedness as the first step while discussing business strategies or making decisions. The direct LoS between competencies and their immediate impact

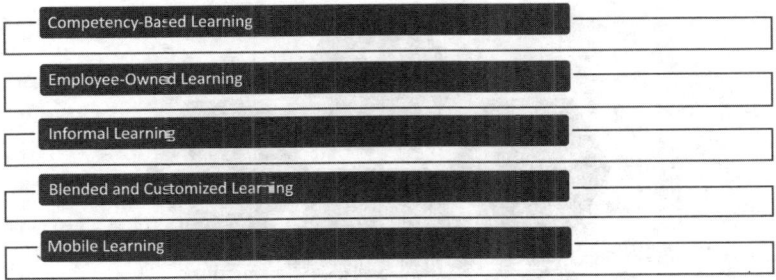

Figure 6.2. Digital Learning: Five Factors

on a business has made it imperative for organizations to direct their learning teams to design and deploy competency-based learning (CBL) strategies.

The advantages of CBL are (a) support to work needs; (b) real-life learning; (c) personalized and customizable learning; (d) transfer of learning; (e) time-, cost- and resource-effectiveness; and (f) performance improvement.

a. *Learning experience—Support to work needs:* The learning needs for CBL are assessed through analysing job profiles, job requirements and employee and stakeholder feedback. The job focus and 360° perspective help the learning expert accurately identify the competencies and the level of the competencies needed by an employee for a job. The programme design and delivery can be enhanced using the ADDIE (Analysis, Design, Development, Implementation and Evaluation) model.

The design and development of a learning programme are based on a few factors, such as expectations of the employees and the reporting manager, time/cost and training infrastructure availability/needs. Factoring in these elements makes it easy for the learning expert to implement the learning programme designed. The participants would find it relevant to their learning needs and show an inclination to actively participate in

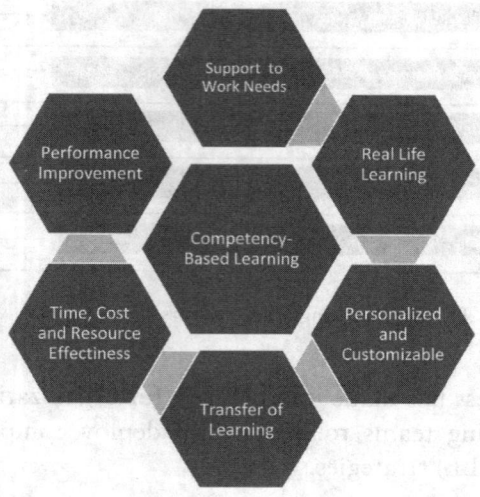

Figure 6.3. Competency-Based Learning: Pay-offs

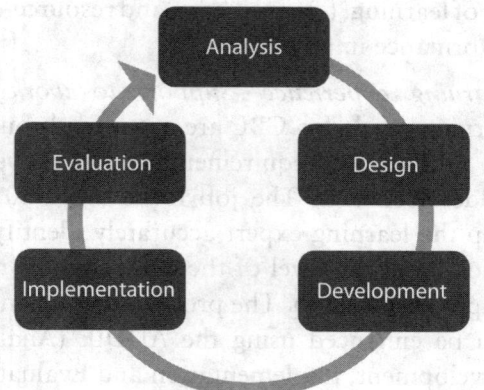

Figure 6.4. ADDIE Model

the learning process. The evaluation process does not throw up any surprises as well. The level of learning and participant feedback would be aligned to the learning objectives for the programme.

b. *Learning experience—Real-life learning:* CBL need not always involve classroom-based learning and can involve on-the-job learning in the form 'microlearning modules' or 'learning bytes'. The digital life, apart from other things, has led to multitasking, and one by-product of this is a reduced 'span of attention'. This aspect is addressed through bite-sized learning or microlearning. The features of microlearning are that it: (a) focuses on the specific learning needs of a learner; and (b) helps the learner perform self-assessment both before and after the learning. The learning would be relevant to the immediate need of the job.

MICROLEARNING AT A BANK

A credit analyst in a large global bank had just moved into his current role from banking operations. The employee wanted to quickly brush his credit assessment skills before diving into the job. He picked up a micro-learning course on 'Moody's Risk Rating Method' with credit assessment and quickly completed the course in 3 hours. The course had an action learning aspect in the form of a micro-project where the employee had to use his learning to assess the balance sheet of a corporate customer and submit his recommendations. The recommendations were assessed based on pre-set assessment criteria and the learner was given a learning score. To bring in learning rigour, the learning module had set the criterion of scoring at least 70% as an aggregate of both the theory and practice assessments. Employees who failed to score 70% would be advised to either retake the course theory or redo the micro-project or both. This inbuilt rigour made it imperative for the learner to focus on the course concepts and applications. At the end of the course, the employee was infused with confidence to do the job confidently and effectively.

c. *Learning experience—Personalization and customization:* CBL helps in customizing learning based on the skills/role of an employee. The combination of digital learning and CBL makes it possible for the learning design expert to design the entire module to address the learning needs of employees. A CBL programme, though comprehensive in its coverage, does not thrust the entire learning upon a learner but delivers learning content based on the current competency/skill level of the learner. The learner is required to take a pre-learning assessment before logging into the learning module. The learner's score would not only indicate their current skill/competency level at both understanding of concepts and their application, but also advise the learner, based on their score, whether to take an entry-level, medium-level, advanced-level or expert-level course. The course, when accessed by the learner, presents both the concepts and applications pertinent to the level of the learner. This aspect enhances their learning experience (LX), as the learner is not burdened with unwanted syllabi or learning that is at a low level and makes them lose interest. If the learning content is at a level much higher than the level of the learner, the learner would find it difficult to cope and would abruptly end/abandon the learning. In both scenarios, the learning effectiveness is low and the learning programme's objectives are not met.

PERSONALIZED AND CUSTOMIZED LEARNING AT A MAJOR INFORMATION TECHNOLOGY COMPANY

The learning team of a large IT organization was working on a programme for competency development of next-generation leaders. The CEO advised them to focus on grooming software engineers with at least 4 years of work experience to be ready for 'project manager' roles in the next 1–2 years. The learning team brainstormed on the project and identified the following methods to identify the learning needs and design the programme objectives:

- Collect and analyse the job descriptions of project manager roles;
- Carry out a focus group discussion (FGD) with existing project managers with varied work experience who are managing projects across various verticals and geographies;
- Study the performance feedback of the software engineers (SEs);
- Analyse the learning and career aspirations of the SEs; and
- Interact with vertical heads to understand their expectations in terms of competencies/skills from young project managers.

The learning team, after collecting data from various sources, analysed the data and discovered the following insights:

- Vertical heads expect project managers to come with domain and prior exposure to respective verticals.
- SEs are focused on aligning themselves to the projects in a specific vertical until they reach the mid-management level, as they want to specialize and get depth in one area.
- A few SEs have completed external certification courses on project management.
- Project managers feel that dipping into 'live' problems would improve learning effectiveness.
- SEs expect bite-sized learning to make it flexible for them.
- SEs want access to learning at their location.
- SEs want live-project cases and not just theories/concepts.

The learning team, after reviewing the insights, decided to design and deliver the learning programme with the following features to address the needs of the learners:

- The programme was to be offered only in the digital format, with a combination of synchronous and asynchronous learning, to allow the learners to choose a learning format based on their needs.
- The programme was to be comprehensive and structured into four modules addressing four levels/types of learners—beginner, medium, advanced and expert levels.
- Each module was to be for a duration of 2 hours.
- Learners would have to take a pre-assessment mandatorily before starting the programme.
- Based on the pre-assessment score, the learner would be provided with access to a learning module at their respective level.
- The learner would have to take a test at the end of the module for certification and to move to the next level.
- Failure of the learner to get a mandated score would necessitate the learner to retake the programme to get the mandated score for certification.

d. *Learning experience and transfer of learning:* Organizations today are pressed for resources, leading to an emphasis on ROI and effectiveness. It would be contextual to discuss Kirkpatrick's model in detail here. The model is a critical source of reference for all in the training system. It indicates four levels of learning effectiveness. The first level is reaction, that is, the behaviour/activity of a learner during the learning programme. Reaction can be gauged through such indicators as body language, engagement during the programme, questions asked to or interactions with the facilitator and fellow learners, etc.

At the second level is learning, which is assessed based on the assessments carried out either during the programme or at the end of the programme. The scores

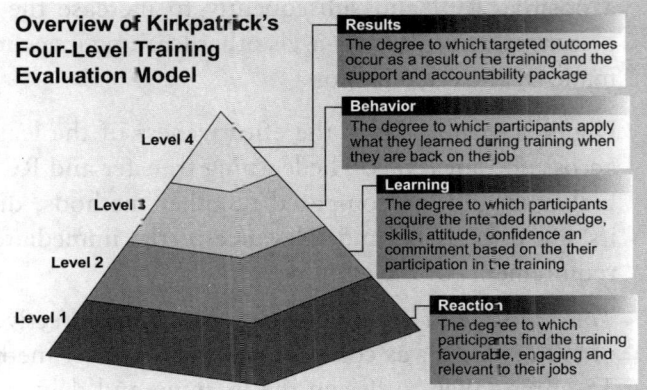

Figure 6.5. Kirkpatrick's Model
Source: https://images.app.goo.gl/5NdLUeEU2Dmprw6P8

of/submissions by the learners would help the facilitator assess the learning by the learner. The facilitator can set threshold levels for learners to qualify to be certified on both conceptual learning and application skills.

The third level focuses on the effectiveness of the 'transfer of learning'. The focus is on analysing the extent of use of the conceptual knowledge and application of the skills by a learner back in their job. The data for this purpose can be collected from three sources using a 'triangulation method'—employee's self-assessment, feedback from the manager and feedback from other stakeholders. The three-dimensional data would help assess the 'transfer' of the learning of the employee to their job. Feedback is sought on both the behaviour/attitude of the employee and its impact on the job delivery.

The fourth level involves the 'ROI' for the organization for the investment made in the learning initiative. The productivity of an employee is compared against the learning investment made on the employee by the organization. The leadership expectation is first to have a positive ROI and subsequently to increase the ROI or comparative ROI vis-à-vis other learning investments made by the organization.

Digital Learning helps the effectiveness of the learning across all four levels. The learning transfer and ROI are higher in CBL as compared to other methods, due to its sharp focus on and relevance to the immediate job requirements of the employee.

e. *Time-, cost- and resource-effectiveness:* The effectiveness of CBL is higher as compared to that of other methods. The time taken to design the learning and deliver it to a learner is much lower, as CBL ruthlessly knocks away content that is irrelevant to the employee. The costs of programme design and delivery are also lower, as out-of-scope content is edited out in both stages. The focused approach towards the programme optimizes resource utilization.

f. *Performance improvement role:* The sharp focus of CBL helps employees pick up the learning (knowledge and skills) that is relevant to their immediate job needs. This leads to higher retention and learning transfer. CBL, if designed in a microlearning or 'on-demand learning' format, would help a learner perform better in their job. The learner would be able to toggle between their job and the learning based on the felt learning need.

Employee-Owned Learning

The learning systems at workplaces have undergone a fundamental shift. Ownership for learning has moved from the employer towards the employee. There are a few factors that have influenced this 'learning shift': workplace pressure, lack of time, increased rate of attrition, increased cost of off-the-job training, etc. Millennials and Gen Z no longer believe in leaving

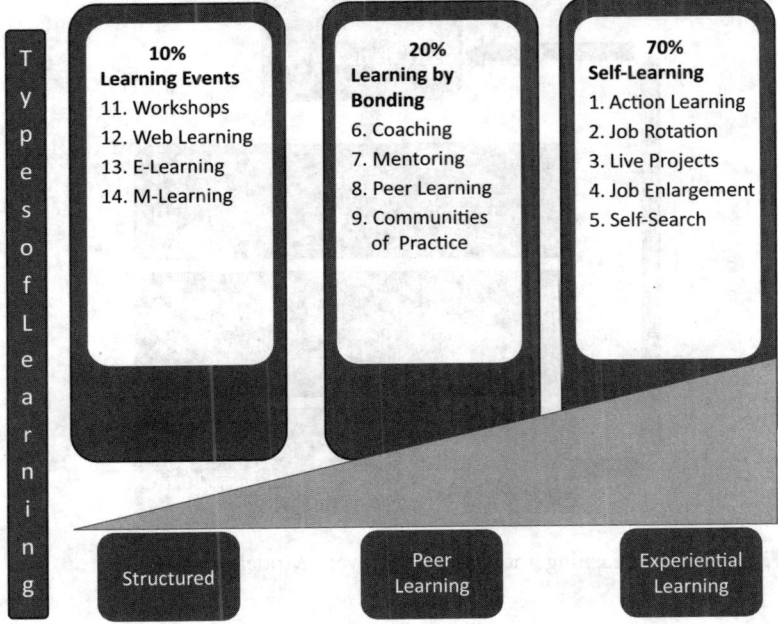

Figure 6.6. Employee-Owned Learning

their career at the hands of their organization. They have a clear focus on their career aspirations and stages. This has led to the predominance of the adoption of the 70:20:10 model by organizations. The primary responsibilities of identifying learning needs, discovering the learning sources and acquiring knowledge and skills are now with the employees.

Employees are expected to take initiatives towards learning based on their career aspirations. They are expected to go through a journey of self-discovery. The first step in this 'self-discovery' is the identification of strengths and areas of development. The second step is 'career discovery', in which an employee discovers their areas of interest and then explores the career options available. The third step is 'learning discovery', where the employee identifies the learning opportunities and

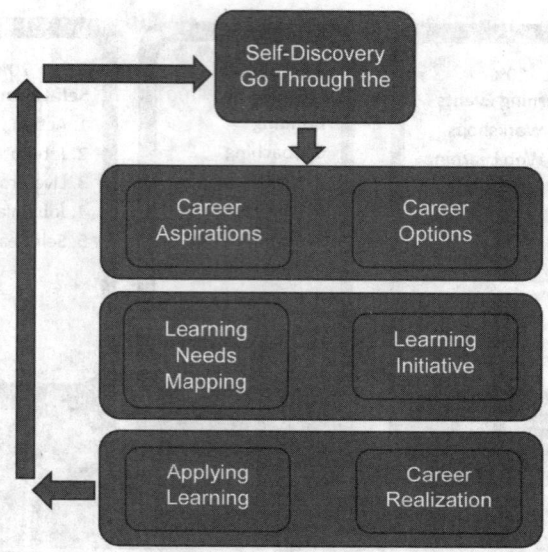

Figure 6.7. Learning and Career Discovery Model

takes the initiative to learn and develop their skills. The next step is 'application and realization', where the employee applies their learning and realizes their career aspirations. The journey is not a one-time phenomenon but is an iterative cycle that the employee goes through. It is not necessary that the employee be successful in every attempt. The journey has elements of 'trial and error'. The learnings from the positive and unsuccessful experiences add up to the self-development of the employee.

Learning Experience and Informal Learning

The learning preferences of employees have undergone a change, due to both organizational and employee-related factors. Organizations are encouraging informal learning, and the stress on the 70:20:10 model across organizations is an indicator of this dimension. Employees, especially millennials and Gen Z, do not like formal learning, as it brings in the constraints of time and power dynamics. This is where 'employee-owned learning' has come into the picture. Formal learning has five distinct features and associated disadvantages, as presented below.

Formal Learning—Factors	Formal Learning—Issues of Learning
Learning framework	The framework cannot be completely customized to the learner's needs.
Learning event	Participation in the learning event may not be feasible for the learner.
Learning facilitator	The facilitator may not be able to address all the needs of the learner.
Learning outcome	The external assessment adds to the stress of the learner.
External validation	Application of learning is subject to external validation.

The disadvantages associated with formal learning take away its sheen and pushes away the learner. Adult learning is based on the 'learning cycle', which has four distinct components.

In formal learning, a learner becomes dependent on external support. In contrast, 'informal learning' allows the learner to go through its steps at their convenience. The employee can go through the steps in the work context, which increases their learning impact. Learning in the informal context has features of 'self-discovery' and brings in a sense of 'empowerment' and 'ownership'. These facets are the cornerstones of 'adult learning'. The iterative nature of the learning makes 'continuous learning' a way of life for the employee. Unlike in the past, when periodic/episodic learning was a sufficient pre-condition for an employee to deliver on their job, in the competitive world

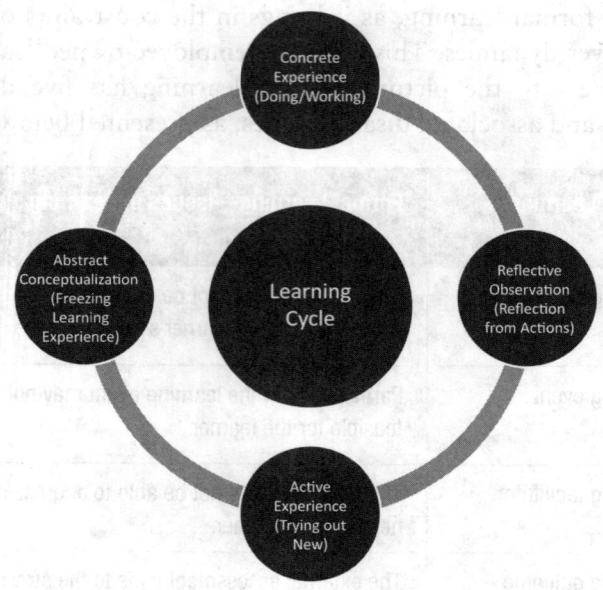

Figure 6.8. Learning Cycle

today where the market is dynamic, the employee is expected to learn and deliver 'on the go'. Realizing this, organizations are inspiring their employees to make 'learning' a way of life and, in the process, transforming their culture into a 'learning culture', where employees thrive by learning continuously.

Learning Experience: Blended and Customized Learning

Skill building and development have become necessary for organizations to stay ahead of their competition. This development has led to the need for organizations to make learning opportunities available to their employees. The other strategic necessity for organizations is to balance the provision of learning opportunities and investment. This has led to the emergence of blended/hybrid learning in organizations. Blended learning is designed using multiple formats of learning:

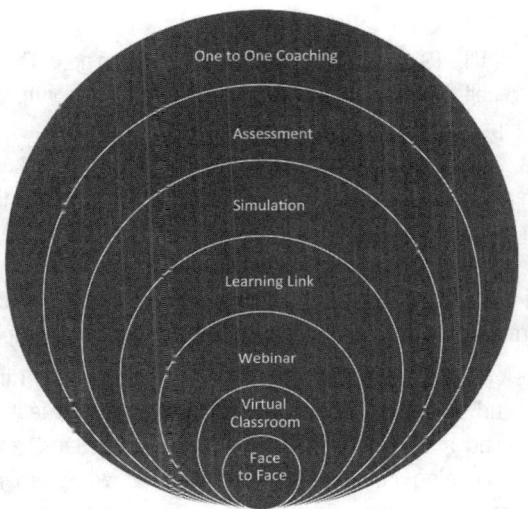

Figure 6.9. Blended Learning: Options

Learning opportunities are made available to employees through multiple formats, to help them choose their learning option based on three C's (context, competence and convenience). Each of these formats can operate in either a standalone or an integrated manner.

> **INNOVATIVE BLENDED LEARNING DURING COVID-19**
>
> A large manufacturing firm in the industrial and infrastructure products space recruited summer interns from across B-school campuses in the country. The organization had planned for a regular format of summer internships, which included classroom training for 1 week, followed by a 1-week on-the-job training, a field-based project that requires interns to interact with the organization's supply chain partners and consumers, 1:1 interaction with the guides and leadership, project presentations and assessments, finally culminating in the award of certification of learning. Depending on the performance of the intern, the organization had planned for either a pre-placement offer or a pre-placement interview.

However, COVID-19 threw the entire planning out of gear. The organization had to halt the internship programme for about a month, as it was a situation that had not been witnessed before by organizations, B-schools or interns. At the end of a month, when it became clear that the lockdown norms were going to stay and that there was no way in which the regular format of summer internship could be offered to the interns, the learning teams went back to the drawing board to offer a summer interning experience using multiple options that digital technologies offer. The completely digital format of the summer internship had the following components:

- A 1-week corporate orientation consisting of HR interaction and leadership address was conducted (the learning team used a virtual classroom for live interactions, and for the remaining components the students were provided with access to online videos on HR policies, systems and product information.).
- The in-company guides used Microsoft Teams to interact with, coach and guide the interns.
- The project was redesigned to help the students carry it out online.
- To collect data, the students used Microsoft Teams to interact with multiple stakeholders, like business heads and managers.
- The students used Microsoft Teams to present their interim progress reports and seek feedback from their guides.
- The final project presentations were carried out on Microsoft Teams.
- The students were given assessment feedback at the end of the internship.

In short, though the organization had to transition to an online internship format, it was able to use multiple online formats and provide online blended learning. This broke the perception that blended learning has to always be a mix of online and offline learning, as the organization showed that it can also be a mix of purely online formats.

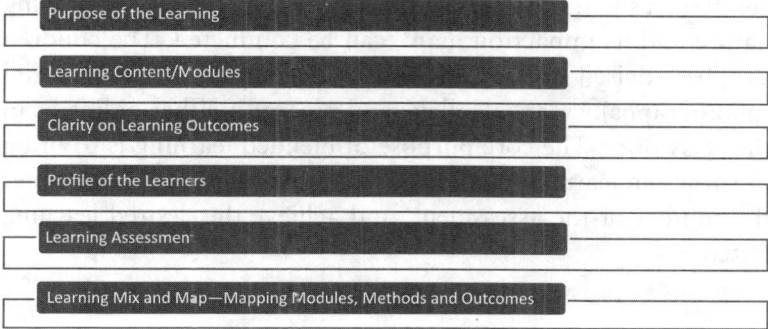

Figure 6.10. Blended Learning: Factors

For blended learning to be successful, the learning expert has to keep in mind a few factors to ensure that the learning programme is effective and delivers the desired results.

The learning expert needs to identify the purpose of the learning. If the purpose of the training is to give an update on a product or a service, the learners could be engaged through a live and interactive online session. Along with it, they could be provided with a reference manual to refer to for further information. The next step is designing the content to be delivered. If the content is long, it would be better to break it into modules. A few modules can be taught in a physical classroom, to establish a comfortable relationship between the facilitator and the learners. The other modules can be offered online or through a mix of offline and online formats.

The profile of the learners is an important dimension impacting the decision on 'learning mix and map'. If the learners are highly learning-oriented and tech-savvy, the learning and assessment can be conducted online. The context of the learning, along with the competence of the learners to be developed, must decide the learning mix. For instance, in the case of adult learners, the learning and assessment can be carried out through a field project (individual-/group-based). In the case of children, a small learning activity, like one on the topic 'studying nature and its impact on man', can be conducted. The children can be advised to collect both online and offline material (photographs), create a collage and present it either online or in the classroom. The core purpose of blended learning is to bring in variety in learning methods, without compromising on either the content or the assessment, and achieve the desired learning outcomes.

Learning Experience: Mobile Learning

Mobile phones entered into a relationship with human beings ever since they were invented, and it was Dr Martin Paul who made the first call using a mobile phone way back in 1973. It was IBM that launched the first smart mobile with an antenna in the year 1993, and Nokia launched the first smartphone without an external antenna in the year 1998. The smartphone revolution came in a big way with the entry of Korean manufacturer Samsung and Apple. The trend got accentuated with the entry of Chinese manufacturers like Xiaomi and Oppo, who have brought down the prices of smartphones along with bringing more features. The transition of mobile network technology to 4G and recently to 5G has increased the speed of smartphones and the possibility of multiple new features being added to them. The combination of technology, affordability and features/ functionalities have made the smartphone a universal favourite. What began as a communication tool has now transformed into a core tool for both personal and professional uses. Their convenience and accessibility have helped mobiles capture several features, such as messaging, applications and service delivery, that were the forte of personal computers and laptops.

The benefits of mobiles have automatically transformed them into a core learning platform. A learning expert, while designing

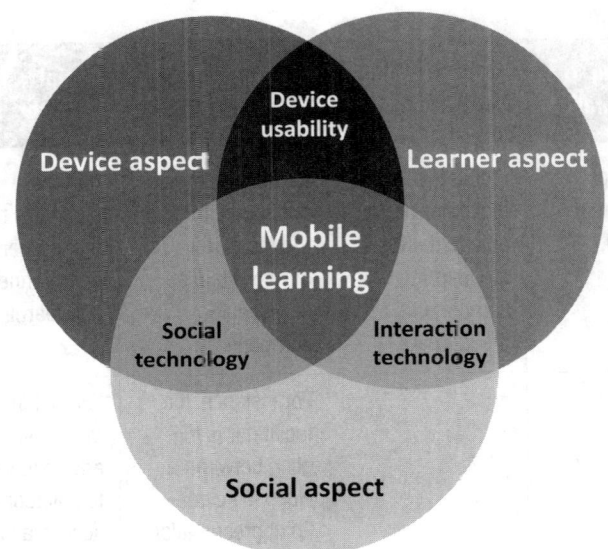

Figure 6.11. Mobile Learning Ecosystem

and deploying a mobile learning solution, has to consider a few factors to make it more effective.

All the dimensions impacting mobile learning can be analysed using the reference points presented below.

Learning Consideration	Device Aspect	Learner Aspect	Social Aspect
Learning component design	Do all the users have mobile handsets with features that support the proposed learning application?	Can all the users access the learning functionality seamlessly?	Do the learning components facilitate social interaction between a learner and their fellow learners?

(continued)

(continued)

Learning Consideration	Device Aspect	Learner Aspect	Social Aspect
Learning component delivery	Would the facilitator be able to deliver the learning components to the learners?	Can the learners connect with the facilitator during the use of a specific component?	Can the facilitator help the learners' peer connection and learning?
	Does the content call for a high bandwidth and a large memory space?	For instance, if a facilitator is toggling between a video, a PowerPoint presentation and a facilitating discussion, would the user be able to seamlessly switch between these pedagogical tools? Can the learner access the content flexibly in a modular manner at their convenience?	For instance, can the facilitator advise learners to collaborate to access a video on a given topic, discuss the topic and stream the video to the class? Can the learner self-learn without much dependence on others? For instance, can they access a discussion thread on a topic asynchronously in a searchable format?
Learning component assessment	Can the device support online assessment?	Would the learner be comfortable with the format	Would the learning assessment call for extensive

(continued)

(continued)

Learning Consideration	Device Aspect	Learner Aspect	Social Aspect
	For instance, the conventional essay format or Excel format followed in exams cannot be supported by mobile handsets.	of the learning assessment? For instance, the facilitator, at the end of their delivery of the learning, may ask the learners to come online and share their thoughts. This may not be feasible for the learning programme executives who are on the field, as the issues such as bandwidth and external noise can be a problem for not just the said learner but also for the entire class.	collaboration between the learners? A quick collaboration for 5–10 minutes could be feasible but not a long discussion, as the latter would lead to weariness and disinterest among the learners.
Learning effectiveness	Would the technology feature be adding only excitement or also actual learning to the users?	Does the proposed learning component enhance the UX?	What is the overall extent of social interaction that is built into the learning solution to balance between distraction and learning through peer interaction?

Mobile learning can be a form of supplementary learning but may not be a primary driver of learning for all learning needs. The learning designer has to keep in mind the aspects like the impact of mobiles on the psychological and physical health of the learner. If the content is asynchronous and can be accessed in a modular and flexible way, mobiles can be used, but trying to use a mobile platform for long-duration synchronous learning would end up being ineffective for both the user and the organization.

Mobile learning, if designed and delivered properly, has several pay-offs:

- **Learning portability:** Learners can access learning irrespective of their geographic location.
- **Personal:** Mobile learning offers the convenience of personal learning experience to the user.
- **Adaptive:** As a learning platform, mobiles can be easily adapted to both formal and informal learning situations. Learners can access online learning modules, discuss with peers informally and take a quick assessment online. The entire learning cycle can be designed into a blended format, balancing flexibility and learning dimensions.
- **Learning effectiveness:** The learning designer needs to develop indicators to track its effectiveness across the stages of mobile learning—access, learning and internalization.
- **Shared learning:** Mobile learning, unlike other platforms, helps learners collaborate and share their learning seamlessly in both formal and informal settings.

Though there are several advantages to mobile learning, there are disadvantages as well. The learner is likely to get distracted by social media chats/messages or incoming calls, which can severely impact the learning effectiveness. These factors raise issues if the organization needs to

Learning Experience: Learning Transformation and Service Delivery

The role of competencies in 'organizational performance' has made organizations realize the importance of the learning function. Learning has been transformed from a supportive function to a strategic function that has a key role in the success of an organization. Organizations can leverage the McKinsey 7S framework to evaluate the current state versus the desired state of the learning function and its integration with their business strategy.

The first step is to study the existing and emergent business strategy of an organization. The learning strategy of an organization would vary based on the life-cycle stage of the organization. An organization that is at the beginning stage would have informal and loosely defined systems that run on informal learning systems, such as peer learning. As the organization matures to the growth stage, the focus would shift to having a robust learning strategy

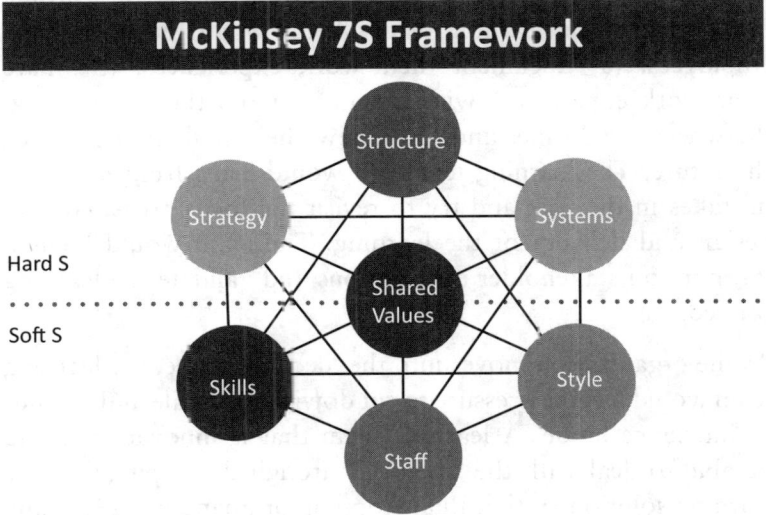

Figure 6.12. McKinsey 7S Framework
Source: https://images.app.goo.gl/2Sp8ZJ3x1KJG3Lw68

and system to support its growth plans. The focus of the learning team would be on two key areas: (a) orienting new hires to the organizational culture and context and the job deliverables; and (b) upskilling existing employees to support the growing needs of the organization. Organizations in the growth stage would look for more growth opportunities for existing employees, along with lateral hires. Existing employees who are moving up the career ladder would have to be upskilled to help them shape up to the next-level role. Lateral hires would have to be facilitated in settling down in their new role and start delivering on the job. The learning team may not have the bandwidth to design robust systems, but the approach must be to design 'workable learning solutions' that fit the bill. Employees who are under pressure to catch up with the organization's growth would be happy with the learning support provided by the learning team.

As the organization moves into the maturity phase, it would transition from a "Rush Hour" to pausing and evaluating strategies, systems and skills based on 'collective learning experiences'. The learning team's focus would be on helping employees: (a) document their work experiences; (b) share their work experiences with others to avoid the 'reinventing-the-wheel' syndrome; and (c) review their skills and plan for the future. The learning team too would learn from its work/mistakes in the past and try to revisit the focus areas, content design and delivery of the learning. The team would focus a lot more on stakeholder expectations and validate the learning offered.

As the organization moves into the 'decline' phase, the learning team would feel the pressure to cut down on its scale and get into maintenance mode. A learning team that is innovative would be able to deal with the situation through developing creative learning solutions rather than stopping or abandoning learning initiatives outright. The learning team would experience loss of

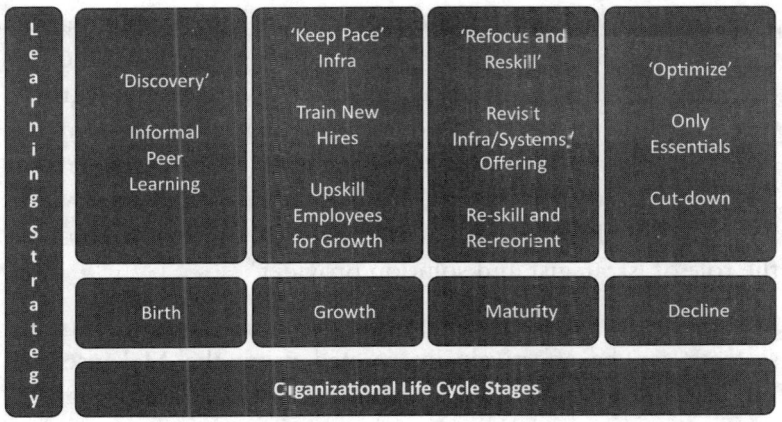

Figure 6.13. Learning Strategies Versus Organizational Life Cycle

space and empowerment due to leadership pressure. The situation can worsen if the style of leadership is autocratic, which can turn the learning team into mere executors of decisions taken by the leadership and do more damage to the learning team and the organization. The learning team members who are creative and enterprising would choose to leave the organization, and those who are okay with being mere executors would stay. This kind of degeneration in the learning team can push the organization into the death stage than help it actually fight and bounce back in the marketplace.

A learning team would sail along with their organization in terms of experience. In the birth phase, the learning team may not exist separately but exist and operate informally with a small team of employees. As the organization enters into the growth phase, business leaders would realize the need to have a dedicated team to handle the learning needs of the organization and would take a personal interest in the learning team. The learning team's priorities are to a certain extent set by the business leadership, and it tends to adopt the role of execution. It is in the maturity phase that the organization's leadership realizes the need to have senior talent in the learning function, who can become a business partner. They look forward to the learning team coming up with end-to-end learning solutions that are aligned with the organization's strategies. The learning team lead would get invited to the business reviews and their views would be sought by the business leadership. They would assume the role of 'strategist and solution provider'.

The linkage between organizational strategy and learning systems can be effectively interpreted using the McKinsey 7S Model, which can be used by the learning team in an organization to perform a quick check of the learning system or formulate an action plan.

McKinsey's Seven S's	Birth Stage	Maturity Stage	Maturity Stage	Decline Stage
Strategy	Non-existent	Focus on training new hires and upscaling of employees to the next level	Comprehensive and covers all the learning needs of the organization and aligns them to the organization's strategy	Limited to bare-minimum and essential learning, to optimize the learning expenditure
Structure	Non-existent	Formal learning in place	Integrated and comprehensive structure to offer end-to-end learning solutions	Restructuring to meet the essentials

(continued)

(continued)

McKinsey's Seven S's	Birth Stage	Maturity Stage	Maturity Stage	Decline Stage
Systems	Non-existent	Emergent systems covering the immediate business needs	Well-structured systems that are reviewed periodically	Maintenance of the scaled-down system and outsourcing of the rest on a need basis
Skills	Partly existing	Learning facilitation skills to take care of needs of the organization; may have to look for external assistance for advanced programmes	The learning team having the skills inventory to take care of most of the learning needs of the organization	Core- and essential-skills inventory retained
Staff	No dedicated set of employees	Staffing always behind the staffing requirements, leaving the training team embroiled in a constant firefighting exercise	Learning team structured in an integrated service delivery format; every learning programme viewed as a product and owned by a product manager	Staff employed on a contract or project basis

(continued)

(continued)

McKinsey's Seven S's	Birth Stage	Maturity Stage	Maturity Stage	Decline Stage
Style	Informal and friendly	Learning team working under a directive leadership; discussions and consultations focusing on the immediate to short-term needs and not so much on the long-term strategic learning needs of the organization	Well-structured team working style, with consensus driven by both internal and external stakeholders	Rigid and directed style of functioning, with not much room for experimentation
Shared values	Shared bonding through working on an entrepreneurship idea	Practicality and 'focus on the now and here'	Balanced view, ensuring that medium to long-term needs are addressed	'Skills for survival and sustenance'

Learning Experience: Learning Styles and Instructional Design

The first step in designing a learning solution is to understand the learning styles/learner orientations. Learning styles are broadly categorized into eight types: (a) physical; (b) verbal; (c) aural; (d) visual; (e) solitary; (f) social; (g) logical; and (h) reasoning. The learning orientation is impacted by the job profile and employee profile.

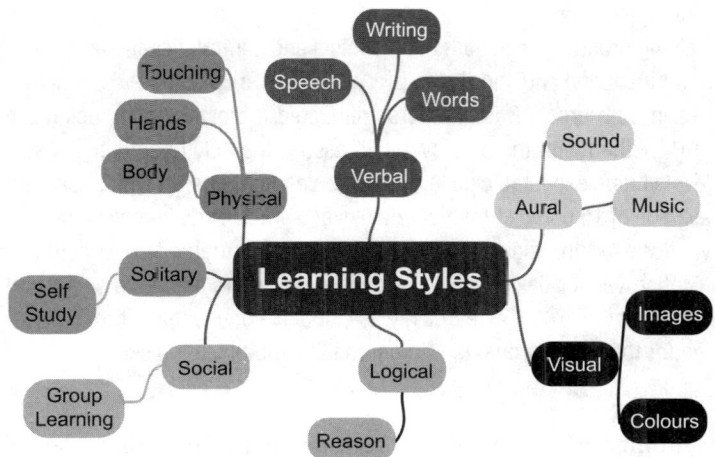

Figure 6.14. Learning Styles
Source: www.absorbonlinelearning.com

LEARNING STYLES AND DESIGN AT A HEALTHCARE INFORMATION TECHNOLOGY–ENABLED SERVICES ORGANIZATION

The vice-president (VP) of a major revenue vertical reached out to the learning head to design a learning solution for his employees. The employees were supporting healthcare organizations in the United States. They were providing tech support for healthcare IT applications of the client. The learning head set up a meeting with the VP to understand the context and the expectations. The VP shared the client feedback that the employees needed to be upskilled in application maintenance and client-servicing communication. The VP indicated that due to the workload and manpower shortage he would not be able to allocate learning time for the employees during working hours. The employees were aligned to a US shift of 6.30 p.m. IST (Indian Standard Time) to 3.30 a.m. IST. The VP indicated that he could advise his employees to log in 2 hours before the working hours began, attend the training and log back in for the job.

The learning head discussed the client expectations with his team and advised them to come back with vendors who could deliver a modular

> training programme in both the technical and communication areas. The team identified and shortlisted two vendors who could train the employees in both areas. Both vendors conducted a dipstick study using the FGD method with the employees, to assess their skill gap (current skill level versus expected skill level). Either vendor came up with a learning solution of 15 hours (1 hour per day) over 3 weeks. The technical training vendor used the logical and reasoning learning methods. The communication vendor designed the learning programme using the social and verbal methods. Social learning was clubbed along with the group learning for the development of interpersonal communication skills.

The ability of a learner to actively participate in a learning process is dependent on the alignment of the learning method with the learner's learning style/orientation. For instance, trying to train a set of medical attendants who are attuned to 'action learning' purely based on an audiovisual method would lead to a situation of learner disconnect. The reason for this is that the learners would have an expectation of receiving practical training on the matters such as first aid, administration of medicines, tracking of patient's vitals on a real-time basis, etc. The disconnect between learner expectations and delivered learning defeats the very purpose of the learning programme, due to a negative LX.

Learning Experience: Methods of Instructional Design

After understanding the learning styles/orientations, the next step for the learning expert is to adopt a structured approach (during the design and delivery stages) in delivering the desired LX. Though there are several methods of instructional design, the top five are explained here briefly.

- **ADDIE model:** The ADDIE model approaches instructional design using an iterative format. The process

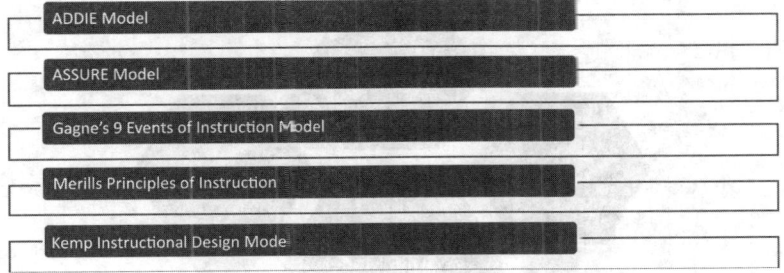

Figure 6.15. Learning Design: Models

begins with an analysis of the needs of the learner. Then, the outline/framework for the proposed learning programme is designed. Learning experts who are seasoned tend to adopt a consultative approach and run the overall programme design through the stakeholders for two reasons, the first being ensuring that the design is aligned with the expectations of the stakeholders and the second being to see if there are any changes needed due to recent and new requirements that might have cropped up. After getting a sign-off, the learning expert goes ahead with developing the programme and delivering it. The last and most important phase is evaluation. It is important for the learning expert to validate the programme on three critical dimensions: (a) meeting of learning objectives; (b) overall LX; and (c) changes needed if there is a gap in either of the first two dimensions.

- **ASSURE model:** The ASSURE model, unlike the ADDIE model, has six steps, but there are overlaps between the two. The first steps of either model are very similar. In the second step, the ASSURE model focuses on the outcomes, which is narrow as compared to the other model. The ADDIE model is broader as it scopes the overall programme design and not just the objectives. The ASSURE model then suggests planning and using support material to drive the learning. Then, the focus

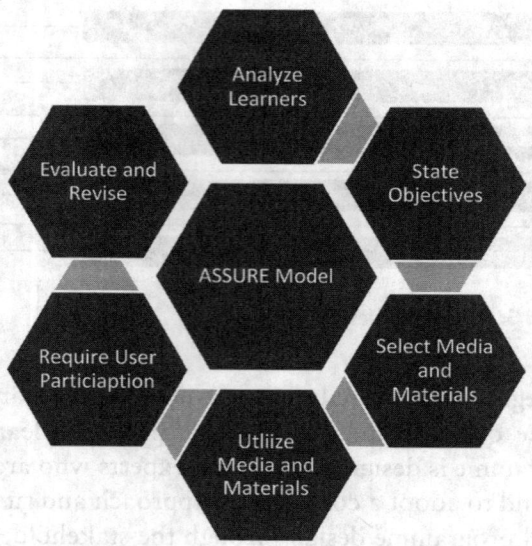

Figure 6.16. ASSURE Model

shifts towards engaging the user. This model explicitly talks about learner engagement and participation. Thus, the focus is clearly on LX. After engaging the learner, the last step stresses on evaluation of the entire learning cycle.

- **Gagne's nine events of instructions:** The Gagne model visualizes the learning process from end to end, comprehensively. The first responsibility of the learning facilitator is 'to get the attention of the learner' at the onset of the learning process. The facilitator uses the methods like warm-up exercises at the beginning of the session, to establish a relationship of trust with the learner. After helping the learners settle down, the facilitator 'shares the learning objectives' sought to be achieved. Learning is akin to a journey, and the learner must know the destination. Otherwise, it tends to become an 'aimless journey', which can lead to loss of focus or interest for the learner. The learner might end up focusing more on guessing the destination than on learning.

Typically a learner when exposed to a new set of knowledge and skills, experiences either 'fear' of or 'flight' from the programme. For such a learner, starting with the known and moving into the unknown gives a sense of comfort and motivates them to discover the unknown set of knowledge and skills. This is achieved through helping the learner 'recall prior knowledge'. An effective learning facilitator uses the principle of 'looped learning' iteratively at every stage of learning, that is, while starting the programme and when helping the learners navigate from one module/level to the next. The looped-learning approach helps the learner: (a) recall and retain prior learning; (b) gain confidence and motivation to move to the next level; (c) see the interrelatedness of the learning; and finally (d) anchor the 'transfer of learning', thus helping them and the organization reap the benefits of the learning investments.

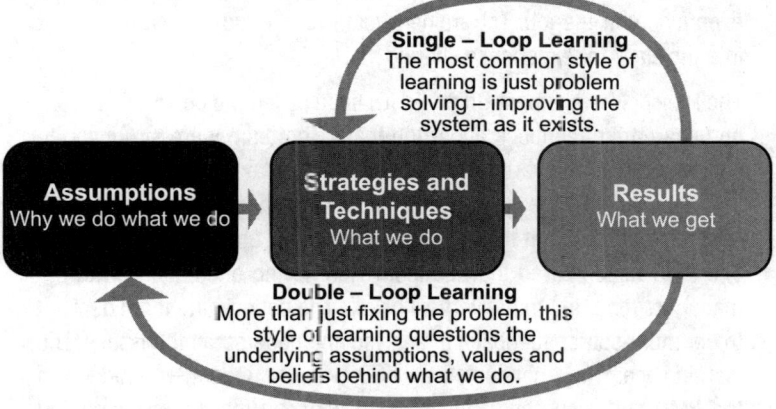

Figure 6.17. Looped Learning
Source: orl9.wordpress.com

There are two types of loops: single and double. The first type is narrow in nature, as it focuses on the 'action–results' linkage and not on the underlying assumptions. This approach may be partly okay in technical training but would be disastrous in behavioural learning, where the learner has to question their underlying assumptions and the impact of these on their actions and bear the consequences of their actions.

LOOPED LEARNING IN PRACTICE

In a large IT major, there was a technical training team and a behavioural training team. The technical trainer was called by the head of IT infrastructure to design a learning programme for his 'Application Maintenance' team. He added that the team could not be off the job and that he would prefer 'on-the-job' learning. The trainer, in order to carry out a 'learning-needs assessment', conducted an FGD with the Application Maintenance engineers. He could identify that they were already receiving 'on-the-job' learning. To formalize the learning process, the trainer designed short learning modules of two hours each. The first half hour would facilitate conceptual discussion, followed by one hour of live experience on the job. The trainer would then bring the learners back into the class for experience sharing.

The Project Management Office (PMO) head called the behavioural team and shared the feedback about the team. The team were struggling to coordinate with the vertical heads and get the data. They were preparing and updating the dashboard. The vertical heads came back with adverse feedback that the data were not correct and were not updated. The PMO head shared that his team was having altercations with the managers reporting to the vertical heads. The behavioural team decided to get multi-source feedback to analyse and understand the issues. The learning team first conducted an FGD with the managers working in the PMO and then conducted an FGD with the managers supporting the vertical heads. They conducted in-depth interviews with randomly selected vertical heads. The key issues were that managers in the

PMO did not plan for data or always placed requests at short notice. They were having transactional and need-based communication with the managers supporting the vertical heads. The vertical heads too had given similar feedback about the PMO managers.

The learning team at the end of the study decided that the learning intervention needed was 'relationship building', which is based on experiential learning, in a modular format, through two modules across two days. The first module would involve participants carrying out self-introspection on their assumptions about relationship building and analysis. The second would focus on providing learning for the participants on approaches to and techniques of relationship building. The participants went back to their work and came back after a month with the insights/learnings. The group came back to discuss about actions along with their outcomes and identified the gaps in understanding and implementation. They went back to the drawing board, worked on revising the learning and came back with a third module to check on the learning and impact of the actions post learning.

The learning facilitator, after identifying that the learners are ready for and conducive to the learning, 'presents the learning content'. Mere presentation of the content in an abstract format would not be useful, as the learners would not be able to relate to it. An effective facilitator would share both the concepts and their applications and 'provide learning guidance'. They would encourage the learners to think of scenarios for the application of the concepts taught. They would also facilitate peer learning by encouraging the learners to share their understanding of the content and interpretation of the content in the context of their own experiences ('experiential learning'). The experiential learning would help the learners perform better, both in the learning situation and in the assessment at the end of the learning programme.

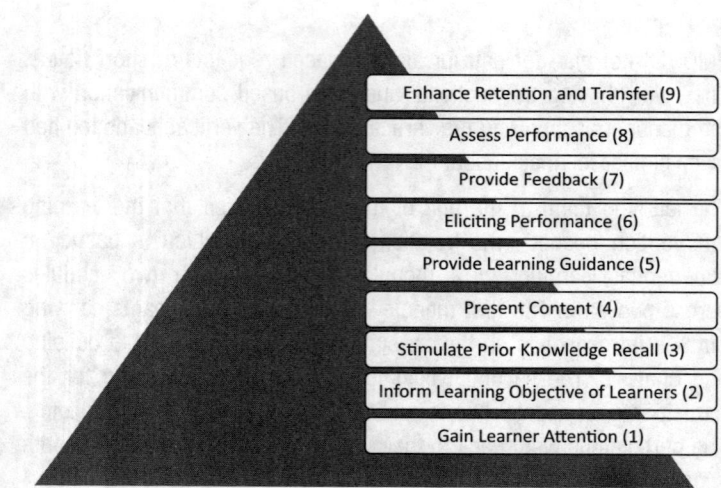

Figure 6.18. Gagne's Nine-Stage Model

A good score in the learning assessment boosts the morale of a learner and has threefold benefits. It encourages the learner to first retain the learning, then strive to apply the knowledge and skills in their job and, most importantly, develop a 'positive behaviour' towards learning in future. A positive learning orientation inspires learners to carry on 'continuous learning', that is, continue the learning with 'on-the-job learning'. Leaders who are keen to build a learning organization, provide platforms for learners to document their learning ('knowledge management' [KM]) and create forums, like 'learning chats' and 'discussion forums', for the learners to discuss and share their learnings, in terms of both application of knowledge and the skills learnt, through both 'off-the-job' and 'on-the-job' learning. This entire process contributes to building a 'learning organization', proposed by Peter Senge in his book *Fifth Discipline*. The five building blocks of a learning organization are: (a) shared vision; (b) systems-oriented thinking; (c) personal mastery; (d) team learning; and (e) mental models. For the learning designer/product owner, having these five elements addressed through the learning life cycle stages is critical.

To anchor the transformation process of the organization, the leadership has the responsibility to create and disseminate a shared vision and communicate the urgency for self-learning and development through a continuous process. This would help the learning team drive the design and implementation of the learning systems/processes in the organization.

It is important for the learners to see/interpret the integrated view of knowledge and application of skills not just in their individual space but also across other work streams (systems thinking). In some learning situations, a few learners engage in learning behaviour just to create an impression on the facilitator, without making an attempt to learn and internalize the learning. This kind of deviant behaviour distracts the fellow learners. Alternatively, a few learners could focus on self-learning to excel in a knowledge/skill area (personal mastery) but may be unwilling to share their expertise with other employees, due to selfish and competitive reasons. Such behaviours by employees could lead to a situation where the organization has individual islands of excellence who are not willing to collaborate and in some cases hurt each other.

In the competitive era, where 'knowledge is the new currency of power', it is likely that learners would retain their learning to hoard power. Learning if not shared can lead to 'personal and functional conflicts', as information on the application of knowledge is not shared between individuals and functions. This is where 'team learning' comes into the picture. Digital workplaces have made it easy for organizations to facilitate shared learning.

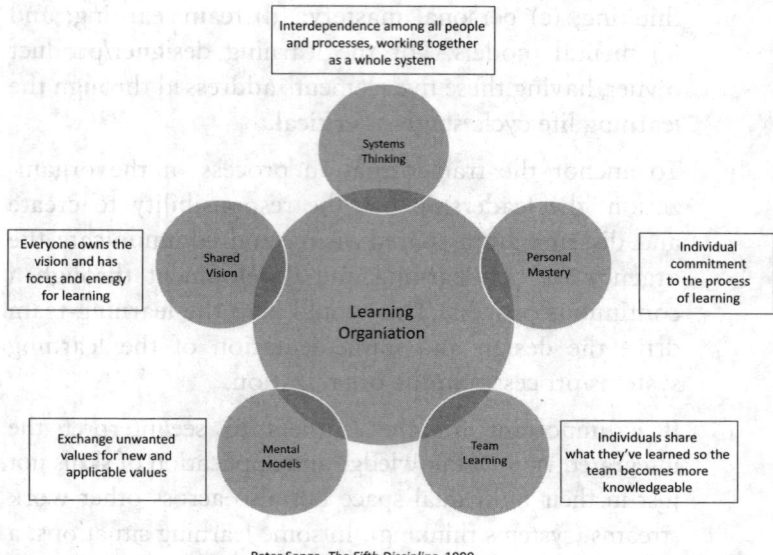

Figure 6.19. Impacting Learning Experience Through the Fifth Discipline
Source: https://images.app.goo.gl/9x53DYntQ9UioMHP6

Shared learning helps teams revisit their old values and assumptions and try to collectively identify new values/assumptions. This periodical exercise would support the agility and innovation process in an organization. Peter Senge's model helps in fostering a positive LX due to its hybrid approach that seamlessly twines strategic and integrated approaches towards learning systems in organizations.

- **Merrill's principles of instructional design:** Merrill's principles are based on 'action learning'. The underlying philosophy is that adult learners value learning that is presented as a solution to a problem that they are trying to solve. The facilitator helps the learners discover solutions to issues that the latter are facing in real life. The facilitator elicits insights from the participants, prioritizes them and takes up a problem that the group as a collective feels is a priority. An inexperienced facilitator might jump straight into the delivery of the learning, which would lead to a disconnect between the facilitator and the learners, as the learners would perceive the learning as being imposed on them and would fail to see the value they derive out of it. This can lower the learner engagement and ultimately the LX. The facilitator then helps the learners recall their existing body of knowledge/application of skills (activation), identifies gaps in learning and motivates the learners to be open to new learning. They then share the new body of knowledge and the benefits of its application in problem-solving for the learner (demonstration).

Leaving a learner immediately after a new learning can lead to issues such as low retention or total loss of learning. Merrill's model in the fourth stage stresses the facilitator supporting the learners in the application of their knowledge through providing opportunities. This could include in-class activities where, after a module, the learners are provided with an application opportunity, which helps them in three ways. The learners can

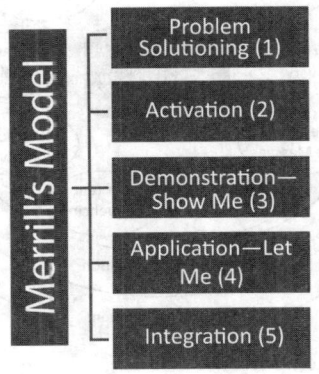

Figure 6.20. Merrill's Model

check on their learning gaps, gain confidence in their application of their knowledge and, most importantly, internalize and reinforce their learning (integration).

- **The Kemp model of instructional design:** The Kemp model, also referred to as the Morrison, Ross and Kemp model scopes four key and interrelated elements into instructional design: learner needs, learning objectives, methods of learning and evaluation methods. It highlights the 'continuous' nature of the process and execution of the four elements through nine stages of the learning cycle. The applicability of the nine stages can considered by the learning designer either independently or collectively. The learners choose to prioritize and emphasize some steps over others, based on the learning context and their needs.

The 'first step' in instructional design is to identify the specific goals and possible issues that could arise due to the learning content, context and infrastructure. The 'second step' is to identify and

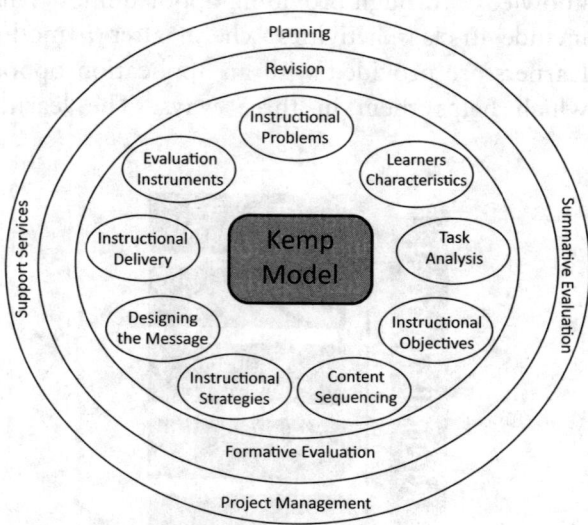

Figure 6.21. The Kemp Model
Source: https://images.app.goo.gl/4K1Vp7ZgDUNmqBom6

analyse the characteristics of the learners, such as their age, tech-savviness and orientation towards the learning. In organizations that are static and bureaucratic, the employees typically have an antipathy towards learning. The facilitator, in the 'third step', presents the task components vis-à-vis the learning goals or the purpose of the course. The 'fourth step' involves defining the course objectives and desired learning outcomes. The 'fifth step' stresses on sequencing the individual instructional units to avoid learner discomfort or confusion. For instance, the basics are presented first to help the learner settle down and be comfortable with learning before advanced learning units are presented. Attempts to present advanced learning units prior to the basics would drive away the learner, due to the difficulty of acquiring entirely new learning and the lack of connection between the existing body of knowledge and the new knowledge delivered. The 'sixth step' involves customization of instructional methods to meet the needs of individual learners, to achieve the desired outcomes. The basic challenge encountered by instructors is the variance in the level of knowledge/skills of the learners. A few might be at either an advanced or a low level, and the majority might be at the average level. An effective facilitator would try to pitch the level of instruction at the average level. The learners at an advanced level could be handled through personal coaching or specific assignments that would challenge them. The 'seventh step' is planning the instructional message and mode of delivery. A facilitator for young children may choose an instruction method that enables them to carry out a small activity and learn. In the case of adult learners, the facilitator can choose the instructional method of a small assignment that would involve learners reading and interpreting lessons and bringing discussion points to the class. In the 'eighth step', the facilitator makes a choice of instruments/methods to assess the traction in learning by the learners with respect to the learning outcomes. In the 'ninth step', the facilitator needs to identify resources that would support them in the various stages of learning.

> **LEARNING FACILITATION IN COVID-19 TIMES AT A B-SCHOOL**
>
> No one in the world has been spared by COVID-19. B-schools have undergone their share of quick resets to move towards digital learning. A leading B-school in India had to embark on digital transition. It identified Microsoft Teams as a good platform for this and signed up with it. Next, it had to train its faculty to get oriented to the system. The faculty had their own set of apprehensions and had to be nudged to adopt digital tools. The next major challenge was the mindset of the learners. The learners of the Executive MBA programme were resistant to the change, as they feared that the online learning experience would not be the same as that in offline learning.
>
> The faculty, after delivering one or two sessions, realized that teaching online was not the same as offline teaching. They understood the need to: (a) reset the content (moderate it); (b) revisit the delivery method (make it more interactive and engaging); (c) design the delivery around action-/discovery-based or experiential learning as anchors for the process; (d) assure the learner of their learning through small learning-level checks; (e) redesign the assessment pattern (both content and format, to a small/bite-sized and application-oriented pattern); (f) get supporting resources, like learning assistants to monitor class participation, submissions, etc.; (g) get technical support to deal with tech glitches at both the facilitator's and the learners' side.
>
> The process was iterative and dynamic, and the LX was monitored periodically at every stage at multiple levels—learning-facilitator level, learner level and tech-service delivery level—to assure a seamless LX for the learners.

Learning Experience: Learning Approaches

Different learning theories/approaches have been emerging over the previous century. The four broad approaches are: (a) behaviourism; (b) cognitivism; (c) constructivism; and (d) connectivism.

Behaviourism assumes that learners are passive and thus there is a need for external processes, like periodic positive reinforcement, to keep them on track. The learning methods are conventional, such as lecture, drill and practice, rote learning, multiple-choice test, etc. The LX delivered by this approach would be low, as the learner is assumed to be passive, which is not the case. A learner, irrespective of their age group, in the contemporary world wants to be an active partner along with the facilitator in the learning process. The only relevant aspect of behaviourism today would be positive reinforcement. The facilitator can enhance the LX by sharing assessment feedback, both formal and informal, to assure the learner of the traction in their learning and that they are keeping up the learning pace. In cases where the facilitator observes low levels of learning, the learners can be motivated through personal touch, individualized coaching and learning support.

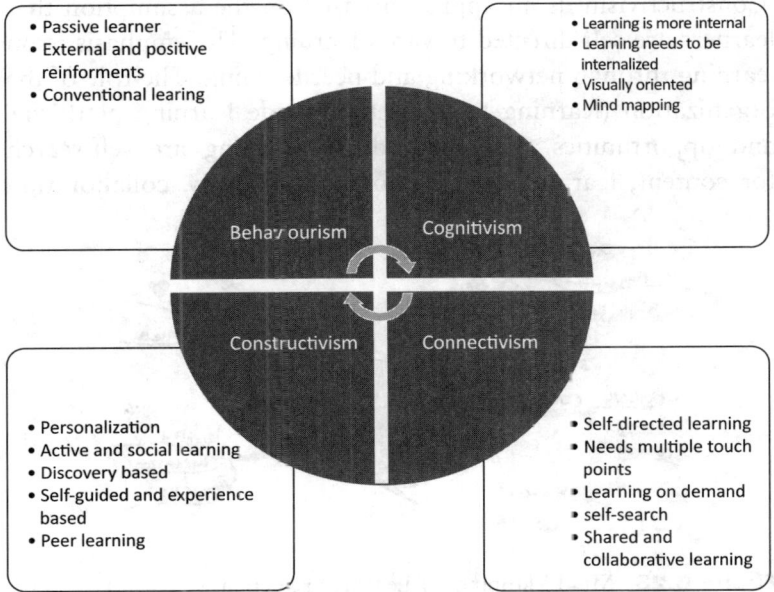

Figure 6.22. Approaches to Learning Design

The 'cognitivism' approach assumes that learning is more of an internal process, and it calls for internalization of learning—retention of the learning in both short-term and long-term memory. The LX is facilitated by the facilitator using visual tools. The usage of visual tools helps the learners form mind maps. Mind mapping is based on the action learning principle. The learners are encouraged to brainstorm, discover the various underlying themes/learnings and identify the interrelatedness and the impact of the points connected by the topic of learning. The effectiveness of the tool is determined by the skill of the facilitator. The facilitator gently nudges the learners to come up with insights and share them with their peers. Thus, the learners are able to see the learning insights of their peers during the facilitation process. The facilitator then shares the output with the learners for their future reference. The collaborative and interactive process and visual imaging help the learners internalize the learning strongly and retain it in both short-term and long-term memory.

'Constructivism' is an approach based on the assumption that learners are self-directed towards learning. The emphasis is on learning through networking and peer learning. The role of the organization (learning team) is to provide learning platforms and opportunities. The methods of learning are self-search for content, learning on the job spontaneously, collaboration

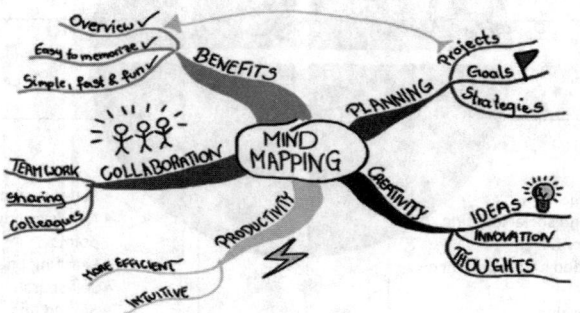

Figure 6.23. Mind Mapping for Learning Experience
Source: https://images.app.goo.gl/UFfLLSgQKmBUJKCk6

with others to create learning opportunities and sharing of the learning. The approach is oriented more towards adult learning and can work in an open, flexible and agile organization, and it may deliver a positive LX to the learners. It may not work the same way in controlled and bureaucratic organizations, where employees are directed towards a way of work and learning. Employees may interpret such an approach as a disinterested or hands-off approach by the organization/leaders/HR team members.

'Connectivism' is based on the philosophy that learners have the capability to learn from their own experience. The role of the learning facilitator is to create opportunities for the learners to come together, share their experiences and derive learning from each other's experiences. This method of learning is called experiential learning. The LX is dependent on a learner getting insights on or making interpretations of the experiences of their fellow learners. The methods of learning involved here are discovery-based learning, collaborative group work, scaffolding, self-guided learning based on personal experiences and peer grading/review.

Learning Experience Through the 'Ladder of Inference'

In andragogy (adult learning), the facilitator taking a supportive role to help the learners discover the learning is a popular method, under the connectivism approach. The facilitator takes the learner through a discovery-based learning process. This method of learning is used majorly for behavioural training and, if planned properly, can be used for analytics/leadership/strategy-related training programmes as well. In the first step, the facilitator helps the learner observe the reality around them by presenting the 'available data'. Then, the focus shifts to 'selected data' when the facilitator helps the learner see the data selected and omitted by them. The objective is to help the learner look at any issue holistically and not jump to considering only one set of data. In the third stage, the facilitator helps the learner 'interpret' the data objectively without any bias. Most problems in life or career crop up because people tend to interpret the available set of data based on their assumptions.

> **LADDER OF INFERENCE IN PRACTICE**
>
> For instance, a learning facilitator, when presented with not-so-great feedback by the learners, tends to attribute it to lack of orientation towards learning among the learners or lack of support by the managers in nominating the right set of learners to the programme. By doing so, the facilitator loses an opportunity to conduct a self-introspection/analysis of 'what went well and what did not' and thus loses an opportunity to improve. In a way, the facilitator tends to get into a self-defence or self-justification mode. This happens with managers/leaders as well when they review their decisions.

In the fourth step, the facilitator helps the learner decide the 'assumptions' for such behaviour or approach towards

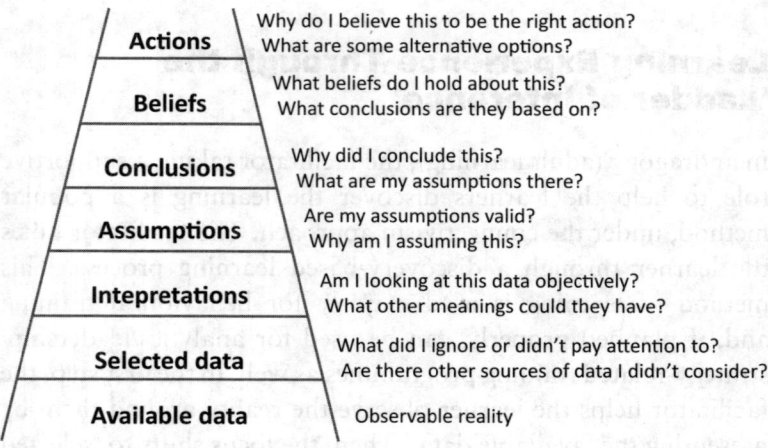

Figure 6.24. Ladder of Inference
Source: https://images.app.goo.gl/xfERsFXZWZzD5aJ3A

analysing a situation. This calls for tactful facilitation and a balancing act, whereby the facilitator gently 'probes/nudges' the learner to discover the reasons for such past assumptions. One key reason for this is that people tend to 'operate from experiences of the past' rather than 'living in the present'. The role of the facilitator is to help the learner identify the internal subconscious dichotomy. In the fifth step, the facilitator helps the learner develop conviction on their 'conclusions'. Quite often, people, when they arrive at decisions/conclusions, tend to arrive at them based on momentary emotions, which are transient. This impacts their commitment to their own decisions, and as a result, people tend to 'waver or vacillate'. Such behaviour can adversely affect one's productivity and credibility at the workplace or in real life. The sixth step is 'beliefs' analysis/introspection, in which the learners take a deep dive to uncover the beliefs that have led them to arrive at a conclusion or position on a given set of data. This step can actually help a learner revisit their conclusion and discover that it was arrived at based on wrong beliefs or is based on false notions. In a way, this step is critical to motivate the learner's resolve to reach strong conclusions. In the learning context, this step is critical from the 'transfer of learning' perspective. The last step is guiding the learners towards 'actions'. This step is akin to carrying out 'scenario building' through learning about a possible set of actions to execute a decision or reach a conclusion. This would help the learners be prepared and not blindly 'jump into action' and face setbacks. From an LX perspective, this step has a major impact. Quite often, facilitators either rush through it or leave it to the learners to figure it out for themselves. The learners might either spend too much time on 'trial and error' or alternatively abandon the implementation of learnings/decisions in the wake of adversities/challenges. Such a situation can lead to the learners losing interest in learning. In 'on-the-job learning' too, the LX can be a facilitator through periodic 'in-person individual/peer conversations' to help the learners share and document their learnings (KM).

Learning Experience and Knowledge Management

The learning transition in organizations has led to the emphasis on the 70:20:10 learning strategy, leading to a situation where 90% of learning happens informally at the employee level. For an organization to be agile and functionally effective, it is imperative to track its learning for two strategic reasons. The first is that the leadership needs to check if the employees are oriented towards learning, if the learning process is active and if the learning is resulting in positive outcomes for the employees and, more importantly, to motivate the employees to share and document their learning. The other reason is to eliminate 'repeated learning', wherein employees tend to learn the same lessons through trial and error, which impacts both their productivity and the operational excellence of the organization.

It looks very simple as a model to design and operate a KM system for creating a positive LX. However, the reality is far

Figure 6.25. Knowledge Management and Learning Experience

from easy. Organizations in the IT space launched KM in about early 2000 and pursued it for some time, but it has faded away or remains as an extant initiative. A few reasons for the lack of success of KM were:

1. Employees saw it as a top-down initiative.
2. Linkage of KM with HR initiatives, like learning rewards, was weak.
3. HR linked KM to just a few learning points.
4. Larger integration of KM with business and HR strategy was missing.
5. Employees never saw it as their initiative.

Questions may arise as to how the situation could be different and how KM could add to LX. To address these, one needs to refer to the changed paradigm of KM. Mobile learning has become the central nervous system for learning in organizations. The earlier system was dogmatic and regimented and restricted employees to documenting and sharing their learning in a specified format. Employees felt the KM was autocratic and intrusive. Organizations today are using 'crowdsourcing' and 'co-creation' as key business strategies, as consumers today do not want to have just off-the-shelf products and services but want customization. Organizations, to enhance CX, are working on getting ideas from them (using crowdsourcing). As a business process, they are adopting a co-creation approach to designing/ delivering products/services.

Employees who have this CX expect a similar approach by their organization. KM can leverage mobile platforms across all four stages of its life cycle. The first step for the learning team is to get ideas on the 'learning agenda' from the employees. A simple survey may not entice the employees (potential learners) to participate and share their thoughts. Gamification and linkage to business strategy would help. The learning team can roll out a 'Learning Ideathon' to support the business strategy. The

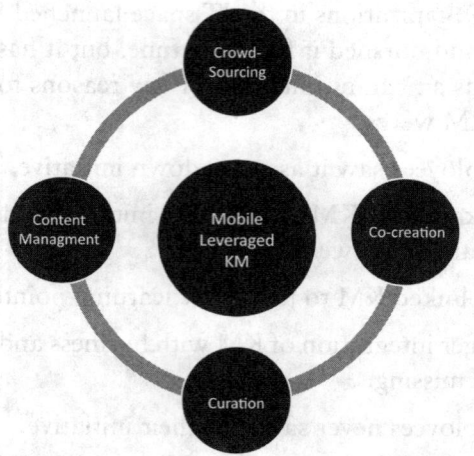

Figure 6.26. Knowledge Management Life Cycle and Mobile Technologies

project can be sponsored by the leadership team, with an award for the best idea. The award need not be just a certificate or a cash prize but can be a project sponsorship to plan and execute the project along with the learning team. This would motivate employees towards 'co-creation', the second step in the KM life cycle. A learning programme created by the users would have better acceptance and buy-in. For a ripple effect, the learning team can roll out business-unit/vertical/function/geographic mini-projects, for a wider spread of KM and learning. Employees can be asked to identify learning resources, go through them and include their LX along with the subject matter documentation. This would help with multiple objectives—a collection of learning material, employee empowerment in learning and development, tracking of employee learning and, most importantly, documentation and sharing of the LX. The content can come in free-flow formats, and the employees can choose multiple formats.

The learning team can play a facilitating and curating role—the third step. The learning team has the responsibility to do a quick quality check on the content. They need not be gatekeeping the structure/format. Employees look for authentic and glossy

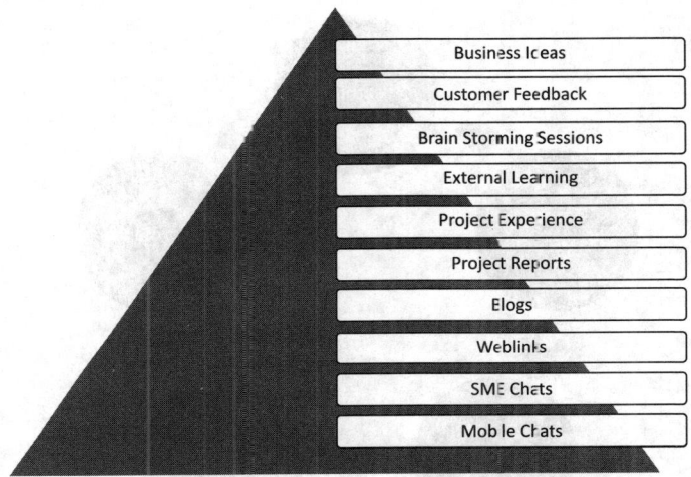

Figure 6.27. Learning Experience and Learning Options

content. Content in the format of chats/discussion threads can be retained in the same format for originality and authenticity. The learning content has to be crisp, authentic and to the point. The role of learning team is to structure the content into a searchable and accessible learning catalogue. The most important aspect is to provide a connection between the learners and the original content creator, for clarification and sharing of insights/learnings. This would link to the fourth step of content management by the learning team. Employees look forward to real-time and constant updates in learning content. The learning team alone cannot handle this responsibility. Thus, it can encourage the employees (learners) to contribute and share regularly.

Partnering for Learning Experience

A frequent cause of the lack of success of learning initiatives is lack of their integration with other HR dimensions, such as performance, rewards and career progression of the employees.

The learning team has to work along with organizational leaders and the HR team. Employee learning needs to happen in sync

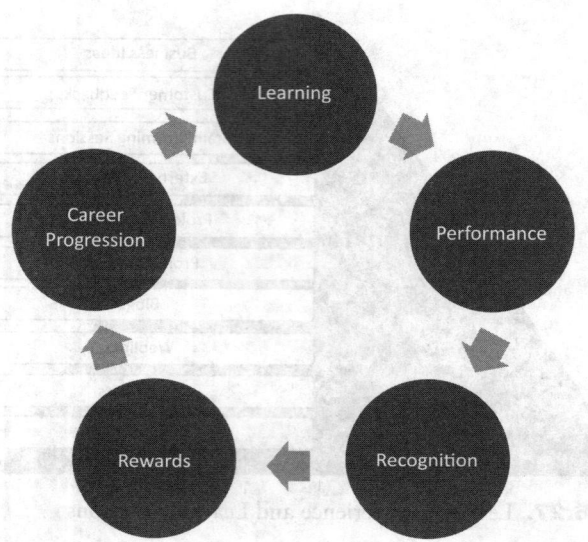

Figure 6.28. Drivers of Positive Learning Experience

with employee performance on the job. Both managers and employees appreciate and value learning when it is integrated into the work context and contributes to an improvement in performance on the job. The performance conversations/reviews need to factor in employee learning and performance. The drive for learning in an employee gets nurtured/accentuated when the employee gets recognized not just for their learning participation and learning but also for their contribution to and delivery on the job.

For an employee to value the rewards of learning outcomes, the first LoS is appreciation by the manager after seeing evidence of the employee's improvement in their job performance. The second level of reinforcement would be recommending employees for reward vouchers that they can encash. The third level of reinforcement would be showcasing employees' learning-linked performance at the team level, like during team get-togethers. The fourth level would be when the manager reviews, gives feedback on and documents employee performance. The

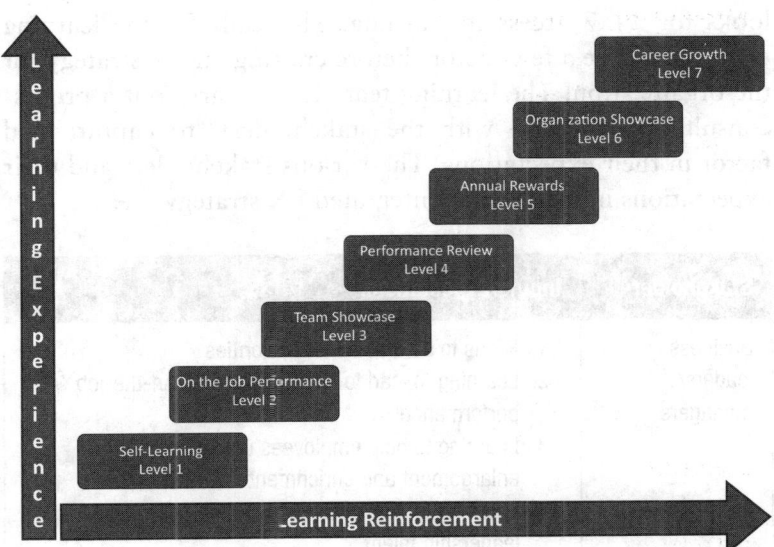

Figure 6.29. Learning Experience Maturity Model™

fifth level would be factoring in and valuing learning-linked performance improvement in annual rewards. The sixth level would be showcasing employee learnings and achievements at the organizational level through forums and events, like town halls and intranet banners, as learning champions/learning ambassadors. The seventh and most important aspect would be giving the employees an opportunity for career progression.

The key to the success in employee learning would be constant communication visibility for employees to see, perceive and commit and continue their continuous learning journey. This calls for a triangular partnership between learning, HR and business.

Integrated Learning Experience Strategy and Execution

The learning systems in organizations have evolved and are still evolving fast due to digital technologies, and today an employee looks for 24x7 access to learning. This calls for the learning team to analyse a few factors before crafting an LX strategy for the organization. The learning team has to carry out a process consultation exercise with the stakeholders, to capture and factor in their expectations. The various stakeholders and their expectations influencing an integrated LX strategy are:

Stakeholder	Inputs/Expectations
Business leaders/ managers	1. Focus to be on business priorities 2. Learning to lead to enhancement of 'on-the-job performance' 3. Learning to help employees upskill for job enlargement and enrichment 4. Learning to help business with the talent pipeline for leadership talent 5. Learning to focus on future skill needs 6. Learning to help with EE
Customers	7. Employees to be ready to provide the CX expected 8. Employees to have the right attitude and orientation 9. Employees to have complete knowledge of product/service delivery
Learners	10. To be helped in gaining knowledge and skills needed for immediate job requirements 11. To be helped in gaining future skills to stay 'on top of the game' 12. To be helped in gaining knowledge/skills needed to move up the career ladder 13. To be provided flexibility in programme design to learn at their convenience 14. Learning method to be customized to their learning style 15. To be provided 'hands-on learning' to help them with 'transfer of learning' 16. Learning from peers to be facilitated

(continued)

(continued)

Stakeholder	Inputs/Expectations
	17. Informal learning to be facilitated through tech-enabled platforms
18. To be provided opportunities to co-create the learning programme
19. To be provided regular feedback on their learning traction to keep them on track
20. Support from manager in implementing the knowledge/skills gained in the learning process
21. To be recognized for contributing to the learning process as an active learner
22. To be recognized and appreciated for implementing the learnt knowledge/skills
23. To be valued and rewarded for upskilling and taking up higher responsibilities
24. To be provided with showcasing opportunities to present the newly acquired knowledge and skills
25. Learning technologies deployed to factor in their constraints and challenges

Based on these expectations, an integrated LX strategy can designed/customized using the generic model below.

About the Model

Learning System Players

The model has all the players involved in the learning system plotted on the Y-axis as learners, business (leaders/managers), external stakeholders (customers, supply chain partners, investors), HR team (of which the learning team is a subset), learning team (the team that owns/anchors the entire learning system

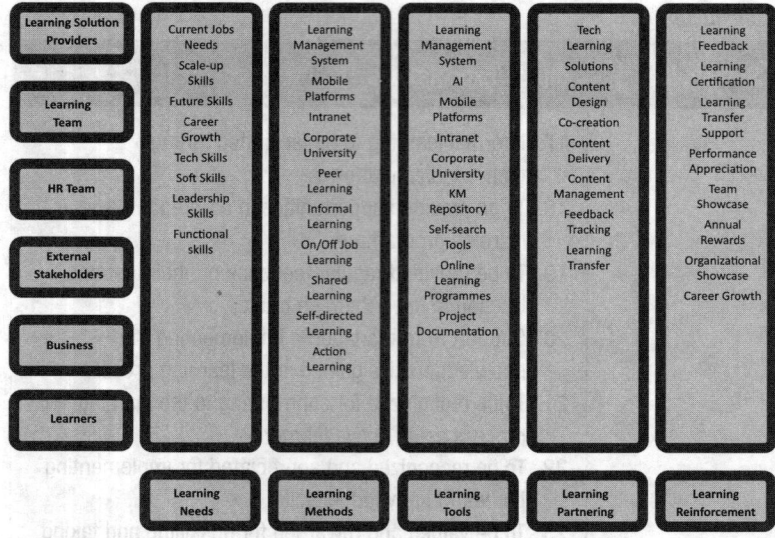

Figure 6.30. Integrated Learning Experience Strategy Model™

for the organization), learning solution providers (providers of learning content, technology like a learning management system, integration platforms, etc). Each of these players has a role to play in the design and execution of the learning system. The players like external stakeholders provide learning expectations in terms of employee performance, skills and future-readiness. The players like HR and business are co-partners in the end-to-end learning cycle management. It is important to scope all these players for an effective and integrated approach.

Learning Enablers

A learning system's performance is supported by certain critical factors, which are termed enablers. The first set of enablers are 'learning needs' (learning expectations/inputs/deliverables), which can also be termed 'learning outcomes'. The second set of enablers are 'learning methods'; organizations want to design and deliver learning solutions that are specific to their context and support the learning process. The third set of enablers are 'learning tools', which would anchor the specific learning process to be designed to deliver the learning to the learners. The fourth set of enablers are 'learning partners'. The learning system, unlike in the past, is dependent on multiple partners today, as the learning function operates on identifying a resource with specific competence and bringing them onboard to support it. It is virtually impossible for learning to cover all the skills needed to operate in the digital learning context, due to the factors such as operating costs, effectiveness, etc. For instance, trying to hire technology-platform creators to run a digital platform may not serve the purpose of a global banking major. The core competency of the bank is the banking business and not learning-technology operations. Hiring external experts based on specific needs would work in the favour of the organization, as they would bring in expertise, contemporary skills and cost advantages. The cost calculations may be considered not on a transaction basis but on an integrated basis, factoring in the costs of hiring, orienting, training and maintaining a resource. It may not be feasible for the bank to design a career path for the learning-tech operations experts. Organizations that did not view learning strategically in the past created an army of learning team experts and had to scuttle them, as they found it unviable to take care of them. The cost of maintaining an integrated and end-to-end learning team is virtually impossible in the digital world.

The last set of enablers are 'learning reinforcements', which refers to the strategies an organization adopts to keep the learners motivated and on track. The key objectives of reinforcement strategies are to motivate the learners to engage in continuous learning and contribute to organizational excellence through improved performance delivery. Reinforcement of the employees is ensured throughout the employee learning cycle—during classroom learning, during the learning process, at the end of the learning process and on the job. It not only covers the four levels of Kirkpatrick's model of learning effectiveness but goes beyond them as well. It covers the aspects like employee recognition/visibility and career growth, which are not addressed in Kirkpatrick's model.

Learning Integrators

The third component comprises learning integrators, who have the role of integrating the learning-system players and the leaning enablers. The strategy provides strategy alternatives across five stacks of learning enablers. The learning team can use this model to conduct a self-assessment and also to plan for the future. While designing and executing the learning strategy, organizations need to ensure that they:

- Provide learning opportunities and options to employees where they are;
- Use the 3C (curate, create, contextualize) mantra as a reference guide;
- Groom managers to own and drive the learning agenda;
- Involve development managers for authentic learner engagement;
- Facilitate, capture and brand the 'Aha!' learning moments to create learning pull;
- Focus on 'action-oriented' workplace learning;
- Identify 'learning role models' and use them as 'learning champions' or 'learning ambassadors';
- Focus on 'personalization of learning' for better consumption and benefits;
- Plan for and deliver 'on-demand learning' through crowdsourcing of learning agendas;

- Customize and integrate tech-enabled learning solutions;
- Devise and implement 'future skills' forecasting and offer learning solutions;
- Nurture 'continuous learning' among employees through 'personal learning scorecards' and link it to their career progression;
- Reorient the learning team to deliver 'power skills' (soft skills), due to their increased importance in the digital world;
- Strive for 'inclusivity' through catering to the learning needs of employees across levels.
- Ensure learning teams adopt a 'mobile-first' learning strategy to provide accessibility and convenience to the users.
- Be cautious of 'encroaching into work-life balance' while designing learning initiatives;
- Ensure 'empowered learning' for learners, to allow them to access learning flexibly;
- Design learning initiatives using gamification, as far as possible;
- Ensure ROI on learning investment through mapping 'learning outcomes' to all the four levels of Kirkpatrick's model;
- Ensure the learning teams plan and prepare for 'gig workers' to create an 'inclusive learning environment';
- Nurture 'data literacy' as a competence among employees across levels, to ensure that the organizations are future-ready;

- Set 'building a learning culture' as the primary objective for learning teams;
- Ensure that 'customer education' falls under the domain of learning teams and undertake immediate planning for the same;
- Be on guard against 'getting lost in content' and have an LoS on organizational priorities; and
- Use 'micro-learning' as an anchor for workplace learning solutions.

Conclusion

Learning has evolved from a backroom solutions team to a strategic solution provider to address the expectations of the different stakeholders across the spectrum of an organization: employees, business partners, customers, investors and supply chain partners. Digital, mobile and AI-enabled learning will gain more ground in the future to support learner expectations of flexibility, personalization and customization. The learning team in organizations would be able to track the learning through real-time dashboards and analytics. This would help in adapting/changing the product 'on the go' rather than holding back changes till the product is fully run, as in the conventional format. Learning systems will move towards a network of specialist service providers. The role of the learning team will become more of aggregating, communicating and tracking. On the content front, learning teams will leverage strategies of 'co-create' and 'curate'. Co-creation can take the form of crowdsourcing from employees and domain experts in the organization. This would make learning an all-pervasive phenomenon, which currently, in most organizations, remains in the realm of the 'learning team'.

Points to Ponder

1. Do organizations in the digital context need to have internal learning teams?
2. How could organizations optimize and strategize learning functions for better ROI?
3. Does creating a 'learner-centric' agenda imply learning teams bequeathing learning to employees?
4. How could organizations optimize investment on LXPs (learning experience platforms)?
5. Does transformation to the 'mobile-first' learning strategy call for radical re-engineering of learning products and processes?

7
Leveraging Employee Experience for Employer Branding

This chapter focuses on how EX can impact the employer branding (EB) of organizations and how organizations can manage a positive EX not just internally but also through social networks. Process re-engineering, digitization of HR processes and orientation of people managers to EX are the three key strategies to build and nurture employee- and experience-centricity.

Why Focus on Employer Branding?

In today's competitive world there is always a slugfest among organizations to get noticed ahead of their competitors. Just like there is an imperative on organizations to brand their products and services amid the competition, there is an equal and compelling need to get themselves noticed to attract and retain talent. Employer branding (EB) is the 'process of attracting and positively influencing prospective candidates, employees and stakeholders of the organization'. The two key objectives of EB are attracting and positively influencing. Now, the question is who and why. The first target audience is the prospective set of talent in the talent market who are trying to identify the best-suited career option for them based on their socio-economic background, personality orientation, skill sets and career aspirations. For instance, an employee from a poor rural background with basic education and technical qualifications would look for a stable job and decent pay in the vicinity of their residence. On the contrary, a candidate coming from an affluent background, with educational qualifications from top educational institutions (may be national/international) and aggressive career aspirations could look for a global brand that launches a happening career for them. A candidate with a similar socio-economic and education profile but with an orientation towards innovation and risk-taking could build a start-up venture that they perceive to have a bright future ahead.

Attracting Future Talent

Organizations, in order to attract attention, would have to position themselves as a compelling option among the competing choices. Candidates evaluate organizations based on the choices they notice or come across. Hence, the first hurdle for organizations is to get noticed and then to explain to the candidates what they have on the table for them. A related question that one may have at this point is: should the organization position itself through all the offerings on the table? Should the positioning and messaging be the same for all sets of candidates or should they be customized and variant for different sets of candidate pools? Why should the organization

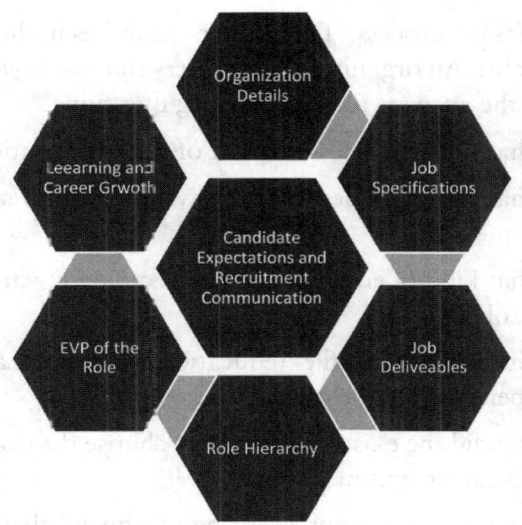

Figure 7.1. Employer Branding and Recruitment Communication

not use a unified and common messaging approach for all the candidates?

The answer to these questions is that in case a standard/unified/common form of messaging is used, the organization would suffer on two counts. First, candidates would not bother to consider messaging that looks 'cluttered'. The general human response is to ignore or look away from a message that one does not find interesting, and candidates would do the same if the message/communication do not highlight what they are looking for while scouting for career options. Candidates expect recruitment communication from prospective employer to factor in what they are looking for and be designed accordingly.

Branding for Candidates

The question now is: how should organizations position themselves in front of candidates in terms of the latter's career-choice decision-making process? The answer to this lies in the profile of the candidates. An organization can carry out employee analysis to identify the answers to the following questions:

- What is the business context of the organization?
- What kind of roles does it have in place to support its business needs?
- What kind of employees does it employ in various types of roles?
- What is the profile (education, skill sets and work experience) of the candidates?
- Why did the existing employees choose the organization as a career option?
- What are the sources/hiring channels/talent markets from which the talent have been hired?
- What kind of recruiting messaging has been used in the past?
- What was the success rate of previous recruitment branding approaches?
- How is the performance of the talent acquired from various sources?
- What is the EX of employees in the relationship with the organization?
- What do the employees like in the organization?

Recruitment Marketing

The answers to the above questions would provide strategic insights for EB or recruitment marketing for the organization. One may have a question at this juncture: is there a difference between recruitment branding and EB, and if yes, how do they differ? Most HR professionals tend to confuse the two terms and use them interchangeably. EB refers to the process

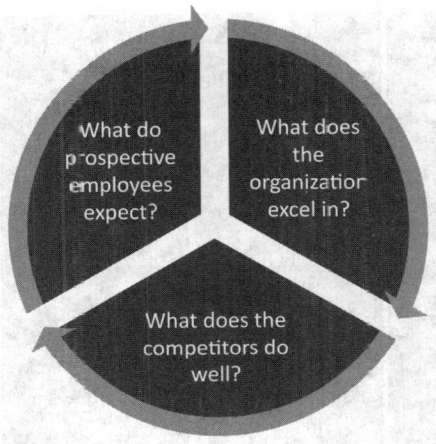

Figure 7.2. Decoding Unique Value Proposition

of communicating the 'employee offerings', also termed as 'employee value proposition' (EVP) offerings, to the prospective talent. For crafting an EB strategy, the organization needs to have clarity on the following questions:

- 'Which' positions/roles does it want to hire for?
- 'Whom' (set of candidates) does it want to hire?
- 'What' are the unique offerings that it offers to the talent?
- 'Why' should the candidates choose to work with it?

The answers to these questions would provide both clarity on and direction for EB strategy formulation. The major challenge in EB strategy design and execution is identifying the EVP offerings of an organization. The EVP offerings have to be 'unique' ('Unique Value Proposition' [UVP]) to make them stand out from those offered by competitors. To identify the differentiating UVP, the organization has to diagnose three major dimensions.

Figure 7.3. Employee Value Proposition: Answers to 'What's in it for Me?'

Employee Value Proposition

A critical analysis of the three dimensions would help the organization to identify its areas of strengths/uniqueness, competitive-position gaps and opportunities to focus on candidates' aspirations. To carry out a deep dive on strengths/uniqueness, the organization needs to analyse its EVP offerings. EVP can be defined as the 'aggregate of pay, benefits, experiences, that the organization promises to offer/offer to return for employment relationship and performance/contributions by the employee'. In the context of RM, it has been defined as 'UVP offerings by the organization, positioned by the organization to positively influence the potential candidates'. In short, it answers the candidate question: 'What's in it for me?' The components of EVP are shown in the figure below.

The EVP diagnosis offers a preview of the comprehensive set of employee offerings by the organization. This leads to the next set of questions:

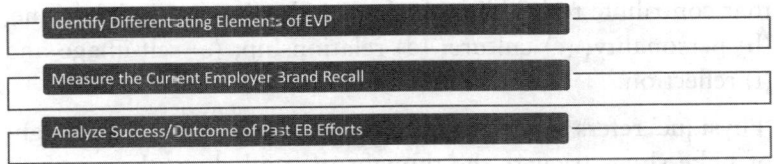

Figure 7.4. Employee Value Proposition and Employer Branding Integration Steps

- Should the organization communicate all the offerings?
- Should the organization carry out customized communication?
- How should the organization plan for customized communication?
- How can the organization improve the effectiveness of its targeted/customized communication?

To get answers to these questions and fine-tune its EB efforts, it is suggested that the organization follow the steps below

The first step for the organization is to identify the EVP components that are unique to it and make them stand out in the competition. For instance, an organization that is in a fast-growing industry and consistently recording higher growth rates in relation to its competitors can use these two dimensions to design a branding campaign around the theme, 'Grow with a Leader in a Happening Industry'. Through such a branding theme, the organization would be communicating three key aspects to the candidate pool. The first aspect is that the sector is a sunrise sector. The second aspect is that the organization is a leader in its space/sunrise sector. The third and most critical aspect is the career growth opportunities for the candidate due to the organization and its operating environment.

Brand Identity Prism and Employer Branding

Kapferer developed and contributed to a structured approach to analysing and developing a brand identity. The six elements

Leveraging Employee Experience for Employer Branding | 255

that contribute to building the brand identity are: (a) physique; (b) personality; (c) culture; (d) relationship; (e) self-image and (f) reflection.

'Physique' refers to the physical aspect; for instance, the thought of Nike shoes triggers the thought of solid shoes that support strong athletic performance. EB refers to the way in which an organization uses its logo and tag line to brand itself as an attractive workplace.

'Personality' refers to the personification of the brand as a living being through its colour, size, orientation and interaction with the consumers. The branding that an organization uses for its marketing purposes actually forms a base for the physical representation of the brand. This in turn gets accentuated by the way the leaders/communication team/existing employees position/interpret the employer brand to prospective employees.

'Culture' refers to the values of an organization that anchor its foundation. For instance, Toyota uses the caption 'The Toyota Way', which emphasizes the focus of Toyota on quality and passion for perfection. Toyota cars are known for their quality, and sheer perfection is demonstrated through them. Consumers

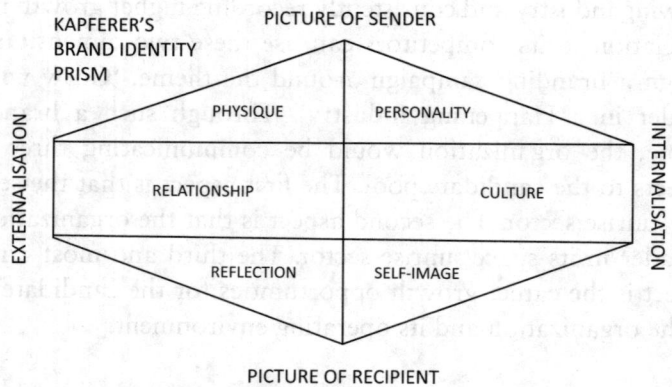

Figure 7.5. Employee Value Proposition and Employer Branding Integration Diagram
Source: https://images.app.goo.gl/Yt5gykagCmU8XKiW8

know for sure that any product they buy from Toyota would provide superior value for money through its quality and superior performance.

Similarly, Pepsi has recently revised its tag line to 'That's What I Like'. The switch in the tag line is based on the fact that Millennials and Gen Z have strong preferences, and this aspect is reflected through the revised tag line. In the cases of both Toyota and Pepsi, the branding used by the companies extends to their EB strategies. The talent looking for career opportunities with Toyota knows for sure that they need to have an eye for quality and perfection to sign up for the organization. Similarly, the existing employees know that their likes/choices get respected at Pepsi. The organization gives space and respect for their likes and allows them to pursue their aspirations/orientations at the workplace, in alignment with its strategy.

'Self-image' refers to the perceived experiences of people as consumers of a brand. The experiences that the consumers have with the brand get codified and communicated through the branding campaign. This helps in positioning a 'brand promise' in terms of the experience that the consumers would have through buying/using/consuming the brand's products. In the case of EB, self-image refers to the EX of employees after

Figure 7.6. Pepsi Branding
Source: https://images.app.goo.gl/euepgP7i8AV2tCG29

choosing a career with the organization. Let us take a look at the EX of IBM employees working in Bangalore (sourced from Glassdoor):

- 'Good work environment And new approaches' (in 2473 reviews)
- 'Flexible working hours, Work From Home option available' (in 2419 reviews)
- 'Relatively low salary payment etc' (in 711 reviews)
- 'Salary hike is comparatively less' (in 642 reviews)

'Pros

o Good work life balance. Company has great values and teaches you a lot in that respect. Great place to learn. Good work environment. Abundant holidays. Flexible work hours.

Cons

o Low pay. Increase in salary to reach a decent pay would take at least three to four years

'Pros

o Very flexible & got opportunities to learn new technologies

Cons

o Too many hierarchies. Need to reduce the management force'

'Pros

o Huge learnings, great technologies, good work-life balance

Cons

- o   Limited and slow growth, complex systems and processes

- **Advice to Management**
- Transform as envisioned by current Global CEO'

(Glassdoor reviews for IBM's Bangalore office.)

Employer Branding and Trust Factor

Employee reviews are a key source of EB for prospective employees. For an organization too, employee inputs on its areas of strength can be used to identify the central themes for its EB. There are multiple pay-offs for the organization in doing so. The first is that from a 'value-centricity' perspective, the organization would be communicating only based on the actual EX of its current employees. This would ensure that candidates do not later face shocks, provided the EB is based on facts/EX that is truly reflective of the current reality in the organization. A second aspect is that existing employees would not experience a trust deficit either, and in fact, the EB would lead to 'trust reinforcement', as they would see the organization carrying out EB based on current realities.

Millennials and Gen Z look for values and trust as top priorities while evaluating organizations. They do not mince words or waver in sharing feedback, on social media and professional networks, on organizations' EB promise versus their experience, conformity or otherwise. Positive conformity of EB promise with CX works in favour of an organization. On the contrary, sharing of non-conformity feedback on social media can lead to adverse and negative EB and can actually undermine the EB efforts of an organization. Thus, it is in the interest of organizations to stay truthful and factual in their EB efforts to attract and win the 'war for talent'.

'Reflection' refers to the efforts of a brand to project its image on consumers. For instance, Pepsi, in its campaign projects, shows all its consumers having fun while consuming its products. The question is, are the customers homogenous in nature? Not really. Despite its global footprint and diverse customer segments, Pepsi tries to project itself through a unified image, drawing from the projective technique in psychology. The projective technique personifies the brand, which tries to strike an emotional chord using the image and colours in its logo and the brand ambassadors it chooses.

In terms of EB, organizations have to build a brand persona for the market and consumers. This makes sense for a couple of reasons. First, the brand persona creates an interactive and reflective relationship between the organization and the talent. The talent sees a reflection of themselves in the projected EB. They derive a sense of happiness and pride that the projected EB actually depicts/reflects them to the external world. This adds credibility and value to their personal brand equity. The 'projective technique' used in branding has its origins in the field of psychology.

Employer Branding: Strategy Innovation

Thanks to the strategies like 'crowdsourcing' and 'co-creation', organizations are trying to leverage support/efforts from employees across levels. For instance, an organization can conduct an 'Ideathon' for its employees to seek inputs on

Figure 7.7. Projective Technique

what dimensions can be emphasized in the crafting of its EB strategy/communication. If the idea is to showcase the career growth or LX of the employees, the organization can conduct a competition among the employees to self-shoot in a whacky way a video of 30–45 minutes describing their career journey or LX. The videos can then be curated and used for a series of campaigns on social media platforms, like Facebook (official page) or the official YouTube channel. Such an approach has multiple benefits. The existing employees feel connected and happy through the inclusive approach of the organization. They actually transform from passive brand consumers into brand champions. The candidates in the talent market would find the EB more authentic and trustworthy, as they can relate to the employees and their emotions.

In the competitive world today, the talent (millennials/gen Z) are very particular about the 'value added' to their CV. Talent demands and market value are directly linked to the value that is reflected on a candidate's profile. The factors impacting personal brand equity for talent, among other things, are: (a) hot skills; (b) right experience; and (c) association with the right organization. These three dimensions are mutually interactive. Organizations that lead in their sectors and are successful would always look for quality talent that have a combination of hot skills and the right experience. Thus, candidates try to upskill and gain experience that has demand and market value.

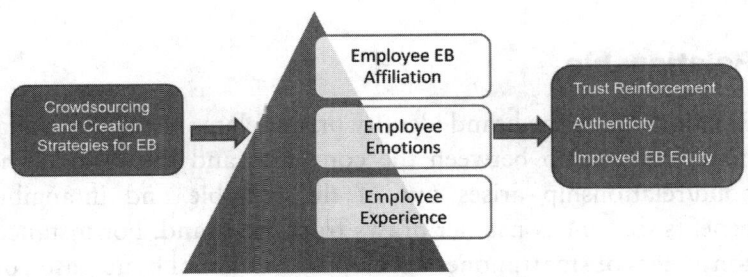

Figure 7.8. Employer Branding: Strategy Innovation

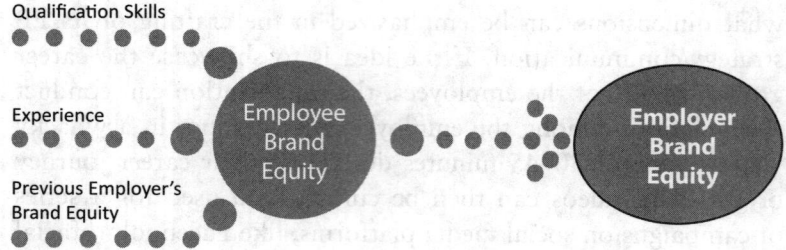

Figure 7.9. Employer and Employee Brand Equity Interplay

The impact on an individual is much higher as compared to that of an organization. In a sense, the candidate adopts a two-pronged strategy of 'career risk minimization' and 'career enhancement'. The candidate gets exposed to career risk if their chosen organization is either not successful or does not provide learning and growth opportunities to its employees. The candidate, unlike in the past, does not blindly trust the official communication but tries to cross-validate it with the EX insights of existing employees. The connected world makes it easy for candidates to access data on social and professional networks. Candidates, on the other hand, stand to benefit through career enhancement by choosing an organization that provides them learning and growth opportunities. Millennials and Gen Z have a clear understanding that learning (skills) and exposure/experience hold the key to their career growth. The link between candidate brand equity and the EB of an organization is depicted below.

Relationship

Relationship in the brand identity prism relates to the emotional bond/relationship between the consumer and the brand. The bond/relationship arises out of the tangible and intangible benefits that the consumer draws from the brand. For instance, consumers of smartphones develop an emotional bond based on the functionality/uses that their phone offers to them. In terms of EB, an employee develops an emotional bond based on the perceived/actual benefits from their employment relationship with their organization. The benefits are an outcome of the EVP offerings by the organization. The more the benefits, the better would be the relationship.

The same EVP offerings may be perceived differently by various talent pool segments. For instance, young talent (campus hires) look for a lot of projects, job rotation, quick learning and exposure. On the contrary, tenured talent who are in the mid-to-late career stage would not prefer a lot of projects and frequent job rotation, as these would interfere with their other priorities in life. An EB enthusiast may query: does one have a comprehensive view of the EB components and methods to cascading and assessing the impact of one's EB strategy?

EB Canvas for Candidates

An EB strategist or execution team can adopt the following integrated view of strategy design and execution. The first set of dimensions comprise the business context and strategy, market leadership, products/services, leadership style and

Figure 7.10. Paytm Recruitment Advertisement
Source: https://images.app.goo.gl/AmK8moARpajCyc7n6.

organizational culture and values. The combination of business context, strategy, market leadership and products/services forms a differentiating business quadrangle for an organization. For instance, PayTM, in its recruitment advertisements, used a combination of all four elements through a 'visual storytelling approach'; as they say, one picture speaks louder than 1,000 words. PayTM combined its industry, products and services and market position into one visual story to communicate them to the fresh talent in the country.

The branding strategy of an established brand and market leader like Microsoft can be quite contrasting to that of PayTM, which is a rising star in the online payments market. Microsoft uses just the logo and the name to communicate with the prospective talent about career opportunities, the reason being that it already enjoys a brand recall value in the market, due to its organizational branding and its products/services.

Employer Branding and Campus Hiring

After freezing the components, the next focus area for an organization is the communication cascade for its EB. This would be dependent on a few factors—the type and profile of

Figure 7.11. Microsoft Branding
Source: https://images.app.goo.gl/vx3Tex744dhvet5HA

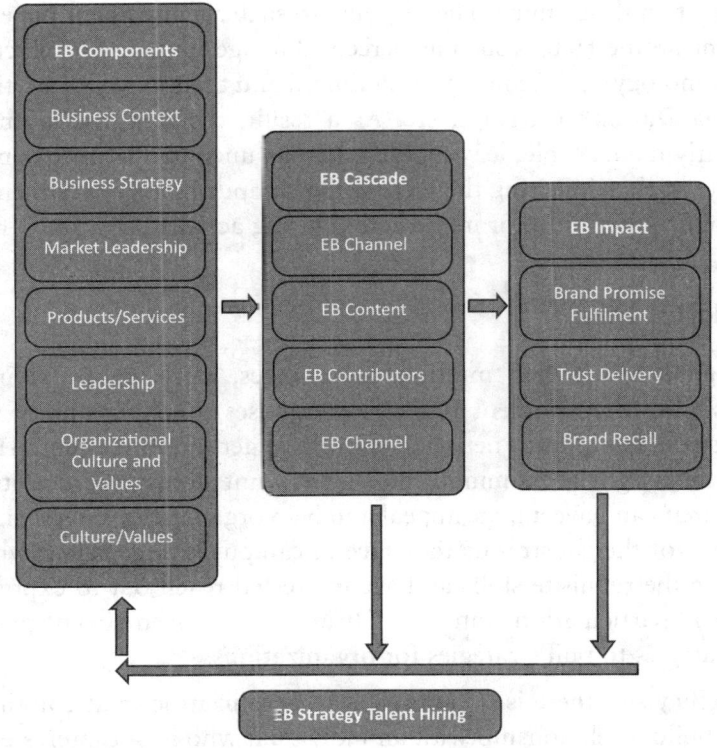

Figure 7.12. Employer Branding and Talent Acquisition

the targeted customer segment, the space that talent is available in or visit quite often and, more importantly, what the talent looks for. For instance, organizations that hire a lot of tech talent from premier engineering institutions, like the Indian Institute of Technology (IIT) and International Institute of Information Technology (IIIT), use coding/hackathon competitions on the campus to attract talent. Digital technology has transformed campus hiring completely. What used to be a heavily campus-driven activity is now moving towards the digital online format for multiple reasons, such as cost, efforts, time, reach and results.

For instance, a campus-hiring campaign of a tech-services company would have a limited reach, restricted to only the talent on the campus. The response to such a campaign is dependent on the factors such as perceived image (industry/products/technology), past connections (alumni and their experience), the organization's offerings, etc. As a result, the response is only partly manageable, leaving the outcome uncontrollable to some extent, thus lowering the ROI of the campus-hiring investments made, either in EB or in the actual hiring activity.

Digital Hiring

Digital hiring has multiple advantages, such as providing visibility across talent markets (campuses) and the ability to cast the talent hunt net wide enough to get in more talent. The termed right to communicate talent hunt across the country format can have a huge appeal and help organizations overcome some of the constraints they face in campus hiring. Talent who have the requisite skills and are interested reach out to express their participation interest. Hiring has moved from push strategies to pull strategies for organizations.

As they say, there is no point for an organization in attempting to build a relationship with an individual who is not interested, as the individual is likely to spurn the offers/attempts by the organization. This is a strategic move that helps organizations have a better 'hiring conversion' and ROI for their efforts. The process also has an impact on talent retention, for the simple reason that talent joins organizations with a positive affinity towards the latter. The impact and reach of digital hiring can be gauged from the following statistics:

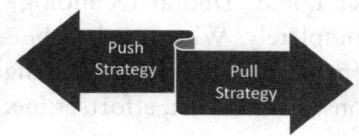

Figure 7.13. Digital Hiring Strategy: Options

- Almost half of the world's population (3 billion people) is on social media.
- Among job hunters, 79 per cent are using social media (Glassdoor).
- Job applicants are rating social media/professional networks on job boards and job advertisements/events (CareerArc).
- Among organizations, 84 per cent are currently using social media for hiring (SHRM).
- Among US consumers, 58 per cent follow brands through social media.
- Among millennials, 73 per cent search for career opportunities through social media (CareerProfiles).
- Social recruiting is chosen by 80 per cent of recruiters for reaching out to passive recruiters (Betterteam).
- Social media is used by 90 per cent of employers to recruit talent (CareerArc).
- Employers believe that social media marketing is an essential skill for HR professionals.

Employer Branding Impact

The success of EB efforts can be assessed at multiple levels. The first indicator that is tangible and can be easily measured is recruitment funnel conversions. An organization with a better EB value would be able to see better overall conversion and critical-stage conversion in the funnel. In the first stage the organization would attract both a superior quantity and a superior quality of applications. Most organizations with a lower EB value tend to suffer in either quality or quality. Quality issues result in a situation where an organization gets loads of applications but, on screening them, finds that it has a weak candidate pipeline across the stages of the funnel. The odd shortlisted candidates who are offered a contract might reject the offer, as they might find another brand with a better EB value and EVP offerings. Such an organization would have a missing 'TAT', and it would be struggling to fill vacancies on time. The hiring manager would be unhappy with the hiring team for its inability to fulfil talent delivery. The fact is that the hiring team is a facilitator and cannot handle the entire EB single-handedly.

A high EB value would result in not just better candidate conversions but also candidates feeling happy about brand fulfilment. The candidates, on joining the organization, would discover not gaps but conformity of the organizational realities with the assurance and claims made through the EB. Thus, they would experience a sense of brand fulfilment. This helps the organization gain the trust of the new hires, who in turn become EB champions or EB ambassadors and create a positive ripple effect in the talent market. The positive experiences sharing by the new hires would result in the organization having a better EB recall value.

Employer Branding Strategies and Employees

The second set of target audience for EB comprises the existing employees who are working with the organization. One might wonder, why should an organization worry about assuring the employees who have already been onboarded about its brand value? Is it not akin to 'preaching to the converted'? The answers to these lie in the concept of the 'cognitive dissonance' (CD) theory. The existing employees have a tendency to validate their choices constantly, to check and get a sense of reassurance that they have made the right choice in their career and are associated with the right organization. Employee behaviour is akin to the behaviour of consumers, as they constantly look for reassurance in their decision of a career choice. A positive sense of self-assurance is based on two factors. Employees get assured by the first-hand experiences that they have in the organization. Second, they look for external assurance based on the experiences of other

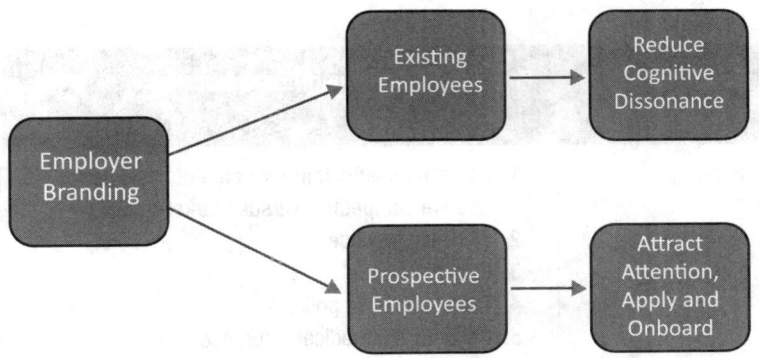

Figure 7.14. Employer Branding and Employer Needs

employees. Digital connectivity and social media have induced a constant sense of comparison among individuals, due to the availability of data on social and professional networks. The tendency to search for data has reached a proportion of addiction among many. Decisions, regarding either purchases or career and life, are being taken based on external data. Very few individuals tend to use their discretion to validate the data available in other sources, which calls for an analytical and objective bent of mind. The fact is that most often, humans are driven by emotions.

The question one may have now is, how do organizations reduce CD? There is no 'one-size-fits-all' solution, and organizations can evaluate multiple options and make a choice based on their context and culture.

Employee Needs/ Expectations	Positive Reinforcement/Experience
Physical	1. Good workplace ergonomics 2. Facilities like canteen/recreation 3. Transportation for remote work location 4. Accommodation in case of remote work location 5. Flexi-work

(continued)

(continued)

Employee Needs/ Expectations	Positive Reinforcement/Experience
Security	1. Pay and benefits that take care of basic needs and are competitive versus market rates 2. Work-life balance 3. Paid-holidays 4. Transparency in policies 5. Benefits like medical insurance 6. Retirement benefits 7. Job clarity and congruity 8. Balanced work pressure 9. Predictable workload 10. Predictable bosses 11. Dependable peers and juniors
Emotional/ belongingness	1. Welcoming and friendly environment 2. Comfortable reporting relationship with the boss 3. Bonding with peers 4. Coaching/support for learning 5. Networking opportunities
Esteem/pride	1. Space/autonomy in the job 2. Recognition for efforts 3. Performance feedback and appreciation 4. Visibility in the organization 5. Opportunity to contribute to the success of the organization
	6. Respect for one's knowledge and skills 7. Pride in working with a happening brand 8. Pride in facilitating achievements by the organization
Achievement needs	9. Contribution through innovation/strategy/ execution 10. Celebration of achievements in the job 11. Scaling of career heights

Both new hires and existing employees tend to experience CD due to different reasons. New hires would first try to validate their experience with the organization through the hiring and onboarding process. The first 180 days are critical for a new hire, as there would be a subconscious comparison in their mind on three counts. The first comparison would be between the EB promise and EX delivery, as the new hire would try to compare what was promised and what is being delivered. Second, the comparison would be between the new job versus other competing job options that the candidate was evaluating. In the event of suboptimal fulfilment of expectations against the promises made, the new hire would develop self-doubts and self-critiquing and start blaming themselves for the wrong career choice/job opportunity. The third reason for CD would be negative results in the comparison between the new job and the old job.

The employee would try to constantly cross-validate the EX with their expectations across all the five major dimensions (cited in the table above). Though they would have a sense of excitement about the new job/assignment, there would always be a lurking fear of change due to the career risk and fear of the unknown in a new environment. The employee becomes cognizant of the fact that they would have to rebuild their identity and image afresh in the new job and would have to let go of their credentials. The value of the previous job credentials would cease to exist after they move into the new job. This constant inner tussle lies underneath the surface and unsettles the employee in the event of an unpleasant EX in any of the dimensions.

In the case of an existing/tenured employee, CD comes into play based on the EX the employee has in their organization. The employee tries to validate their current experiences against previous experiences in the same organization. If the quality of the current EX is lower than that in the past, it triggers a sense of CD. The employee would start thinking along the following lines:

- 'Maybe I'm not valued any more'.
- 'Maybe it is time to move on in life'.
- 'Maybe the organization is subtly signalling to me to move on'.
- 'I do not deserve to be undervalued as against my peers'.

Such thoughts would bring in a change in the attitude and consequent behaviour of the employee. The experiences of employees influence their perception and beliefs, which in turn impact their attitude and resultant behavioural change.

Thus, organizations would have to focus on EX, as it has a cascading impact on the EB promise and EB value. Unlike in the past, organizations today live in a transparent world where their every action directed at EX gets shared instantly on social/digital media. Thus, it is not enough for them to make EB promises through strategic branding communication; organizations also have the huge responsibility to live up to the promises made to the candidates and the existing employees, as both talent pools are interconnected.

DNA of Employer Branding

The DNA of EB can be understood to begin with the strategic analysis of the fundamental elements of an organization. The analysis must not just relate to the people dimension, and the organization needs to first question and interpret its core identity and the purpose of its existence. These questions sometimes are bound to rattle even the top leadership, as questions are not very comfortable to deal with, and are brushed aside when dealing with more pressing business needs. However, the fact is that without discussing these questions, an organization may never get to act cohesively on the design of any of its elements (7S framework)—strategy, structure, systems, style, staffing, skills and shared values—except perhaps for shared values, which get formed and internalized by the leadership and core team over time in the evolutionary process of the organization.

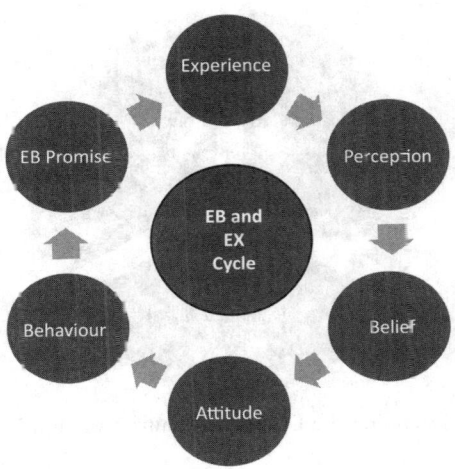

Figure 7.15. Employer Branding & EX Life Cycle

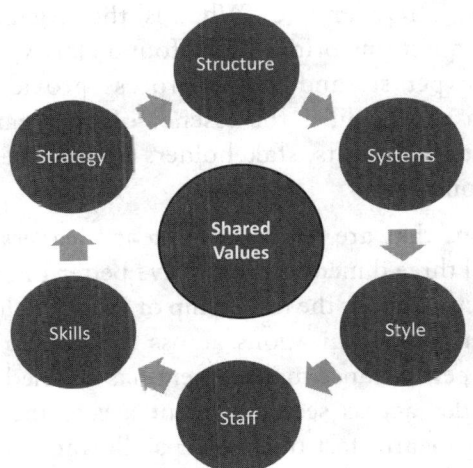

Figure 7.16. McKinsey 7S Model
Source: McKinsey 7S model.

One may wonder about the foundational/fundamental questions that the leadership needs to answer not just for EB but also for the overall business strategy/operations, as both of them are closely interlinked. The three fundamental questions

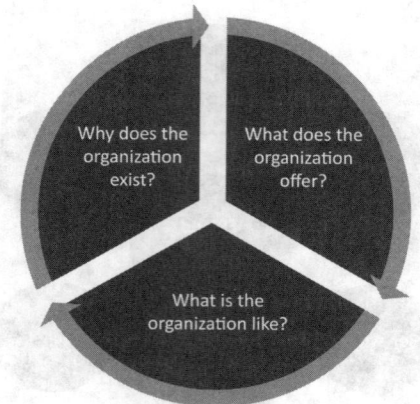

Figure 7.17. Decoding the DNA of Organization and Employer Branding

are: (a) Why does the organization exist? (b) What does the organization offer? and (c) What is the organization like? Each of the questions brings in profound clarity to decode the organization per se, and in the process provides clarity on EB. EB in a way codifies the essence of an organization and communicates it to its stakeholders (employees, suppliers, investors, consumers).

Organizations that are led by enlightened leaders would have clarity on all three dimensions and have better EB. For instance, General Electric, under the leadership of Jack Welch, has become a trendsetter for organizations across the world. Its focus on quality and performance management has enabled it to become a world leader across sectors. Talent across the globe aspire to join GE to learn, fast-track their skills and get exposure to diverse projects.

DECODING THE DNA OF RELIANCE INDUSTRIES LIMITED

The first question in decoding the DNA of an organization is: why does the organization exist? This question helps get clarity on the existential purpose of the organization. It brings to focus the vision/mission of the organization. In a dynamic world, the vision/mission too gets modified over time. For instance, Reliance Industries Limited (RIL), on its journey, initially had the vision of building and operating one of the world's largest and integrated petrochemical projects, to lead the space. But now when we look at its motto, 'Growth is Life', it aptly reflects the spirit of the organization. The answers to the second and third questions(what do we offer and what are we like) are interlinked in the case of RIL. The core value proposition of the organization is 'customer value', which is at the core of everything it does as an organization. The core value 'stakeholder respect' is interpreted by RIL as: 'We believe that without respecting all our stakeholders there can be no Reliance. We acknowledge that there may be a difference of perspectives but there must always be respect'.

By defining its values in an interlinked way, RIL has defined and presented an integrated picture of its identity. The values of customer value, ownership, respect, integrity, team spirit and excellence define 'RIL' for its stakeholders, and more so for its current and prospective employees. 'Customer value' gets primacy as the first value and sets the tone for the

Figure 7.18. Values at Reliance Industries Limited

other six values. If we were to analyse RIL's business strategy and customer offerings, it always offers 'value for money' across all the businesses it operates, be it telecom, retail, apparel or footwear. This is possible through the 'ownership' mindset among RIL employees. Every employee is expected to approach their role with an ownership mindset, which infuses a sense of accountability and empowerment. The employees are expected to be proactive and take initiatives on what is necessary to balance the organizational objectives and provide value to the stakeholders.

The Indian value of respecting others, 'Atithi Devo Bhava', is a value the organization expects everyone to possess. The ownership and empowerment are linked to integrity, as the employees are expected to uphold the organization's values and work in its interests. RIL projects are always very large and aggressive, for which teamwork is critical. All the teams/employees are expected to work in a collaborative way to deliver on collective (organizational) goals. RIL as an organization always aspires to be a leader in every segment that it ventures into. This calls for orientation towards and sharing of the value of 'excellence', to make it possible for the organization to realize its goals.

Its motto and values have helped RIL transform into a global powerhouse and a conglomerate that has perfected the art of conquering the business segments it ventures into. The aggregate of all these factors has helped RIL build a high EB value. The centralized HR service delivery approach has helped it live up to and deliver on its EB promises to both the existing and aspiring employees. As a result, the EB of RIL is high

Source: https://www.ril.com/OurCompany/About.aspx

EB can be analysed and understood through its building block/components. The six major building blocks of EB are: (a) employer brand attributes; (b) EX of the existing employees; (c) EVP offerings; (d) market visibility and branding; (e) CX; and (f) brand recall in the talent market. The EB attributes of a corporate include its logo, the demand for its products/services, visibility/recognition of the top leadership and awareness of its culture and values. These EB attributes provide the foundation for the employee life cycle stages or the employee journeys in the organization. Thanks to the digital world, employees leave a digital trail/footprint of their experiences, which can either contribute to or damage the EB of an organization. The focus here is not on what the organization offers to its employees, but how it is offered to the employees.

For instance, an organization may be awarding a annual hike/rewards to its employees but may be doing so well past the timelines in a hurried way, without any communication either at the leadership level or at the level of the managers. In such a situation, the entire experience negates the financial value of the rewards due to two key failures of the organization: not adhering to the schedule as per the annual calendar and not valuing the employees' emotions around the rewards. In some cases, the rewards might simply be paid out along with the monthly salary or the employee might receive a PDF (portable document format) file of the CTC revision/annual rewards much later than expected. The employee would end up guessing or relying on grapevine information about the purpose of or logic behind the payout. The employee, instead of hearing the news from their reporting manager, ends up getting it from

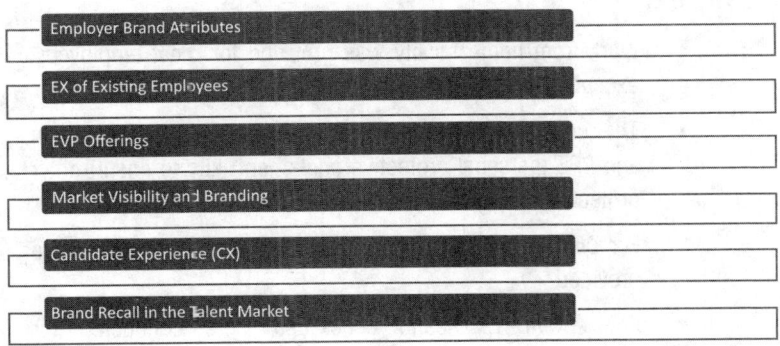

Figure 7.19. Employer Branding and Employee Experience Linkages

the grapevine, which is mostly distorted and disturbs the mind/perception of the employee.

The third dimension of EB comprises the set of EVP offerings by an organization for its employees. The EVP can be a mix of both health and motivational factors. The competitive differentiation in EVP can be arrived at using a mix of both. For instance, Google offers free snacks/drinks to its employees, while other tech organizations limit themselves to providing subsidized food in their canteen. The EVP mix and offerings are dependent on the business context, leadership and culture of the organization. For instance, the benefits like work from home, remote work or flexi-work, which were offered by IT organizations, are now offered by organizations across sectors during COVID-19.

> **EMPLOYEE VALUE PROPOSITION OFFERINGS DURING COVID-19**
>
> Organizations across the globe have suddenly woken up to the reality that the EVP offerings made by them to their employees do not meet the needs of the new normal. They had to go back to the drawing board and come up with new initiatives to take care of their employees. The details of EVP offerings across segments are briefly presented here:
>
> **Physical**
>
> - Work-from-home facility was provided for most employees, except for critical-mission employees.
> - The critical employees were provided with transportation and PPE (personal protective equipment) kits to ensure their protection.
> - For outsourced employees, food and accommodation were provided.
> - Free COVID-19 health check-ups were conducted for employees and their families.

- Medical treatment was provided to employees and their dependents in case they were diagnosed with COVID-19.
- Financial support was provided to employees for 'home office infrastructure', such as Internet facility, office table, chairs and other facilities needed to work from home comfortably.

Security

- Steps were taken for safety in communication during COVID-19.
- Flexi-work opportunities were provided to help employees balance their personal and professional needs.
- The employees were paid their full salary during the period of lockdown, though the productivity was suboptimal. In cases where the fiscal conditions did not permit full salary payment, the employees were provided with part salary, to ensure that their basic needs were met.
- Medical insurance plans were extended to cover COVID-19 treatment for employees and their families.
- Permission was given to employees to travel back to their native place and be with their family.
- Pharmacy supplies were provided to take care of the medical needs of employees and their dependents.

Emotional

- Employees were constantly updated on the status of COVID-19.
- Leadership connect sessions were organized, and leaders shared details of the organization to protect the physical, emotional and social needs of both employees and their families.
- Telemedicine and counselling facilities were provided for employees and their dependents.

Social

- Virtual team meetings were conducted to help employees connect and bond with each other.

- Team celebrations, like birthdays/festivals, were conducted online.
- Opportunities were provided for employees to participate in or contribute to community service activities (either online or physical).

Esteem

- The CSR activities undertaken by the organization to help needy people (provision of medical treatment, food and ration, free fuel for emergency medical vehicles, setting up of COVID-19 treatment centres) were communicated.
- Upskilling programmes were held to help employees pick up skills in the new normal.
- EB communication on initiatives taken by the organization in the new normal to discharge its corporate citizenship role was held.

Achievement/Self-actualization

- Opportunities were provided to employees to come up with ideas to take care of themselves and the business interests of the organization.
- Ideas were developed and projects were conducted on people/business/supply chain/business resilience.

file:///C:/Users/GIM/Downloads/COVID-19_Employee_Benefits_Checklist_for_Employers.pdf

In short, organizations had to reinvent their EVP offerings, to demonstrate their care for not just the employees but also their families and the extended community. This set of initiatives have helped organizations better their EB value and recall among both internal and external stakeholders.

Organizations used various media channels to cascade the efforts undertaken by them during the new normal, including press releases and leadership interactions with print/electronic and digital/social media. The employees were regularly communicated with, and a number of organizations launched special mobile apps to share updates on COVID-19 and business and organizational updates.

The interaction of the leadership with media to share steps to work with their industry partners have them to present their thought leadership and responsible and caring citizenship behaviour. Organizations have undertaken massive individual campaigns to share their efforts across the stakeholder spectrum (employees, businesses, community, etc).

NRG Energy in its campaign shared details of its efforts to support protect and health warriors, its support for the community to bounce back to normalcy and its financial support to educators to continue with online education teaching. TCS, India's leading technology services provider, has offered its education software to educators worldwide to help them continue their learning facilitation online, uninterrupted, and it has carried out a branding campaign showcasing its efforts.

Organizations have realized the need to not just contribute but also showcase/brand their efforts for two reasons: to communicate to the internal and external stakeholders about their efforts and to ensure the visibility of their efforts. The need for strategic communication was felt by organizations during COVID-19, for the simple reason that in the competitive world it is important to not just do the right things to care for internal and external communities but also demonstrate this to the world through constant communication using multiple channels/platforms, with an aim to build and nurture a positive brand recall value.

Employee Experience and Employer Branding Canvas

Having looked at and understood the importance of EB both during normal times and in the new normal (COVID-19), one may have the following questions:

- What is the link between EX and EB?
- How many stages of EX should an organization focus on for its EB?
- Should the organization customize its EB efforts based on employee needs and its context?

One needs to understand that the relationship of an employee with their organization starts right from their acceptance of the employment offer and continues till the end of their journey in or association with the organization. In the connected world, the association is extended even after the employee leaves the organization, as alumnus. In short the Ex through the employee journey both with and after being with the organization. The expectations of employees in terms of EX and EB are captured and presented briefly below.

The above image comprehensively captures the touchpoints in an employee's journey, right from their joining an organization

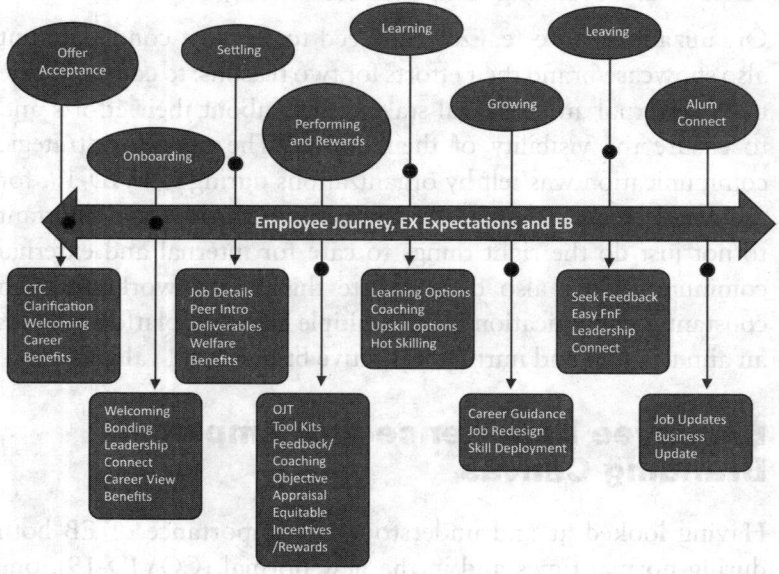

Figure 7.20. Employee Experience and Employer Branding Canvas

to exiting it and also after exiting it. The EX at each touchpoint has an impact on the EB of the organization, as the employees would share their feedback on social networks, both positive and negative. Positive feedback would enhance the EB value, which would be lowered if there is negative feedback.

Offer Acceptance

At the time of offer acceptance, a candidate expects to have a point of contact (PoC) in the HR with whom they can connect and discuss queries that they may have. The candidate expects the HR PoC to reach out proactively and share/discuss such details as CTC break-up, tax planning, relocation and connecting with the new reporting manager/team. For a positive EX, the HR PoC is required to constantly be in touch, to build and nurture the relationship with the candidate. The twin advantages of doing so are candidate comfort and predictability of the candidate joining and thus improving the offers-to-joining ratio.

Onboarding Stage

During the onboarding stage, an employee expects a warm welcome from their organization (HR PoC/reporting manager/ buddy). The first 100 days are critical for a new hire to establish connections and settle down in the organization. Onboarding provides an opportunity for organizations to innovate and offer a wow experience. For instance, instead of being crammed with packed sessions, thanks to digital technologies, candidates can be encouraged to adopt a gamification-based orientation towards understanding the systems, culture and workplace practices. Organization are experimenting with interactive 'career pathing' or 'career discovery'. The employee can take tests, share their thoughts/aspirations with a chatbot and create a customized career path. Along with the career path, the upskilling journey can be self-designed by the employee. These kinds of HR innovations can induce a long-term career relationship rather than a transactional relationship that results in early/infant attrition.

Settling-Down Stage

The reporting manager and peers have a significant role to play in helping a new employee settle down in their new role. Carrying out a 10-minute briefing session or handing out a document to read through is not going to help the employee. Provision of a semi-structured plan to interact with various stakeholders and regular interactions with the reporting manager would help the new hire get to know the place and have the gaps in their understanding of their role addressed. Organizations with an open culture tend to offer better EX to new hires. Employees joining not-so-open/closed organizations experience a feeling of dealing with an iron curtain and struggle to get information or support from tenured employees (peers), who refuse to cooperate or share information.

Performance and Rewards Stage

The EX during the performance and rewards stage is based on expectation fulfilment in the areas such as on-the-job training and learning. A job that challenges an employee to learn on the go inspires/motivates them more than a job that is routine and monotonous. The reporting manager has the responsibility to understand the skill level and skill utilization of the new hire and co-create/design the latter's role through periodic/real-time enrichment. Regular and instant feedback would help the employee understand their standing on performance against the expectations. Positive feedback would help the employee scale up and perform better. Developmental feedback on performance slips can help the employee get their act together and improve their performance. This could include the provision of guidance on learning resources and the assignment of a buddy mentor to help the employee rise up the learning curve. Employees

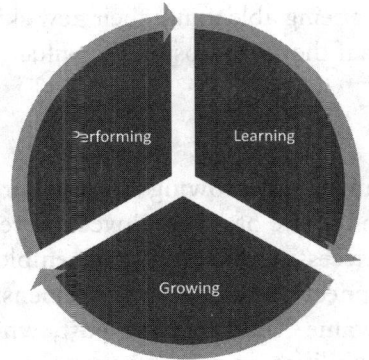

Figure 7.21. 3 Dimensions of Performance

expect a fair and objective evaluation of their performance. A holistic performance evaluation is expected to scope the career pathing and developmental conversation. Employees can see through a robotic/mechanical appraisal versus one engendering empathy and a human touch. For their performance experience to be complete, employees expect that the rewards allocation be transparent and equitable. For instance, if there is a difference in rewards allocation between two employees with a similar profile and performance, it would lead to discontent/frustration, which can lead to a negative EX and consequently a negative EB for the organization.

Learning Stage

The competitive landscape and digital technologies have transformed learning, which used to be largely episodic and static in nature but has now transformed into a strategic and continuous process following the 70:20:10 model. Organizations have the responsibility to create digital-learning access/facilities, provide guidance for learning and initiate semi-formal/developmental conversations to motivate and help employees with their learning. They have the responsibility to provide opportunities to their employees to scale up or cross-scale in their job through using the new skills learnt. Nothing could be more frustrating for an employee than not being able to use their new skills, which would make them feel as if they were lost in the wilderness.

Growth Stage

Performing, learning and growing are the three points in the golden triangle in the life of an employee, more so in the digital age. These are a necessity for not just the employee but also the employer. Disconnect between these dimensions can lower the EX and EB value. Unlike in the past, when only the HR had these responsibilities, in contemporary organizations, every people manager wears the HR hat and is accountable for these dimensions of their direct reports. People managers who focus only on performance, without balancing it with the other two elements, would deliver a negative EX, as the employee would perceive the organization (through the manager) to be exploitative. The employee would perceive the organization to lack interest in their development.

Leaving Stage

There is a notion in employee circles that the true colours of the bosses, peers and the organization come into the picture only when an employee announces the intention to leave the organization. The conventional approach of ostracizing or ignoring an employee the moment the employee announces their intention to leave is passé. Such an approach would result in a negative EB, as the employee is bound to share the negative experience on social networks. Unlike in the past, today organizations consider and value their ex-employees (alumni) as a talent pool for future talent needs, for multiple reasons, including that the employee has proved their mettle on KSA (knowledge, skills and attitude) and, more importantly, is used to the culture and way of life in the organization. These elements significantly lower the organization's 'TAT' and 'cost for OPL' (optimum productivity level). They (alumni) thus contribute to

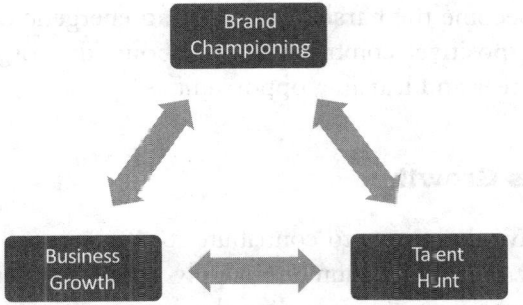

Figure 7.22. Alumni and Employer Branding Triangle

lowering the talent acquisition and onboarding costs for the organization.

Alumni Connect

'Out of sight is out of mind' is an adage that applies to anyone, and more so in the case of ex-employees as they move on in their life. Organizations have the responsibility of staying in touch with and keeping the alumni informed of their developments. Different organizations have different terms for alumni. Deloitte uses the term 'colleagues for life', and others are using the terms like 'boomerang employees' and 'comeback employees' for returning alumni. The focus on alumni relationship is driven by three strategic reasons, as shown in the figure below.

Brand Championing

Alumni with a positive EX champion the EB for their former organization through sharing their positive experience in both formal and informal ways. They share their experiences with their friends and networks informally, apart from sharing them on social media. It is similar to a 'ripple effect', as each alumnus would create small positive ripples that add up and contribute to the EB of the organization. The departing talent has the potential to either become the harshest critic or an energetic cheerleader spreading positive communication about the organization, culture, career and learning opportunities.

Business Growth

Alumni have the power to contribute to the business growth of an organization as consumers, supply chain partners, professional network service providers, business partners or leaders in other organizations. A happy employee is the first consumer of the products/services of an organization. The alumni would not only be consuming but also actively advocating the organization's products/services to potential consumers. In these days of entrepreneurship, they can start their own venture and become a business partner through joining the supply chain partner. In the manufacturing environment, it is quite common to see leaders branching out and starting their ventures as auto-component manufacturers. Due to their association, they contribute by offering quality components.

Talent Hunt

Hiring talent from known sources is a win-win both for the organization and for the individual concerned, as they are known to each other and the previous information about each other would eliminate surprises and lower the adjustment time. Alumni, apart from forming the talent pool, can be leveraged for referral programmes as well. Online forums, like Glassdoor and Ambition Box, are demonstrating the power of the 'voice of alumni'. Potential talent these days first refer to employee/alumni reviews, to evaluate an organization, before arriving at a decision of whether or not to apply.

It is this increased importance of alumni that is guiding organizations to have robust alumni programmes, as shown through a few examples:

Organization	Strength of Alumni	Alumni Connection Initiatives
BCG	20,000 globally	Virtual training opportunities; quarterly newsletter; networking groups on LinkedIn and Facebook; and live chats on social media
Deloitte	300,000 globally	Networking opportunities; alumni showcasing on professional networks; quarterly communications; and training on resume writing and interviewing
Microsoft	36,000 across 50 countries	Discounted prices for Microsoft products; and opportunity to become business partners
Oliver Wyman	11,000	Annual conferences; happy hours; charity events; offer of dedicated alumni partnership to manage alumni relationships
Sodexo	9,000	Naming of the alumni network as 'Reconnexions', centrally managed by the talent acquisition team; invitation to exiting employees to join the network and gain access to Sodexo's micro-career website that posts career opportunities, showcasing of alumni in Sodexo's publications

Source: https://www.shrm.org/hr-today/news/hr-magazine/0418/pages/corporate-alumni-programs-mean-never-having-to-say-goodbye.aspx

In short, alumni have become part of the core business and talent strategy of organizations, due to which the latter are investing time and resources to carefully craft their EVP offerings, the key objectives being to create a positive EX and to build a better EB value and recall for the organization.

Impact of Employee Experience on the Employer Branding Framework

The EB framework is designed around the needs and experiences of employees, who form the central lever for the EB strategy. The factors to consider in EB strategy formulation are employees': (a) persona; (b) career aspirations; (c) job search behaviour; (d) positive and negative drivers; (e) social and life channels; (f) decision influencers and (g) trust and information sources.

'Employee persona' refers to the socio-economic background, education and skill sets of an employee. The EB strategy for blue-collar talent would be different from that for white-collar talent. Blue-collar talent looks for job stability, as they would prefer to stay within the same geography for the reasons such as social and cultural affinity, family bonds and friendships. They look for organizational support in upskilling them. For them, the key drivers are job stability and assured income. On the contrary, white-collar talent from better-off social and economic strata are well-educated and exposed to a broader set of opportunities across the country they live in or globally in the connected world. They are self-driven and capable of identifying emerging career opportunities in their domain and acquiring skills to stay on top of the game.

'Career aspirations' vary across talent pools and markets. Engineering graduates look for experience and exposure to new technologies, opportunities for innovation, recognition for their tech skills and alignment of their roles with their projects/clients. If their organization is not able to recognize this and facilitate such alignment, they move on in search of roles/organizations that offer these job and learning experiences. Tech organizations, in terms of their branding design, need to focus on gaining an edge in technology, opening up tech career opportunities in hot-skill areas, attracting relevant clients/projects and retaining tech talent.

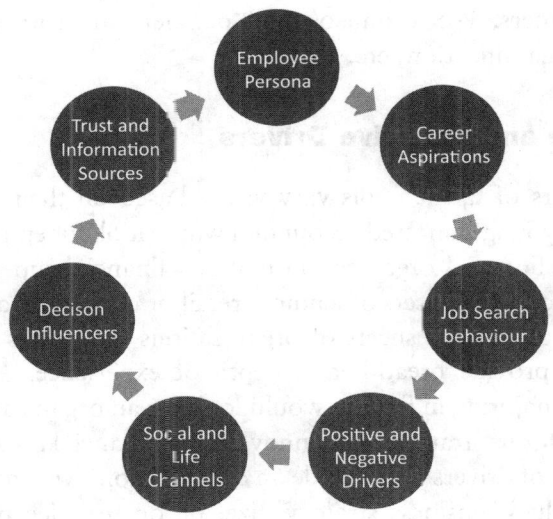

Figure 7.23. Factors Impacting Employer Branding

B-school graduates, on the contrary, evaluate organizations based on the factors such as sector/domain, business strategy, leadership and alumni, learning and fast-track career opportunities. Leadership & Alum connect and showcase is the key strategy driver, as the talent trusts/believes talent based on information that comes from source directly than any other source.

Job Search Behaviour

Organizations must keep a track of the channels/sources through which talent scout for job/career opportunities—do the talent search for jobs on their mobiles or desktops or participate in job fairs (physical/virtual)? The EB for mobile devices would be different from that for desktops. On mobile phones, the EB would be brief and bit-sized and happen through visual communication. On the contrary, the EB through desktops would happen through banners, anecdotes, experience narratives, leadership profiling, etc. The EB in job fairs would be through sleek banners, PoS (point-of-sale) danglers, in-store banners, activities/gamification, etc.

Positive and Negative Drivers

The drivers of talent pools vary vastly based on their persona/profile. A young chartered accountant would look for employment in a large financial organization that is a financial supermarket, is active across all facets of lending, retail or corporate, and gives exposure to balance sheets of organizations of various sizes, as it would provide breadth and depth of experience. An MBA graduate majoring in finance would look for an organization that is known for its strategies and innovation in financial instruments. The range of drivers can include an organization's vision/mission, culture/values, business strategy, size, product/service portfolio, learning and growth opportunities, type of leadership/peers, supply chain partners, etc.

Social and Life Channels

Millennials and Gen Z spend their time largely on social media. They like to explore the world virtually, connect and form new relationships. They love to share their feelings and emotions with their network and the world openly. As a result, they spend a lot of time on the platforms such as Facebook, Twitter, Instagram and YouTube. Each of these channels is known for its uniqueness in content and communication. YouTube, which began only for entertainment, has now diversified into people sharing their hobbies, entertainment and video content on a whole range of topics. Facebook is known as a platform for the communication/exchange of feelings and emotions by people either within their private network or with people at large. Instagram is a visual platform containing largely pictures, and people use it to share their emotions and feelings. LinkedIn has evolved into an intellectual capital sharing platform from a pure-play networking and job portal.

An organization, as part of its branding strategy, first needs to identify the uniqueness of a platform, carry out competitor analysis for differentiating opportunities, identify its unique EVP components and customize its EB communication.

Decision and Trust Influencers

As people go through their life cycle stages, the importance they attach to various stakeholders varies. A young adult in their early 20's would give more weight to information/guidance from friends/peers, as they emotionally connect with and easily relate to individuals at a similar life stage. They value the inputs coming from their friends/peers more than those from any other source. A middle-aged person values their relationship with their family and professional peers over other relationships. An organization, while deciding on its EB strategy, has to identify these decision influencers and communicate the EX through them. For instance, EB during campus hiring is anchored through alumni, as students find them to be more reliable than any other source. In the case of mid-career professionals, they trust and value information from leaders and people in their professional network. Channelling the EB communication through them would be more impactful than through any other source.

Employer Branding Strategy and Execution—A Mix of Employee Value Proposition and Employee Experience

The advent of social media and digital channels has moved the focus of both organizations and employees, from 'what is being offered' to 'how is it offered'. This has made it necessary for organizations to emphasize not just what they offer to their employees but also what the employees feel/experience when availing the EVPs.

Figure 7.24. Employer Branding Paradigm Shift

An organization needs to take a structured approach in the process of EB transition. The steps involved in the transition are:

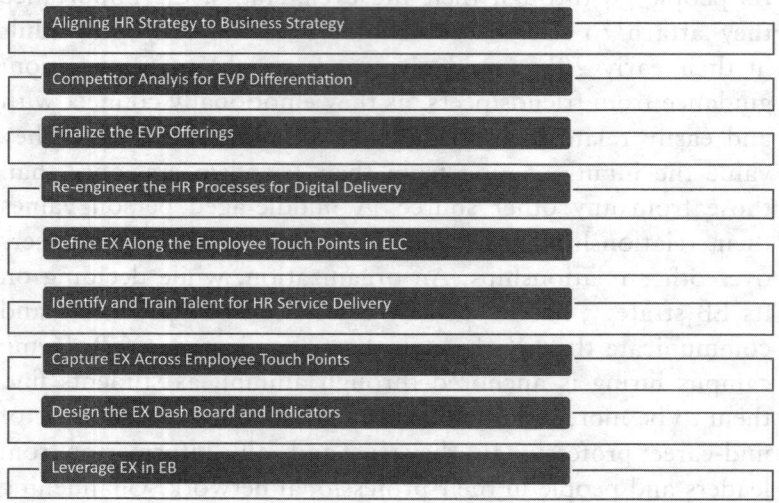

Figure 7.25. Employer Branding and Employee Experience Steps

The first step for the organization is to define the HR strategy based on its business context. To define the HR strategy, the organization needs to carry out a competitor analysis, through a commissioned compensation survey to identify the EVP offerings by its competitors, and accordingly decide on its EVP offerings. However, this is just half the job. The elements impacting EX include 'how it will be offered' and 'who will deliver it'. The analysis and seamless integration of these three elements hold the key to successful delivery of EVP with a positive EX.

Organizations tend to weak their EVP offerings, but tend to ignore the **"How" & who"** part and as a result, they fail to derive

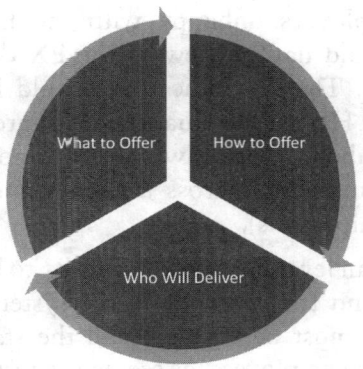

Figure 7.26. Employee Experience Factors

the benefits. Digitization can deliver transparency and a positive EX only when the process is designed for the same. For instance, an organization can digitize its leave management process to help its employees apply for leave. However, if the system does not scope in such elements as leave availability, leave history and leave approval status, the employees would end up still being dependent on the HR or their reporting manager for the same. The desire to be independent and empowered is not just limited to millennials and Gen Z but cuts across generations.

The HR team or people managers who are part of the HR service delivery process need to be oriented/trained on the process, to ensure that they do not end up becoming bottlenecks in the EX delivery to the employees. The orientation could include training on the KSA of employees, depending on their profile. Most organizations focus on knowledge and skills, ignoring attitude. Lack of employee-centricity can adversely impact the EX delivery to the employees.

EX delivery, like any other service delivery, needs to be tracked, and accountability needs to be fixed to the HR service delivery providers through linking EX delivery to their KRAs and performance planning and reviews. The lack of linkage of performance to service providers can lead to gaps in EX delivery, leaving the employees unhappy with the EX. The question then is who would have a view of the EX delivery indicators and dashboards. The EX indicators should include employee feedback on the HR service quality and aggregate and analyse the data. A dashboard with raw data is of no use unless it has comparative dimensions (across timelines and across business units or leadership teams).

Organizations can leverage the opportunity to bring in employee empowerment and transparency in the system. The indicators and dashboards must be visible to all the stakeholders in the process, that is, to employees, as seeing the results is believing in them, and to HR/people managers to check on their effectiveness with people. The data from the dashboard needs to be linked to the performance scorecard of the employees. The top leadership should make it a point to review the EX delivery indicators, along with employee feedback.

For instance, an FMCG (fast-moving consumer goods) organization with a large part of its workforce as field employees would have a different HR strategy from that of an IT services organization. The focus of the organization would be to attract, reward and retain talent who have knowledge of and a grip on the marketplace for the products the organization offers. The field sales force would operate away from office and would not be able to come to office for any HR service. Hence, the organization would have to design its HR systems/processes to be delivered using digital technologies. These employees were initially operating with only mobiles and physical paper for collection of customer/supply chain details. Then, they had to come to office to key in the details and update the system. The employees were spending more time feeding data into the management information system (MIS) than on actual relationship management, which was frustrating for them.

Thanks to digital technologies, most organizations have transitioned to appification of business processes, to help the employees capture business details and update them on the system. This has resulted in multiple advantages. Organizations get real-time

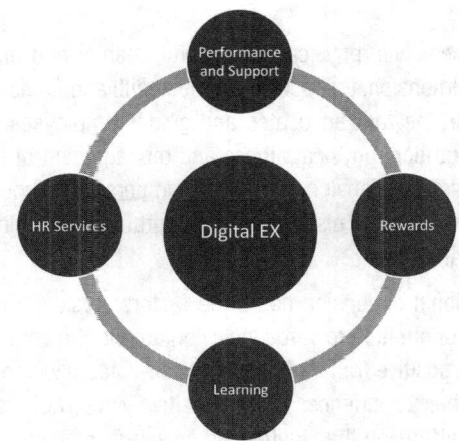

Figure 7.27. Digital Employee Experience Factors

updates on employee performance, and the employees are relieved of redundant work. The reporting managers can review the performance of employees on a real-time basis and provide continuous feedback to them.

The reporting manager can recommend/award performance incentives based on an employee's performance. The employee can query and reach out to the manager for performance support, even 'on the go'. Employee can access details like criteria and details performance incentives awarded on real time. They can access the HR services like leave processing and salary and benefits processing without struggling to reach out to anyone. They can reach out to their reporting manager/peers for 'on-the-job learning' and can send in their queries and seek views/responses while working on a job/assignment. Organizations are delivering micro- and bite-sized learning in appified format.

> **UNILEVER EMPLOYEE WELL-BEING FRAMEWORK**
>
> Unilever, as part of its integrated EX, designed and rolled out a 'Well-being Framework'. It attempts to service employee expectations on four

major dimensions: physical, purposeful, mental and emotional. In the physical dimension, the focus is on the health and fitness of the employees. The framework advocates and guides employees on the aspects such as nutrition, physical fitness and management of one's energy. In the purposeful dimension, it tries to align personal purposes with a sustainable living plan. This is done to integrate the sustainability strategy of the organization.

The emotional dimension has three factors: positive mindset, self-esteem and orientation towards inclusion among the employees. Employees with a positive frame of mind and self-esteem would try to view and interpret their experiences from a positive view. Their happiness would be more self-driven than influenced by external factors.

The mental dimension aims to nurture qualities of focus in one's efforts, flexibility and agility and a higher level of mindfulness to live and interpret one's experiences fully. By integrating the four dimensions, Unilever has transformed itself from a passive EX seeker to an EX co-creator. The employees thus contribute to EB as well, as those with a positive EX are likely to share their positive experiences with others. The employees thus become strong advocates for EB and actually champion EB.

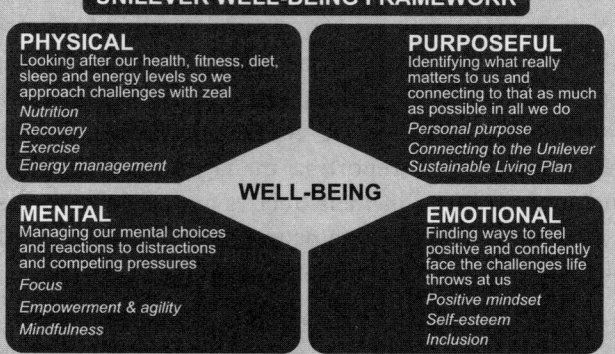

https://www.unilever.com/sustainable-living/enhancing-livelihoods/fairness-in-the-workplace/improving-employee-health-and-well-being/

Conclusion

HR services for employees have expanded beyond the designing of HR policies/systems and their implementation. Employee engagement surveys that capture employee feedback are passé and redundant in the dynamic digital world. Today, an employee looks for positive and fulfilling experiences at every touchpoint through the stages of the employee life cycle. Organizations are taking an integrated approach by defining EVP in the context of business and HR strategy, re-engineering HR processes, aligning them to digital applications, orienting HR and people managers and linking their KRAs to EX indicators, tracking EX at the organizational level and leveraging EX feedback by linking it to EB initiatives for authenticity.

Points to Ponder

1. How does EX contribute to the EB of an organization?
2. How is the paradigm shift from EVP to EX impacting the EB of organizations?
3. How can digital transformation of organizations in HR service delivery and EX take place?
4. What factors should the leadership of organizations be mindful of in delivering a positive EX?
5. How could organizations use 'co-creation' and 'crowd-sourcing' in leveraging EX for EB?
6. How do EX indicators and dashboards contribute to EB?

8
Employee Experience of Gig Employees

The phenomenon of earlier days of all employees being full-time workers is passé, and today both employees and organizations are getting used to the gig economy. There has been a paradigm shift in organizations, which have transitioned from treating gig workers as a good-to-have talent component to treating them as an integral part of the talent mix critical for business success. This chapter discusses in detail the context of gig workers and strategies adopted by organizations to leverage them.
It discusses in detail the EX design and delivery strategies adopted by organizations to offer an 'inclusive and equitable EX' to gig employees.

Advent and Impact of the Gig Economy

LIFE AND GIGS

Aditi is a project manager with a leading IT services provider in Bengaluru. She has been working with her current employer for over 6 years and has been assigned to lead a digital-transformation project for a leading European bank. She leads a team of 55 IT professionals with different skill sets. This is the nth project in her career spanning over 15 years. Her employer has given her flexible-login and work-from-home options. Her husband, Sujit, works with a captive IT unit of a large global bank as VP (business transformation). The couple have two children, a boy aged 10 and a girl aged 12, who are in classes IV and VI, respectively. Both children study in an international school.

On a day when Aditi has to work from her office, she wakes up at 6.00 a.m. to get the children to do their homework and logs into work to oversee project tractions and submissions by her team, to prepare for a team meeting at 9.00 a.m. At 7.00 a.m., she realizes that she does not have time for preparing breakfast; she logs into the Zomato app, checks with the children and orders a pizza for them and *idlis* for herself and her husband.

Sujit, who usually drops the children to the school on his way to the office, tells Aditi to manage the task on that day, as he needs to reach office early for an important meeting. Aditi has long given up driving her car to office, due to the nightmarish traffic snarls in the city. She gets ready, books an Uber cab and sets the school as the destination for dropping the children and heads to her office. She logs into work as she is travelling (in the cab) to catch up on mails she could not check the previous day. She gives instructions to her children and asks them to have food in the school canteen, and then she books an Uber for them to come home after school.

Around 4.00 p.m., between meetings, she checks if the children have reached home and orders burgers for them. Around 7.00 p.m., she books an Uber for herself to head back home. En route, she realizes the need to book medical check-up appointments for the children (eyesight), herself and her husband (annual health check-up) and books slots for the weekend with doctors through Practo. Then, she speaks to her in-laws and discovers that her father-in-law has sprained his leg that evening and books a physiotherapist online for the same evening. She then calls her mother and discovers that the latter has been having a problem with her fridge for over 2 days. Aditi logs into a services aggregator app and books a fridge repairman to visit her parents' place the next morning.

She then reviews the status of her housemaid, sourced through an app, tracks her performance over the last few days and makes the monthly payment to the maid services provider.

As she waits for the traffic on her way home to clear up, she looks at her watch and notices that the time is 15 minutes past 8. Realizing the need to arrange for dinner for her children, she orders roti rolls and salads, through Zomato yet again. She realizes the need to stock up on groceries and places a grocery order to be delivered the next morning through Amazon.

As she prepares to end her day, Aditi looks back at her life after the digital and gig economies and thanks them for making her life manageable through remote multitasking. She briefly ponders quitting her high-paying full-time job to become a freelancer, but then she factors in the financial commitments, like EMIs (equated monthly instalments) for the flat and two cars and the children's current and future expenses that the couple are likely to plan for. Of course, other plans around retirement savings and lifestyle too crop up in her thoughts.

Aditi knows that for scores of professionals like her, the *jugalbandi* between life and career has to go on and becoming a gig worker is a pipe dream that she cannot afford to pursue, due to a range of responsibilities, and perhaps psychological insecurities as well. The only mantra for professionals like her is to rely on gig workers to do the balancing act in life. In short, professionals like Aditi are opening up doors for scores of gig workers, who were battling with unorganized and unpredictable incomes but now lead a more organized and respectable life with improved predictability of income. Thus, both worlds can coexist peacefully, and gig workers are bound to swell in numbers over the years, due to the changing socio-economic and cultural patterns across the globe.

> The gig world is helping improve standards of income and life for people who were living on the fringes of society. Would today's frontline gig workers like their next generation to become gig workers in the same space? It is unlikely, as they would aspire for their children to lead a life with improved socio-economic standards.

Economic (National) Impact

Is the gig economy just a recent phenomenon or has it been in existence through the ages? If we look at various civilizations, like those in Rome, Nile or the Indus Valley, these civilizations had artisans who were working as freelancers in their respective crafts (pottery/arts/crafts); these were the original gig workers. In recent times, in both rural and urban areas, we have had people working in crafts at the bottom of the pyramid, working as freelancers and earning their living. The question one may ask is: why is there so much noise about the gig economy? Is it not 'old wine in a new bottle'?

The answer lies in digital technologies, which have converted informal, intangible and invisible freelancers into a semi-formal, tangible and visible part of the economy. Digital technologies (app-based services aggregators) have brought distributed talent onto one platform. The organizational design, which used to be largely centralized, transitioned to a hub-and-spokes format, with the hubs being manned and operated by on-roll/permanent employees and the spokes, which are customer-facing,

Figure 8.1. Economy Shift

being manned by gig employees. In a sense, organizations have transformed into a hybrid-talent powerhouse and are experimenting with talent mixes of various intensities based on their business and people strategy.

In the United States, the total number of gig employees has reached 60 million, and it is projected that 44 per cent of the US workforce would comprise gig workers in the next few years. In India, the number of gig employees, which was at 8.5 million during the year 2016, almost doubled to 15 million by the year 2018 (ASSOCHAM Report).

The first focus area and challenge for governments around the world, those in both developed and developing countries, is to create employment opportunities for their population. The percentage of employed population versus that of unemployed population has a bearing on the GDP, social security costs, consumption of products and services and the quality of life for citizens. A high rate of unemployment has the potential to create social and political unrest in countries, which can threaten to topple elected governments. There has been reduction in employment by governments and the public sector, as the socialist model of governance was found to be ineffective and

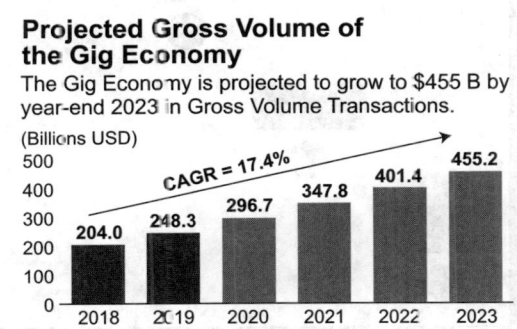

Figure 8.2. Gig Economy: Growth Projections

Source: https://community.nasscom.in/communities/talent/future-of-jobs/gig-economy---a-new-trend-in-employment.html

inefficient. The world has largely tilted towards the capitalist form of economies, allowing free enterprise and demand–supply dynamics to run the marketplace. The traditional form of large organizations in market economies has proved to be non-viable due to their lack of agility/flexibility. This is where the gig economy has assumed importance.

Such organizations as Amazon, Uber and Zomato have a talent mix in the 40:60 ratio (permanent employees to gig workers), while traditional IT/IT services companies, which are supposed to be trendsetters, have gig talent constituting less than 10 per cent of their workforce. In a sector like insurance, we have freelancers, like insurance advisors/surveyors, supporting the operations of insurance companies. One may wonder why such disparity exists and why there is lack of a uniform trend across sectors.

The fundamental trend indicates that organizations tend to opt for a higher proportion of gig talent for roles that require low

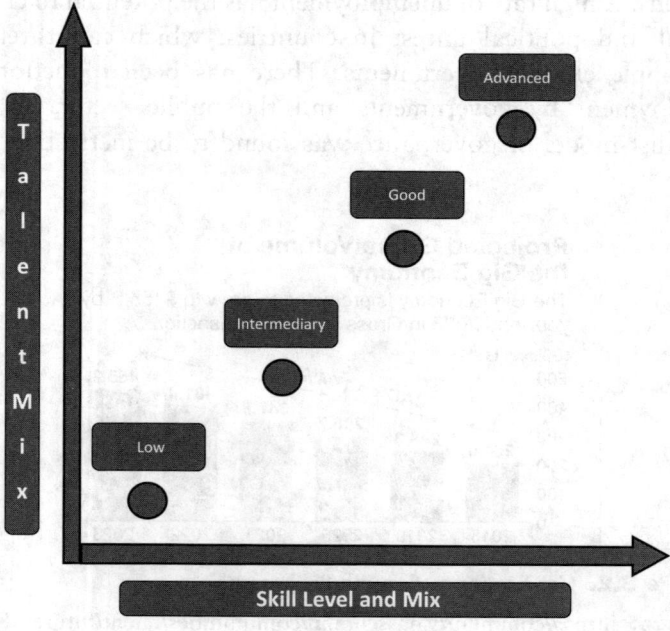

Figure 8.3. Skill and Talent Mix Strategy

and intermediary skills, and they tend to lower the proportion of gig talent as the skill requirements move to a higher level. One may have the following deeper questions:

- Are there multiple reasons for this kind of differentiated approach?
- Is there a strategic reason underlying this approach of organizations?
- Are organizations less empathetic and ruthless with junior employees?
- Are talent demand–supply anomalies impacting these trends?
- Is it the gig talent's agility and flexibility that influence these strategies?
- Is risk aversion driving the gig-talent strategy?

The answer to all the above questions is yes, and all these factors are impacting the gig-talent strategies of organizations. The key factor is that organizations have large sets of talent at the bottom of the pyramid. The agility and performance of an organization in today's competitive economy depends on its ability to have flexibility in tweaking a large portion of its workforce.

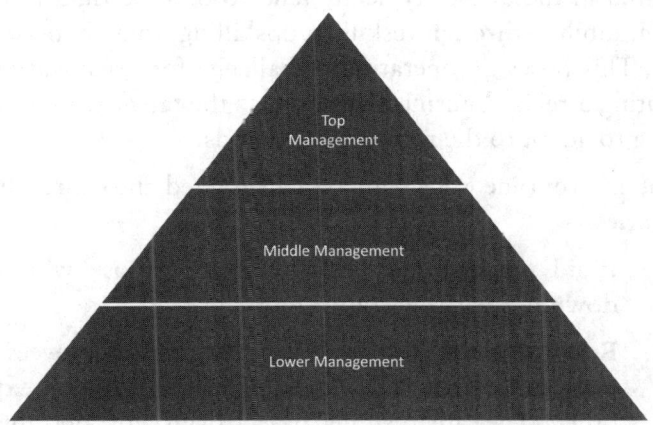

Figure 8.4. Gig Talent Mix and Organizational Pyramid

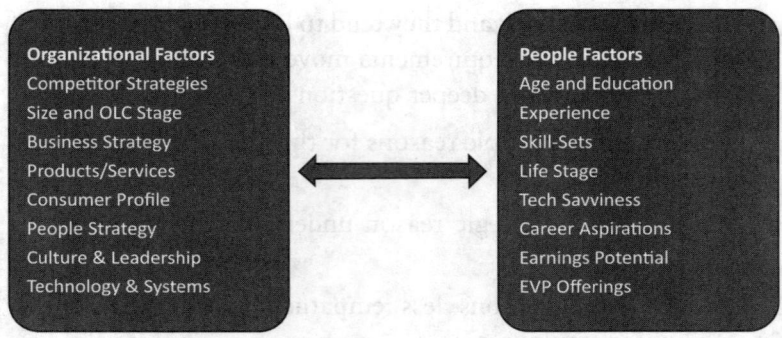

Figure 8.5. Gig Talent and Impacting Factors

The skill sets of talent at the bottom of the pyramid are available in abundance, as they can be trained and deployed easily. The most critical reason for this is that the roles/jobs are repetitive in nature. An organization would be going for overkill if it hires talent with a higher skill level for these roles, which would also lead to multiple challenges for the organization.

The cost of acquiring and servicing the talent would increase, and the profitability/spreads would be eaten away by the increased people costs. The other major challenge is that employees hired in these roles typically tend to become rigid in terms of adaptability, through reskilling/upskilling, to a changed situation. This poses an operational challenge for organizations in executing a revised business strategy, as the talent would not be willing to adapt to the new business needs.

Talent in frontline roles can be categorized into three broad categories:

1. **Rigid talent:** Rigid talent comprise those who settle down in their role comfortably.
2. **Restless talent:** Restless talent comprise employees who tend to outgrow their role and would like to explore others. They are frustrated by lack of growth opportunities, pose challenges, like high attrition, creating instability in

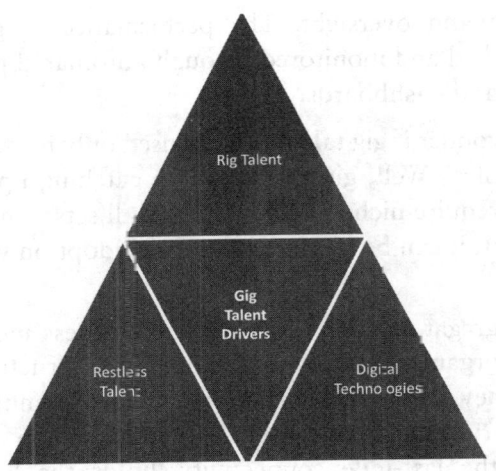

Figure 8.6. Gig Talent and Influencing Factors

operations. These talent issues form one set of drivers that motivate organizations to look for gig talent for these roles.

3. **Digital-technologies talent:** The fast-paced evolution of digital technologies has standardized the skills for roles in the domain, eliminating the complexity that existed earlier. The employees in frontline roles had to be trained on products/services, and processes as well. This is not the case anymore, as the entire information is stored at the backend and made available on apps for handheld devices, using which the talent can access information and execute their job. Te role of frontline employees can be seen as undergoing 'commoditization', which can be taught easily; thus, it has become easy for digital-tech organizations to source, train and deploy frontline talent.

Unlike in the conventional format, digitized work processes help organizations track and guide frontline gig workers on task/role deliverables. The deployment of AI/ML technologies, coupled with big data, has eliminated the challenges around supervision and oversight. The performance of gig workers can be tracked and monitored through automated performance indicators and dashboards.

One may wonder if gig talent is to be used only for frontline and low-skill roles? Well, gig talent is also catching up with other areas that require niche and advanced skill sets. On an analysis of gig talent, it can be observed that role adoption varies across sectors.

'Online aggregators' by virtue of their business model, like to keep their organization design and operating structure lean and flexible. They facilitate connection between manufacturers of products/services and consumers. The supply chain distribution, especially the last-mile connectivity, holds the key to these organizations. Their talent needs, to help them connect with and service customers, are large. Most frontline roles are repetitive and provide no added value. Thanks to digital automation, these organizations can easily track the performance and delivery of frontline employees remotely and cross-validate them with customer feedback as well. Also, they follow a strategy of keeping themselves 'asset-light' and less capital-intensive. Hence, they hire talent for the delivery fleet as gig employees. The players like Amazon which use smaller vans to transport goods use the 'lease–hire' format to lease vehicles and pay to the owners the monthly lease charges. In the case of two-wheelers for last-mile delivery, the gig talent are mandated to use their own vehicles. Thus, the most critical last-mile infrastructure in terms of both talent and delivery fleet is deployed on the 'gig format', which makes the organizations' operations flexible. The cab aggregators like Uber and Ola use a similar format of engaging drivers and vehicles in gig format, to expand their footprint in a less capital-intensive way, to reduce the asset stress on both talent and vehicular fleet. The cab aggregators' e-commerce firms have expanded the gig talent in manifold times. Perhaps, it can be said that they have 'mainstreamed' gig talent in the global economy.

'Healthcare services providers' (health-tech firms) are emerging as major sector employing medical and paramedical professionals to offer medical services on a gig format. The kinds of talent they employ are diverse; on the one hand, they have medical professionals who are highly skilled and valued and who place a high premium on their skills. On the other hand, they employ paramedics who operate at lower levels of knowledge/services. Trying to acquire the talent on roll would inflate their cost of operations. On the contrary, if they were to engage the talent as gig employees, with contracts where the payout is estimated on a pro rata basis, this would help the organizations balance costs and help the talent get paid on a pro rata basis.

'Professional-services firms' like consulting firms (strategy, finance advisory, tax advisory and investment advisory) lead the transition to the adoption of gig talent. This can be analysed through the underlying reasons such as niche skills, cost of engaging talent full-time and desire of the talent to be independent and get a share of project revenue rather than a mere salary that puts them at a disadvantage. The talent working in professional-services firms typically look for regular roles up to 10 years of work experience for adding value to their CV, gaining experience/exposure across sectors/geographies. The competition is tough in professional-services firms, and only a few can rise up the ranks. As a result, employees who do not like to report to erstwhile peers tend to move out and operate in the gig format, as it gives them an opportunity to work as equals with leaders in their previous organizations. Also the contacts and the network they had built help them start their own gig operations, unlike employees in other sectors who tend to struggle to find their footing and stabilize their income.

Legal professionals, by virtue of the nature of their profession, tend to prefer majorly to operate as freelancers having their own firms. The sector has law firms (corporate and individual) offering their services to the clients. Legal professionals, just like finance professionals, tend to go through the learning curve with

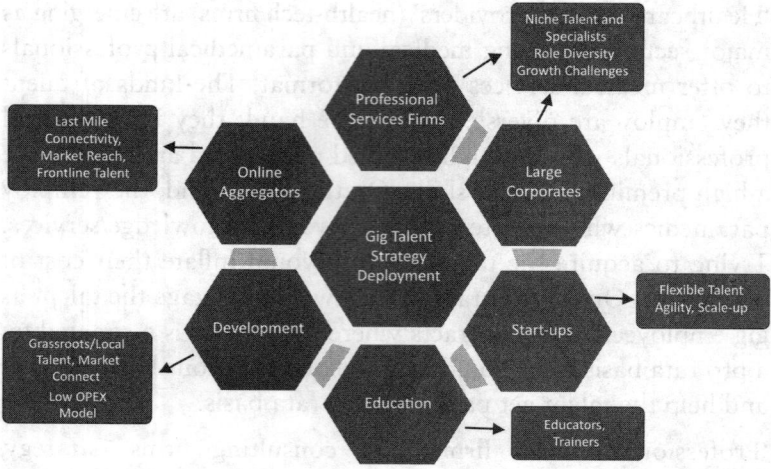

Figure 8.7. Gig Talent: Driving Forces

a senior legal professional (either operating as an individual or running a firm with a couple of partners). After they gain experience/expertise, they prefer to operate as gig lawyers, as this would provide them with an opportunity to service a larger number of clients to maximize their learning. The advent of outsourcing (legal process outsourcing [LPO]) has opened up opportunities for legal professionals to support global clients of LPOs. Working as full-time employees leads to their opting out of practice, which poses a career risk, as they end up losing their client base that they had built up assiduously over time.

'Large corporates' are the next set of organizations that are employing gig talent for multiple reasons. They have large talent pools and large needs, which gives them an opportunity to experiment with and explore different talent mixes in their journey to the next level of operational efficiency. Strategy diagnosis helps them identify roles that offer both opportunity and advantages through their transitioning to a gig-talent mix. The type of roles chosen for gig employees are the repetitive roles at the front line, where they struggle to retain full-time employees. Gig talent are also employed in niche roles that are typically individual-contributor

(IC) roles. The talent in these roles are focused on their skills and career, thus self-limiting their career opportunities. The skill and career orientations of niche talent constrain organizations, makes it necessary to moderate their EVP offerings viz., compensation, role diversity and career growth options.

Niche talent typically tend to stagnate after 10–12 years of work experience in formal roles. This gives them the financial comfort and CV value to take a career risk and venture out as a gig talent. It is a win-win strategy for both organizations and the talent, as the organizations get access to the talent's skills/expertise on a need basis and the employees get the freedom to work on their terms and on parallel assignments that satisfy their need for experience diversity. IT services organizations, which are undergoing digital transformation, have adopted the 'non-linear growth' model to drive business growth without the latter being linked to headcount growth. They are using 'gig talent' in both routine and hot-skill areas. For instance, in the areas like project management and application development and maintenance where the talent needs are large, they are deploying gig talent. Also, some of these roles are getting phased out or merged with other roles.

For instance, roles in application maintenance and workforce management are getting phased out through digital automation using AI/ML technologies. As a result, organizations are encouraging existing employees to transition into gig workers, with a strategy to align talent with emerging business needs. Similarly, talent in the hot-skill areas like AI/ML and hacking are being hired on a gig format, due to such reasons as demand–supply mismatch, need for quick scaling up of business and preference of talent to operate as gig talent due to their aspiration for career independence and maximization of their earning potential. On talent diagnosis, it can be noticed that most of the talent working in hot-skill areas are millennials or Gen Z, who love freedom and nurture a desire to experiment, as unlike those of their previous generations (baby boomers and Gen X) their basic needs (physical/security needs) are met thanks to parental support. Their belonging needs are met thanks to their networking and bonding through social networks. Their emotional needs are met primarily through friends/social networks and secondarily through family/friends. This makes it easy for new-generation talent to operate their career as gig talent.

'Start-ups' in their initial stages face challenges in terms of physical infrastructure and hiring of 'full-time talent', due to budgetary constraints. They cannot afford to 'burn cash' on routine operations, and cash is reserved for critical business needs, like technology innovation/acquisition and market expansion. They also have the need to keep their talent/operations flexible/agile to adapt to emerging needs, as they have a high amount of risk exposure in terms of acceptance of their products/services, and they have to constantly innovate/change their business model to get it right and then quickly scale up. These issues make start-ups a fertile ground for adoption of the gig-talent strategy. The target talent mix for them would be tenured talent/senior talent (with an experience of 10–12 years) who have experience working with large corporates and are looking to experiment with gig work. The other set of target talent for start-ups comprise millennials and Gen Z, who love workplace freedom, empowerment at work and opportunities to work on cutting-edge technology (hot skills).

The 'education sector' is a fertile ground for gig talent, as educators are creative and freedom-seeking professionals. Their drive for learning and passion for their work is not linked to their organizations. Traditionally, educators in formal employment experience bureaucracy and shackles, which trigger in them a need for operational independence. The advent of online education aggregators (education technology [EdTech] firms) has emboldened educators to branch out as gig workers. Digital technologies have done away with geographical constraints, due to which educators can reach out and offer their services to learners across countries.

Educators can be broadly classified into four learning categories: (a) child learning; (b) adult learning; (c) professional learning and (d) tech learning. Child learning facilitators focus on teaching children at the school level languages or specific subjects. Adult learning comprises education for young adults who are at the

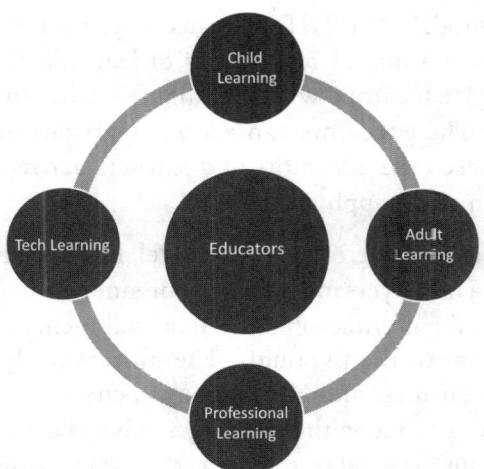

Figure 8.8. Gig Talent: Learning Needs

undergraduate/postgraduate level and look for learning support, either for distance learning or due to their dissatisfaction with the learning services provided in the formal learning set-up.

Professional learning includes learning by working professionals to develop themselves in specific knowledge, skill and attitude areas. The skill level and talent value increase proportionately from child learning to adult learning. Child/adult learning facilitators tend to offer basic learning in the form of tutorials that supplement the students' learning. The educators offering professional/tech learning tend to have both expertise and experience, which are valued. The maturity of the learners ensures that they are updating their knowledge/content and skills.

Technical learning is focused specifically on the learning of tech skills by either aspiring or existing tech professionals to equip themselves with the emerging 'hot skills' and to meet their career objectives of 'staying on the top of the game', 'staying employable', 'transforming into hot talent', 'growing into new tech domains' and 'improving their pay'. The educators who were operating independently received a 'shot in the arm' with the advent of 'EdTech' firms, which have also adopted the aggregator model. The EdTech firms, based on their business models, focus on one or more areas of learning. They identify and onboard educators who are aligned with their business focus areas. The educators can access, aggregate and facilitate connect between the educators and learners across geographies using the demand–supply analytics.

The 'development sector' by its model has specifics that are unique to it. The players include social organizations (NGOs) and development finance/microfinance/financial inclusion (financing for the bottom of the pyramid). The players in the sectors, as part of their business and HR strategy, focus on sourcing talent locally for connecting with their targeted beneficiaries. Trying to import/implant external resources as their representatives would impair their efforts. Trying to onboard the local talent on a full-time basis would add to their costs and rigidity in managing the talent. Engaging gig talent is a win-win for both the talent and the organization. The talent are engaged in such activities as developing the business to reach out to potential beneficiaries, delivering products/services and tracking the progress/impact of the efforts of their development organization.

Post COVID-19, a number of jobs are projected to grow in the gig format. The jobs and profile fit are mentioned below:

- **Freelancers:** Such professionals as content writers, graphic designers, web designers, social media managers, developers and marketers would become assets of the economy.
- **Artificial intelligence developers:** AI and ML have been in great demand. Working in this field may get a person up to $115.06 per hour. A normal bachelor's degree and a postgraduate degree are enough for the same, and a job in this domain would be the highest-paying of all jobs.
- **Blockchain architects:** A blockchain freelancer can make up to $87.05 per hour with proficiency in C++, Python and other languages. The demand for them would grow due to an increase in the popularity of this sector.

- **Robotics engineers:** Robotics engineers earn up to $77.46 per hour and requires degree in mechanical engineering, with proficiency in 3D modelling, photo view, etc.
- **Virtual and augmented reality developers:** Such specialists are required by such companies as Facebook, Google, Apple and Microsoft, which might pay them up to $50.18 per hour. Ones who are passionate about programming and coding would be benefitted.
- **Instagram marketers:** Little professional training is needed to qualify for this job description, and Instagram marketing would help many millennials who are keen about social media.

Source: https://community.nasscom.in/communities/talent/future-of-jobs/gig-economy---a-new-trend-in-employment.html

The increased importance of gig talent has led to the emergence of specific talent markets that focus on niche gig talent based on their job profile and the skill sets needed.

Talent Market (Portal)	Gig Opportunities/Profiles
https://www.upwork.com/	The website offers talent across careers tracks, including web developers, mobile developers, web designers, design architects, creative professionals, freelance writers, administrative support staff, customer service professionals, marketing experts and finance and accounting experts.
https://www.freelancer.com/	It offers gig opportunities in entry-level jobs for professionals with relevant skill sets, including web designers, Ad word experts, e-commerce experts, software experts, programming professionals, freelance writers, supply chain experts and graphic designers.

(continued)

(continued)

Talent Market (Portal)	Gig Opportunities/Profiles
https://www.guru.com/	It offers gig opportunities to programming and software developers, writing professionals, designers, artists, administrative and secretarial staff, sales and marketing experts and business and finance experts.
https://www.taskrabbit.com	It offers gig opportunities for frontline workers in the supply chain delivery area, such as food delivery, online-shopping delivery, transportation of goods and services, etc.
https://www.toptal.com/	It is a talent market for professionals with niche skills at the higher end of the talent value chain. The talent profiles covered are software developers, UI/UX developers, visual and interaction designers, financial experts with deep skills in financial modelling, start-up funders, chief financial officers, those in market sizing, project managers with expertise in SCRUM and digital projects management and product managers with experience in sectors like banking and e-commerce.
https://www.flexjobs.com	It is a talent supermarket that facilitates the connection of gig workers across the spectrum, including finance professionals, administrative/secretarial staff, writing professionals, hospitality professionals, professionals in personal care and beauty, HR, sports and fitness trainers, medical professionals, journalists, engineers, marketers and educators.
https://www.fiverr.com	It is an exclusive talent market for creative professionals in both technology and non-technology areas. The gig profiles include graphics and design, digital marketing, writing and translation, video and animation, music and audio, etc.
LinkedIn ProFinder	LinkedIn the professional network, which is in sync with the talent and market needs, launched.

These talent markets offer gigs across skill sets in every career track. Large brands, such as Microsoft, Airbnb and General Electric, are shopping for talent through these talent markets. The talent too, realizing the gig-career opportunities, are scouting for gig opportunities in these portals.

Employee Value Proposition: Regular and Gig Employees

We have seen the positive aspects of the gig economy, but as the adage goes, 'All that glitters is not gold'. There is a flip side to the happening gig story, which we realize has shades of grey on deeper analysis. The key issues that organizations and aspiring gig professionals need to keep in mind are described next.

Talent Uncertainty and Business Impact

Organizations may avail the benefit of flexibility in staffing through hiring gig workers, but there are issues that have serious implications on the business of the organization. Inability of the organization to take care of staffing uncertainty can seriously

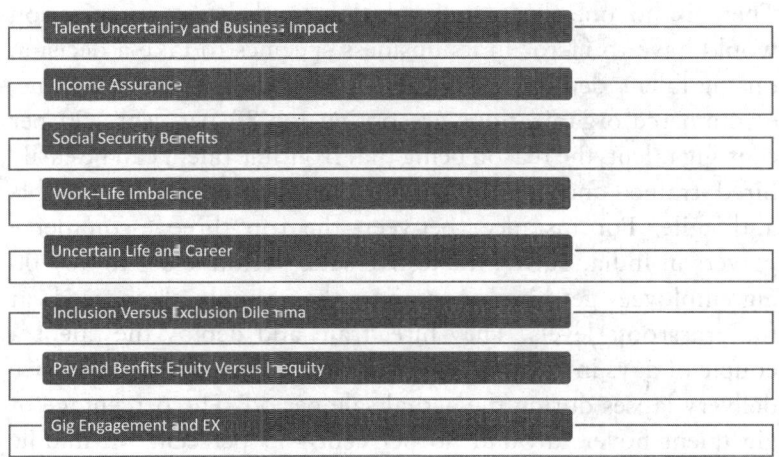

Figure 8.9. Gig Talent: EVP Needs

Employee Experience of Gig Employees | 319

impact its service delivery. For instance, a retail hypermarket chain can take the decision of hiring gig talent for its floor support and billing staff, due to the reasons like seasonality of its business. Say, as a gender inclusion strategy, the organization takes a decision that 70 per cent of its frontline staff would be women and preference would be given to women who have been on a career sabbatical for personal reasons. From a talent perspective, it may sound great, but the organization could face operational issues, like unauthorized absenteeism by the staff, which can throw its customer service delivery out of gear, resulting in a negative CX, which in turn can adversely impact its festive-sales revenues. At this juncture, one may face the following questions:

- What should be the proportion of gig workers in the talent mix?
- What would be the ideal talent mix for an organization?
- How could an organization de-risk its business from gig-talent uncertainty?
- What is the right trade-off between talent/cost optimization and business risk?

There is no one-size-fits-all solution, and every organization would have to factor in its business specifics to take a decision on gig-talent deployment in its operations. In the front line, e-commerce organizations are opting for 80 per cent –90 per cent gig talent, the reason being that frontline talent can be easily hired, trained and deployed. They keep their operations flexible and agile. For instance, between the top three e-commerce players in India, during the festive-sales period, close to 30,000 gig employees get hired to support their supply chain needs at the grassroots levels. They hire, train and deploy the talent a couple of days in advance, carrying out dry runs to avoid service delivery lapses during the actual sale period. The percentage of gig talent hovers around 30 per cent –35 per cent in middle management, and it comes down to less than 10 per cent at the

Figure 8.10. Gig Talent and Organization Preparedness

top-management level. In the IT sector, professionals for roles such as project management, user interface/user experience (UI/UX) design and application development, opt for gig roles.

'System preparedness' refers to the organizational dynamics such as organizational culture, leadership, technology alignment/integration, business process effectiveness, orientation of regular employees and performance rigour. If an organization has a closed mindset and is very bureaucratic in nature, it would be an uphill task for it to integrate gig talent into its workstreams. From a quick glance at the types of organizations that are adopting gig talent, it can be noticed that the majority of them belong to the knowledge services industry (IT/ITeS/consulting) and are young organizations. Organizations with a long history and those in manufacturing or traditional sectors tend to opt hire talent who have worked on a full-time basis as gig talent, due to the factors such as loyalty, relationship and familiarity with the business. They find it difficult to accept a complete stranger as a gig associate.

'Leadership' has a major role in preparing an organization for employing gig talent. An engaging and strong leader would be able to communicate to and convince the rest of the organization about the imperative to bring in gig talent. They would be able to explain the strategic reasons and advantages for the organization. Without buy-in from employees, it would be a herculean task for an organization to create an inclusive, open and welcome environment for gig workers.

In terms of 'technology alignment', in relation to organizations that are less tech-integrated, organizations with a high level of tech preparedness are able to integrate gig talent, providing the option of remote or flexible login. Gig talent prefers to operate on their own terms, and trying to enforce conventional workplace rules would discourage them from looking for opportunities with an organization. Also, there might be operational issues, like creating physical workspaces for them. Organizations are using co-working spaces in some cases to accommodate gig workers, as the physical space needed can be rented at a lower cost through pro rata payment. Co-working spaces offer equal ambience as regular workspaces in organizations at a lower cost.

'Process effectiveness' refers to the capability of an organization to break work processes into manageable portions, assign them to gig workers and integrate their work to derive business results. It brings in performance rigour, with the ability to track the performance of employees (irrespective of their role/location) through automated performance indicators.

Gigs workers, unlike regular employees, face issues around 'income assurance', as in today's competitive world it is unlikely that gig workers would be able to get assignments/work on a continuous basis. The level of transparency in the identification/selection of gig workers has a long way to go. Organizations, whether small or big, tend to show personal biases in the selection process, due to referrals of networked employees or powerful stakeholders tending to bag opportunities over the

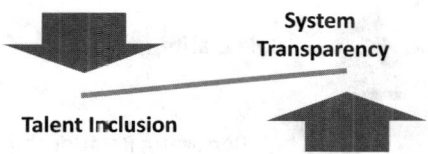

Figure 8.11. Gig Talent: Winning Elements

rest. The extent of work available to a gig worker is directly related to the power of their network.

Gig workers are largely creative and freedom seeking individuals who are mostly introverted. Their personality orientation is a key factor that drives them away from the political realities in formal organizations to create an independent space for themselves. But if their network/connectedness is the factor impacting the availability of work for them, it defeats the very purpose of their career orientation. Professional networks/digital talent markets must bring in transparency and inclusivity in the gig workers sourcing processes within organizations, through visibility and equal opportunity. The internal process of selection and oversight of gig workers needs to be robust to ensure that there is no disparity between perceived and actual inclusion and transparency by an organization in dealing with gig workers.

Orientation of Regular Employees

The EX of gig workers is dependent on how the regular employees respond and reach out to and treat them at the workplace. If the regular employees treat them as a threat to their careers, they are unlikely to welcome them. They would instead display non-cooperation and try their best to sabotage the efforts of gig workers. Leaders and HR have a major role in helping the regular employees understand the role and importance of gig workers. Full-time employees need to understand in detail the difference between their roles and those of the gig workers. Second, reporting relationships can become complicated if care is not taken in deciding them.

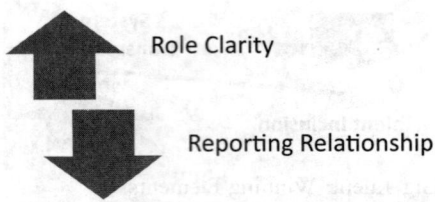

Figure 8.12. Two Dimensions Impacting the Employee Experience of Gig Workers

Making a regular employee report to a gig worker can lead to multiple challenges. The regular employee would find it difficult to report to a gigging manager, as the latter is transient. Having a temporary manager can lead to a sense of insecurity in the minds of regular employees, due to the issues such as: (a) lack of full-time availability of the manager; b) the employees feeling that their role has been diluted; (c) performance reviews by the gigging manager not carrying weight in the organization; and (d) the regular employees perceiving that their role too can get moved into the gig format. These are the reasons why organizations prefer to have gig workers in IC roles.

The other scenario could involve gig employees having a gig manager. Both the gig employee and the gig manager would be operating under similar relationships with the organization, which makes it possible for them to align with each other. On the flip side of such an arrangement, the employees and the manager, sharing a similar relationship with the organization, are likely to take each other lightly. The extent of commitment and accountability could be low. There are operational risks involved in organizations entrusting their business operations to a team and manager who are both working on a gig basis. The question then is: how could organizations balance such a scenario when having such a talent mix becomes inevitable? There are three broad strategies that organizations could adopt to deal with the situation. The first approach is based on the talent mix, and the second on technology, and the third is a hybrid approach. Adopting the strategy based on the talent mix,

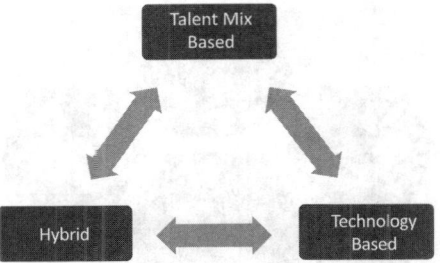

Figure 8.13. Gig Worker Performance (Employee Experience) Management

an organization would assign the gigging team and manager to a regular employee who is placed at a higher level in the hierarchy. The role of the IC manager would be limited to performance coaching and oversight, while the regular-employee manager would be assigned the responsibility of performance management. The gig employees would have a dual reporting relationship, with the weight to their performance ratings given by the gig and regular manager being distributed.

In organizations, which use tech-based performance management, they tend to use AI-enabled performance dashboards that monitor the gigging team's performance and provide them feedback. The performance indicators can be linked to their contractual payout, thus bringing the concept of 'self-managed teams' into practice in the organization. In the hybrid strategy, a mix of talent-based and tech-based management is used, through leveraging technology for operational performance indicators and having a regular reporting/reviewing manager carry out the strategic performance reviews.

Performance Rigour

A critical factor impacting the success or failure of an organization to optimize the benefits of its gig strategy would be the performance rigour in its systems. The performance rigour in an organization is a function of several sub-factors that include culture, leadership, role clarity, performance communication

Figure 8.14. Gig Workers and Performance Rigour

(communication of KRAs and conduct of regular reviews), leveraging of technology for oversight and linking of rewards to performance results.

Organizations leveraging gig talent score higher in relation to those that do not, in terms of creating and nurturing a culture and systems that drive performance rigour. First, the leadership has a clear view of strategy design and execution.

> **JEFF BEZOS AND PERFORMANCE RIGOUR AT AMAZON**
>
> Jeff Bezos, with respect to leadership connection, shares three critical mantras for creating a culture of performance excellence at Amazon. He emphasizes having performance standards that have a high level of stretch built into them. Organizations that aspire for and set high standards would be able to align their employees to delivering higher levels of performance. Organizations that do not have a culture of high standards would have even their employees with potential adjusting to a lower level of performance delivery.
>
> The second mantra is setting clear expectations and communicating to employees what level of 'quality' is expected. At Amazon, unlike in

other organizations, there are no PowerPoint presentations. Instead, employees are asked to come up with a six-page performance memo that includes a narrative of how they have approached performance quality in the job. Unlike PowerPoint presentations, memos cannot be created in an hour or two; employees, while writing their memos, realize that documenting their performance calls for intense introspection and self-engagement. The memo-writing process takes a couple of days for the employees.

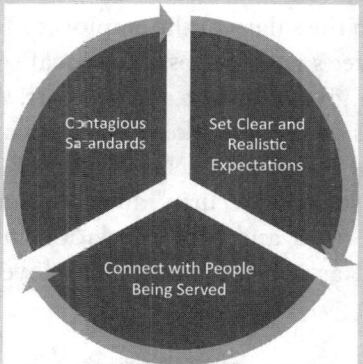

Leaders/employees should be encouraged to stay connected with their organization's end customers. Bezos personally reads all the emails in his mail box received through the public jeff@amazon.com. This is a way for him to have a view of 'customer experience and feedback'. For Bezos, customer feedback holds more value than competitor data. He tries to cross-validate his company's performance indicators with customer feedback. The inputs from the cross-validation help him in formulating a 'feedforward and response strategy' to stay ahead of the competition.

Source: https://www.entrepreneur.com/article/312374

Social Security Benefits for Gig Workers

Employees, when they sign up for a full-time job, get access to social security benefits, which are provided by their employers.

These benefits include retirement benefits (provident fund, gratuity), apart from the benefits like medical/accident/death insurance for both themselves and their dependents. The question here is: should the decision of an individual to opt for a gig career automatically result in their losing these benefits?

Social security has psychological, physical and financial dimensions. Organizations offer social security in three major dimensions. The first is individual subscription to subscription and the organizational contribution to the social security benefits, based on the salary of the employee. The group security is due to employee's need for psychological security, to be part of a team, which gives comfort and support. An individual has basic social needs and would like to relate to a set of individual, through a formal relationship. Unfortunately, in the case of a gig worker, this sense of security does not exist, as the person does not have a fixed and formal relationship but a nomadic relationship, and as a result the gig employee constantly gets

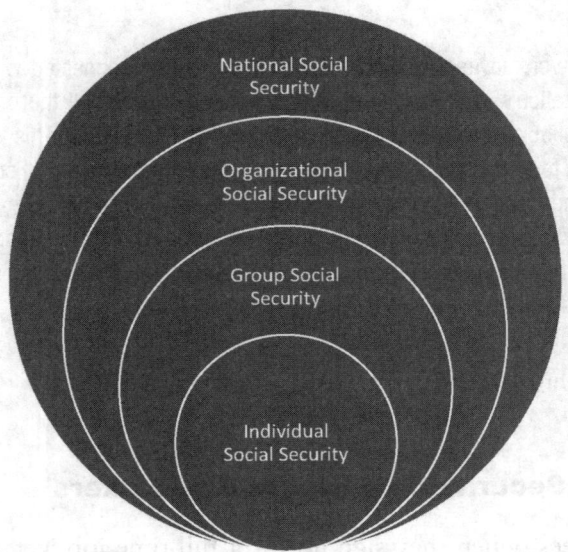

Figure 8.15. Gig Workers and Social Security Levels

into temporal relationships as a transient member. The regular employees with whom the gig employee works would not accord lower preference to their relationship with them as compared to their relationships with regular employees.

Regular employees get retirement benefits, like gratuity, that are designed to provide financial security at the end of their formal working life, to partly meet their financial needs of old age. In addition, they get other benefits, like medical insurance and group/personal accident insurance, that take care of the psychological and financial needs of the employees and their dependents in the event of health issues or mishaps, like an accident, that result in partial/total disability or death. In the case of gig workers, they do not have access to these benefits because of the nature of their contractual relationship.

National security benefits are the set of benefits that the citizens of a country get from their national/state government. The range of benefits include medical/disability insurance, unemployment support, etc. In the United States, social security is termed as OASDI (Old-Age, Survivors and Disability Insurance), which gets administered through the payroll taxes and federal contributions. Developing economies, due to their weak financial position, have not been able to extend comprehensive and robust financial support to their citizens. In countries like India at the bottom of the pyramid, employees working in the organized sector have access to some of these benefits; for instance, the Employee State Insurance Act (ESI Act) in India guarantees certain benefits, but the percentage of employees getting covered through this is minuscule compared to the overall population.

Thankfully, the trend is changing across economies, as countries have realized the need to step in and offer social security to gig workers, as their proportion in the workforce is rising rapidly. It is imperative that countries create a conducive environment to take care of gig workers, both from health and economic perspectives, to ensure that their citizens are encouraged to opt for gig work without being worried about their social security benefits, which are mixed. In the United States, during a federal investigation, it was reported that independent contractors had not paid taxes worth USD 3.9 billion, and on-demand workers had not paid taxes amounting to USD 2 billion. The reasons for this include misreporting and employees not realizing the need to report their earnings. As a result, gig workers are forced to pay for their social security. In a sense, the social security net is getting weaker for gig workers.

In India, recently, the government realized the need to take care of both employees working in the unorganized sector and gig workers and legislated a regulatory amendment in the form of four labour codes. The Code on Social Security, 2020 identifies four major types of workers: employees in the formal sector, employees in the unorganized sector, gig workers and platform workers. The old labour acts were designed around formal-employment contracts. The gig employees working for app-based aggregators were not even defined as employees. Such employers did not specify the working hours either, and the gig workers chose the number of hours they would work based on their earning needs. Most gig workers were defined as independent contractors, which made it difficult for them to be covered with benefits under various acts. The new code has taken care of these loopholes. It mandates the establishment of national- and state-level boards for administering welfare schemes for workers in the unorganized sector. The National Social Security Board has representation from four major segments:

- Five representatives of aggregators, nominated by the central government;
- Five representatives of gig workers and platform workers, nominated by the central government;
- The Director-General of the Employees' State Insurance Corporation (ESIC); and
- Five representatives of state governments.

The board shall periodically consider the needs of gig and platform workers and advise the central and state governments on the steps to be taken towards their welfare.

Uncertainty in the Life and Career of Gig Workers

Gig workers experience a high level of uncertainty in their life of gigs. Unlike full-time employees, who have an assured income and a defined life, gig workers are always on a roller coaster. Their life has aspects of 'living in the moment' and not worrying about the next day. It may sound like a romantic way of leading life, but the reality is far from this dreamy picture. Millennials and Gen Z find it easy to relate to and explore the gig lifestyle, as they have parental support to fall back on. This is not the case with tenured professionals who are in their late 30s or mid-40s, who have responsibilities towards their family. Trying to support a family without having a fixed income is like starting on a voyage on a ship with limited fuel. The ship can be rocked any time for want of fuel. The key challenges faced by gig workers are:

Figure 8.16. Gig Workers and Challenges

Gig workers have a serious 'work–life imbalance', as they are under constant pressure to impress their client/organization to get their contract extended. The competition among gig workers is so hard that for any opportunity there are scores of gig workers competing with each other to bag the contract. They have to deal with the issues like not being part of a network or being an outsider while competing for work. Second, the performance pressure on gig workers is always high, as organizations try to optimize their ROI for gig payouts. As a result, the supervision of gig workers is much higher as compared to that of regular employees. The gig workers end up agreeing to aggressive timelines for delivery of projects/completion of work. The life of a gig worker is akin to that of entrepreneurs, who have to struggle to prove themselves to both the self and the world.

Further, 'financial pressure' adds to the pressure on gig workers, especially in the case of those who come from a weak financial background. The factors such as their lifestyle, life stage and responsibilities/commitments add to the pressure on gig workers. In the case of millennials/Gen Z, since their focus is on getting instant gratification and chasing momentary pleasures, they tend to blow their income as fast as they earn. Their level of indebtedness is high, as they easily opt for credit purchases through EMI payments. Trying to make EMI payments without having an assured income or with a vacillating income is like having the sword of Damocles hanging over one's head. In the case of tenured professionals, they have to deal with regular payouts, such as rent, EMIs for home/vehicles, children's education, healthcare for themselves and their dependents, etc. The financial commitments add to the financial pressure, which in turn forces gig workers to overstretch, losing work-life balance.

When gig workers, as part of their job contracts, deal with organizations/employees, they tend to feel like an outsider, especially in large/bureaucratic organizations that have large clearances for outsiders to get access to their systems/people. They may get temporary access, which obviously would have restrictions. Quite often, they end up becoming dependent on employees even for small issues, like having a conference room booked for a meeting or reaching out to stakeholders who are not part of their regular contact list. They tend to experience the dilemma of whether they are an outsider or an insider. The situations like the COVID-19 pandemic have exposed the perils or the uglier side of the gig life.

EMPLOYEE EXPERIENCE OF AN OLA CAB DRIVER

Brijesh is a migrant from the district of Muzaffarpur, in the state of Bihar, India, who is now living in Delhi NCR (National Capital Region), India. He is the eldest sibling, followed by three sisters. His aged parents live in his native place and survive through farming three acres of land inherited from their ancestors. He is married and has two young children. His wife works as a domestic help in a nearby colony.

He was earlier working as a driver for the CEO of a large firm (through an outsourced contractor) and has over five years of work experience. He was paid a salary of ₹20,000 that included statutory payouts like PF, ESI, etc. He made a living from hand to mouth, as he had to take care of not just his immediate family but also his aged parents. He had long working hours, from 8.00 am to 11.00 pm.

After hearing from his friends about opportunities to earn better (between ₹70,000 and ₹80,000) through joining as a driver-partner with a cab aggregator, he took the plunge to become a driver-partner and bought a car. However, his dreams turned sour, as the cab aggregator lowered his incentives. His initial income, which was around ₹70,000, came down sharply to ₹30,000 per month. He had to pay a vehicle EMI of ₹10,000 and handle costs of maintenance and repairs, which went up to ₹5,000 per month. The net result was that his overall income came down to ₹15,000 per month. To get his incentives, he had to drive for long hours through the serpentine city traffic, which never ended and was full of pollution. He had to work for between 13 and 15 hours to meet the mileage and earnings criteria, in order to be eligible to get the incentives. His health suffered hugely, as he faced back problems due to the long and continuous hours of driving without being able to take breaks even for biological needs or to have food. In addition to the back problem, he was suffering from acidity and a gas problem as well.

> His life had 'jumped out of the frying pan into the fire'. Brijesh wondered if he had taken the right decision to work as a driver-partner. He toyed with the idea of selling his car and returning to a regular driver profile or to his native place, to either become a farm labourer or cultivate his agricultural land.

Gig workers experience an 'identity crisis' in their lives. They may flash their independence and autonomy, which they gained through trading off their regular careers, but they do not have the glamour attached to working with a large organization. In a country like India, which has seen high levels of poverty and suffering in the initial days of its independence, people attach a lot of importance to having a regular job, as it signals financial safety and security. In fact, initially, preference was given to only government jobs, as people considered them as a lifetime assurance for a safe life. It was only after the liberalization in the 1990s, with the reduced number of opportunities, that people looked at private jobs as a safe alternative to government jobs. In lower and middle classes, one who would not married, if one were to on his own, as the prospective bride's father would not like to risk the life of his daughter with a man, who had no stable income.

Gig workers' peers and social circles tend to treat them as being in the 'in-between-jobs phase' and make such remarks as, 'Oh, why did you give up such a good job?', 'You were getting a good salary. How will you manage now without any stable earnings?', 'You have taken such a huge risk to start something on your own' and 'You have committed a big mistake'. Such remarks take away the sheen from the life of gig workers and tend to push them back into introspection—'Have I taken the right decision?'

The members of a society go through three major stages to be identified as part of a social group and have their social identity defined. In the first step, they get classified on the basis of a given

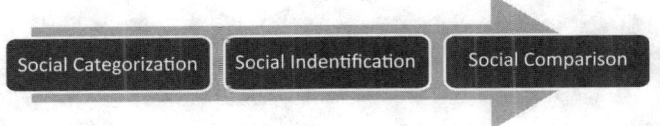

Figure 8.17. Social Identity Stages

dimension or a set of dimensions. For instance, all employees working in a society could be classified as government employees, banking professionals or IT professionals, based on the type of organization they are employed in.

Employees working in different sectors carry the identity of their respective sectors. For instance, those in the IT sector are classified as IT professionals and are accorded a high level of prestige in society due to the factors such as their knowledge, earnings, exposure and work-like balance (5 days of work in a week). Employees working in the public sector are identified as individuals with a high level of social prestige, due to their assured retirement benefits like pension and free access to healthcare services.

In the comparison stage, members of a group compare and contrast themselves with those of other groups in terms of the benefits/privileges they have over the latter. For instance, IT professionals may rank themselves better due to their pay and benefits, international exposure and fast-track career path. They tend to carry out a comparison to assure themselves individually and collectively of their superior conditions in relation to those of members of other groups.

Gig workers may identify themselves as such and claim to have benefits, such as freedom, earning potential, work-life balance and the ability to take risks and innovate. This is the 'perceived identity' that they use to project and create a 'projected identity' for themselves. Their reality is far from this, resulting in an 'identity crisis' among gig workers—their actual situation may be quite in contrast to their projected identity. Gig workers are bound to

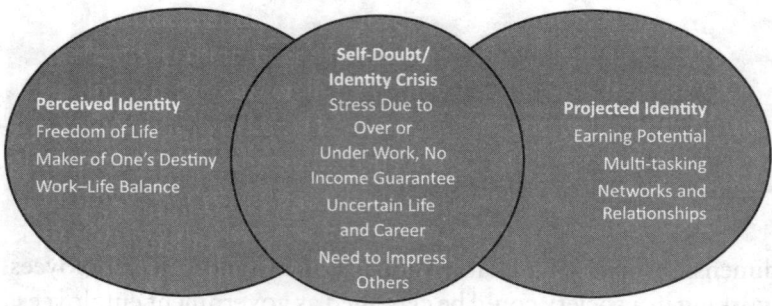

Figure 8.18. Identity Crisis of Gig Workers

suffer from a lack of 'identity cohesion', as their projected identity is not in sync with their reality, and they have 'role confusion'—confusion on whether they are employees or not.

Gig workers tend to constantly experience identity crisis and self-doubt on three major counts. The first aspect involves their inability to meet their own aspirations about being a gig worker. None of their aspirations—freedom in life, ability to make their own destiny, work-life balance, choice of work—gets fulfilled. They are forced to choose work/projects in demand, to assure themselves through the income. They have to do overtime to impress their clients/employers and get more work or positive references in the future. They experience stress due to their projected identity of having earning potential, multitasking ability, networks and assurance. They feel obligated to live up to the expectations that people around them have towards them based on the projected identity they have created for themselves.

Gig workers also experience stress due to being overworked, as they do not like to say no to the jobs coming their way. Saying no to jobs/projects would imply subjecting themselves to the risk of displeasing the employer/client, which can impact their relationship with them and consequently impact their future projects. In the alternative scenario, the gig workers would have less work, which can lead to frustration. The unpredictable flow of work impacts their income flow, which adds a high level of uncertainty to their life. When they see their peers in regular jobs with an assured income scaling up the career ladder, they start questioning their decision to be a gig worker. Their family and social networks complicate their life through constant comparisons that often take the angle of critiquing, which can push the gig workers deeper into self-doubt. Negative life events, like ill health in the family or job loss of another family member, can accentuate the stress, on both psychological and financial counts.

Gig workers, by virtue of being on their own, realize the need to demonstrate socially acceptable/responsible behaviour to maintain positivity in relationships, which holds the key for them to keep their networks/job contacts intact. This is in sharp contrast to the general belief that one does not have to always be politically correct as a freelancer. In regular jobs, employees are under constant pressure to please peers/bosses and other stakeholders to ensure that they are not labelled as politicking and bickering employees who are difficult to get along with. In contemporary workplaces, perceptions tend to overpower performance and can seriously impact employees.

Gig workers' experiences on the count of 'work-life balance' tend to add to their identity crisis, as they see themselves slogging for long hours in comparison to regular employees. The comparison is made not just by them but also within the social circles around them. The comments from family members and friends like, 'Oh, you were better off as an employee than you are as a gig worker. You seem to be working long hours now, not sure if you are making commensurate income', push them into a state of 'self-doubt'. They tend to perceive a sense of 'lack of control' over their life. Instead of realizing their aspiration of being in control of their life, they end up being caught in the grind of competition and income assurance and completely lose sight of 'work-life balance', which defeats the very purpose of being a gig worker.

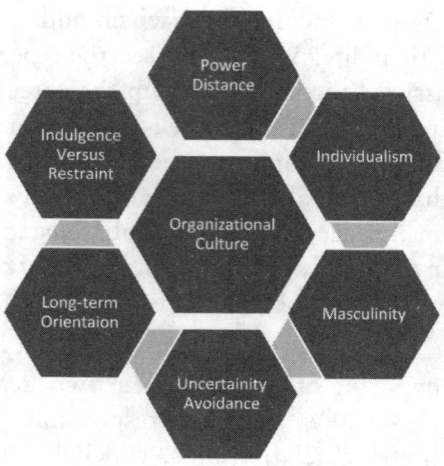

Figure 8.19. Gig Workers and Organizational Culture

The gig workers' state of being part of a team and yet not being a part of the team puts them in a constant dilemma of 'inclusion versus exclusion'. They would wonder whether they are really a part of the team. They would often discover that regular employees would have team bonding while they get treated as an outsider, though they equally contribute to the success of the team/organization. The cultural dimensions in an organization can impact their inclusion-versus-exclusion dilemma and EX.

An organization with a high level of 'power distance' is likely to differentiate between regular and gig employees. The latter would perceive a clear sense of segregation and may end up feeling like second-class citizens. The regular employees are likely to collude to create a sense of superiority among themselves and may attempt to boss over the gig workers to get a feeling of being in control and perpetuate/legitimize their power. Typically, large organizations with a rigid bureaucracy would exhibit such indicators. One can find organizations in manufacturing, large conglomerates and, more importantly, those in the public sector and the government to have these issues. Gig workers end up having a negative EX in such organizations.

Gig employees working in an organization with a high level of 'individualism' would find it easy to relate to it and work, as the organization's employees would not have a group identity. Organizations operating in the knowledge sector, such as in the IT/ITeS, consulting, research and academic areas, would have cultural indicators, due to the high level of individualized self-identity of the employees which comes from their high level of skills and expertise. Such employees do not have to depend on the organizational identity to derive strength for their self-identity. Such an environment is conducive for gig workers, who are also skilled professionals trying to make their mark and living on their own. The commonalities in their personality and their approach towards life and career would make it easy for gig and regular employees to gel well with each other. An organization with this dominant cultural dimension would offer a positive EX to gig workers.

Organizations with a high level of *masculinity* will have-its employees exhibit behaviors such as high ego orientation, emphasis on money material things, core focus of life is work, and focus on material prosperity will have love-hate relationship with egos. Gig workers, by virtue of their orientation towards independence and deep and clear sense of self-identity, would have relatively high levels of ego. There is bound to be a situation of tension and unease when they come across individuals with similar traits; as the adage goes, 'like poles are bound to repel each other'. The emphasis on success and materialistic things would add to the conflict between the gig and regular workers. It would be difficult for the leaders and HR managers to manage the situation, as their job would be akin to 'keeping two warring parties at bay'. Gig workers are bound to have neutral-to-negative EX in such organizations. Organizations operating in highly competitive sectors would have these cultural traits; examples of these are players in the FMCG sector, like Pepsi, which operate in an environment of cut-throat competition which makes them ruthless and success-oriented. In the process, they take away or lower the human elements like showing empathy and being accommodating, as not doing so would sound the death knell for their business.

Organizations with high levels of 'uncertainty avoidance' would be a difficult place for gig workers to fit in, as the regular employees would have low affinity to uncertainty in situations around them. Gig workers, by the design of their relationship with organizations, bring in transience in the relationship and induce uncertainty. The regular employees would find it difficult to digest the uncertainty brought in by the gig workers into the system. The latter would have to fight hard to get a buy-in for themselves. The key challenge for the gig workers would be to get a buy-in and prove their worth and need, more than their work/contributions. It would be an uphill task for them to gain acceptance and get opportunities to contribute. The EX of gig workers in such organizations would be defined by tension and stress, which make it largely negative. Given an opportunity, gig workers would prefer to stay away from such organizations, due to the 'negative EX'.

Organizations with a 'long-term orientation' would have a long-term focus and would have their employees sacrificing short-term gains for future benefits for both them and the organization. The work ethics of the regular employees and gig workers would be aligned. The latter would have sacrificed the elements like job security and income assurance to make a mark for themselves and create a space/opportunity to do what they like in life, be it in the personal or the professional space. Along with them, the regular employees would be able to appreciate the long-term pay-offs to the organization and themselves through the gig strategy adopted by the organization. The responsibility of the leadership/HR in such organizations would be to have a continuous narrative of and conversations around the need for and importance of employing gig workers. The gig workers may have a 'positive EX' in such organizations.

Organizations with *high levels of indulgence* will have its employees looking for instant gratification and those with restraint will its employees being perseverant and sacrificing in nature and approach both in personal and professional lives. Gig workers would find instant acceptance in such organizations, as they offer instant help to solve the latter's problems around the issues like talent and skill shortage. They would bring in support to deal with the excess workload immediately, and there would be no long-term issues with them. Organizations with *high level of restraint* with its employees being appreciate of organizational needs to right size to optimize the talent, preferring of gig talent over hiring regular talent, to adjust to the organizational strategies. Gig workers would have a positive EX in organizations with an orientation towards indulgence or restraint.

Being employed and yet not being part of the employee group inflates the identity crisis and role confusion of gig workers.

These cultural dimensions were identified by Hofstede in his seminal cross-cultural research across different countries in the world. Thanks to globalization and digitization, national cultures are undergoing a transformation through the processes of diffusion and integration. The digital world is breaking the barriers between countries and cultures, making the world truly boundary-less. In the contemporary workplace, it is but natural to see cultural diversity in both form and spirit. Cultural diversity in form is being viewed as a strategic necessity by organizations, who are tracking it through a talent diversity index. The talent diversity index has become inclusive from two perspectives: (a) through including gigs; and (b) through measuring diversity considering gig workers as a sub-component of the talent pool. These initiatives are helping to create a favourable environment for gig workers to be welcomed into workplaces and slowly increasing their representation in the talent pool across various dimensions.

Employee Experience Strategy for Gig Workers

It is easy for an organization to join the bandwagon and employ gig workers, but being successful in this endeavour calls for meticulous planning for effectively leveraging and integrating the latter into the system. In the first place, the leadership/organization needs to be clear about the business context and strategy for which it wants to deploy gig talent. For instance, employing of gig drivers fits well into a digital market place model-based organization, as they run their business boundary less across geographies, as they offer to facilitate the buyers and sellers of the sellers of products/services. This is the reason why the players like Amazon and Uber could effectively deploy the gig strategy to run their operations—because their business model is a hybrid of centralized and distributed architecture. The core functions that facilitate the connectivity and monitor the operations have been centralized, while the rest of the operations have been allowed to be distributed geographically. This was done for three reasons: (a) operational and supply chain effectiveness; (b) agility and scalability; and (c) cost-effectiveness. The COVID-19 pandemic has made these companies rethink their core functions as well. They have allowed their employees to operate remotely from home. This has given them an opportunity to revisit their strategy for hiring and engaging talent. The original idea was that talent working in core areas had to be centralized and had to operate from the controlling offices. This is not the case anymore, since employees can now operate from home; this has raised strategy questions for the digital-marketplace players:

1. Should these employees be from the same geography/place?
2. Why cannot these talents comprise gig workers?
3. Why cannot gig workers be hired and allowed to operate remotely?

Currently, most of these players offer 24x7 services, which requires them to pick up and drop regular employees safely, especially those working late hours. The second dimension is that most of them have gender diversity as high as 50 per cent, which makes it necessary for them to ensure that the female employees are picked up and dropped safely, especially during the late hours. In one sense, the operational logistics of picking up and dropping employees has become as large as that of managing employees' work in the office. Due to the two factors discussed above, these organizations are outsourcing employee logistics to third parties, which consumes a fair amount of their time, cost and resources.

The question is: should these organizations be investing so much energy in non-core operations. Third, in the event of a natural disaster or any other urban phenomenon, like social disruptions, their operations get impacted, as they face challenges in picking up and dropping their employees, leaving them vulnerable to external events. This leaves their service delivery adversely impacted. Having a business model that is challenged to manage the BCP/DRP (business continuity plan/disaster recovery plan)

Figure 8.20. COVID-19 Pandemic—Strategy/Staffing Issues

adds risks to their business which might impact their customer relationship and servicing adversely. Managing the majority of operations remotely has opened up new avenues for them, mainly for those organizations in the digital and knowledge services space. It has opened a window of opportunity to them and made them rethink the staffing question and ask themselves: should we not leverage the pandemic experience to revisit our fundamental assumptions on having all employees working in the office and managing work-life balance and diversity inclusion (gender, differently abled, etc.)? Most organizations in the digital and knowledge services space face the issue of managing the work-life balance of their employees. In large cities, employees tend to spend an equivalent of about 25 per cent of their office time in commuting to the office. Now if this element can be removed, employees would get significant savings on their time, which would add positively to their work-life balance, thus improving their engagement and motivation levels. A recent survey indicates that more than 50 per cent of the working Indian population would prefer remote working becoming a permanent feature for them, even if it means a slight reduction in their compensation.

The competitive digital world calls for agility and flexibility in operations and talent management, which has brought into focus a new phenomenon termed 'flexpertise', which refers to organizations being able to identify and engage experts (gig talent) in a flexible way. For an organization to design and deploy the flexpertise strategy, it needs to have three components in place.

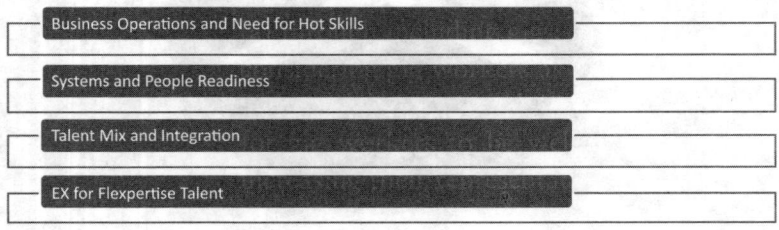

Figure 8.21. Gig Workers and Flexpertise

The first step for the organization is to identify the areas of business operations where it needs to leverage and deploy flexperts. The second step is to decide whether it wants to hire and deploy flexperts or gig workers for its talent needs. It needs to have systems/technology in place to seamlessly integrate gig workers into the workflow. The people dynamics would be more conducive in remote working as compared to physical co-location of talent. Employees, when they work remotely, are likely to be more open to working with gig workers/flexperts, as they themselves are working remotely in a flexible way. Trying to have peer employees, who are on flexi terms (gig employees) is easy for employees to relate and work with.

The organizational design and the need for and importance of gig workers/flexperts must be clearly articulated to all the employees, and the employees must be advised to create space for the gig workers/flexperts. The core of this talent strategy is 'job design/redesign'. The conventional job design focused on aggregating job elements into one block and consequently into roles. In a complex environment, it may not always be feasible

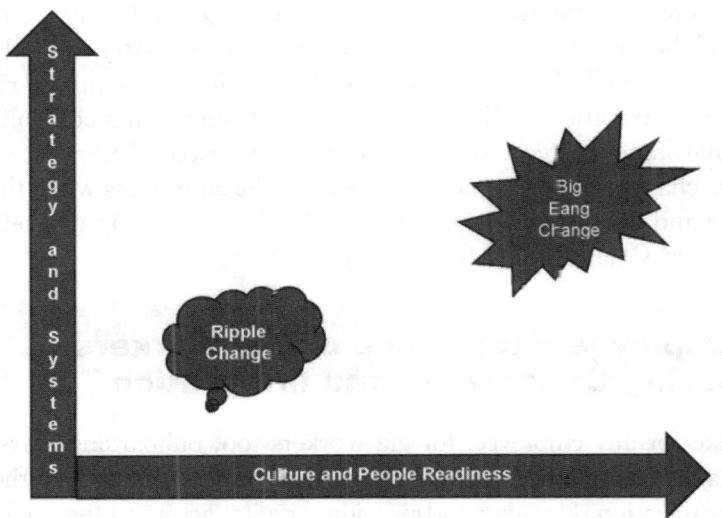

Figure 8.22. Gig Strategy and Change Management

Employee Experience of Gig Employees | 345

for organizations to have talent who are multi-skilled, or there could be an operational need to have skill diversity within the same job. This may call for redesigning of jobs into diverse and distinct job elements. This may sound radical but could be the order of the day in the future with digital and remote workplaces. Employees who are used to viewing jobs in the conventional format of integrated job elements need to prepare for this radical organizational transformation. Depending on the culture of an organization, it could opt for either a 'big-bang transformation' or a 'ripple transformation'.

An organization adopting the big-bang approach would undertake a one-shot transformation of jobs and deployment of gig workers/flexperts. This would expose the organization to huge risks on all fronts: operational, systems and people risk. Not many leaders would be comfortable in exposing their organization to such a high risk. On the contrary, through adopting the ripple approach, the organization would identify small areas of operations, design systems and jobs, train and orient the existing employees towards the change and execute the change. The success of small ripple efforts would be widely showcased in the organization for it to gey buy-ins from internal and external stakeholders and scale up/expand the transformation to other areas as well. The ripple approach helps the leadership de-risk the organization, by limiting the trials of change in a controlled environment, create success and make it visible. Acceptance of the change is likely to be higher among the employees when they see and hear about the positive impact/success of gig workers'/flexperts' deployment in their organization.

Employee Experience of Gig Workers During Onboarding and Integration

Like for any employee, for gig workers too, onboarding plays a major role in how they join, settle down in and integrate with their organization. Planning and providing digital access to the organizational culture and ethos, designed in an interactive format, would help the gig workers understand the organization's business strategy/structure and systems. Gig Employee's introduction/orientation designed on a self-learning format, with elements of gamification and AI, would make it easy for the gig workers to learn at their own pace. Conducting a self-assessment and tracking the learner score would help both the gig workers and the organization evaluate the effectiveness of the learning from the orientation.

> **WOW EXPERIENCE AND DIGITAL ONBOARDING FOR GIG WORKERS IN E-COMMERCE ORGANIZATIONS**
>
> For the large e-commerce players like Amazon and Flipkart, the majority of CX is delivered at the customer's place. The CX design includes small things, such as the delivery partner calling up the customer before reaching their place, to check on the customer's availability and inform of their arrival, greeting them while delivering the package and taking the customer's signature as an authentication of receipt of the package. Amazon and Flipkart have thousands of delivery partners working gigs across the length and breadth of the country. The question is: how do the e-commerce players carry out the orientation for these delivery partners? The challenge for the HR and learning team would be to reach and train these delivery partners, who have poor Internet bandwidth and quite often no access to the gadgets like laptop or desktops, at a low cost.
>
> The learning team would have to depend on the appification approach using AI to orient the gig workers. They can schedule a virtual onboarding event for delivery partners from diverse locations to help them experience a grand welcome. This would induce in the latter a feeling of being part of a large organization/team and give them a wow experience at the time of their welcome. Arrangement of a brief session for them addressed by one of the operational leaders would send the message to the gig workers that they are valued and honoured for them to be able to interact with one of the leading members in the organization.
>
> The learning team can leverage the app of the organization to ensure that the gig partners go through micro-videos, which can

> be accessed in English or the vernacular language, to help the latter understand the nuances of interacting with customers while servicing them. They can be trained through interactive videos on identifying customer locations, updating about completed deliveries on the app and, in the case of return of a package, checking the details of the goods to be returned by the customer on the app, checking the status of the goods being returned by the customer and authenticating it on the app, and sending confirmation of the goods' return and the refund status to the customer, through an AI-linked supply chain management process, all monitored in a centralized way by the e-commerce players. The learning team would have to work with the operations and technical teams to create training communication and videos as and when the organization carries out a process change, to ensure that the delivery partners are on board with the changed process.

The manager and team members, if they are preoccupied with their jobs/tasks, either forget to extend a welcome or end up extending a plastic welcome to a gig worker on the latter's first day, which gives a negative EX to the gig worker. The HR would have to set up a welcoming interaction for the gig worker with the manager and the team, to ensure that they get introduced to each other properly and the gig worker does not scramble in the new place trying to relate to the team. Small initiatives, like setting up a tea or snacks session after the introduction, would ensure that the orientation process has an icebreaker in an informal setting which makes it easy for the team/employees and the gig workers to connect with each other. In a remote working environment, the HR can schedule a digital meeting to ensure that the onboarding experience is as smooth as physical onboarding.

The three key players during this onboarding process are the HR, reporting manager and peers. The HR needs to have constant and triangular conversations with the gig workers/ flexperts and the reporting manager, to set the role expectations in terms of operational nuances and deliverables. In case of regular employees, HR typically tends to assign the resource to reporting manager and leave between employee and manager and carry out a periodical dip to check on the status/comfort of the new hire. In the case of gig workers, the HR would have a major role to play. Trying to adopt an approach similar to that for regular-employee facilitation would not yield the desired results and instead could lead to a fiasco. HR role needs to transform to integrate and ensure that the gig settles and the relationship becomes a win-win, both for the organization and the gigs.

The first focus for the HR is to facilitate the gig workers' relationships, to ensure that the latter experience themselves to be an integral part of the organization. The regular employees, by virtue of their relationship with the organization, tend to settle down easily into their roles, due to the group and relationship dynamics between team members at the workplace. The gig workers, on the other hand, have a differentiated relationship with the organization. If they were to operate in the remote working format, it would add new dimensions to the relationship. The regular employees and gig workers would not be located at the same place and would be working remotely on their jobs. In this situation, the regular employees are likely to warmly welcome the gig workers and accept them as part of their teams, in contrast to the situation in the physical workplace. Millennials/Gen Z, who are used to digital networking and relationships, would find it easier to bond with gig workers than Gen X, who have spent most of their work lives working in

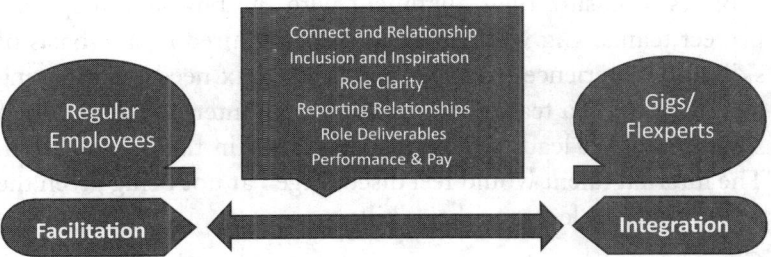

Figure 8.23. Gig Strategy and Change Management

traditional roles and in organizational designs/structures that are traditional.

Role Clarity and Performance System

The first step for the HR would be to introduce the gig worker to all the internal stakeholders that the latter would have to deal with as part of their role. At the same time, the HR has to ensure that the gig worker is introduced to the external stakeholders as well. The HR would have a critical role in clarifying the reporting relationships of the gig worker with the managers, to ensure that the gig worker does not face issues in understanding their role. The process of role clarification, along with clarification on the reporting relationships and performance goals, needs to be undertaken jointly by the HR PoC and the reporting manager. Clarifying the performance goals, along with the performance management system, is key to aligning the gig worker to the performance system.

Pay and Rewards Predictability

The pay and rewards strategy of organizations for gig workers vary based on the level at which the gig talent are hired by them. The other factors affecting the strategy include the culture- and people-centricity of the organization and the regulatory norms guiding it. For instance, organizations in the IT sector engage gig workers as project consultants and map them to specific projects to ensure their alignment with the business in specific project teams. Gig workers are also being hired on the basis of skill and experience mapping and talent mix needs. Employing a gig worker in a team that already has an internal talent with a similar skill set leads to talent redundancy in the organization. The internal talent would feel discouraged at not being given the opportunity to leverage their skills.

Gig talent at the top- and middle-management levels are being hired for specific durations for either a monthly consolidated pay or payouts linked to stages of project completion, or a hybrid of both. A monthly consolidated pay would be a win-loss arrangement between a gig worker and an organization; the former would get an assured income/payout from the latter, but the organization would find it difficult to link the performance of the gig worker with their traction. Typically, such an arrangement is restricted to specific professionals, like legal or taxation professionals. Such professionals are hired on a retainership-fee basis, with an upper limit on the number of cases/projects and type of service delivery undertaken by the gig talent with niche skills. Talent with niche skills and senior level talent not like to short-changed on payout Vs extent of skill service delivery offered by them.

For technical professionals, such as civil engineers, domain consultants and tech professionals, the engagement and payout terms are a mix of fixed monthly payouts and performance incentives linked to project completion. The type of performance-linked incentives could vary between plain vanilla incentives and those linked to project completion and timelines. Organizations with performance rigour build stretch performance incentives into the variable pay for a gig consultant, to motivate the latter's better performance through early completion of projects, positive client feedback, etc. This is a win-win situation for the gig worker and the organization, with the former drawing a fixed monthly payout to meet their operational/living expenses and also being motivated to stretch and contribute better performance for incentives.

The e-commerce organizations Ola, Uber, Big Basket, Zomato, Amazon and Flipkart between them employ close to 1 million

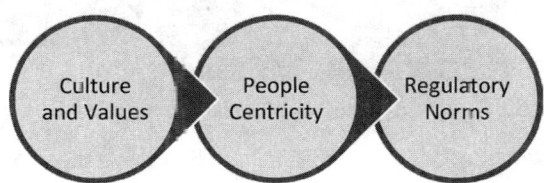

Figure 8.24. Factors Impacting Gig Pay Strategy

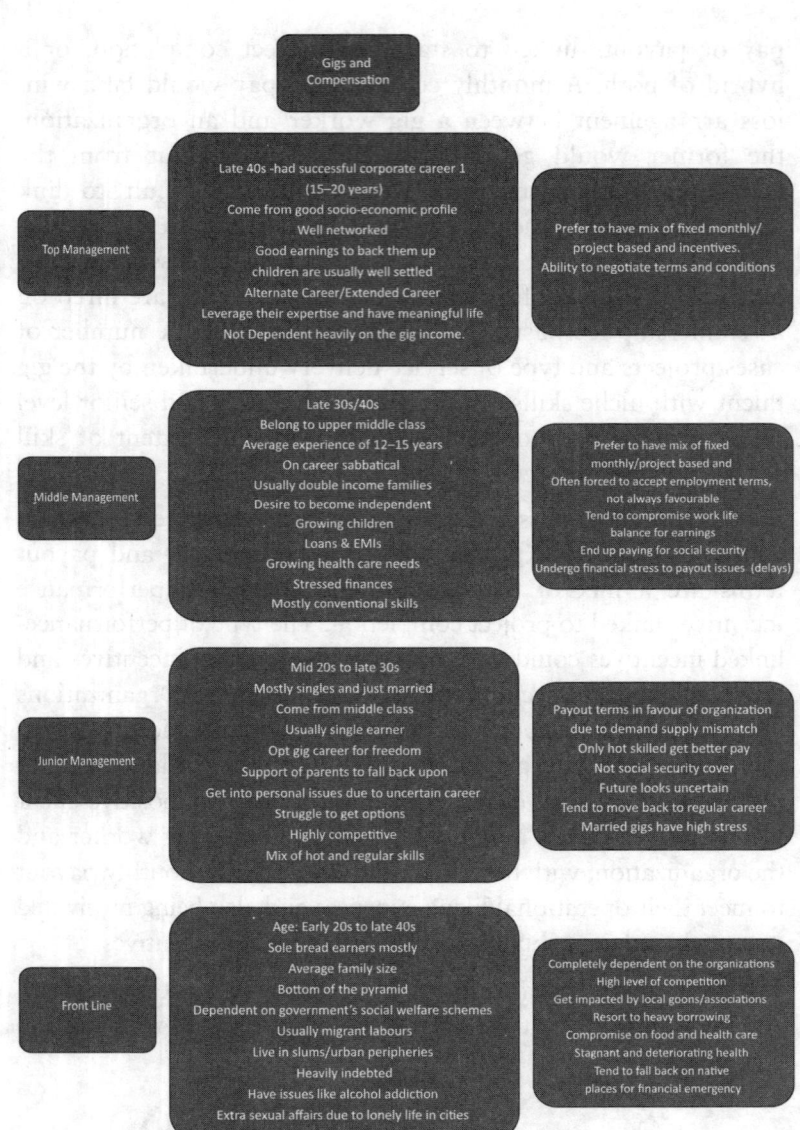

Figure 8.25. Gigs: Ecosystem and Issues

partners across India. Except for drivers, who were initially being paid close to ₹80,000 per month, the other partners were earning anywhere between ₹15,000 and ₹20,000 per month; most of the earnings were in the form of performance incentives, and there was no fixed component. This led to a situation where driver-partners ended up working 18–20 hours a day to earn their incentives. Their monthly earnings came down drastically to ₹25,000, due to the factors such as reduction of incentives, increase in the number of drivers, which reduced the number of rides per driver per day, terms and conditions attached to the incentives, increased percentage of commission charged by the cab aggregators, city traffic conditions that made it almost impossible for them to meet the incentive payout terms and conditions, ageing due to high usage of vehicles in adverse conditions and increase in the cost of repairs. The players like Big Basket discovered a high churn among their delivery partners, which adversely impacted their operational efficiency. They realized the need for introducing a hybrid payout system that balances both the fixed-income needs of the partners and the variable incentives that take care of the performance needs of the organization.

The above ecosystem indicates that except for gig workers operating at the top-management level, those at all other levels are facing severe financial stress in their lives. The extent of the impact may vary across levels of management, and gig workers face the intense stress at the frontline level. The COVID-19 pandemic has exposed the financial distress of gig life, and it has delivered a severe blow to the transition of economies to gig economies across the world.

Governments too have realized the need to take care of gig workers. Developed economies, like the United States and Europe, have in place well-designed social-security systems offering unemployment pension and health coverage to take care of gig workers. The issue is more serious in the developing economies across Asia and Africa, where the levels of income are low. The governments are financially stressed and offer sparse social-security support to their citizens. The countries like India have initiated legal reforms aimed at gig employees' welfare. India's Code on Social Security, 2020 has helped create welfare boards at the national and state levels. The Indian government has extended universal health insurance ('Ayushman Bharat Yojana') to driver-partners working with cab aggregators.

The government recently introduced more welfare measures for the welfare of driver-partners, such as health and life insurance. Cab aggregators are required to provide medical insurance of ₹500,000, starting immediately, and the insurance cover is to be extended progressively by 5 per cent every year to meet the inflationary needs of expenses related to medical treatment. Driver-partners are to be provided with a life insurance cover of ₹1 million to take care of the financial-security needs of their dependents in the event of the driver-partners' unfortunate death.

Gig Workers' Employee Experience: Insights and Issues

The percentage of gig workers in the overall workforce has been progressively increasing over the years. Employees across age groups, especially millennials and Gen Z, are opting to be gig workers by choice. Gen X are opting to become gig workers due to career and personal needs. The definition of old age for employee classification has come down to the early 40s from the late 50s couple of years. The average age of developing nations tend to be in the young age group, to their advantage, due to which employers are preferring fresh gig talent, who bring in energy and hot skills at a lower price point, over tenured talent. Irrespective of the reasons for the growth of gig workers, the gig economy is here to stay, and there is a felt need across all levels—individuals, organizations and governments—to mainstream and strengthen the gig-worker engagement process.

The strategies for gig workers are aimed at meeting not just their basic needs but those across all five levels of Maslow's hierarchy:

physiological needs, security needs, belongingness and love needs, esteem and self-actualization. Before looking at strategies aimed at the EX of gig workers, it would be pertinent to take their pulse on their current experiences across levels.

SNEAK PEEK INTO DRIVER PARTNERS' LIVES/FEEDBACK

'There is no time to balance family life income also very low incentives also need to improve drivers have to spend 12 to 14 hours in a day to get minimum salary'. —Uber driver

'Stressful, bad managers recently not giving respect to teams always need to work for whole eight hrs top management needs to be changed not worthy manager'. —Former city team lead

No value of delivery boy.

It's the best opportunity to earn more than 30,000 per month to undergraduate persons.

Overall very bad and poor experience through this pandemic situation because I did not get any help from you but your company deducted ₹800 from me. This was not fair with me so I stopped working with you.

This is my third organisation and the best organization ever in India. Overall work experience was very good as I worked in many departments and I saw the organization when it was growing very fast. I started work with logistics when we received only 3,000 from all cities of India; after that I saw that phase also when we started to receive two lakhs orders in a day. The working environment was perfect and the culture was unbelievable as we all celebrated all festivals together. If I am talking about career then everyone had equal to opportunity for growth. This was the only company who was paying the highest salary to employees. Finally I had work satisficiton at Zomato. —Senior Associate

Zomato layoff me during covid our manager always take burdens on us am working with full effort during lockdown but Zomato layoff me – Executive

All team leader good and back support team work is excellent but i am and others riders not happy because payout.

Unnecessary work pressure, seniors support – Senior executive

Working criteria is cool ..and a cool environment of working...this is a platform have to take leadership on your own job, if you want your personal and professional life to be cool.. —Logistics executive

I am very happy to work there beacuse there is very good work environment and culture. —Data entry operator

I haven't got any support from zomato . instead of supporting us zomato cut down the payout very badly by which I m forced to quit the zomato compny —Delivery boy

Teammates are supportive .Good work environment and culture. —Senior executive/team leader, anonymous

Management doesn't address our issues and there is a lot of politics

Some time when i needed a leave or senior not approved. It's not fault of Zomato It was the fault of our senior. Seniors was not analyzing the work according to ur hard & smart work. They only analysed, how many times hv u called them. If u have no issue, u r working since 2 years obviously u didn't have any issues and any question related to work. Thn why will u call and disturb him. Everything else was good.

Well career growth is slow, nd job security – Process associate, anonymous

Company always reduce your rate card. As a food delivery your career is not grow up- Food executive, anonymous

Source: https://www.ambitionbox.com/reviews/zomato-reviews

Gig Workers' Experiences and Expectations

It is important to analyse gig workers' current experiences before designing a workplace EX solution for them. Research was carried out to collect the workplace experiences shared by gig workers on various online portals, and a word cloud has been created to analyse the major points/insights from these experiences.

Gig workers face issues around having a 'good work environment'. The first focus area for them is getting pay and benefits commensurate with their efforts. The key grievance among them, especially among those in frontline and blue-collar jobs, is that organizations tweaked their financial incentives randomly, deviating from the initial norms. This has resulted in severe hardships for many of them. Such abrupt and sudden change lowers their trust in their employer, whom they perceive as

Figure 8.26. Gig Experience: Word Cloud

Employee Experience of Gig Employees | 357

being not dependable, and they find that their earnings and consequently their lives have become uncertain and risky, due to the career choices they have made.

The reason why most full-time employees quit their full-time job and choose to operate as a gig worker is to move away from the daily 'tyranny of bosses'. Unfortunately, life continues, and bosses continue to impact even their careers/lives as gig workers. In the case of gig workers at junior levels, the reporting manager has a say on their EX. The first aspect is work allocation, whereby bosses tend to allocate lower workloads to their favourites in contrast to others. Bosses need to be fair in work allocation, performance reviews and recommending for incentives to their team members. These issues continue to haunt employees even in the gig life as much as in the full-time life. The impact of bosses is much higher for gig workers, as the latter do not have a well-developed grievance mechanism like regular employees do. Thus, leaving major decisions to the discretion of only the reporting manager has its perils.

Organizations can moderate these negative aspects by strengthening supervision and oversight, through a mix of both technology and human interventions, over decisions on 'pay and benefits'. For instance, the service delivery quality indicators like service TAT and customer feedback can be calculated automatically using AI to score employees on their performance. The incentive calculations can be streamlined through backend linkage between them and performance indicators. Lack of social-security benefits is another area of concern for gig workers. In order to offer social security benefits to gigs employers could look at options offered by the government or team up with insurance service providers offering the co-payment option—payment of insurance premiums jointly by the employer and the employee. Portability of the insurance policy would be the key to ensuring the continuity of coverage. Ownership of the policy needs to be in the name of the gig employee, unlike in the case of regular employees, where the insurance coverage tends to lapse along with the employment contract.

The 'work-life balance' of gig workers is dependent on mutual collaboration. The primary onus of ensuring it rests with them and not so much with the organizations they work with. A gig worker has to calculate the time to be allocated for gigs to make earnings. Having said that, organizations have the responsibility to ensure that gig workers' job contracts and performance indicators are balanced and are not loaded against them. For this purpose, while deciding on the gig workers' workload, organizations can carry out an internal benchmarking exercise with regular employees. Gig employees tend to compare to weigh their pay & benefits Vs workload of regular employees. Along with internal benchmarking, it would be pertinent to carry out external benchmarking with competitors to ensure that there is external parity.

Employee Experience Model for Gig Workers

The integrated EX model has to identify the touchpoints across the ELC stages for gig workers and tech-enabled processes have to be designed to offer a wow EX to gig workers.

The execution of experience action items by an organization at each touch-point can be validated using the gig-worker EX checklist below.

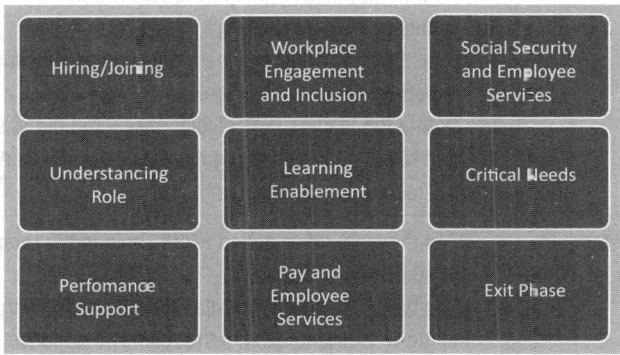

Figure 8.27. Gig Journey and Touchpoints

Gig Career Journey	Gig EX Validation Pointers
Hiring and joining	1. Does the organization have a gig hiring strategy, policy and process in place? 2. Is the hiring process transparent? 3. Do the gig opportunities get hosted on online forums? 4. Does the organization have cross-functional teams in place? 5. Does the organization have policies on compensation and benefits in place? 6. Does the organization consider internal equity and parity on compensation fitment? 7. Do the gig workers get the freedom to structure their compensation based on the personal cash flow? 8. Are the detailed employment terms and conditions communicated and explained to the gig workers? 9. Do the gig workers get assistance with the transfer of social benefit schemes from a previous employer (if any)? 10. Does the organization periodically audit its gig-hiring practices through a third party? 11. Do the gig workers have a structured onboarding process? 12. Is there a PoC with the defined responsibility to handle the hiring process? 13. Do the gig workers get briefed on the culture and values of the organization? 14. Does the organization have a gig-worker-welcome-experience tracker in place? 15. Do the top leaders periodically review the hiring status and hiring and onboarding experience of gig workers in their periodical reviews?
Understanding of role	1. Does the gig worker get an HRBP assigned to them for assistance on HR issues? 2. Does the HRBP share the role brief document with the gig worker and explain the role expectations/ deliverables of the latter?

(continued)

(continued)

Gig Career Journey	Gig EX Validation Pointers
	3. Does the HRBP organize a role clarification workshop with the reporting manager? 4. Does the gig worker get introduced to all the internal and external stakeholders? 5. Does the organization capture, analyse and act on gig workers' feedback on their role design periodically?
Performance support	1. Does the reporting manager undertake a goal setting exercise with the gig worker? 2. Does the gig worker get briefed on performance standards and the incentives attached? 3. Does the organization have a digital and AI-enabled performance system in place to track gig workers' performance? 4. Does the gig worker undergo periodical performance reviews by the reporting manager? 5. Does the gig worker get learning and performance coaching support based on the performance reviews from the reporting manager? 6. Is there a separate performance dashboard for the gig workers in the organization (across levels/businesses/projects)? 7. Does the HR carry out random audits of gig workers' performance systems?
Workplace engagement and inclusion	1. Does the HR plan and conduct engagement initiatives for gig workers along with those for regular employees? 2. Do gig workers get treated at par with regular employees in terms of access to the facilities like sports and other facilities offered by the organization? 3. Are gig workers provided with the benefits like uniform, etc. at par with regular employees, while representing the organization in front of its clients?

(continued)

(continued)

Gig Career Journey	Gig EX Validation Pointers
	4. Does the HR periodically take gig workers' feedback? 5. Do the gig workers have an established process to voice their issues? 6. Does the organization have defined TATs to address the issues of gig workers? 7. Do gig workers get invited for leadership connect events along with regular employees? 8. Do gig workers get the opportunity to interact informally with other team members? 9. Do gig workers get the opportunity to interface with clients/customers at par with regular employees?
Learning enablement	1. Do gig workers get access to the free learning resources offered by the organization? 2. Do gig workers get opportunities to be trained on functional and power skills critical to their role? 3. Do senior gig workers get an opportunity to be learning resource persons in internal training programmes? 4. Do gig workers get trained on product/service delivery as and when the organization rolls out new products/services?
Pay and benefits services	1. Are the pay and benefits offered to gig workers according to the timelines agreed upon? 2. Do gig workers get an opportunity for personalized tax planning for their income from the organization? 3. Do gig workers get leave and other benefits in proportion to their work as part of their job contract? 4. Do gig workers who work on a contract or tenure basis get details, like payout details, transparently, without having to ask for them?
Social security and employee services	1. Do employees get support in subscribing to insurance benefits, like health and accident insurance, on a payment basis? 2.

(continued)

(continued)

Gig Career Journey	Gig EX Validation Pointers
Critical needs	1. Do gig workers get support in accessing medical services for their health needs? 2. Do the dependents of gig workers get assistance in claiming death benefits? 3. Do the dependents of frontline (blue-collar) gig workers get financial support for funeral expenses upon the latter's death while on duty?
Exit phase	4. Is the attrition rate of gig workers tracked and analysed periodically? 5. Does the organization have a structured full-and-final-settlement procedure in place? 6. Do gig workers get their settlements on time? 7. Do gig employees have access to identified resources, to share their grievances/issues on final 8. Does the organization have systems in place to capture exit-interview feedback from gig workers? 9. Is the exit-interview feedback of gig workers analysed and acted upon?

Conclusion

The digital trends in the world and across global organizations have transformed gig workers from being a peripheral part of the talent strategy and mix to becoming part of the core operations and central to the business strategy and design of organizations. Organizations cannot blindly adopt the gig strategies of other organizations or their competitors. Such an approach can backfire instead of helping them. Digital technologies, such as appification, big data and AI, are helping organizations seamlessly integrate gig workers into the modern workplace. The EX of gig workers is as important as that of regular employees. In their attempts to create an 'inclusive and equitable experience' for gig workers, organizations are streamlining touchpoints in the latter's employment journey. Talent dashboards today have lead and lag indicators depicting the success and impact of gig workers in an organization.

Points to Ponder

1. Is gig talent strategy another management fad that will fade away?
2. Will the COVID-19 pandemic signal the end of the road for the gig economy?
3. Is the gig strategy a big no-no for conventional organizations?
4. How does the government balance between interventionist and welfare approaches towards gigs?
5. Does EX focus on gig workers help ROI for organizations?
6. Does HR have a differentiated role towards gig workers?
7. How do the leadership and culture of an organization impact the inclusion of gig workers?
8. How could organizations offer customized EX to gig workers?

9
Employee Experience Analytics: Tracking and Measuring Employee Experience Indicators

This chapter covers how organizations could adopt an integrated approach towards EX data and analytics. It covers comprehensively the strategy insights and operational details such as how to identify, deploy and track EX indicators and establish EX's linkage to business performance.

EMPLOYEE EXPERIENCE AT A BANKING SERVICES FIRM

A global bank had its back office in a South Indian city and had a large headcount of over 10,000 employees working in it across various divisions, including retail banking, corporate banking, technology services and HR shared services. Each unit had an employee headcount ranging from 400 to 800. It had strong HR practices in place across the employee life cycle stages, starting from the recruitment, learning and compensation/rewards areas.

The organization followed a 100-day-delight plan to make sure that the new hires got oriented and settled down well. The HR shared services (HRSS) team was one of the critical units, which supported the HR needs of the 100,000-plus employees the bank had globally. The HRSS team was structured into departments like Hiring, Talent Management, Employee Services, HR Analytics, etc. The VP of one of the verticals hired an assistant VP (AVP) to head the global talent management office.

The new hire went through a 5-day structured induction programme conducted by the learning team, along with new hires. On one of the days, as was the practice in the organization, the VP came to the induction unit, introduced himself to the new AVP and took him for a coffee. After completion of the induction, the AVP reported to the VP in the office. The VP called for a quick team huddle and introduced the new hire to the entire unit.

The VP advised the new hire to spend time with each sub-unit and get to know about the operations. The new hire was advised to set up schedules on his own, to get introduced to the external stakeholders (head HRs) of key global divisions. He had to get the email IDs of the stakeholders, introduce himself and seek appointments. In the second week, the VP checked with the new hire and shared the feedback that his introduction with the external stakeholders could have been better.

The new hire was asked to prepare his KRAs based on the understanding of his role. The trusted team members of the VP told the new hire that the VP expects his direct reports (DRs) to come to the office before he does and leave after he leaves the office. The VP made it a point to attend all the weekly meetings that the AVP had with his team. The AVP was made to listen to the advice of the VP along with his team. The VP joined in all the informal team lunches every day and made it a point to listen to the informal conversations of the team.

The VP organized a team event on the weekend and advised all the team members to attend the event without fail. The new hire, who had made plans to travel to his native place to be with his family on the weekend, had to cancel his plans. The VP reviewed the performance of his teams every week along with his DRs. It was observed that the DRs of the new hire were reporting to the VP on all matters, bypassing him. The AVP was expected to consult the VP and take his approval on all operational decisions.

The new hire reflected on his experiences during the first 3 months of his association with the organization and wondered if he had any role in the team and if it made any sense for him to continue in his role without any empowerment and operational freedom. He wondered if had made the right choice to leave his previous assignment and join the current organization. He felt that the organization was good in terms of HR practices, but he did not feel the same way about his experiences with his immediate manager and team. He wondered about the relevance of the employee engagement (EE) survey that his team had conducted for the entire bank worldwide (it was termed as Global People Survey and was conducted in partnership with leading engagement survey services providers). The EE survey showed all the indicators to be in place, but the EX indicated otherwise. Some of the AVP's team members too shared their discomfort with the 'state of affairs'. The organization reported high engagement scores.

Do annual engagement surveys really measure the true pulse of the employees?

Do they capture the EX of employees?

How could organizations capture, measure and track EX continuously?

Why Measure Employee Experience?

Changing Sociocultural Trends

In the digital world, individuals are exposed to customized experiences as customers when they shop for products and services. Customers are getting personalized assistance across the purchasing life cycle, including when comparing options and cross-checking the feedback of other customers on the products and services. Consumers today are not shopping for products/services based on just their technical features. Technology created by one organization gets adopted by another organization within no time, and hence organizations no longer have competition, as the digital world has taken away the value around information. During the early stages of the technology revolution, the focus of individuals and organizations was on sharing information. Organizations and systems were designed around flows of information, to support business needs.

Organizations investing in creating a brand image around their experience and technology become an enabler in the entire customer journey. Social media has given rise to a sociocultural trend of sharing of emotions and experiences more than sharing of information. The cultural divide that existed between the

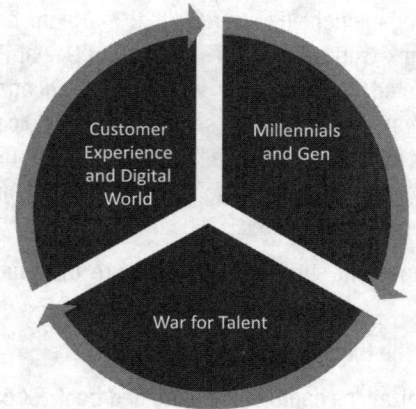

Figure 9.1. Drivers of Employee Experience

Figure 9.2. Experience-Centricity and Paradigm Shift

Oriental and Western cultures does not exist anymore, and the cultures of different countries have actually converged. Social media leaders, such as Facebook, Twitter and Instagram, have ushered in the cultural revolution.

Organizations have realized this consumer's need hear about experiences of other consumers and are integrating them into their branding strategy design and execution. Customers are encouraged to share their experience at each stage, through their social media profiles. From the perspective of consumers, the sharing occurs due to two major inherent needs, to share their experiences with their network and to influence the thoughts or decisions of other consumers. People today have realized the power they have to influence others (in both their personal and public networks).

These needs of consumers are being tapped by organizations for the latter's branding strategies. Consumer experiences shared on personal profiles are getting linked to the social media profiles of organizations. The official pages/handles of organizations are leveraging AI and digital technologies to aggregate and analyse insights of consumers about their experiences and present them to prospective consumers. The experience of the consumer is measured and leveraged by organizations for the latter to gain a competitive edge. In other words, social media is driving a convergence between the informal and formal worlds.

Millennials and Gen Z

Millennials and Gen Z are slowly replacing Gen X at the workplace. The digital native generation (Millennial/Gen Z) culturally attuned to sharing their experiences, both within their private networks and outside them. They do not have inhibitions in sharing their experiences openly. They do not hesitate before sharing their work experiences openly on social networks. They review the feedback/experiences of existing or previous employees before taking up a career opportunity with any organization. They trust information from informal sources more than that from formal sources. It has become imperative for organizations to be cognizant of employee feedback or posts on their experiences. Annual employee engagement surveys have lost their flavour. An employee's participation or sharing of feedback is dependent on two sets of factors: organizational factors and employee factors.

Organizational Factors

The 'level of trust' in an organization is a major determinant of employee morale and motivation. Trust is engendered when employees perceive equity and transparency in the dispensation of justice to them through the HR policies/systems. Employees are likely to repose trust in their organization when the HR policies are clear and leave no room for ambiguity. Quite often, organizations tend to leave room in the design of HR policies for 'flexibility' in dispensation or interpretation. However, this flexibility is likely to be used by the 'powers that be' to make decisions according to their biases and convenience. Though the leaders or managers may attempt to justify their actions, employees can see through the 'disconnect' and choose to respond in two ways: giving negative feedback or withdrawing and remaining silent. In the first response, there is the risk of the employee being identified and victimized by the leaders, which would make it difficult for them to thrive in the organization. The second response is a less risky option for the employee, who can bid time till they get another option to move on in life, rather than 'messing up their life' themself.

'Authenticity' in an organization is interpreted by employees in terms of the 'alignment of words and deeds'. If the leaders 'walk the talk', employees would feel encouraged to participate and share their feedback. For instance, during COVID-19, leaders may have advised an employee against travelling but later on may have granted leave and permission to other employees to travel and operate from their native locations. Employees, through such actions, can identify the level of authenticity. In another example leaders/managers, during their goal setting exercise, promise appropriate rewards on performance delivery, but they tend to go back on their promise, during the performance period, citing organizational constraints. Correctly conveys the essence.

'Opportunity to participate' refers to the efforts/initiatives by an organization to help its employees share their feedback. Organizations that have an autocratic leadership would not

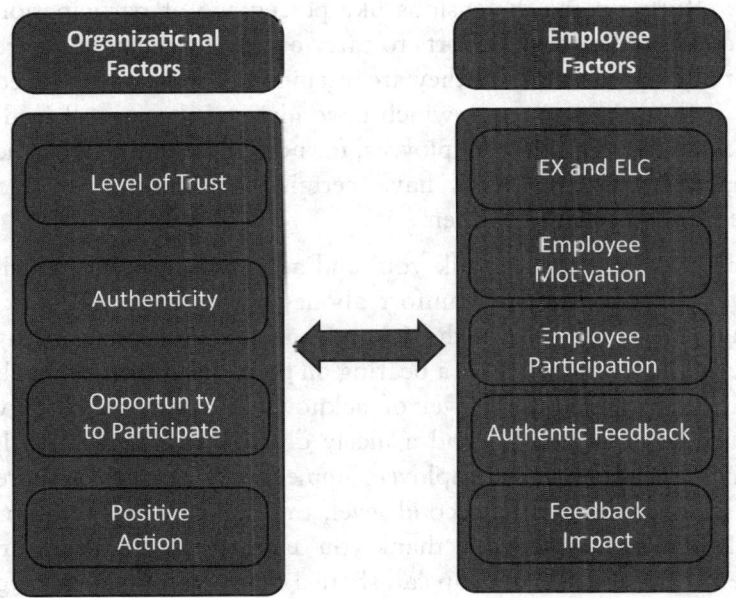

Figure 9.3. Employee Feedback Equilibrium

even attempt to create an opportunity for employees to share their feedback. Benevolent leadership will collect the feedback, but would always play with data, to engender support to their leadership (not a true reflection of the reality). In fact, employees find such an environment very artificial and hypocritical, leading to their levels of participation being really low or, alternatively, their sharing of feedback that is musical to the ears of the leadership, for fear of being victimized. New-age organizations that are tech-driven and have young talent provide multiple opportunities to employees to share their experiences, through formal/semi-formal/informal approaches, using the tech tools that are available. It is not technology per se but the attitude/orientation of the leadership which is critical in the delivery of EX.

'Positive action' refers to the response of an organization to employee feedback. Organizations design systems to capture employee feedback as part of their HR practices but tend to focus the efforts on the dimensions like percentage of participation and overall feedback. Efforts to carry out detailed diagnosis are not attempted or even if they are attempted, they tend It is used to analyse the segments, which have lowered the overall feedback and victimize the employees, for not falling in line with the organization. Employees have certain expectations around the feedback shared by them.

Employees expect a 'thank you' and acknowledgement, which gives them a sense of comfort about sharing their feedback. The quality and type of the acknowledgement are analysed by the employee, which have a bearing on their sharing of feedback in future. At the first level of acknowledgement, technology could be leveraged to send a nicely drafted 'thank you' mail, personalized for each employee, immediately after they share their feedback. At the second level, the reporting manager or unit manager can send a 'thank you' mail to the employees in their team/unit. Leadership can share a thank you mail, sharing the overall participation and the employee efforts to be a part of organizational efforts to change for the better.

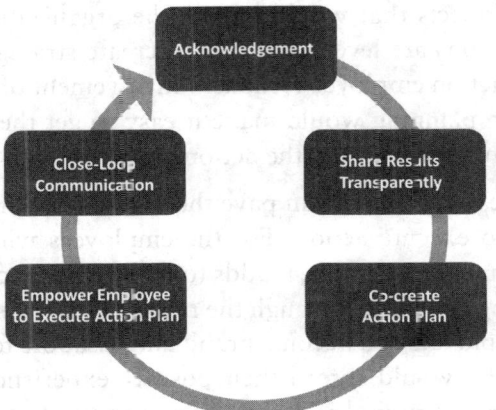

Figure 9.4. Feedback and Employee Experience

The second dimension of positive action would be the top leadership's sharing of the overall employee feedback and feedback analytics with the employees, indicating the 'positives' and 'call for action' areas. Most organizations tend to share cryptic details through a generic mail, which employees find disinteresting, as they perceive these details to be superficial and lacking sincerity and more of a show-off ritual. The grapevine comments about the feedback would be along the lines of: 'Oh, it had to be window dressed or shared for the heck of it'. The leadership's acknowledgement needs to contain the next steps and timelines and set the tone and direction for triggering change in the organization. It could indicate the inclusive approach that the organization may want to adopt in the proposed actioning process.

The action plan in most organizations tends to be centralized and created by the leadership or a select team. This approach tends to lower the trust of the employees, as they remain mere spectators in the process. An organization-wide process consultation exercise could be undertaken. The leadership/HR can plan Focus Group Discussions with employees to brainstorm on the current issues faced along with possibly implementation plans. The employees would feel happy at being involved and consulted in the creation and execution of action plans. Millennials and Gen Z love to be part of projects that would impact the organization positively. Organizations are leveraging the 'co-create strategy' to prepare plans to act on employee feedback. Involvement of employees in the action planning would make it easy to get their buy-in and support in implementing the action plan.

Employee involvement can pave the way for 'employee empowerment' to execute action. For the employees who are part of the implementation team, it adds to their experience, apart from them being benefitted through the revised HR systems/processes. These employees can become brand ambassadors for the organization, who would spread their positive experiences with their peers in their personal and professional networks and contribute to building brand equity in the organization.

Employees, unlike in the past, expect a 'continuous closed-loop communication' on matters relating to the organization and more so on issues relating to them. The traditional leadership believed that dashboard monitoring the performance of employees, organization and critical issues be reviewed during periodical; meetings. This is not the case anymore. In the new schools of leadership thought, there is a felt need to make the process transparent, to make the dashboards visible to the employees, as it is a way to help employees understand the strategies and direction of the organization. The employees would have sight of not only the long-term strategy but also the current reality, in terms of both the business and people dimensions. Millennials and Gen Z do not want to be restricted to being sweatshop workers who just deliver what is assigned to them. They would like to know the answers to the following questions:

- Why are they assigned to their job?
- How is their job linked to the long-term strategy of their organization?
- How is the organization going to help them in executing the job?

- How would their peers and the rest of the organization be connected to their job?
- How would the job outcome impact them personally and professionally?
- How would their job outcome be important for and impact the organization?
- How are other employees performing in their jobs?
- What are the experiences of other employees in their job and in the organization?
- Do employees working in the organization feel good, bad, okay or great about their experiences?

The leadership today is expected to be inclusive in 'information and experience dissemination' in their two-way communication with employees. Sharing information comprehensively using dashboards adds significant value to the overall experience of the employees. The leadership or organizations can customize the 'inclusive information experience' for the employees using AI/ML. The technology applications like virtual dashboards

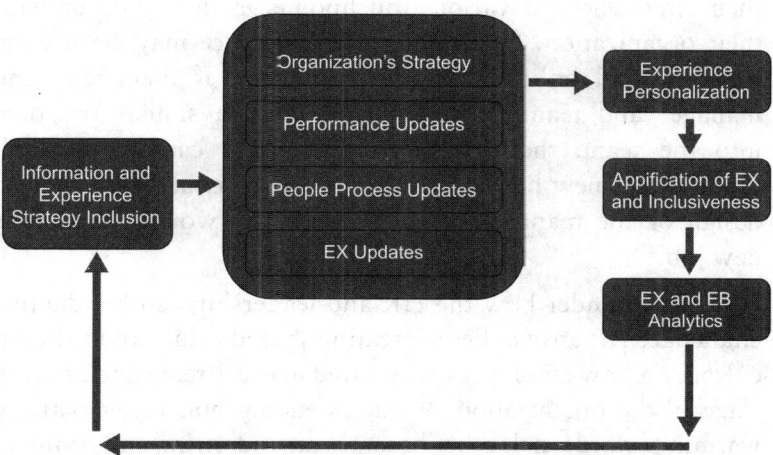

Figure 9.5. Employee Experience Analytics Framework

Employee Experience Analytics | 375

can be made available to the employees on the intranet. For instance, an IT firm, as part of its information and experience inclusivity strategy, can create an app for all the employees. One of the features of the app could be information and experience customization. The employees can be provided with a standard dashboard that is customized to their respective levels. They can be given the drop-down menu option for them to make a choice about the information dimensions that they would like to see in the dashboard. This would significantly enhance EX due to the employees' empowerment.

Employee Factors and Employee Experience

Leaders and organizations should be cognizant of the factors impacting their employees. The overall 'EX' through the HR touchpoints across the employee life cycle stages is the first critical dimension that needs to be measured and tracked by an organization. Technology has made it easy for organizations to design and track EX indicators and capture the factors impacting EX. The level of an employee's motivation is a function of their experiences at various touchpoints in their journey with their organization. For instance, an employee may get a wow welcome and onboarding experience, but if their reporting manager and team do not extend them a similar welcome into the team, the employee's motivation can be lowered. Quite often, new hires tend to quit due to issues with the job design or the manager or teams that they work within their new job.

One may wonder how the HR and leadership can handle this challenge. The answer lies in creating shared values and a shared culture on how employees get treated in every team and at every stage in the organization. When extending human, empathetic warmth towards each other becomes an underlying and common value among all employees, it is possible for them to have positive

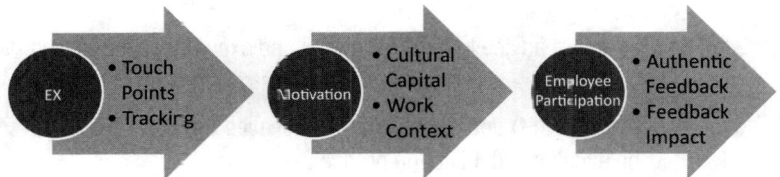

Figure 9.6. Employee Experience Analytics: Key Dimensions

experiences at the workplace. This dimension is linked to what is being measured in EX to track the prevalent 'cultural capital' of the organizations. In the digital world, the success of human capital is dependent on cultural capital more than ever before. 'Cultural Capital' connotes the way of life ('work context') for employees, both the formal and informal aspects of their workplace interactions, relationships and business and people processes. Workplace context has two key dimensions impacting it: 'employee-centricity' and 'customer-centricity'. An organization that is woven around and gets its act right on these dimensions would be able to build and nurture a culture of excellence. The analytics dashboards need to focus on these dimensions and link them to all facets of business and people processes. Typically, the leadership in organizations tends to focus on customer-centricity more than on employee-centricity. This can adversely impact their EX. For instance, Amazon tends to focus excessively on customer-centricity, with 'customer obsession' being the lever for its business strategy and execution. All its dashboards are designed to capture and deliver a wow customer experience, due to which it has been able to consistently charm customers and expand its footprint across geographies. However, its EX has a different story to tell. Amazon has a high level of attrition, with its employees complaining of burnout, pressure and exhaustion. The company's leadership has realized and acknowledged these dimensions and has suggested adopting an integrated approach for Amazon's employees.

> **Jeff Bezos says his advice to Amazon interns and execs is to stop aiming for work-life 'balance'—here's what you should strive for instead**
>
> - Amazon CEO Jeff Bezos says he believes the term 'work-life balance' is a 'debilitating phrase'.
>
> - Bezos revealed that one of the top pieces of advice he offers new Amazon employees is that they shouldn't view the two as a strict tradeoff.
>
> - Instead, Bezos thinks of his personal and professional pursuits as a 'circle' rather than a balancing act.

Source: https://www.businessinsider.in/tech/jeff-bezos-says-his-advice-to-amazon-interns-and-execs-is-to-stop-aiming-for-work-life-balance-heres-what-you-should-strive-for-instead/articleshow/63976703.cms

Did Amazon's employees get this message and are they ready to create a positive EX for themselves? Perhaps not as yet, the reason being that at the employee level, their external dependencies tend to override their priorities at the workplace. While one may argue philosophically that one can, through the internal locus of control, be able to create and enjoy positive experiences around themselves, there is a long road ahead in the journey of self-development. Plus, how much is the organization willing to invest in it? Are the employee well-being initiatives focusing on dimensions like stress management, or are they superficial and transactional in nature? Tracking and monitoring superficial things does not help an organization deliver a sustainable and positive EX to its employees.

'Employee participation' refers to employees' sharing of their experiences (quality) with their organization, which is primarily a function of three elements: authenticity/receptivity, opportunity to share one's EX and the impact of feedback shared earlier. In an organization where the climate around employees is hypocritical and artificial, it is unlikely that they would come forward to share their experiences.

> EX Sharing = Authenticity/Receptivity × Opportunity × Impact

The top leadership have the responsibility to create an authentic climate through their own behaviour, apart from coaching and monitoring the people management behaviours of all people managers. Employees are quick to notice the behaviours of leaders/managers and decide whether to share their experiences and, if yes, whether it should be real or faked. If an employee senses unease in their manager while the latter receives their feedback on their experiences, it is unlikely that the employee would give authentic feedback. If employees of a sizeable number undergo similar experiences, they are likely to share it in the grapevine, and the collective response would be to either not share their EX at all or, if made to share, do so superficially, defeating the entire endeavour to track and analyse EX.

The opportunities for employees to share their experiences impact the quality and quantity of data for EX analytics. In the digital world, people are used to sharing experience feedback instantly and on the go. Technology tools, such as chatbots, apps and text messaging, are being integrated to provide opportunities for people to share their feedback instantaneously and in real time. Digital natives, like millennials, are impatient and may walk away if the feedback-capturing system has negative UX features, like login requirements, and if the time taken in and ease of sharing feedback were not kept in mind when designing the system. For instance, an organization after roll-out can share a link to its customized app, through which employees can avail 'employee self-services' (ESS) from the organization, such as joining-formalities completion, onboarding, customization of pay structure and components, linking of bank account for salary, learning about the organizational culture through bite-sized videos and setting of performance and learning goals.

Employees can be provided with the opportunity to share their feedback on their experiences. After submission of feedback on experience, employees like to be know the real time experience indicators. Real-time EX aggregation would induce confidence in the employees that their experience is being tracked constantly. The EX indicators dashboard must be made visible to all the employees, with a drill-down option for them to check the EX indicators for their business. While it would be a feel-good factor for the employees to access overall EX indicators for specific HR services, they would be keener to know the state/details of their business unit/function. In other words, the EX dashboards should have the feature of 'hyper-localization' (HL). HL as a concept is being increasingly adopted for marketing and offering customized services. Google, for instance, offers localized news to its customers. The question is: are the leaders and HR aware of this reality and are they acting on it? Most organizations have launched HR ESS solutions, but these end up having only the basic features of provision of HR

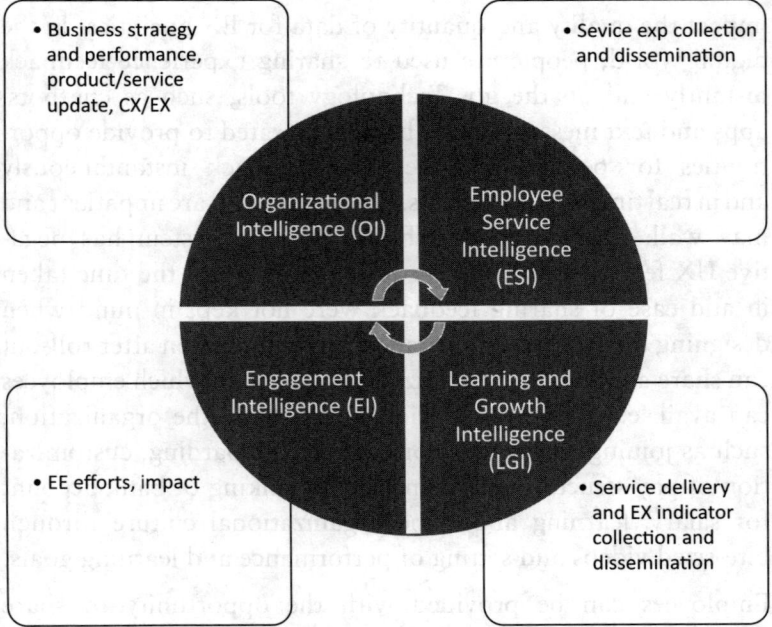

Figure 9.7. Employee Experience Intelligence and Hyper-localization

services and feedback collection. These organizations are far from using HL as a feature to offer a wow experience to their employees.

The four dimensions of 'EX intelligence and HL' for an employee are: (a) organizational intelligence (OI); (b) employee services intelligence (ESI); (c) learning and growth intelligence (LGI); and (d) engagement intelligence (EI). Employees like to be informed about the business strategy of their organization and also about how their organization has performed in relation to its competitors. The EX would be high when the employees get first-hand information about their organization rather than being dependent on the grapevine, either internal or external. It is frustrating for employees to struggle to get clues on where their organization is heading. EX indicators and analytics should capture whether the employees are being regularly provided with information relating to the organization and their responses. Employees feel glad to know about the positive outcome of customer experience delivered. More importantly for employees, they would be keen to know how their peers are feeling about being associated with the organization. The availability and

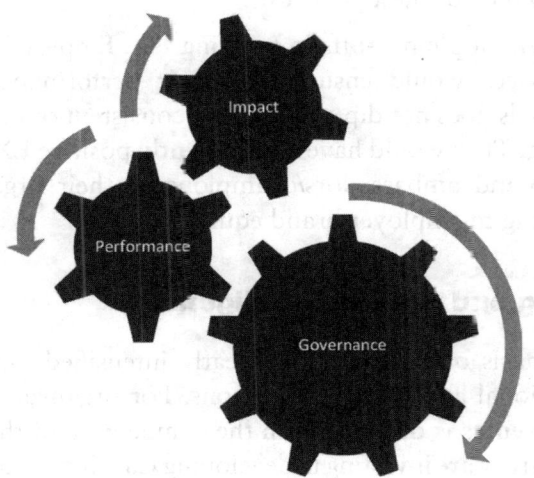

Figure 9.8. Organizational Intelligence and Employee Experience

Employee Experience Analytics | 381

quality of such information have an impact on the overall EX level in the organization.

Employee Services Intelligence

Employees avail themselves of a whole range of services, such as salary payouts, leave and the benefits like medical insurance and services for their well-being. While signing up for an organization, they would be curious to know the answers to the following questions:

- How long have these services been offered by the organization?
- What is the experience of employees availing of mandatory services?
- What percentage of employees are subscribing to optional services?
- What are the benefits of subscribing to optional services?
- What are the credentials of these service providers?
- What has been the experience of employees who have availed of these services?

There are multiple pay-offs in tracking ESI. Employees availing these services would ensure that their performance bar on service levels does not dip and is either consistent or consistently improving. They would have a consistently positive EX and thus become brand ambassadors/champions of their organization, contributing to employer brand equity.

Learning and Growth Intelligence

The emphasis on learning has greatly intensified due to both organizational and individual reasons. For organizations, their competitiveness is dependent on the competence of their talent, and hence they are investing in developing learning infrastructure. Unlike in the past, when learning needed heavy investment in

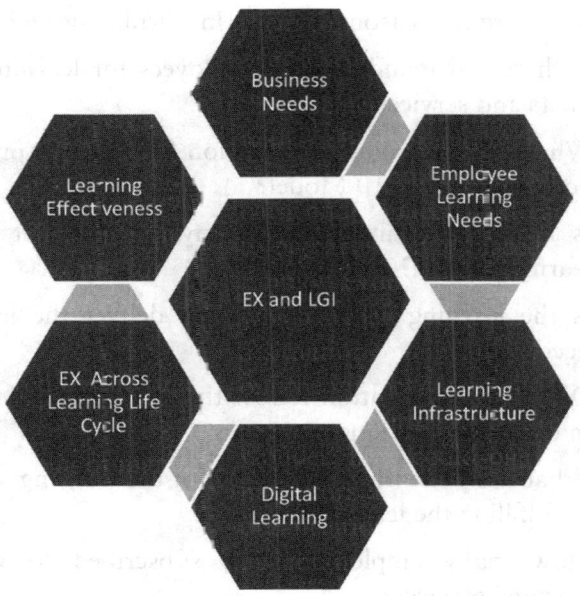

Figure 9.9. Employee Experience and Learning and Growth Intelligence

physical infrastructure, digital technologies have made it easy to design and deliver learning to employees anytime and anywhere. Earlier, organizations had to wait for learner response for want of data for analytics. Digital learning has made it easy for organizations to carry out analytics on employee feedback and experience across the learning life cycle instantaneously.

The analytics' dimensions are:

- What are the learning needs of employees as perceived by the business leadership?
- Are employees perceiving the same learning needs as their priority?
- What are the learning needs of employees?
- Is there alignment or a gap between organizational and employee needs?

Employee Experience Analytics | 383

- What are the reasons for gaps in learning needs?
- Is there a demand among employees for learning products and services?
- What is the learning subscription for learning products across the 70:20:10 Model?
- Is there a demand skew in any specific part of the learning model?
- Is the learning system geared to deliver the learning needs?
- Does the organization follow the 'co-creation' strategy in delivering learning services?
- What has been the effectiveness of the learning services in fulfilling the learning needs?
- How many employees have subscribed to various learning services?
- Is the learning strategy supporting the talent and growth needs of the employees?
- What is the EX of employees at every stage of learning (subscription, learning and application)?
- Is the organization deriving a positive ROI on its learning investments?
- Does the organization have an integrated learning and growth dashboard?

The key paradigm shift in the learning space has been the involvement and empowerment of employees. Employees today, unlike in the past, want to actively avail the learning services. They would like to have a say in the design and delivery of learning services, as they are cognizant of the impact of learning on their career growth. For instance, an employee who signs up for a learning course would be keen to know how many peers at their level have signed up for the course and what have been the latter's learning experiences before

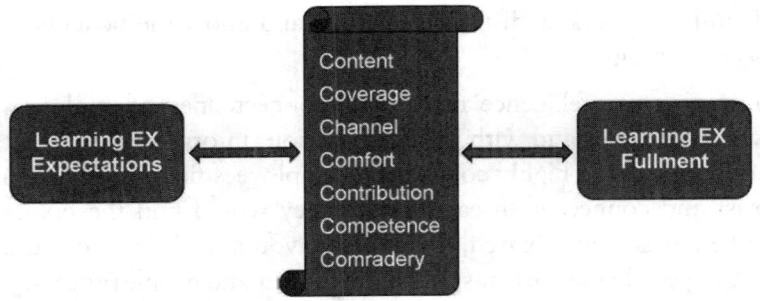

Figure 9.10. Employee Experience and Learning Management System - Analytics Focus Areas

and after attending it. An appified LMS needs to have these functionalities, as employees today like to being informed. Employees look for good experience at every stage in their journey and like to know about the experiences of their peers as well.

Employees have defined expectations around their learning and career growth. They want to analyse the content of the learning offered to validate if the learning would help them gain cutting-edge skills. For instance, learning programmes in such emerging areas as analytics, big data and AI would have more takers than the conventional learning programmes. Employees analyse not just the title per se but also the scope and learning objectives of a programme. They like to be informed about how a programme compares with those in the open market and what its USP (unique selling point) is. They look at learning flexibility and the ability to learn at their own pace as key aspects of their LX and look for bite-sized and modular programmes that they can take at their convenience.

Employees, before signing up for a programme, look for positive answers to the following questions: Would the competencies developed through the programme be useful for their current and future career growth? How have previous learners benefitted from the programme? Would the programme allow them to network with fellow learners and allow the benefits of peer learning?

'Engagement intelligence' refers to the connectedness of employees with each other and with the organization. In organizations that are political and highly competitive, employees find it difficult to trust and connect with each other. They would find the bosses to be partisan and biased, doling out favours to their favourites. Employees do not see transparency in the HR and people processes, which are left open to interpretation by the decision-makers. Such a situation is unhealthy from the EX perspective, and negativity on the grapevine would rule the roost. Employees who are keen on bettering their careers compete with each other. One may wonder: how could one create positive engagement, collect EX indicators and share it transparently with the employees? Well, organizations can conduct spot pulse surveys randomly and instantaneously share them with the employees. This would result in twin advantages. First, the leaders/managers would become aware of the EX delivered by them to their team members and would strive to be fair, transparent and empathetic in leading their team. Simultaneously, employees would become confident and repose trust in the leadership and systems in the organization. The levels of insecurity and mistrust among the employees would be lowered. This would create a positive and collaborative environment among them. One may wonder: which EX indicators should organizations be focusing on to track ESI?

The following questions identify the EX indicators to be tracked:

- Are the HR policies perceived as transparent by the employees?
- Do the employees find their leaders/managers to be fair and ethical?
- Do the employees trust their leaders/managers on what they speak?
- Do the employees find their leaders/managers supportive of their learning and growth?

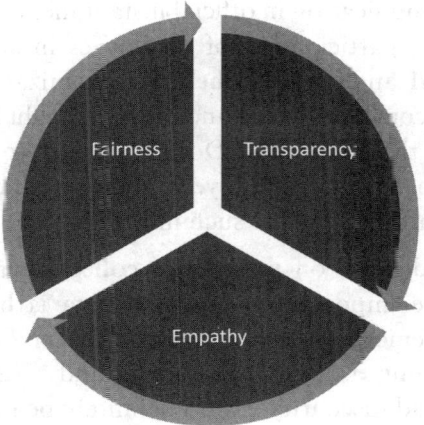

Figure 9.11. Employee Experience and Employee Satisfaction Influencers

- Do the employees find their leaders/managers reaching out to them during 'critical moments' in their life/career?
- Do the employees find their leaders/managers empathetic in dealing with them?
- Do the employees rejoice the success of their team/organization?
- Do the employees celebrate the success of their peers?
- Do the employees reach out to their peers and support each other?
- How frequent are the collaborations, competitions and conflicts among the employees?

One may wonder: is it not a herculean task for an organization to collect employee feedback on these indicators directly and regularly, as it could lead to feedback fatigue and the employees may stop sharing their feedback once it loses its novelty after some time? The question then is, how then would one track these indicators? Digital and AI technologies can be used to collect information on these dimensions. The data can be collected and analysed using official mail exchanges between employees, employee communication in official instant messenger or project documentation, participation of employees in shared learning etc. Though AI analytics can help an organization track ESI, would not the constant surveillance and oversight lead to a sense of fear among the employees? Does it amount to a breach into the informal space of the employees, and is it ethical on the part of the organization to collect such information?

The answers depend on process of collecting and analyzing data and more importantly, how the data is being used for people management. If the employees perceive the data and analytics as being used for victimizing and targeting them, a sense of fear and insecurity would definitely be instilled among them, and the ESI, which is supposed to deliver a positive EX, would end up being counterproductive for the organization. Well then, how would one balance these dichotomies in the ESI design and execution? Some EX indicators in the ESI may be discomforting for the leaders or managers. Given an opportunity, leaders would like to skirt around or ignore these questions derived from the collected feedback. These questions lead back to the three indicators that we began with: fairness, transparency and ethics in the culture of the organization. If these indicators are at a good level, then the ESI would spin the organization into a trajectory of improved EX delivery. Otherwise, it would end up delivering a negative EX. Organizations can leverage integrated EX systems through their official social media presence for EB. Linking employee feedback to social media would induce trust among both the existing employees and prospective talent.

Organizations are trying out pulse surveys, but the benefits are limited, especially if the trust level of the employees with regard to the leadership and the organization is low. Employees are unlikely to participate and provide authentic feedback to the organization if they feel that their feedback would not be listened to and acted upon by the leadership of the organization.

Business and Employee Experience Strategy Alignment

EX per se may be a generic concept, but its interpretation varies across organizations, akin to EE, which is approached by different organizations with varying objectives. Some organizations participate in global EE surveys for the sake of market visibility and branding. Other organizations participate with a genuine interest in taking the pulse of their employees and attempt to work towards providing a better working environment to their employees. Organizations in the IT and knowledge services sector participate to get external validation and showcase their people practices and the impact of these on their employees.

EX calls for a more integrated people strategy aligned to the business strategy at every stage of both business and people processes. For instance, an organization in the hospitality industry has to focus on the profile and skills of its employees to ensure that they are having a positive experience, without which its employees cannot offer positive experiences to the organization's clients.

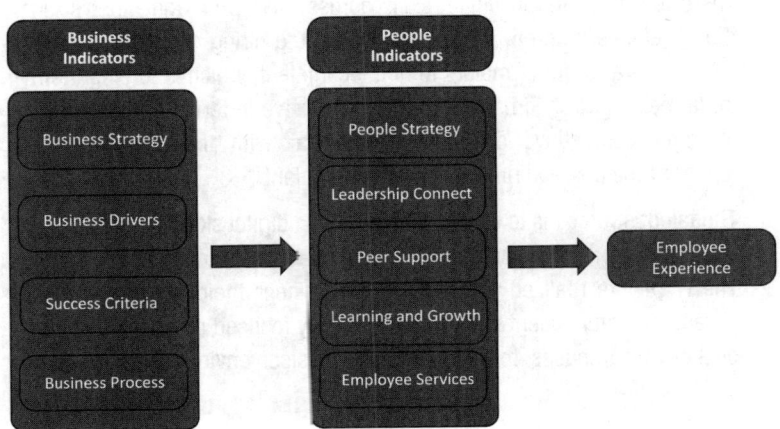

Figure 9.12. Business Strategy and Employee Experience Alignment

INFORMATION TECHNOLOGY INDUSTRY: STRATEGY AND EMPLOYEE EXPERIENCE

According to NASSCOM (National Association of Software and Service Companies), an IT-industry body, the growth of the Indian IT industry would be muted due to the COVID-19 pandemic—it would continue to be non-linear and would be centred on the digital-transformation services provided by IT firms to their clients. Clients are reducing their traditional IT expenditure and trying to increase their digital spending, to adapt to the digital trends. The industry is facing a double whammy of a strict visa regime by the US government, on the one hand, and clients' transition away from pure-play automation to business transformation using digital technologies, on the other.

IT majors were operating on a people strategy based on body shopping and headcount (HC). To meet their HC target, they hired aggressively from engineering campuses, trained the talent across skill domains and leveraged the talent to bag projects from clients.

The HR strategy of IT organizations is to attract and retain talent with digital skills in social media, big data analytics, AI and cloud computing. According to Pravin Rao, COO (Chief Operating Officer) of Infosys, 'We are aligning our talent base in the changed scenario'.

There is a shortage in digital skills across the world, and more so in the developed markets. The restriction on the hiring of talent is making it imperative for IT majors to hire local talent, which is forcing them to: (a) become truly cross-cultural and inclusive in terms of talent mix; (b) offer competitive compensation at par with their competitors; (c) offer projects requiring hot skills to the talent.

The talent strategy is to hire linear talent with digital skills, as the industry operates primarily through gaining a talent-based competitive edge. The IT majors realized the need to re-engineer their EX approach to attract and retain talent with 'hot skills'. They focused on building state-of-the-art campuses to offer a 'wow physical environment' to their talent. Their business and HR strategy is now making it necessary for them to focus on the cultural and technological environment.

The EX of talent with hot skills is primarily anchored on the cultural and technological dimensions. The cultural dimension includes the aspects of inclusivity, flexibility and empowerment of the talent. The technological environment is dependent on the organization's business strategy, its focus on digital skills and its ability to offer projects in the 'hot skills' area. In a sense, the IT majors are facing a 'chicken-and-egg' situation. Their clients would not offer them projects if the companies did not have talent with hot skills, and the talent would not look at them as a career option unless they got projects in the 'hot skills' area.

Unlike in the past, when IT majors were keen on having their leadership talent based in only India, today they are open to hiring leadership talent using the 'offshoring approach, especially in the key markets like the United States. This strategy works in three ways: (a) the leadership talent would be able to convince clients; (b) the IT majors are able to attract and retain top leadership talent; and (c) they are able to attract and retain local talent, as the latter gain confidence on seeing the leadership talent around them.

What to Measure in Employee Experience and How?

The conventional approach for organizations in the area of EX was to focus on transactional and tangible metrics. The conventional HR metrics were focused more on the organizational needs than on the employee needs. For instance, the hiring strategy previously focused on factors such as talent availability, conversion, cost per hire and TAT. These metrics are undoubtedly important for the organization, but are they important for the candidates? If not, what are the focus areas or areas of importance from the EX perspective? Organizations

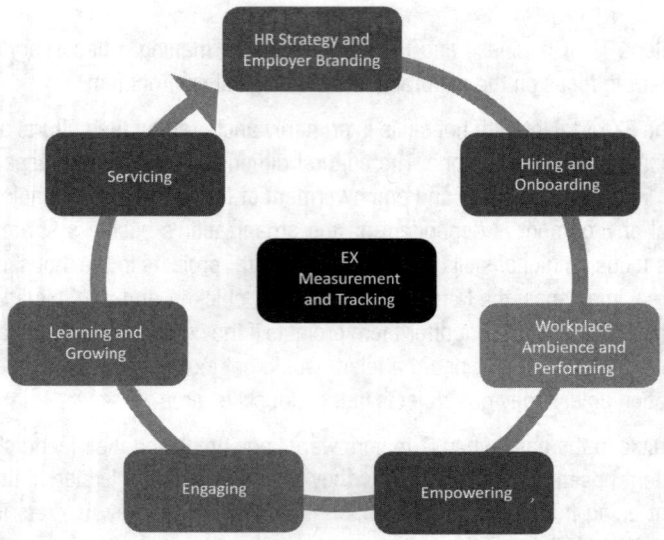

Figure 9.13. EX Measurement: Steps and Tracking

need to focus on HR metrics across the HR life cycle stages: hiring, onboarding, work environment, performance monitoring, engagement and growth. The new HR life cycle would have the components of EB, employee empowerment and employee servicing as the EX drivers.

EB is akin to a double-edged sword, being both a driver and outcome of HR strategy. The integration of HR strategy with EX is critical for the addition of a third dimension to the two dimensions of the former—'what to offer to the employees' and 'when to offer to the employees'; the third dimension would be: 'how to offer to the employees'. The 'what to offer' aspect would determine the HR service offerings to the employees, including the work environment (physical, emotional and cultural) in the organization. The physical aspect refers to the ambience of the workplace and the facilities (hygiene and differentiators). For instance, in the pre-pandemic period, the focus was on providing a state-of-the-art physical environment. During and post pandemic, since remote working has become a norm than exception, 'work from home' which was an exception and a differentiator has now become a hygiene factor.

The HR's energies are invested in recreating 'emotional connection' with the employees, especially in a situation where the latter are experiencing depression and frustration due to social distancing and isolation norms. The earlier challenges for employees were long hours of commuting through the horrifying city traffic and extended working hours. Now, the employee challenges revolve around how to stay focused on work and have work-life balance. It has become challenging for working mothers to balance work with their young children around them. As a result, young mothers are focusing on their children during their waking hours and extending work into the wee hours, which is resulting in sleep disorders and health issues among them. Expecting employees to be available for all meetings during regular office hours may work for neither organizations nor their employees. The leaders/managers need to limit meetings, in terms of both the number of meetings that an employee is expected to attend and the duration of the meetings. In fact, this is a golden opportunity for organizations to get over the menace of meetings, which mostly guzzle time rather than offering productive outcomes. In the era of instant messaging, should not the instant messaging and chat facilities be used for workplace communication and collaboration? Doing so would free the employees from unproductive login hours and offer them flexibility to focus on their deliverables more effectively.

In the pre-COVID-19 situation, employees were provided with tech tools and infrastructure at the office, and there was no need for the organization to offer these facilities when an employee was offered the 'remote working' facility. Now, in the post-COVID-19 situation, organizations are finding it imperative to offer the facilities like Internet-expenses reimbursement and home-office furniture purchase incentives to all their employees. Similarly, employee assistance programmes (EAPs), which were

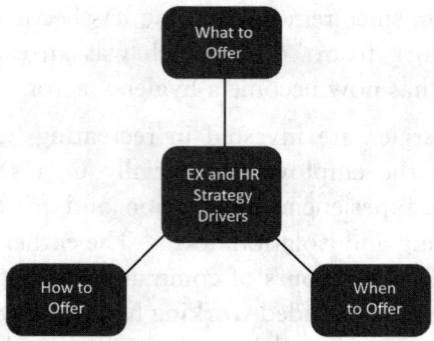

Figure 9.14. EX: HR Strategy Drivers

offered in the office to the employees, are now offered to the latter virtually. Employee well-being services, like meditation services, have now been extended through corporate subscription to meditation apps that are available to the employees. Town halls, which involved a lot of fanfare and expenditure on EE, are now being conducted at near-zero expenditure, thanks to digital platforms like the Zoom and Microsoft teams. Today, the top leaders have more opportunities to connect and engage with their talent than ever before.

The changes in the HR strategy focus areas and the consequent impact on the HR metrics and analytics, which now focus on EX, are explained below.

Human Resources Life Cycle Stage	Old Paradigm	New Paradigm
HR strategy and employer branding	The prime focus was on how to align the HR strategy with the business strategy, with an emphasis on organizational needs.	The prime focus is on EX alignment with the business strategy. EX-anchored EB is a core element of the HR strategy.

(continued)

(continued)

Human Resources Life Cycle Stage	Old Paradigm	New Paradigm
Hiring and onboarding	The prime focus was on improving the efficiency of processes through hiring a good quantity of quality talent.	The hiring strategy is experience-centric. EX, CX and EB are leveraged as drivers of the recruitment process. CX is tracked across all stages of the RLC, through the application, screening, interview, employment offer and onboarding stages.
Workplace ambience and performance	The focus was on the physical ambience, and goal setting emphasized organizational needs. Performance evaluation was akin to a post-mortem.	The focus is on employees' psychological and emotional well-being. Performance goals are co-created along with employees through balancing organizational needs and employee aspirations. Agile and real-time performance management is ensured, which allows both the organization and the employees to track, calibrate and get feedback without being intrusive. An employee need not be dependent on their manager for performance diagnostics, as the performance dashboard provides them to the employee.

(continued)

(continued)

Human Resources Life Cycle Stage	Old Paradigm	New Paradigm
Empowerment	The quality initiatives like Kaizen and Six Sigma existed partly in organizations. Empowerment was transactional and was restricted to the immediate work context.	Empowerment is a core factor impacting the experience of employees across levels, especially in the case of millennials and Gen Z. Employees are provided opportunities to participate across the spectrum, strategy design, execution and beyond their immediate work context.
Engagement	Engagement agendas and initiatives were built around the organization's strategies and were largely driven by either the HR or the organization's leaders. Engagement was based on post-mortem analysis. The engagement strategy was based on fun elements at the workplace.	Engagement is based on the deeper experience of employees at the workplace. Fun elements are just one part of the engagement process. The engagement of employees is driven by their workplace experiences.
Learning and growth	Learning was largely reactive and was adopted as a top-down approach. It was delivered in	Learning is designed around LX and there are aspects like flexibility and 24x7 access to learning resources in

(continued)

(continued)

Human Resources Life Cycle Stage	Old Paradigm	New Paradigm
	the one-size-fits-all mode. It was showcased as a privilege offered to employees. The employees faced a trade-off between work and learning and were dependent on their manager's permission to attend learning programmes.	organizations. Organizations provide access to learning on the job which is need-based. The hybrid/blended design of learning resources—offline/online and informal/formal—has enabled employees to have a positive experience with the learning. Not only is learning is linked to the immediate job needs, but employees can also customize their learning based on the career tracks that they have carved for themselves.
Servicing	Employees had no defined TAT, as the HR policies/procedures were either opaque or bureaucratic in nature. The employees were completely dependent on the leadership or HR teams. The reactive nature of the system made it difficult for the employees to reach out with queries or provide feedback on the HR services provided to them.	Organizations are designing HR services with a service delivery orientation focused on employee empowerment and experience. Most HR services are offered in an appified format, to help employees apply and access and track the status of their application. Employees can customize the services like compensation and benefits and services around well-being.

Employee Experience Analytics and Touchpoints in the Employee Journey

EX is not episodic but is a continuous process in organizations. An employee tends to evaluate their relationship with their organization based on their experiences (both positive and negative) with the latter. Employees in the digital world do not hold back their feelings about experiences but tend to share them with their internal and external networks using digital platforms. Organizations can adopt three approaches to collect data and track EX indicators across all the key touchpoints in an employee's journey. The first approach is to collect feedback on the EX through the HR services availed. Thanks to digital technologies and appification, feedback on EX can be collected immediately after the employees' availing of HR services. Employee inclination will be positive and high on three counts (a) sharing the experience feedback (b) sharing the authentic feedback and (c) curtailing employee instinct to experience externally. Feedback collected instantaneously would be authentic and useful for the organization to get real-time data reflective of the reality. This feedback can quickly be fed forward to the HR service delivery

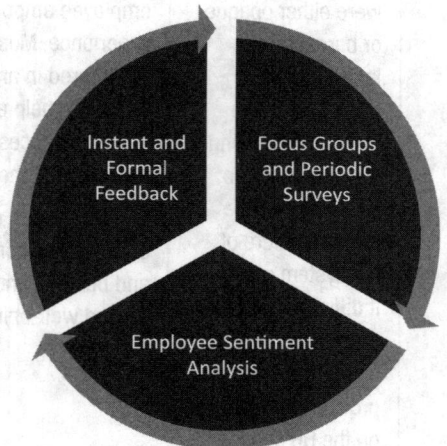

Figure 9.15. Employee Experience Indicators and Triangulation Method

team for the latter to undertake course correction. Efforts by the organization to collect feedback, acknowledge it, act on it and close the communication loop would help it proactively track and manage EX without adverse impacts, either internally or externally. In the absence of an outlet mechanism, employees, swayed by their emotions, would share their experiences through the grapevine. The negative experience tend to catch up like wildfire and will cross the boundaries of an organization, in a truly boundary-less and connected world.

From an EX perspective, it is critical for an organization to connect with its employees and collect EX data continuously. Organizations could use a combination of FGDs and skip-level meetings with the employees. The advantage of these interactions over instant, appified collection of experience feedback is that they provide the opportunity to get details on the context of the issues around employee experiences. Employees might instantaneously give emotional feedback that could be biased due to their preconceived notions/judgements/biases. For instance, an employee who has had negative experiences with their performance rating and annual rewards over the years is bound to react negatively and offer negative experience feedback, as they would aspire to get even with the perceived injustice of the past. The facts and data could be contrasting, as the employee could have been rated low and given fewer annual rewards due to their lower relative performance. Hence, it is advisable for an organization to adopt a triangulation method of collecting EX data, cross-validating them and carrying out EX analytics. The advantage of FGDs and skip-level meetings is that they make employees feel valued and involved in the process of developing solutions to their issues and offer an enhanced EX. From being an external party, employees become part of the service design and delivery. Employees have transformed into process owners from being clients. This led to paradigm shift in the EX design and delivery process, and from the employees' perspective, due to their process ownership and involvement, their view and

Figure 9.16. EX Paradigm Shift

interpretation of their EX undergo a radical change for the better.

The periodical pulse survey can be made more interesting by making it focused and thematic. The employee groups at which these surveys are aimed can be varied to eliminate survey fatigue among the employees. The employees targeted for collection of experience feedback can be differentiated or common, based on the EX theme on which data are to be collected and analysed. Feedback on the hiring and onboarding experience can be collected based on the hiring volume or seasonality. Organizations that witness high volumes of hiring throughout the year, due to either aggressive business expansion or high attrition, can collect EX feedback on a monthly basis and include the hiring EX feedback in its monthly HR dashboards. For the services like learning, organizations can conduct a combined feedback survey, collecting EX data on performance feedback and learning goals. LX feedback can be collected immediately after employees complete the formal learning. Data related to employees' experiences with informal learning, can be collected quarterly or annually.

Employee sentiment analysis (ESA) is the third and most important angle of EX analytics using the triangulation method. The advantage of ESA over the other two angles is that it takes a scientific and holistic approach to analysing EX data. The first two angles have a high level of human element, and hence the possibilities of data and analytics disruption are high, due to the human biases of the people involved in the EX data collection and analysis.

Sentiment Analysis, Employee Feedback Surveys, Services and Laws of Attraction

Figure 9.17. Employee Feedback and Sentiment Analysis
Source: https://images.app.goo.gl/fKedv9nv8QmMZpTu8

ESA's origin is linked to customer sentiment analysis. It leverages AI and ML to collect and analyse employee sentiments on identified EX indicators and visualizes the data. ESI makes it easy for leaders and HR teams to include the data in the EX dashboards. Apart from its objectivity in data collection and analytics, ESA is easy to operate and less resource-intensive, making it less stressful for organizations to track EX indicators on a regular basis. It goes without saying that ESA is a powerful

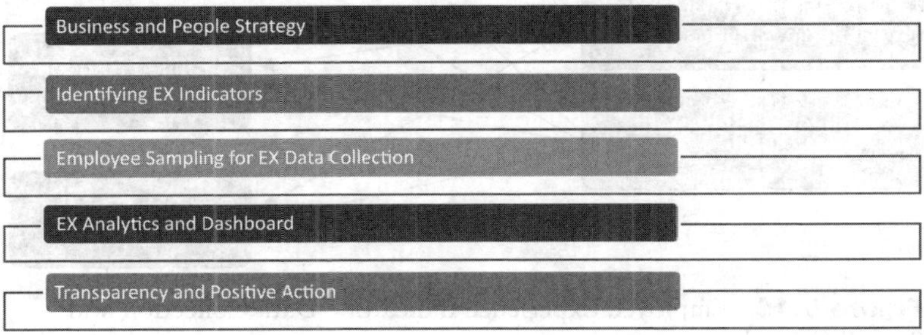

- Business and People Strategy
- Identifying EX Indicators
- Employee Sampling for EX Data Collection
- EX Analytics and Dashboard
- Transparency and Positive Action

Figure 9.18. Employee Experience Analytics: Steps

tool, but its effectiveness depends on the ability of an organization to follow certain critical steps.

The first step for an organization in designing its EX dashboard is to analyse its business and HR strategy in order to identify the business priorities and business drivers. The next step would be to identify EX indicators across the employees' journey stages. The third step would be to identify an employee sampling procedure for assessing the EX indicators. The sampling procedure could vary across the three dimensions of the triangulation method used in the collection of the EX data. Organizations can attempt collection of 'instant and formal feedback' from all its employees availing its HR services. Participation could be low initially but would pick up over time. The higher the employee participation, the better would be the EX analysis and insights.

In the case of FGDs, the participants can be selected based on random sampling method, depending on the objective for which EX data are to be collected. For instance, if an organization wants to carry out a deep dive of the EX feedback from the campus

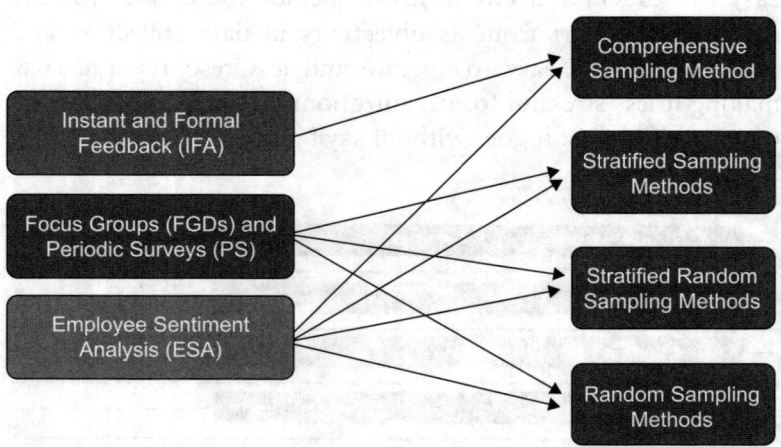

Figure 9.19. Employee Experience Indicators: Data Collection and Sampling Methods

hires it has recruited in a year, it can conduct separate FGDs for engineering and B-school campus hires, as the expectations and experiences of the two groups would be different. The engineering grads would expect to be trained on the latest technologies and assigned to projects that are aligned with their skills and interests. The B-school hires, on the contrary, would expect their jobs/roles to be in their areas of their interest. In case the organization hires from campuses at different tiers, the sampling strata can be further categorized on the basis of top-tier and non-tiered campuses. There are pros and cons of sampling method on the EX analysis. It is but natural for organizations to differentiate their EVP offerings to campus hires based on the tier of the latter's college. However, maintaining the tier system even in the FGD sample selection could be construed as being discriminating by new hires from non-tiered campuses. On the other hand, hires from top-tier campuses can feel slighted if they are grouped with hires from non-tiered campuses. Organizations can moderate these perceptions and consequently the employee expectations, as well as the EX, through communicating and setting expectations right at the stage of the orientation, to avoid misgivings in the future. Those that have a highly inclusive culture manage the signalling in unequivocal terms.

The choice of the sampling method for the 'periodic surveys' would be dependent on the EX analytics' objective. If the objective of an organization is to collect EX feedback from frontline employees on the annual performance processes and the incentive systems in place, the organization can design a questionnaire customized to the needs of the frontline employees and collect their EX feedback. The questionnaire can specifically collect data on the employees' quality of interactions with their reporting managers, the kind of performance support received by them, the equity in the distribution of annual incentives, issues in the existing incentives system and possible solutions to improve the design of the system. Mixing up the sampling through including employees from other levels would lead to mixed feedback, which would lead to false decision insights for the leadership. The sampling method for ESA must be comprehensive, as ESA helps organizations get an overall view of the EX feedback. ESA provides the opportunity for an organization to later carry out a deep dive into the analytics for various segments, based on specific insights, which if not done would trigger feedback fatigue, in which case the organization would be forced to reach out to its employees for collection of data.

Employee Experience Data and Analytics Model

The success of EX data and analytics is dependent on the data collected and the touchpoints covered in an employee's journey with their organization. It is important for an organization to collect data from employees right from the stage of talent acquisition till the exit phase. Each phase has multiple touchpoints between the employees and the organization which contribute to the former's overall experience. The 'EX Data and Analytics Model™' adopts an integrated approach towards designing and executing the EX data and analytics strategy.

About the Model

The model maps the employee-journey stages and the critical components of the EX analytics journey of an organization in a grid format, creating an EX analytics matrix that can be used for the design and execution of the EX analytics journey of an organization. The effectiveness of any data-based analytics is anchored on three V's: 'volume', 'variety' and 'velocity'. 'Volume' refers to the quantity of data the organization is able to collect for carrying out analytics. Variety refers to the multiple varieties of data which can come from different sources, sample mix, which makes it easy for the organization to analyse data, by applying multiple filters, and be able to arrive at multi-dimensional decision

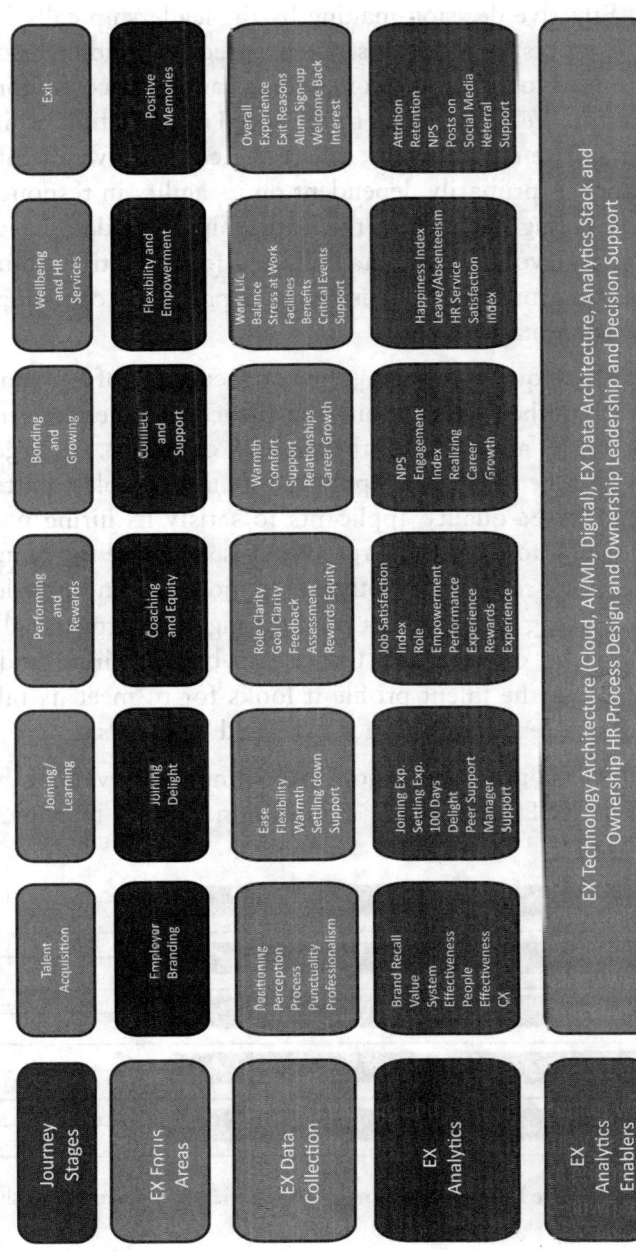

Figure 9.20. Employee Experience Data and Analytics Model™

insights. Effective decision-making by the leadership calls for a variety of inputs, as decisions taken based on unidimensional views can lead to decision errors, which can prove costly for an organization. 'Velocity' refers to the speed of collection of data. In a competitive environment, where the competitiveness of an organization is primarily dependent on its agility in responding to and predicting the market, the leadership needs data insights based on large volumes of data collected from multiple sources and capturing multiple dimensions at a pace that can support quick decision-making.

In the 'talent acquisition stage', the key focus area of EX analytics is the EB of the organization. The efficiency and effectiveness of hiring efforts are based on the strength of the EB. An organization with a better brand reputation would be able to attract good quantity & quality applicants to satisfy its hiring needs. For instance, Infosys in India receives close to twice the number of applications received by other IT majors for an entry-level position. Having a large talent pool through numerous applications allows an organization to raise its bar on hiring and be selective about the talent profile it looks for to meet its talent needs. EB in talent acquisition is impacted by five Ps.

It is critical for an organization to continuously evaluate how it positions its EB versus the competition. Trying to copy the

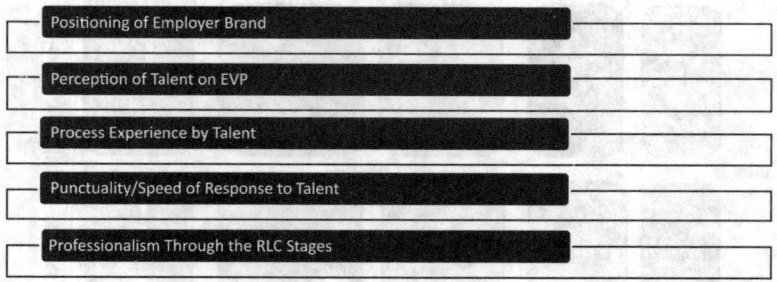

Figure 9.21. Five Ps Impacting Employee Experience in Talent Acquisition

competition without unique differentiation would lead to talent not noticing the brand altogether and, as a result, choosing to ignore the opportunities with the organization. Talent's EB perception can be assessed through the number of applications received for any position. Their perception of EVP can be assessed using a 'perception analysis framework'. The requirements for such analysis are: (a) understanding the needs/preferences of the prospective talent; (b) devising a customized EB approach to address the talent's needs; and (c) capturing the talent's response to the EB communication using both online and offline channels. To analyze the impact of candidate experience on EB, organization can collect feedback from candidates if the details stated in the adverts have covered all the details that are looking for before applying for the job. The kaizen approach can be adopted to constantly improve hiring communication. The process experience feedback must cover the details like the ability of the talent to get the information they need and to get their queries clarified before applying. Data to be collected on punctuality refers to turn around time (TAT) taken to respond to the applicant on the status/outcome of the process/step in a defined TAT, without a long wait period or needing constant follow-ups. Professionalism can be assessed through collecting data on candidates' experience when dealing with the hiring PoC and interview panel.

EX analytics in talent acquisition needs to focus on: (a) brand recall value; (b) system-effectiveness; (c) people-effectiveness; and (d) overall CX. For instance, an FMCG organization while conducting a campus hiring drive can ask the students how many times the latter have heard about the organization and through which channels. Both the content and channel of communication play a dominant role in the EB recall value. They provide inputs to the EB team supporting the hiring process. System-effectiveness can be assessed using the TATs (overall process and for each step). People-effectiveness can be analysed based on the hiring manager's satisfaction with the hiring support and candidate feedback.

In the 'joining stage', the focus of an organization in terms of EX would be to analyse its ability to create joining delight among new hires. Here, data are to be collected on dimensions like 'ease' and 'flexibility' of joining. Organizations are appifying much of the joining process. Candidates, after accepting an offer, are provided with a link to a joining app, using which they complete the joining formalities with ease at their convenience. Feedback must be collected on the qualitative dimensions like the warmth experienced by them during the joining and onboarding process. Data are to be collected from new hires on whether they have been able to settle down comfortably and, if yes, whether they have been able to get the required support from the people they have been interfacing with. The EX analytics needs to cover the dimensions such as overall joining/settling-down experience, 100-day delight and peers' and manager's support.

In the 'performance and rewards' stage, the EX focus must be on the coaching and equity dimensions. Data must be collected on whether the employees are clear about their roles and the goals to be delivered by them. It is important to check whether the employees are getting constant and quality feedback from their managers. Automated and appified processes make it easy for the HR team to track these dimensions. The quality of the performance feedback and assessment can be gauged through the appraisal comments and chat communications between managers and employees. Data on the level of equity in rewards can be collected using internal and external equity analyses, by comparing both the profile and performance of the talent against the payouts made to them. Direct feedback from employees on salaries/annual increments/incentive calculations can be collected using a pulse survey after the annual rewards exercise. EX analytics here must focus on the overall job satisfaction of the employees, the extent of empowerment enjoyed by them in their roles, their overall performance experience through the performance management life cycle and their overall rewards experience on the dimensions such as fairness, transparency and equity.

EX analytics in the bonding and growth stage must focus on the 'connection and bonding' experienced by the employees. Employee feedback must be collected on the dimensions like the warmth/comfort and support they receive from their bosses and team members. Employee's perception of their organization is always influenced by their experiences in their immediate work environment. If the employee does not experience a sense of warmth/comfort or does not get the needed support for their role, it is unlikely that they would have a positive EX. The quality of their workplace relationships holds the key to an employee having a positive experience. EX analytics here must focus on three dimensions: NPS (Net Promoter Score), engagement index and career growth realization index. NPS indicates the desire or propensity of an employee to positively recommend their organization in their network. The engagement index consists of periodical engagement surveys conducted by an organization using both the quantity and quality dimensions of employee participation. The analysis can also be extended to track the percentage of employees who have been able to achieve career growth both horizontally and vertically in their roles.

Employee experience in terms of well-being and HR services is centred on their 'flexibility and empowerment'. EX data collection in this regard should focus on work-life balance, stress at the workplace and facilities and benefits and support provided during critical moments. For assessing work-life balance, data can be collected on the average number of hours logged in by the employees per day. Thanks to technology infusion into workplaces, it has become easy for organizations to track the number of hours logged in by their employees. The latter's productivity can be correlated with the number of hours logged in and analysed. Most leaders/managers think that there is a direct relationship between working hours and productivity.

The managers extend their teams' working hours and in the process send wrong signals to the latter. This kind of wrong assumption disturbs the work-life balance and induces stress in the employees, resulting in the latter's negative experience. Collection and analysis of the data need to be followed up with a discussion during business review meetings, to ensure that the leadership get their misconceptions corrected. In France, the government has brought into force a new law restricting the working hours to 35 hours per week, as against 39 hours per week. During COVID-19, though employees initially enjoyed working from home, most realized that they were working longer hours due to two reasons: guilt of the employees for not going to work and the attitude of managers that employees need to work longer hours in return for the remote working facility. It is time to realize that it's not a benefit for employees, but has equivalent benefits for employers as well, with reduced operating expenses.

Employees today like to avail of HR services at their convenience. Digitization and appification have made it possible for employees to avail of most HR services online. The focus of most organizations has been on the digitization of services, and not many focus on EX; as a result, employees tend to face similar issues as when availing services physically. The reason for this is lack of process re-engineering efforts by the HR team. To analyse the EX around well-being and employee services, the HR dashboard needs to capture the indicators such as happiness, leave and absenteeism and satisfaction with HR services. The employee happiness index can be maintained leveraging AI/ML and text analytics tools. The employees' chats on instant messaging platforms can be analysed to take their pulse.

EX focus during the 'employee exit' stage must be on the 'positive memories' of the departing employee. Efforts must be made to capture the overall experience of the employee during the exit interview. Their experience during the exit process can turn even a positive or neutral experience into a negative one.

Planning and facilitating an interaction with the leadership can positively impact the exiting employee. The willingness of the employee to stay connected as an alumnus and their openness of being welcomed back into the organization in the future can help determine the EX. Most employees tend to share positive feedback while leaving but choose not to respond to alumni communication. Lack of reciprocation by alumni can help an organization gauge the latter's EX.

Analytics on EX in terms of exiting employees must focus on the indicators like types of attrition (voluntary/involuntary/high-performers). Retention of critical and HiPo (high-potential) talent may indicate that an organization has been successful in delivering a positive EX to the talent, which would also have contributed to the success of the organization. AI/ML can be used to carry out a sentiment analysis of exiting employees. The other analytics components can be the percentage of boomerang (returning) employees among the new hires and the support of alumni to the hiring referral programme.

'EX data and analytics enablers' play a crucial role in the maturity or capability of an organization to deal with EX data and analyse them. EX technology architecture, which includes the technologies such as cloud computing, AI/ML and digital technologies, makes it easy for an organization to deal with EX data and analytics. It's relatively easy for an organization to take decisions related to data architecture for managing EX related data. It calls for clarity among the leadership on the issues such as the following:

- What is the source of the EX data?
- What are the points on which data are to be collected?
- What data are to be collected from which sources and at what periodicity?
- How would the data be stored and retrieved?
- What are the controls in place for the aspects like data accessibility and control to guard against data distortion?

- Who would be responsible for deciding on the EX points on which data are to be collected?
- Should Ex data be handled by external resources and the cost-benefit trade-off?

Most organizations tend to focus on transactional data and analytics and in the process tend to miss the opportunity to realize value from their efforts. It is important for organizations to map the types of analytics to the value added to the leadership decision insights.

The descriptive analytics of Ex across ELC Stages would capture and analyze transactional data like TAT like rolling out offers to candidates, communication timelines vs adherence. In the case of HR services, it would focus on TAT compliance/deviance.

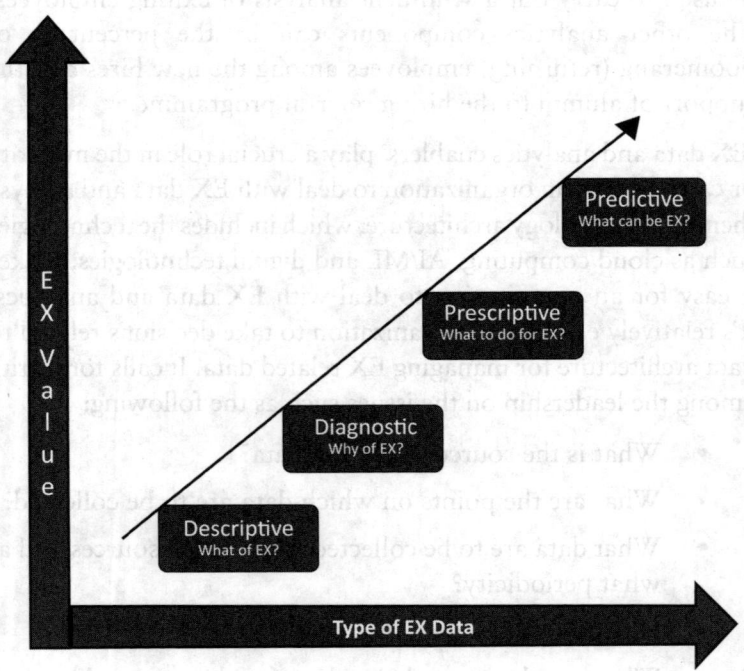

Figure 9.22. Employee Experience Data and Analytics Capability Model™

In the case of CX data, it would capture the overall CX in the hiring process. Carrying out current stage diagnosis is the first step an organization to determine the kind of EX it is offering to its employees. Quite often, organizations do not even track EX and hence are clueless about the EX they offer. The next stage of evolution is diagnosis, where the organization needs to carry out a Why-Why analysis for both hits and misses. It is important for organizations to know the reasons for slips/dips in their EX. More importantly, the 'Why-Why' analysis would help them understand the reasons for positive EX, which would help them plan to scale up to the next level of EX analytics, which would require predictive capability.

Designing and executing HR initiatives in a trial-and-error mode is okay if it is an experiment/initiative completely new to the organization/sector/market. In the case of HR initiatives, it is imperative from a strategic perspective for an organization to have predictive capability, to assure itself of the cause–effect relationship. For instance, the introduction of appified versions of certain HR services has resulted in a positive EX for employees. It is critical to determine whether there is a need to tweak the delivery model or if it could be scaled up as it is, and to determine the model's consequent impact on the EX delivered by the organization.

The analytics team would be in the service delivery mode until they operate at the predictive level. For EX analytics to assume strategic importance, it is critical for the analytics team to acquire the capabilities to prescribe HR initiatives that can help an organization deliver superior EX to its employees. For the analytics team to operate at this level, it needs to focus on acquiring tech tools expertise, domain expertise, analytical skills and strategic-diagnosis and -forecasting capabilities.

Most analytical professionals score high on tech tools expertise and analytical skills. However, they remain dependent on SMEs (subject matter experts) to provide inputs. As a result, they end up being executors of instructions, offering analytical insights

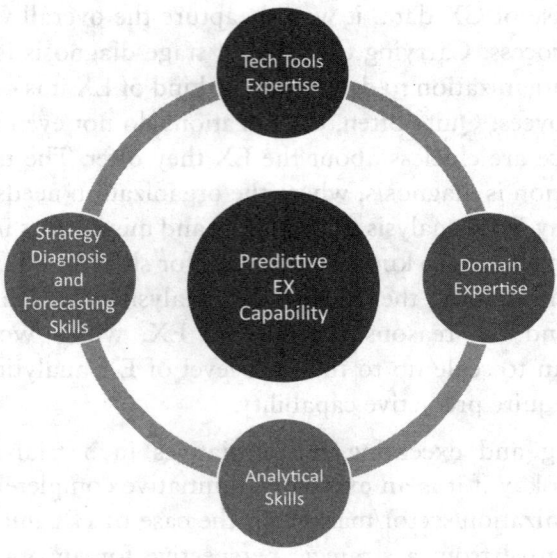

Figure 9.23. EX Prediction: Enablers

at either the descriptive or the diagnostic level. For the analytics team to transition to the predictive and prescriptive levels, it is important for them to acquire domain expertise of the HR function and understand its scope, deliverables and impact on the business. This would aid them in taking a holistic view of the context, needs and application of analytics to support the business needs.

The pure play technical background of the members working in the EX analytics team becomes a challenge for them in relating to both the domain area and the strategy linkage and impact. A combination of management skills and technology would make it easy for the analytics team to transition into the predictive and prescriptive levels. Analytics professionals with a management background could offer better support. Organizations, when they select the analytics team, need to keep these issues in mind and ensure skill and profile diversity. Otherwise, HR teams would end up providing constant coaching and support to the analytics team, which would impair their bandwidth and end up lowering their performance delivery. A good skill and profile mix would help the analytics team offer consultation/problem-solving support to both the HR team and the leadership in such areas as HR process re-engineering and decision insights and support. They would bring a sense of end-to-end ownership towards EX analytics. Organizations can choose to outsource EX analytics for cost control, but it would not be viable or sustainable in the long run. EX and EX analytics now form the core of organizational design, impacting the latter's importance. In terms of outsourcing, it would be fine to outsource non-core and peripheral aspects but not core and critical dimensions. Outsourcing the latter would lead to both operational risks in the short run and strategic risks jeopardizing the performance and capability of the organization in the long run.

Conclusion

Organizations have realized the need for and importance of EX to attract and retain talent but are still operating in the trial-and-error mode, learning through evolution. For organizations to be successful and effective in realizing their EX objectives, it is important for them to adopt a scientific approach and discipline towards the same. EX data and analytics have to be taken seriously. Viewing the data only once in a while and crunching would end up in organizations adopting a randomized approach towards EX, which can lead to negative EB for them. Having a full-fledged and dedicated team for realizing EX objectives would help the HR, the leadership and the organization transition to higher levels of maturity in dealing with EX data and analytics.

Points to Ponder

1. How do EX data and analytics help an organization create a positive EB value?
2. How do EX analytics help an organization in designing and executing its talent strategy?
3. How could organizations leverage digital technologies for EX design and delivery?
4. What are the strategic trade-offs between outsourcing EX analytics and handling EX analytics through an internal team?
5. How could EX analytics help an organization in realizing excellence in its business strategy and performance?

About the Author

Professor (Dr) Devaguptapu Naga Venkatesh is a seasoned HR (human resources) professional with close to three decades of experience. He has worked across sectors, including in logistics, banking, IT/ITES and social sectors. He has essayed leadership roles as an HR generalist and specialized roles, like talent management and learning and development, across organizations (Gati, RBI [IDRBT], SITEL, HSBC, BASIX, Standard Chartered and Akshaya Patra).

He has managed large employee strengths, of over 10,000, and has worked on multiple HR process improvement projects such as process re-engineering and design and deployment of digital HR process.

Currently, he is working as a professor in OB (organizational behaviour) and HR management at Goa Institute of Management (GIM), with which he has been associated for the last six years. In his current role, he is involved in:

- Designing and delivering courses for PGDM and EMBA students in the area of HR;
- Designing and delivering management development programmes/entrepreneurship development programmes (MDPs/EDPs) for working executives in the area of HR;
- Offering HR consulting services to organizations across the country; and
- Leading the corporate relationship for GIM, as placement chairperson.

He has published two books and has authored close to 50 research/strategy papers. The vision drafted by him for IDRBT was included in 'RBI Financial Sector Vision 2020'. He is actively involved with industry bodies like CII (Confederation of

Indian Industry) and the Goa Management Association (GMA). He is currently a member of the HR Subcommittee of CII, Western Region, and is heading the skilling initiative for SMEs across the states of Goa, Maharashtra, Gujarat and Madhya Pradesh. He is also a member of the Executive Committee of GMA.

STAY ENCOURAGED
STAY CREATIVE
STAY MOTIVATED

Keep abreast of the most cutting-edge thinking driving businesses today.

For special offers on these books and more visit **stealadeal.sagepub.in** **Steal A Deal** YOUR ONE-STOP-SHOP FOR LOWEST PRICE

www.sagepub.in